teach yourself

bulgarian

michael holman and
mira kovatcheva

For over 60 years, more than 40 million people have learnt over 750 subjects the **teach yourself** way, with impressive results.

be where you want to be
with **teach yourself**

For UK order enquiries: please contact Bookpoint Ltd, 130 Milton Park, Abingdon, Oxon OX14 4SB. Telephone: +44 (0)/1235 827720, Fax: +44 (0)/1235 400454. Lines are open 9.00–18.00, Monday to Saturday, with a 24-hour message answering service. Details about our titles and how to order are available at www.teachyourself.co.uk

For USA order enquiries: please contact McGraw-Hill Customer Services, P.O. Box 545, Blacklick, OH 43004-0545, USA. Telephone: 1-800-722-4726. Fax: 1-614-755-5645.

For Canada order enquiries: please contact McGraw-Hill Ryerson Ltd, 300 Water St, Whitby, Ontario L1N 9B6, Canada. Telephone: 905 430 5000. Fax: 905 430 5020.

Long renowned as the authoritative source for self-guided learning – with more than 30 million copies sold worldwide – the *Teach Yourself* series includes over 300 titles in the fields of languages, crafts, hobbies, business, computing and education.

British Library Cataloguing in Publication Data
A catalogue entry for this title is available from The British Library.

Library of Congress Catalog Card Number: on file

First published in UK 1993 by Hodder Headline, 338 Euston Road, London, NW1 3BH.

First published in US 1993 by Contemporary Books, a Division of The McGraw-Hill Companies, 1 Prudential Plaza, 130 East Randolph Street, Chicago, Illinois 60601 USA.

This edition published 2003.

Typeset by Transet Limited, Coventry, England.
Printed in Great Britain for Hodder & Stoughton Educational, a division of Hodder Headline, 338 Euston Road, London NW1 3BH by Cox & Wyman Ltd, Reading, Berkshire.

Hodder Headline's policy is to use papers that are natural, renewable and recyclable products and made from wood grown in sustainable forests. The logging and manufacturing processes are expected to conform to the environmental regulations of the country of origin.

Impression number 10 9 8 7 6 5 4 3 2
Year 2009 2008 2007 2006 2005 2004

contents

About the authors

Mira Kovatcheva was born in Sofia and studied English at Sofia University, where she is now Senior Lecturer in the Department of English Studies. Her field of research is English historical linguistics and languages in contact. She also has a special interest in the teaching of Bulgarian to native speakers of English. Between 1989 and 1992 she was on secondment to the universities of Leeds and Sheffield where she taught Bulgarian to English students.

Michael Holman is of mixed English and Russian parentage and was born in Kent, where he now lives. Between 1966 and 1999 he lived in Yorkshire, where he was latterly Professor of Russian and Slavonic Studies at the University of Leeds. He has taught Bulgarian, translated from Bulgarian into English and sought to promote Anglo-Bulgarian cultural interchange. He holds the 'Order of Stara Planina' (First Class) and is an honorary Doctor of Letters of Sofia University. His wife, Dorothea, without whom none of this would have been possible, was born in Sofia of mixed Bulgarian and Macedonian parentage.

Acknowledgements

It would be impossible to thank all our relatives and friends and also colleagues, past and present, who have helped us directly or indirectly with this book. We would, however, like to single out for special mention Christo Stamenov and Vladimir Filipov, both lecturers at Sofia University, who assisted us greatly in the latter stages of our work on the first edition. To everyone who has written to thank us for the book and to make suggestions for its improvement, we are grateful beyond measure. The responsibility for outstanding imperfections in this new edition, however, remains firmly with us.

introduction

Teach Yourself Bulgarian is a complete course for beginners in spoken and written Bulgarian. It has been designed for self-tuition, but may also be used for study with a teacher. It aims to teach you to understand and use the contemporary language in a variety of typical, everyday situations. Above all it is functional, enabling you to communicate and interact, using the language for positive, practical purposes. Although intended primarily for people with no knowledge of the language, you will also find it useful if you want to brush up or extend some previous knowledge.

The course is divided into 20 carefully graded and interlocking units. Each unit is devoted to a particular topic or situation and each successive unit builds naturally on material covered in previous units. In Unit 1, for example, you will learn how to introduce yourself, to use some simple greetings and to say 'please' and 'thank you'. In Unit 2 you will discover how to ask questions, and in Unit 3 you will learn how to answer questions saying where you come from, what you do for a job and indicating whether or not you are married. Unit 4 teaches you some numbers and how to use them when telling the time.

The first half of the book, up to the end of Unit 9, is a basic grammatical and thematic 'survival kit'. The emphasis here is on the present tense and on immediate situations you may well find yourself in on a visit to Bulgaria. Thus, Unit 5 enables you to describe your language knowledge – or lack of it! Unit 6 deals with wanting and asking for things and with changing money, Unit 7 with shopping, Unit 8 with eating out and Unit 9 with getting about and both asking for and giving assistance.

From Unit 10 on you progress to less immediate, but no less important matters. You will learn to ask about future events, inquiring about the weather, for example, or putting together a plan for the days ahead. You will also learn how to talk about things that happened in the past, how to make complaints and tell people what to do. And as your vocabulary and grammatical knowledge increase, you will be able to make more use of the tables and lists in the Appendix at the back of the book.

Each unit is divided into distinct but interlocking sections. An initial Dialogue is followed by a vocabulary with the new words and phrases and a few short questions in Bulgarian based on the Dialogue. Then (up to Unit 11) comes a short section (marked with i) of cultural comments and topical tips for first-time visitors to the country. This is followed by useful phrases relevant to the theme of the unit and worth learning by heart. Then come grammatical explanations which all proceed naturally from the new words and constructions used in the Dialogue. Finally there come the Exercises – lots of them, varied, practical, with all the answers in the back – so you can test yourself and see how you are doing. At the end of the Exercises there is always a second dialogue, that takes you on a little further, incorporating material you will have already covered plus a few new words and phrases.

In the dialogues we have tried to concentrate on the activities of a limited number of characters, both English- and Bulgarian-speakers, whose paths cross in Bulgaria one year in May. First there is Michael Johnson, a man of entrepreneurial disposition from Chelmsford, UK. Mr Johnson is in Sofia for the first time and has wisely learnt some Bulgarian in preparation for his visit. He is on a two-week business trip, establishing contacts, especially with Boyan Antonov, director of a newly established but already quite large, Sofia-based advertising agency. You will also meet members of Mr Antonov's staff: Nadya, his hard-working secretary, Nikolai Dimitrov, a junior colleague, and Milena Marinova, an artist. (Particularly watch Nikolai and Milena...) Then there is a married couple from Manchester, Victoria and George Collins. Victoria is an interpreter and George is a teacher. They too are visiting Bulgaria, but not for the first time. Victoria speaks Bulgarian well. Nevena Petkova is the hotel receptionist. Nevena, too, is entrepreneurial! There are other characters as well taking part in a variety of situations and locations, from Sofia in the west to Plovdiv in the south and on to Varna and the Black Sea in the east. Good luck, and remember, *practice makes perfect* or, as the Bulgarians say, **опитът пра́ви ма́йстора**.

How best to use this book

Before starting Unit 1 you will need carefully to work through the sections on the alphabet and pronunciation. Look, too, at the section on pronunciation and spelling at the beginning of the Appendix. Despite the different script, you will soon find that there are many Bulgarian words you recognize, both in their written form and when you hear them on the recording which accompanies *Teach Yourself Bulgarian*.

Dialogues or other sections marked with ▶ are included on the recording. We strongly advise you to use it. As you listen to the native speakers and imitate their pronunciation, so your own pronunciation will improve. Keep the recording in the car and listen to it on your way to and from work. Repeat the words and phrases as often as possible so as to get your tongue round the foreign sounds. Before going on to a new unit, listen again to the dialogues recorded from the previous unit. The more you listen and the more you speak, the better you'll be!

Learning techniques obviously vary and you will probably need to experiment a little before adopting the procedure that suits you best. However, since each unit follows the same pattern, you might find the following procedure worth trying for a start.

Dialogue

Read the English introduction at the beginning of the opening *Dialogue*. This will establish the context for you.

If you have the recording, listen to the Dialogue and see how much you understand.

Now work through the Dialogue, reading aloud as you go. The vocabulary after the Dialogue gives you the meaning of all new words and key phrases in the order in which they occur. (If, as you work through the book, you find this initial vocabulary doesn't list a word you cannot understand, turn to the Bulgarian–English vocabulary at the back of the book. All the words are listed there or in the Appendix. If you are searching for the Bulgarian equivalent of an English word, try looking in the English–Bulgarian vocabulary. This contains most of the words used in the different units and a good few more besides.)

Listen to the recording again, following the text of the Dialogue in the book.

Questions

Now read aloud the questions that follow the Dialogue and try and answer them individually as you go.

Notes

For a little light relief have a look at the *Notes*.

Grammar

Now study the *Grammar* section. In some units this section is longer than in others. Always, however, the grammatical explanations refer to material used in the Dialogue. The usage should, therefore, already be familiar to you. And since many of the examples used in the Grammar section are taken from the Dialogue, this should help further to consolidate your knowledge. The English translation is always given with words introduced for the first time in the Grammar section.

How do you say it?

Go over the *How do you say it?* section. Try to memorize as many of the words and phrases as possible.

Exercises

Once you feel you have a reasonable understanding of the material, test your knowledge by working through the *Exercises*. They have been designed not only to be useful and communicative, but also to test your mastery of the grammar. They are a vital part of the learning process, so try to do them all! The answers in the back of the book will give you an idea of how you are doing.

Do you understand?

After the exercises in each unit there is a second Dialogue. New words and phrases occurring in this Dialogue are listed at the end of the unit, but try and see how much you understand without reference to the vocabulary, by reading the Dialogue aloud. You should work through this second Dialogue as you worked through the first one.

Finally, before proceeding to the next unit, listen again to all the recorded material of the unit you have just been working on. If you do not have the recording, read through the Dialogues aloud, making sure that you have understood everything.

Abbreviations

Abbreviations used in this book are: adj = adjective, f = feminine, m = masculine, lit. = literally, n = neuter, nn = noun, p. = page, pl = plural, vb = verb, T = true, F - false.

alphabet and pronunciation

Bulgarian is spoken by more than ten million people worldwide and is the official language of the Republic of Bulgaria. It is not a difficult language for English-speakers. In fact, of all the Slavonic languages, which include Russian, Ukrainian, Polish and Czech, its structure makes it one of the easiest for us to learn. True, the Cyrillic alphabet of 30 letters, which takes its name from the ninth century scholar and holy man St Cyril, may at first seem a bit of a barrier, but it is not difficult to master. The alphabet is very logical, extremely efficient and well adapted to rendering the sounds of Bulgarian. In the main, unlike English, the pronunciation is straightforward.

The letters can be conveniently divided into three manageable, easy-to-learn groups. They are:

1 letters that look the same in Bulgarian and English
2 letters that look different
3 letters that look the same, but are, in fact, pronounced very differently. These are the 'false friends' which, initially at least, cause the greatest difficulty.

Look at the alphabet table on pp. xii–xiii and see if you can decide which letters fall into which group.

Bulgarian has six simple vowels: **А**, **Е**, **И**, **О**, **У**, **Ъ** – one more than English – and two letters, **ю** and **я**, that really stand for a consonant plus a vowel – **й** + **у** and **й** + **а**, respectively.

The Bulgarian alphabet

Printed letters		Written letters	
capital	small*	capital	small
А	а	А	а
Б	б	Б	б
В	в (*в*)	В	в
Г	г (*г*)	Г	г
Д	д (*д*)	Д	д
Е	е	Е	е
Ж	ж	Ж	ж
З	з	З	з
И	и (*и*)	И	и
Й	й (*й*)	Й	й
К	к	К	к
Л	л (*л*)	Л	л
М	м	М	м
Н	н	Н	н
О	о	О	о
П	п (*п*)	П	п
Р	р	Р	р
С	с	С	с
Т	т (*т*)	Т	т
У	у	У	у
Ф	ф	Ф	ф
Х	х	Х	х
Ц	ц (*ц*)	Ц	ц
Ч	ч	Ч	ч
Ш	ш (*ш*)	Ш	ш
Щ	щ (*щ*)	Щ	щ
Ъ	ъ	Ъ	ъ
**	ь	**	ь
Ю	ю	Ю	ю
Я	я	Я	я

* The letters in brackets in the second column frequently replace their small printed counterparts in printed texts and public notices.

** The letter **ь** never comes at the beginning of a word, so it is not used as a capital.

Approximate English sound		Bulgarian example	English meaning
a	as in 'art' (but shorter)	Áна	*Anna*
b	as in 'book'	бана́н	*banana*
v	as in 'vice'	вода́	*water*
g	as in 'good'	годи́на	*year*
d	as in 'dot'	да́та	*date*
e	as in 'elephant'	е́сен	*autumn*
s	as in 'pleasure'	жена́	*woman*
z	as in 'zigzag'	зи́ма	*winter*
i	as in 'inch'	и́ме	*name*
y	as in 'yes'	йод	*iodine*
k	as in 'king'	как	*how*
l	as in 'label'	легло́	*bed*
m	as in 'man'	млад	*young*
n	as in 'not'	новина́	*news*
o	as in 'offer'	о́коло	*around*
p	as in 'pet'	па́пка	*folder*
r	as in 'rat'	рестора́нт	*restaurant*
s	as in 'sister'	сестра́	*sister*
t	as in 'tent'	то́рта	*cake*
oo	as in 'foot'	у́тре	*tomorrow*
f	as in 'fifteen'	факс	*fax*
h	as in 'horrid'	ху́бав	*nice*
ts	as in 'fits'	цве́те	*flower*
ch	as in 'church'	че́рква	*church*
sh	as in 'ship'	ша́пка	*hat*
sht	as in 'fishtail'	ща́стие	*happiness*
u	as in 'curtain' (but shorter)	ъ́гъл	*corner*
y	as in 'York'	Ко́льо	*Kolyo*
you	as in 'youth' (but shorter)	ю́ли	*July*
ya	as in 'yarn' (but shorter)	я́года	*strawberry*

Pronouncing Bulgarian

The English sounds you see in the table on p. xiii are only very rough guides to correct Bulgarian pronunciation. Listening to native speakers and copying them is the best way to get things right, so try listening now to the pronunciation guide on the recording. To begin with you might find it helpful to put a ruler beneath the lines with the individual letters and words and move it down the page as you listen and repeat. Later you can just listen, trying to think of the shape of the individual letters as the words are read out.

Stress

You will notice that in each word of more than one syllable, for example **ю́ли** *July*, **годи́на** *year* and **ресторáнт** *restaurant*, we have put an accent above one of the vowels. We have done this to help your pronunciation. Although Bulgarians don't put in the accent when they write, when they speak they pronounce one syllable in every word more distinctly than the rest. (You probably noticed this as you listened to the recording.) This is the 'stressed' syllable. As you can see, the stress can fall on any syllable, just as in English. And as in English, if you stress the wrong syllable, the word will sound very odd, sometimes even incomprehensible. On the rare occasions when a word has two stresses, we have marked this too. So when you learn a new word, make sure you note which syllable is stressed.

You will find some additional notes on pronunciation right at the beginning of the Appendix, but for now it will be enough if you note the following points:

1. Unlike the vowels in English, the Bulgarian vowels don't differ in length. (They are all a little longer than the English short vowels and a little shorter than the English long vowels.)
2. The Bulgarian letter **р** is always rolled, 'r-r-r', as the Scots pronounce B**r**enda and B**r**uce.
3. The sound of the Bulgarian **х** is not found in standard English. It is very like the Scottish **ch** in lo**ch**, and is pronounced nearer the front of the mouth than the English letter **h**.
4. There is no equivalent English letter for **ъ**. We do almost have the sound, though, in a slightly longer version in the **u** in c**ur**tain and f**ur**, or in the letter **e**, when read quickly but clearly in the word th**e**, for example. (Read aloud the last part of this sentence from the word 'or', and you will get the **ъ** in 'the' about right.)

Writing Bulgarian

There are four things to note when writing Bulgarian:

- While there is very little difference between the capital and small letters in the printed script, the printed and the handwritten letters differ considerably. You will, however, come across longhand letters, more rounded in form, used in printed texts alongside their more angular printed counterparts. These are the letters in brackets on p. xii. (You will find examples under 4 below and in the brochure extract on p. 148.)
- Compared with English, both in the printed and handwritten forms, Bulgarian has fewer letters that extend above and below the line. It is important to observe the relative height of the letters.
- When you write the letters **л**, **м** and **я** in longhand, you must make sure you begin the letters with a little hook:

  л *м* *я*

  This makes it impossible to join them to a preceding **о**.
- In general, Bulgarian avoids double consonants, even in foreign words. For example, Mr and Mrs Collins play a large part in this book, and their surname is written **Ко́линс**. Note too that it is written with a final **с**, not a **з**. More about this in the note on pronunciation in the Appendix! Now it's time for a little practice.

Trying out what you have learnt

To help you recognize the letters and to practise your pronunciation, here are some international words, many of them names, and written out in their Bulgarian spelling. We have given both their printed and handwritten forms and have arranged the words in the three different groups mentioned earlier. You should have little difficulty in identifying their English equivalents. Check whether you've got them right by looking up the Key to the Introduction at the back of the book. You might also try writing out the words yourself. Watch the height of your letters!

1 Letters that look the same in Bulgarian and English (at least in their printed form, but see 4 below):

А	**А**ля́ска	*Аляска*	**а**дре́с	*адрес*
Е	**Е**сто́ния	*Естония*	**е**спре́со	*еспресо*

К	**К**ана́да	Канада	**к**ре́дит	кредит
М	**М**ила́но	Милано	**м**ину́та	минута
О	**О**та́ва	Отава	**о**мле́т	омлет
Т	**Т**екса́с	Тексас	**т**елефо́н	телефон

The handwritten forms of the Bulgarian letters **к** and **м** differ slightly from the English, while the Bulgarian handwritten **т** is completely different and confusingly resembles an English **m**.

2 Letters that look different:

Б	**Б**ерли́н	Берлин	**б**ар	бар
Г	**Г**ла́згоу	Глазгоу	**г**ара́ж	гараж
Д	**Д**ако́та	Дакота	во́**д**ка	водка
Ж	**Ж**ене́ва	Женева	**ж**у́ри	жури
З	**З**амбе́зи	Замбези	Ари**з**о́на	Аризона
И	**И**стамбу́л	Истанбул	**И́**нд**и**я	Индия
Й	**Й**орк	Йорк	Ма**й**о́рка	Майорка
Л	**Л**о́ндон	Лондон	Ба**л**ка́н	Балкан
П	**П**ана́ма	Панама	**п**оли́ция	полиция
Ф	**Ф**ра́нкфурт	Франкфурт	Со́**ф**ия	София
Ц	**Ц**ю́рих	Цюрих	Доне́**ц**к	Донецк
Ч	**Ч**ад	Чад	**Ч**ър**ч**ил	Чърчил
Ш	**Ш**е́филд	Шефилд	**ш**оу-би́знес	шоу-бизнес
Щ	**Щ**у́тгарт	Щутгарт	Бу́дапе**щ**а	Будапеща
Ъ	**Ъ́**пдайк	Ъпдайк	Б**ъ**лга́рия	България
Ь	шоф**ь**о́р	шофьор	син**ь**о́ра	синьора
Ю	**Ю́**кон	Юкон	Лийдс **ю**на́йтед	Лийдс юнайт
Я	**Я́**лта	Ялта	**я́**нки	янки

3 Letters that look the same, but are pronounced differently ('false friends'):

В	**В**ие́на	*Виена*	**В**и́**в**иан	*Вивиан*
Н	**Н**ами́бия	*Намибия*	Ва́р**н**а	*Варна*
Р	**Р**и́чард	*Ричард*	Йо́**р**кшир	*Йоркшир*
С	**С**ина́тра	*Синатра*	А́м**с**тердам	*Амстердам*
У	**У**нга́рия	*Унгария*	Ли́верп**у**л	*Ливерпул*
Х	**Х**айд парк	*Хайд парк*	Са**х**а́ра	*Сахара*

Note that unlike the English letter **c** in **cat**, the Bulgarian letter **c** is always pronounced soft as in **Cincinnati** and like the English letter **s** in **S**inatra. It is, therefore, only partially a 'false friend'.

You will notice that the Bulgarian pronunciation of names and 'international' words differs slightly from the English. Sometimes, too, a different syllable is stressed, **телефо́н** and **паспо́рт**, for example. And do remember that Bulgarians say **Со́фия** (*Sófia*, not *Sophía*!)

And talking of 'international words', it has to be said that Cyrillic is increasingly under siege from the Latin script. Sometimes there is considerable uncertainty which script to use. This is particularly the case in business, commerce and communication technology. The Bulgarian mobile phone system, for example, is called GSM, email addresses can only be given in Latin script, and the word 'email' itself still needs an accepted Cyrillic equivalent. You will notice too that Latin script is frequently used alongside Cyrillic in brand and business names and in shop signs.

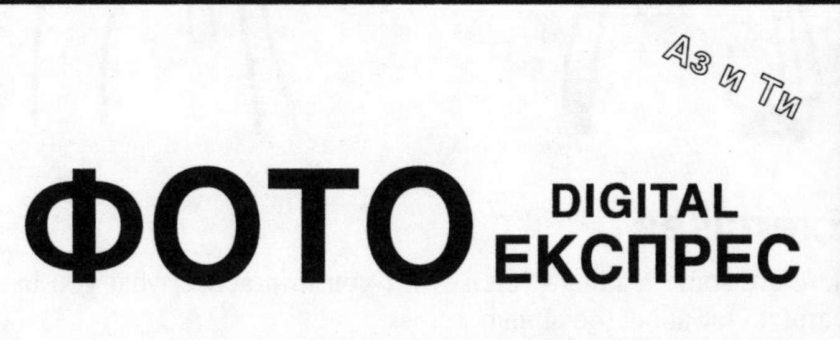

4 Here, side by side, are some words written using both the angular and the more rounded, longhand letters. All the words appear in the previous lists. See if you can recognize them:

адрéс/адрéс, еспрéсо/еспрéсо, телефóн/телефóн, крéдит/крéдит, Отáва/Отáва, гарáж/гарáж, минýта/минýта, Донéцк/Донéцк, шоу-бúзнес/шоу-бúзнес, Бýдапеща/Бýдапеща, Бúйтълс/Бúйтълс, Вúвиан/Вúвиан, Áмстердам/Áмстердам.

Saying *yes* and *no* – a vital word of warning

Another form of communication is non-verbal communication and it is very important in Bulgaria. In most European countries, you nod your head to say 'yes' and shake it to say 'no'. In Bulgaria, a shake of the head – actually often more a rocking of the head from side to side – means *yes* (**да**), while a nod – usually starting with a brisk, dismissive, upward movement of the head – means *no* (**не**).

Whether you are buying an ice-cream, booking an excursion or doing a deal, interpreting the head movements correctly and making them correctly yourself will make all the difference to your negotiations! Have fun and start practising straightaway.

Exercises

Here are some reading exercises for you to practise what you have learnt so far about the alphabet.

1 Read the following place names matching the names in English

with their Bulgarian equivalents. (In this exercise each English letter is replaced by a single Bulgarian letter.)

a	America	**i**	Ло́ндон
b	Amsterdam	**ii**	Саха́ра
c	Arizona	**iii**	Фра́нкфурт
d	Balkan	**iv**	Аме́рика
e	Berlin	**v**	Аризо́на
f	Frankfurt	**vi**	Пло́вдив
g	London	**vii**	Ри́ла
h	Plovdiv	**viii**	Во́лга
i	Rila	**ix**	Ва́рна
j	Sahara	**x**	Балка́н
k	Varna	**xi**	Берли́н
l	Volga	**xii**	А́мстердам

2 Do the same with this list. You might need to replace certain combinations of English letters by a single Bulgarian letter. (Remember that Bulgarian rarely uses double letters!)

a	Charing Cross	**i**	Вие́на
b	Chelmsford	**ii**	Ю́кон
c	Donetsk	**iii**	Че́лмсфорд
d	Shell	**iv**	Ню Йорк
e	Shetland	**v**	Ча́ринг крос
f	Stuttgart	**vi**	Ше́тланд
g	Vienna	**vii**	Доне́цк
h	Yalta	**viii**	Шел
i	New York	**ix**	Щу́тгарт
j	Yukon	**x**	Я́лта

3 Here, concentrate on the sound; read the Bulgarian and identify the English equivalent. Sometimes one English letter needs two letters in Bulgarian and vice-versa.

a	Ли́йдс	**i**	Richard Burton
b	Елизабе́т Те́йлър	**ii**	Beatles
c	Хе́лзинки	**iii**	Helsinki
d	Ли́върпул	**iv**	Oxford
e	Джеймс Бонд	**v**	Liverpool
f	Португа́лия	**vi**	James Bond
g	Чарлс Ди́кенс	**vii**	Scotland
h	О́ксфорд	**viii**	Leeds
i	Би́йтълс	**ix**	Charles Dickens
j	Ри́чард Бъ́ртън	**x**	France
k	Ко́рнуол	**xi**	Geneva
l	Гла́згоу	**xii**	Cambridge

m	Женéва	**xiii**	Cornwall
n	Шотлáндия	**xiv**	Elizabeth Taylor
o	Кéймбридж	**xv**	Glasgow
p	Фрáнция	**xvi**	Portugal

4 If you rang the following numbers, what service would you expect to answer? Read the Bulgarian words out loud!

201	ФАКС	205	БАР
202	РЕСТОРÁНТ	206	ТАКСЍ
203	РЕЦÉПЦИЯ	207	ИНФОРМÁЦИЯ
204	ФЍТНЕС ЦÉНТЪР	166	ПОЛЍЦИЯ

5 What are the names of (**a**) the snack bar, (**b**) the restaurant, (**c**) the hotel and (**d**) the café on the following notices?

a	СНЕК-БАР «СИРÉНА»	**c**	ХОТÉЛ «ШÉРАТОН»
b	РЕСТОРÁНТ «БЕРЛЍН»	**d**	КАФÉ «ОРИÉНТ»

6 When does your plane take off if you are flying to:

a Milan
b Geneva
c Frankfurt
d Paris
e Berlin
f Zurich
g Budapest?

Цю́рих ______	15.40
Бýдапеща ____	16.10
Фрáнкфурт____	16.35
Женéва ______	17.05
Милáно ______	17.25
Парúж ______	18.05
Берлúн ______	18.30

здраве́йте! как се ка́звате?

hello, what's your name?

In this unit you will learn

- **how to say *hello***
- **how to give your name and nationality**
- **how to say *please* and *thank you***
- **how to say *yes* and *no* in answer to *is there?* and *are there?***

Michael Johnson, a businessman from London, arrives at his hotel in Sofia. When he enters the vestibule he is greeted by the doorman with the words **Заповя́дайте, мо́ля!** meaning, here: *Welcome, do come in, please.* (**Мо́ля** can also mean *I beg your pardon* and *Don't mention it.*)

You will often hear **заповя́дайте** and **мо́ля** in Bulgaria, used separately and together with a variety of meanings. They are always polite and welcoming words. Together with the two words for *thank you* – **Благодаря́** and **Мерси́** (*Merci* – as in the French!), and the word for *there isn't* **ня́ма** – they are what for you will probably be the five most important words in the Bulgarian language.

Dialogue

Michael goes up to the reception desk and is greeted by the receptionist, Nevena Petkova.

Неве́на Петко́ва До́бър ден!
Ма́йкъл Джо́нсън Здраве́йте! И́ма ли свобо́дна стá́я?
Неве́на Петко́ва (*Nodding.**) Не, ня́ма.
Ма́йкъл Джо́нсън И́ма ли свобо́ден апартаме́нт?
Неве́на Петко́ва (*Shaking her head.**) Да, и́ма. Тури́ст ли сте?
Ма́йкъл Джо́нсън Не, не съм тури́ст. Би́знесмен съм.
Неве́на Петко́ва И́ме?
Ма́йкъл Джо́нсън Мо́ля?
Неве́на Петко́ва Как се ка́звате?
Ма́йкъл Джо́нсън Ка́звам се Ма́йкъл Джо́нсън.
Неве́на Петко́ва Англича́нин ли сте?
Ма́йкъл Джо́нсън Да, англича́нин съм.
Неве́на Петко́ва Паспо́рта, мо́ля.
Ма́йкъл Джо́нсън Заповя́дайте!
Неве́на Петко́ва Благодаря́!
Ма́йкъл Джо́нсън Мо́ля!

*If this confuses you, look back to the vital word of warning on p. xviii.

До́бър ден!	*Good morning/afternoon.*
Здраве́йте!	*Hello!*
И́ма ли свобо́дна стá́я?	*Is there a room free?*
Не, ня́ма.	*No, there isn't.*
свобо́ден апартаме́нт	*a free apartment*
Да, и́ма.	*Yes, there is.*
Тури́ст ли сте?	*Are you a tourist?*

Не, не съм турúст.	*No, I'm not a tourist.*
Бúзнесмен съм.	*I'm a businessman.*
úме	*name*
Мóля?	*(I beg your) Pardon?*
Как се кáзвате?	*What is your name?*
Кáзвам се...	*My name is...*
Англичáнин ли сте?	*Are you English?*
Да, англичáнин съм.	*Yes, I am (English).*
Паспóрта, мóля.	*Your (the) passport, please.*
Заповя́дайте!	*Here you are/There you go.*
Благодаря́!	*Thank you.*
Мóля!	*Not at all/don't mention it/ my pleasure.*

Questions

Before answering these questions, listen to the recording again (if you have it), once without looking at the dialogue and once following the text as you listen. It would also be a good idea to read aloud the questions before you answer them.

You'll find all the answers in the Dialogue – except to **1** (**c**)! The answers are also in the Key at the back of the book.

1 Try to answer the questions

- **a** Úма ли свобóден апартамéнт?
- **b** Úма ли свобóдна стáя?
- **c** Как се кáзвате? (Give your own name.)

2 True or false?

Write out correct versions of the false statements. Michael Johnson says:

- **a** Англичáнин съм.
- **b** Турúст съм.
- **c** Бúзнесмен съм.

i Greetings

The most frequently heard greeting, and the one to use on formal occasions when addressing people you do not know, is **дóбър ден!** Literally translated it means *Good day*. You can say **дóбър ден!** at any time of the day except the early morning, when you should use **добрó ýтро!** *Good morning*, and the evening, when you say **дóбър вéчер!** *Good evening*.

Здраве́й! and **Здраве́йте!** are rather less formal and are used when you would say *Hello* or *Hi!* in English. Literally the words both mean *May you be healthy*. **Здраве́й!** is a singular form and **здраве́йте!** is a plural. You say **здраве́й!** to a friend or someone you know well. When greeting more than one person or someone you know less well you use **здраве́йте!** (Plural is always polite!) You might also use **здраве́йте!** (instead of the more official **до́бър ден!**) when addressing someone you know well but whom you still address with the polite, formal form. Both **здраве́й!** and **здраве́йте!** can be used at any time of the day, or night.

You will notice that the only difference between **здраве́й!** and **здраве́йте!** is the addition of the two letters -**те** to the greeting you use when meeting a friend. In fact, these two letters distinguish the plural (formal) from the singular (familiar) forms. They are found on the end of other 'polite', 'non-familiar' forms too. You will notice them, for example, on the end of the word **Заповя́дайте!** used by Michael Johnson when he gives Nevena Petkova his passport. (If Michael knew Nevena better, he would say **Заповя́дай!** without the letters -**те**.) You will also see them on the end of the words used by Nevena when she asks Michael his name: Как се ка́зва**те**? and inquires whether he is English: Англича́нин ли **сте?**

How do you say it?

- Asking somebody's name, and giving yours

Как се ка́звате?	*What is your name?*
Ка́звам се Ма́йкъл Джо́нсън.	*My name is Michael Johnson.*
Ка́звам се Неве́на Петко́ва.	*My name is Nevena Petkova.*

- Greeting people at different times of the day

Здраве́йте!	*Hello!* (polite or more than one person)
Здраве́й!	*Hello!* (informal, one person)
Добро́ у́тро!/До́бър ден!	*Good morning.*
До́бър ден!	*Good afternoon.*
До́бър ве́чер!	*Good evening.*

- Saying *please*, *thank you* and *(I beg your) pardon*?

Мо́ля!	*Please; don't mention it; not at all!*
Мо́ля?	*(I beg your) pardon?*
Благодаря́/Мерси́.	*Thank you.*

- Welcoming someone or extending an invitation

Заповя́дай!/Заповя́дайте!	*Won't you please...?; here you are; there you go!*

- Answering *yes* or *no* to *is there?* and *are there?*

И́ма ли свобо́дна ста́я?	*Is there a room free?*
Да, и́ма.	*Yes, there is.*
И́ма ли свобо́ден апартаме́нт?	*Is there a free apartment?*
Не, ня́ма.	*No, there isn't.*

- Confirming your nationality

Англича́нин/англича́нка ли сте?	*Are you English?*
Да, англича́нин/англича́нка съм.	*Yes, I am English.*
Америка́нец/америка́нка ли сте?	*Are you American?*
Да, америка́нец/америка́нка съм.	*Yes, I am American.*
Кана́дец/кана́дка ли сте?	*Are you Canadian?*
Да, кана́дец/кана́дка съм.	*Yes, I am Canadian.*

Grammar

1 Things as *he*, *she* and *it*: gender

All words naming things, whether living or not, are referred to as *he*, *she* or *it* in Bulgarian. This means that all naming words, also called nouns, belong to one of three groups or genders: masculine, feminine or neuter. It is not difficult to recognize them:

masculine nouns usually end in a consonant or **-й**
feminine nouns usually end in **-а** or **-я**
neuter nouns usually end in **-о**, **-е** or sometimes **-и**
words of foreign origin ending in **-и**, **-у** and **-ю** are also neuter.

Masculine			
америка́нец	*an American man*	англича́нин	*an Englishman*
апартаме́нт	*a flat*	българин	*a Bulgarian man*
ден	*a day*	музе́й	*a museum*
мъж	*a man*	тури́ст	*a tourist*
Feminine			
америка́нка	*an American woman*	англича́нка	*an English woman*
българка	*a Bulgarian woman*	ста́я	*a room*
жена́	*a woman*		
Neuter			
кафе́	*coffee, café*	море́	*a sea*
меню́	*menu*	такси́	*taxi*
писмо́	*a letter*	у́тро	*a morning*

2 Adjectives

Describing words that tell you about a thing's qualities are called adjectives. Adjectives acquire similar endings to the nouns: consonants for masculine adjectives, **-a** for feminine ones and **-o** for neuter. You can see this in the expressions дóбъ**р** де**н**, свобóдн**а** стá**я**, добр**ó** ýтр**о**. This repetition of endings often seems to create semi-rhyming groups of words, especially in the feminine and the neuter. Here are some examples:

Masculine	добъ**р** англичáни**н**	*a good Englishman*	свобóде**н** де**н**	*a free day*
Feminine	добр**á** българк**а**	*a good Bulgarian woman*	свобóдн**а** стá**я**	*a free room*
Neuter	добр**ó** ýтр**о**	*good morning*	свобóдн**о** мя́ст**о**	*a free place*

3 Свобóден съм *I am free*

Also, an expression like *I am free* will change depending on whether a man or a woman is speaking. Michael Johnson will say of himself:

свобóде**н** съм. — *I am free.*

Whereas Nevena will say:

свобóдн**а** съм.

And you would say of them:

Невéна е свобóдн**а**. — *Nevena is free.*
Мáйкъл Джóнсън е свобóде**н**. — *Michael Johnson is free.*

A good-looking (but immodest) man might say of himself хýба**в** съм, while a good-looking (and equally immodest) woman would say of herself хýбав**а** съм.

4 Англичáнин ли сте? *Are you English?*

To ask questions which require answers *yes* or *no* you need to add **ли** immediately after the word, or group of words, to which your question is directed:

Англичáнин **ли** сте? — *Are you English?*
Да, англичáнин съм. — *Yes, I am English.*
Не, не съ́м англичáнин. — *No, I am not English.*

Тури́ст **ли** сте? — *Are you a tourist?*
Да, тури́ст съм. — *Yes, I am a tourist.*
Не, не съм тури́ст. — *No, I am not a tourist.*

By moving **ли** from one word to another you can shift the emphasis of your question. In English, you do this by changing your intonation.

Ма́йкъл **в Со́фия ли** е? — *Is Michael **in Sofia**?*
Ма́йкъл ли е в Со́фия? — *Is **Michael** in Sofia?*

5 Ѝма and ня́ма *There is* and *there is not*

The Bulgarian equivalent of both *there is* and *there are* is **ѝма**. The negative *there is not* and *there are not* is simply **ня́ма**:

Ѝма свобо́дна стá я. — *There is a room free.*
Ня́ма свобо́дна стá я. — *There isn't a room free.*
В Ло́ндон **ѝма** река́. — *There is a river in London.*
В Со́фия **ня́ма** река́. — *There isn't a river in Sofia.*

And if you want to ask a question you again add **ли**:

Ѝма **ли** свобо́дна стá я? — *Is there a room free?*
Да, ѝма. — *Yes, there is.*
Ѝма **ли** река́ в Ло́ндон? — *Is there a river in London?*
Да, ѝма. — *Yes, there is.*

6 Не съм – saying *not*

The negative word in Bulgarian is **не**. It is normally placed immediately before the verb:

Не съм бъ́лгарин. — *I'm not a Bulgarian.*
Англича́нин съм. — *I'm an Englishman.*
Не съм бъ́лгарка. — *I'm not a Bulgarian.*
Англича́нка съм. — *I'm an English woman.*

Не is never stressed when followed immediately by a verb. Here **Не съм** is read as one word with emphasis on **съм**.

Exercises

1 This exercise, as far as **шофьо́р**, is on the recording at the end of the Pronunciation guide. Read the following 'international' words out loud in Bulgarian. This will help your pronunciation and build up your vocabulary.

a аге́нция
b адре́с
c аспири́н
d ба́нка
e би́знес
f би́ра
g во́дка
h компю́тър
i лимона́да
j му́зика
k по́ни
l пробле́м
m со́да
n спорт
o то́ник
p тури́ст
q фи́рма
r фу́тбол
s шофьо́р
t при́нтер
u о́фис
v факс
w ви́део
x ксе́рокс

Which words are feminine and which are masculine or neuter?

2 How would you say *hello!* (**здраве́й!** or **здраве́йте!**) to:

a a good friend?
b your parents?
c your boss?
d a shop assistant?
e a little boy?
f a little girl?
g a group of students?

3 How would you greet the hotel porter at the times shown on the pictures?

a (Добро́ у́тро *or* до́бър ден?)

c (Добро́ у́тро *or* до́бър ден?)

b (Добро́ у́тро *or* до́бър ден?)

d (До́бър ден *or* до́бър ве́чер?)

4 Match the questions and answers. If you don't recognize a word, look it up in the Bulgarian–English vocabulary at the end of the book.

i	Америкáнка ли сте?	**a**	Не, не съм българин, англичáнин съм.
ii	Българка ли сте?	**b**	Да, англичáнка съм.
iii	Българин ли сте?	**c**	Да, англичáнин съм.
iv	Англичáнин ли сте?	**d**	Не, не сýм америкáнец, англичáнин съм.
v	Америкáнец ли сте?	**e**	Не, не сýм българка, англичáнка съм.
vi	Англичáнка ли сте?	**f**	Да, америкáнка съм.

5 Answer the following questions with yes or no (**Да, и́ма** or **Не, ня́ма**):

a	И́ма ли кафé?	Да, ________
b	И́ма ли тóник?	Да, ________
c	И́ма ли сóда?	Не, ________
d	И́ма ли джин? (*gin*)	Не, ________
e	И́ма ли таксú?	Да, ________
f	И́ма ли бúра?	Не, ________

6 Repeat the dialogue, which inquires whether there is any mineral water, using the following:

a	уúски	*whisky*	**c**	лимонáда	*lemonade*
b	бúра	*beer*	**d**	чай	*tea*

Сáндра И́ма ли минерáлна водá?
Николáй Да, заповя́дайте.
Сáндра Благодаря́!

7 Make your choice of drink following the model below:

Боя́н Джин илú (*or*) вóдка?
Кен Джин, мóля.
Невéна Вóдка, мóля.

a	**Боя́н**	Уúски илú джин?	**c**	**Джон**	Капучúно илú еспрéсо? (*espresso*)
	Кен	________		**Виктóрия**	________
	Невéна	________		**Боя́н**	________
b	**Боя́н**	Бúра илú Кóка-Кóла?	**d**	**Виктóрия**	Кафé илú чай?
	Кен	________		**Джон**	________
	Виктóрия	________		**Невéна**	________

8 First read aloud and then say in English who is admiring what or whom. Remember that **хýбав** can mean many things – *good-looking*, *nice*, *beautiful*, *lovely*. You could think up other words meaning *nice* which are appropriate to the object.

a	**Мáйкъл Джóнсън**	Хýбав хотéл!
b	**Невéна**	Хýбав мъж!
c	**Джýли**	Хýбаво морé!
d	**Сáндра**	Хýбава бúра!
e	**Трéйси**	Хýбаво úме!
f	**Кен**	Хýбава бъ̀лгарка!

Now, using **хýбав**, **хýбава** or **хýбаво**, express your own satisfaction with your room, your apartment or the lovely Bulgarian wine (бъ̀лгарско вúно):

g ——— стáя!
h ——— апартамéнт!
i ——— бъ̀лгарско вúно!

9 Michael Johnson has to sign the register at the hotel – in Bulgarian, of course – filling in his name and home address. Try writing out what he entered in Bulgarian longhand:

Йме:	Майкъл Джонсън	*Michael Johnson*
Адрéс:	4, Маунт Драйв	*4, Mount Drive*
	Челмсфорд	*Chelmsford*
	Есекс	*Essex*
	Англия	*England*

He also needs to send his Sofia address to his wife, so that she can address the envelope in Cyrillic. Have a go in longhand yourself! Notice how, in Bulgarian, the address is usually written back to front, following the actual route of the letter, moving from the country to the town, to the hotel and the apartment, and finally the addressee:

България	*Michael Johnson*
1000 София	*Apartment 8*
хотел «Родина»	*Rodina Hotel*
апартамент 8	*Sofia 1000*
Майкъл Джонсън	*Bulgaria*

Now write your own name and address in Cyrillic, placing the various components in the Bulgarian order. In actual fact, the Bulgarians are better at deciphering the English script than we are the Bulgarian, so you can get away with addressing your letters in English.

Do you understand?

В ресторáнта *In the restaurant*

Read the following conversation and answer the questions in English:

Сервитьóр	Дóбър вéчер!
Мáйкъл Джóнсън	Дóбър вéчер! Úма ли свобóдно мя́сто?
Сервитьóр	Да, úма. Заповя́дайте!
Мáйкъл Джóнсън	Хýбав ресторáнт! Úма ли шотлáндско уúски?
Сервитьóр	Да, úма. Сóда?
Мáйкъл Джóнсън	Не, минерáлна водá, мóля. Úма ли телефóн с фонокáрта тук в ресторáнта?
Сервитьóр	Не, ня́ма. Съжаля́вам.

мя́сто	*a place*
сервитъóр	*waiter*
хýбав, хýбава, хýбаво	*good-looking, nice, lovely, beautiful*
шотлáндско уúски	*Scotch (whisky)*
телефóн с фонокáрта	*phonecard telephone*
тук	*here*
съжаля́вам	*I'm sorry*

Questions

1 What time of day is it?
2 Is there a place free?
3 What kind of whisky does Mr Johnson want?
4 Does he order anything else?
5 Is there a phonecard telephone in the restaurant?

02 как сте? и́мате ли вре́ме?

how are you? do you have a moment?

In this unit you will learn

- how to ask simple questions using **как?** *how?* and **кога́?** *when?*
- expressions with **и́мам** *have* and **ня́мам** *have not*
- how to respond to **какво́ е това́?** *What is this?* and **как сте?** *How are you?*

Dialogue

Boyan Antonov, manager of an advertising agency in Sofia, calls in at the office to see Nadya, his secretary.

Анто́нов Здраве́й, На́дя.
На́дя До́бър ден, господи́н Анто́нов!
Анто́нов Как си днес?
На́дя Благодаря́, добре́ съм. А Ви́е как сте?
Анто́нов И аз съм добре́. Какво́ е това́?
На́дя Това́ е те́лекс от Ло́ндон.
Анто́нов Кога́ присти́га господи́н Джо́нсън?
На́дя Той присти́га днес.
Анто́нов Кога́ и́ма самоле́т от Ло́ндон?
На́дя В се́дем часа́.
Анто́нов Мно́го добре́. Тук ли са Никола́й и Миле́на?
На́дя Не, те не са́ о́ще тук.
Анто́нов Ни́що. Това́ е вси́чко засега́.
На́дя И́мате ли вре́ме за едно́ кафе́?
Анто́нов Ня́мам вре́ме, съжаля́вам. Днес и́мам мно́го ра́бота.
На́дя Дови́ждане, господи́н Анто́нов! Прия́тен ден!
Анто́нов Благодаря́! Дови́ждане!

господи́н Анто́нов	*Mr Antonov*
Как си днес?	*How are you today?* (familiar)
Благодаря́.	*Thank you.*
Добре́ съм.	*I'm fine.*
И аз съм добре́.	*I'm fine too.*
А Ви́е как сте?	*And how are you?* (formal)
Какво́ е това́?	*What is this?*
Това́ е те́лекс от Ло́ндон.	*It's a telex from London.*
Кога́ присти́га господи́н Джо́нсън?	*When does Mr Johnson arrive?*
Той присти́га днес.	*He is arriving today.*
Кога́ и́ма самоле́т от Ло́ндон?	*When is there a plane from London?*
в се́дем часа́	*at seven o'clock*

мно́го добре́	*very good/fine*
Тук ли са Никола́й и Миле́на?	*Are Nikolai and Milena here?*
Те не са́ о́ще тук.	*They are not here yet.*
ни́що	*never mind*
Това́ е всичко засега́.	*That's all for now.*
И́мате ли вре́ме за едно́ кафе́?	*Have you time for a coffee?*
Ня́мам вре́ме.	*I haven't time.*
И́мам мно́го ра́бота.	*I have a lot of work.*
Дови́ждане.	*Goodbye.*
Прия́тен ден!	*Have a nice day!*

Questions

1 Try to answer the questions.
Looking back to the dialogue, answer these questions instead of Nadya:

- **a** Здраве́й, На́дя. Как си днес? Добре́ ли си?
- **b** (*Picking up the printout*) Какво́ е това́?
- **c** Това́ те́лекс от Ло́ндон ли е?
- **d** Кога́ и́ма самоле́т от Ло́ндон?
- **e** Днес ли присти́га господи́н Джо́нсън?

2 True or false?
Write out correct versions of the false statements.

- **a** На́дя не е́ добре́.
- **b** Това́ е те́лекс от Ло́ндон.
- **c** Никола́й и Миле́на не са́ тук.
- **d** Господи́н Анто́нов и́ма вре́ме за кафе́.
- **e** Господи́н Анто́нов ня́ма мно́го ра́бота.

i Mr, Mrs and Miss

The traditional Bulgarian equivalents of the English *Mr* and *Mrs* are **господи́н** (masculine) and **госпожа́** (feminine). When written, **господи́н** is abbreviated to **г-н** and **госпожа́** to **г-жа́**. You address an unmarried woman as **госпо́жица** (*Miss*).

When you address someone without using their surname, you use the words **господи́н**, **госпожа́** and **госпо́жица** in their special address forms: **господи́не**, **госпо́жо** (note the stress change) and **госпо́жице**. So you say:

До́бър ве́чер, **господи́не!**	*Good evening.* (to Mr)
Дови́ждане, **госпо́жо!**	*Goodbye.* (to Mrs)
Здраве́йте, **госпо́жице!**	*Hello.* (to Miss)

When a surname is used, the special address form is obligatory with the Bulgarian word for *Miss*, so you say: **Здраве́йте, госпо́жице Петко́ва!** *Hello, Miss Petkova*. For *Mrs* you can either say **госпожа́** or **госпо́жо Бори́сова**, but for *Mr* with a surname the special form is never used, so you can only say: **До́бър ве́чер, господи́н Анто́нов!** *Good evening, Mr Antonov.*

Bulgarian does not yet have the equivalent of *Ms*.

Surnames

Masculine surnames usually end in **-ов** or **-ев**, while feminine surnames usually end in **-ова** or **-ева**. Thus Mr Antonov's wife is called **г-жа́ Анто́нова**, while Nevena Petkova's father is **г-н Петко́в**. The stress in feminine surnames is not necessarily on the **о** or **е** preceding the **в**. So, although you do say Петк**о́**ва, for example, you have to say Ант**о́**нова, Бор**и́**сова, Ков**а́**чева and Ст**а́**нева.

How do you say it?

- Asking someone how they are and saying you're fine too

Как си? Как сте?	*How are you?*
Добре́ съм.	*I'm fine.*
И аз съм добре́.	*I'm fine too.*

- Asking *What is this?* and answering *This is...* or *This is not...*

Какво́ е това́?	*What is this?*
Това́ е факс.	*This is a fax.*
Това́ не е́ писмо́.	*This is not a letter.*

- Asking *When?*

Кога́ присти́га г-н Джо́нсън?	*When does Mr Johnson arrive?*
Кога́ и́ма самоле́т от Ло́ндон?	*When is there a plane from London?*

- Saying *Goodbye*

Дови́ждане!	*Goodbye.*

- Expressing good wishes on parting

Прия́тен ден!/Лек ден!	*Have a good day.*
Прия́тна ра́бота!	*Have a good day* (*at work*).
Прия́тна почи́вка!	*Have a good rest.*
Прия́тен уикенд!	*Have a nice weekend.*
Вси́чко ху́баво!/Вси́чко добро́!	*All the best.*

- Expressing regret

Съжаля́вам.	*I'm sorry.*

Grammar

1 Еди́н and English *a*

Normally, no equivalent of the English indefinite article *a* or *an* is necessary in Bulgarian. Compare:

Това́ е и́мейл.	*This is **an** email.*
Това́ е хоте́л.	*This is **an** hotel.*
Тук и́ма рестора́нт.	*There is **a** restaurant here.*
Аз съм англича́нин.	*I'm **an** Englishman.*

However, when the English *a* means *one*, *a certain* or *a single*, you need to use the Bulgarian word for *one* – **еди́н**. **Еди́н** is a counting word, a numeral. It is also an adjective and has different forms for the masculine, feminine and neuter.

Masculine	**еди́н** англича́нин	***one*** *Englishman*	**еди́н** и́мейл	***one*** *email*
Feminine	**една́** би́ра	***one*** *beer*	**една́** стая	***one*** *room*
Neuter	**едно́** кафе́	***one*** *coffee*	**едно́** мя́сто	***one*** *place*
	едно́ писмо́	***one*** *letter*		

If you use the numeral on its own, you have to use the neuter form, as: ста́я но́мер **едно́** *room number one*.

2 *I*, *you*, *he/she/it*, *we*, *you* and *they*

Bulgarian has almost the equivalents of the English words for these subject pronouns, but there are two small differences. First, the Bulgarian **аз** *I* is written with a small letter and, second, Bulgarian has two different words for *you*: **ти** for the singular, familiar form and **ви́е** for the plural. Moreover, when addressing just one person in the polite, formal mode, Bulgarians use the plural form and, when writing, spell it with a capital letter: **Ви́е**.

Singular		**Plural**	
аз	*I*	**ни́е**	*we*
ти	*you*	**ви́е/Ви́е**	*you*
той	*he*		
тя	*she*	**те**	*they*
то	*it*		

If you are using a verb, you can usually omit the subject pronouns, for the ending of the verb makes it clear who is involved. The only times you *must* use the subject pronouns are for emphasis or to avoid ambiguity:

Как си? Добре́ съм. — *How are you? I'm fine.* (No emphasis here!)
А **Ви́е** как сте? — *And how about* ***you****?* (Emphasis)
И **аз** съм добре́. — ***I'm*** *fine too.* (Emphasis)

3 Съм *I am* and the verb *to be*

Verbs, or action words, in Bulgarian have no neutral or basic form corresponding to the English infinitive. There are, therefore, no equivalents of the English 'dictionary' forms *to be* or *to have*. Instead, in Bulgarian dictionaries, verbs are listed in the *I* form (1st person singular) *I am*, *I hav*e, etc.

Here are all the forms of **съм** in the present tense:

(аз)	**съм**	*I am*	**(ни́е)**	**сме**	*we are*
(ти)	**си**	*you are*	**(ви́е)**	**сте**	*you are*
(той)	**е**	*he is*			
(тя)	**е**	*she is*	**(те)**	**са***	*they are*
(то)	**е**	*it is*	*pronounced **(те съ)**		

You have already come across **е** in the question какво́ **е** това́? and the answer това́ **е** факс. Here are some more examples illustrating all forms of **съм**:

Аз съм в Со́фия. — *I am in Sofia.*
Ти си тук. — *You are here.*
Джон не е́ в Ло́ндон. — *John is not in London.*
На́дя е добре́. — *Nadya is well.*
Ни́е сме добре́. — *We are well.*
Ви́е сте тук. — *You are here.*
Те не са́ тук. — *They are not here.*

Note that the usage of the Bulgarian equivalent of *to be* differs from the English in two important ways:

(***a***) the negative marker **не** always comes before the verb

(***b***) when the subject noun or subject pronoun is omitted, you cannot begin the sentence with **съм** or any of its other forms. This means that the different forms of **съм** come second after an introductory word or group of words:

	В Со́фия съм.	*I am in Sofia.*
but	Не съ́м в Со́фия.	*I am not in Sofia.*
	Тук сме.	*We are here.*
but	Не сме́ тук.	*We are not here.*
	На́дя е добре́.	*Nadya is well.*
but	Добре́ е.	*She* (or *he*) *is well.*

4 И́мам/ня́мам *I have* and *I have not*

One unusual feature of Bulgarian is that the negative of **и́мам** (*to have*) is not formed by placing **не** before the verb. Instead, a different verb is used: **ня́мам** (*not to have*). Otherwise, as you can see in this table and in the following examples, the two verbs have identical endings.

аз	**и́мам/ня́мам**	*I have/haven't*	**ни́е и́маме/ня́маме**	*we have/haven't*
ти	**и́маш/ня́маш**	*you have/haven't*	**ви́е и́мате/ня́мате**	*you have/haven't*
той	**и́ма/ня́ма**	*he has/hasn't*	**те и́мат/ня́мат**	*they have/haven't*
тя	**и́ма/ня́ма**	*she has/hasn't*		

И́мам мно́го ра́бота днес.	*I have a lot of work today.*
И́маш писмо́ от Ло́ндон.	*You have a letter from London.*
Г-н Анто́нов ня́ма факс.	*Mr Antonov does not have a fax.*
На́дя ня́ма мно́го ра́бота.	*Nadya does not have much work.*
Ни́е ня́маме вре́ме за кафе́.	*We don't have time for coffee.*
Ви́е и́мате ли вре́ме за кафе́?	*Do you have time for coffee?*
Те и́мат мно́го ра́бота днес.	*They have a lot of work today.*

The verbs **присти́гам** *to arrive*, **съжаля́вам** *to be sorry* and **ка́звам се** *to be called* also follow the pattern of **и́мам**:

Г-н Джо́нсън присти́га в се́дем часа́.	*Mr Johnson arrives at seven o'clock.*
Съжаля́ва**ме**, но ня́ма**ме** вре́ме.	*We are sorry, but we have no time.*
Как се ка́зва**ш**?	*What is your name?*

In Bulgarian, there are three basic verb patterns. This one is the **а**-pattern. (You'll find out more in Unit 4.)

5 Asking questions

как?	*how?*	**Как**	**са те?**	*How are they?*
какво́?	*what?*	**Какво́**	**е това́?**	*What is this?*
кога́?	*when?*	**Кога́**	**присти́гаш?**	*When do you arrive?*
къде́?	*where?*	**Къде́**	**е той?**	*Where is he?*

6 Counting to ten

0	ну́ла		
1	едно́	6	шест
2	две	7	се́дем
3	три	8	о́сем
4	че́тири	9	де́вет
5	пет	10	де́сет

7 *И and, also* and *too*

The little word **и** can have all these meanings in Bulgarian. Normally it is used to join two or more similar things and simply means *and*, as in:

Никола́й **и** Миле́на са тук. — *Nikolai **and** Milena are here.*

Sometimes though, you'll find it used for emphasis to mean *also* and *too*:

И аз съм добре́. — *I'm fine **too**.*

The word **a** can also mean *and*, but only when there is an element of contrast implied:

Той е добре́. А Ви́е как сте? — *He is fine. And (But) how about you?*

Тя е тук. А те са в Ло́ндон. — *She is here. And (But) they are in London.*

Exercises

1 Replace the personal names with the correct subject pronoun: **той**, **тя** or **те**.

- **a** Къде́ е госпожа́ Джо́нсън?
- **b** Господи́н Анто́нов е добре́.
- **c** Как е господи́н Джо́нсън?
- **d** Къде́ са Джон и Кен?
- **e** Неве́на е в хоте́л «Роди́на».
- **f** Господи́н Анто́нов и́ма ра́бота.
- **g** Тук ли са Никола́й и Миле́на?

2 Read the following dialogues out loud completing them according to the model:

Тури́ст Аз съм Пол Те́йлър.
Неве́на Мо́ля? Как се ка́звате?
Тури́ст Ка́звам се Пол Те́йлър.

Note that **мо́ля** here is used to mean *I beg your pardon.* (**тури́стка** = *tourist* woman; **тури́сти** = *tourists*)

a	**Тури́стка**	Аз съм Джу́ли Дже́ймсън.
	Неве́на	Мо́ля? Как се ка́звате?
	Тури́стка	________
b	**Дете́** (*child*)	Аз съм То́ни.
	Неве́на	Мо́ля? Как се ка́зваш?
	Дете́	________
c	**Анто́нов**	Аз съм Боя́н Анто́нов.
	Неве́на	Мо́ля? Как се ка́звате?
	Анто́нов	________
d	**Тури́сти**	Ни́е сме господи́н и госпожа́ Ко́линс.
	Неве́на	Мо́ля? Как се ка́звате?
	Тури́сти	________

3 In the previous exercise you asked questions in the singular and plural, as well as in the plural of formal speech. Bearing in mind the distinction between familiar and formal forms, ask the following people their names:

a a little girl
b an elderly lady
c a young couple

4 Read the following signs at the stop (**спи́рка**) for the tram (**трамва́й**) and the trolleybus (**троле́й**):

СПИРКА Трамвай № 1

СПИРКА Тролей № 3

Now read the words on the sign, changing the tram number to 2, 5, 6 and 8, and the trolleybus number to 1, 4, 7 and 9.

5 You are staying in room number 7. Nevena has rung through from reception. Read the following dialogue and then answer instead of Mrs Collins giving your own name and room number:

Неве́на	Ви́е ли сте г-жа́ Джо́нсън?
г-жа́ Ко́линс	Не, аз съм г-жа́ Ко́линс.
Неве́на	Ви́е в стáя де́сет ли сте?
г-жа́ Ко́линс	Не, аз съм в стáя но́мер о́сем.

6 Ask questions to which the following could be answers, using either **как?** or **какво́?** (Don't forget to change from **аз** to **ти** and **ни́е** to **ви́е!**)

Model: Това́ е автобу́с. (*bus*) (Какво́ е това́?)
Аз съм добре́. (Как си ти?/Как сте Ви́е?)

a Това́ е такси́.
b Тя е добре́.
c Те са добре́.
d Това́ е музе́й. (*museum* is masculine)
e Добре́ съм.
f Това́ е троле́й (masculine)
g Ни́е сме добре́.
h Това́ е фи́тнес це́нтър. (*fitness centre*)

7 To test your knowledge of the question words **къде́?** *where?* and **кога́?** *when?*, read out loud, matching the questions and answers:

i Къде́ е той?
ii Кога́ и́ма самоле́т от Ло́ндон?
iii Кога́ присти́га той?
iv Къде́ са те?
v Къде́ е Че́лмсфорд?

a Той присти́га в три часа́.
b Той е в Со́фия.
c Че́лмсфорд е в А́нглия.
d Самоле́т от Ло́ндон и́ма в се́дем часа́.
e Те са в Шотла́ндия. (*Scotland*)

8 Using the model that follows, ask for the places (**a**)–(**e**) in Sofia. And reply each time saying it is *over there*.

Тури́ст	Това́ ли е хоте́л «Пли́ска»?	*Is this the Pliska Hotel?*
Българин	Не, хоте́л «Пли́ска» е там.	*No, the Pliska Hotel is over there.*

a рестора́нт «Криста́л»
b булева́рд «Ле́вски» (*Levski Boulevard*)
c Центра́лна по́ща (*the Central Post Office*)
d хоте́л «Хе́мус»
e у́лица «Рако́вски» (*Rakovski Street*)

9 Complete the answers with **и́мам** or **ня́мам**:

a И́мате ли резерва́ция (*reservation*), госпожа́ Ко́линс?
Не, ________.
b И́мате ли българска ви́за (*visa*), госпо́жо?
Да, ________.
c И́мате ли ка́рта (*map*), господи́н Джо́нсън?
Не, ________.
d И́мате ли биле́т (*ticket*), госпо́жице?
Да, ________.
e И́мате ли паспо́рт, господи́не? Да, ________.

10 Mr Johnson wants to post a letter. He asks a passer-by: **Мо́ля, къде́ и́ма по́ща** (*post office*)? What would you say if you wanted to find:

ресторáнт
бáнка
телефо́н
по́ща
тоале́тна
фи́тнес це́нтър

a

b

c

d

e

This last is not on the recording:

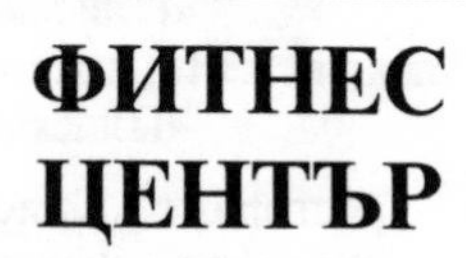

f

11 Complete the answers, using the correct forms of **съм**:

a Ви́е англича́нин ли сте?
Да, аз ... англича́нин, а той ... шотла́ндец (*Scot*).

b Ви́е англича́нка ли сте?
Да, аз ... англича́нка, а тя ... шотла́ндка (*Scotswoman*).

c Ти америка́нец ли си?
Да, аз ... америка́нец, а той ... бъ́лгарин.

d Ви́е от Ма́нчестър ли сте?
Ни́е ... от Ма́нчестър, а те ... от Лийдс.

e Ви́е от Ло́ндон ли сте?
Аз ... от Ло́ндон, а тя ... от Гла́зго́у.

Do you understand?

На информа́цията *At the information desk*

Read the conversation below and then answer the questions on p. 24. It is not essential that you understand every word, but you should find all the new words in the vocabulary also on p. 24.

Michael Johnson is asking the woman at the information desk the way to Vitosha Boulevard. Together they examine this map of Sofia.

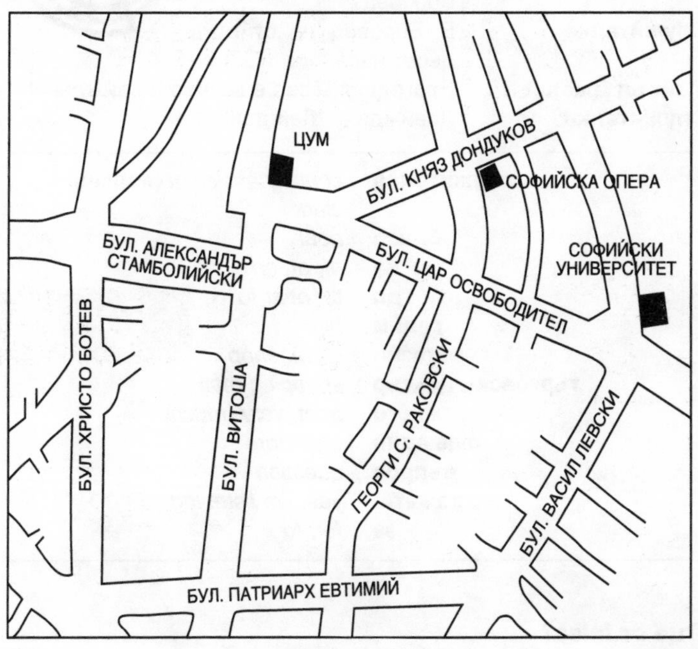

Ма́йкъл Джо́нсън До́бър ден! Мо́ля, къде́ е булева́рд «Ви́тоша»?

Служи́телка Булева́рд «Ви́тоша» не е́ бли́зо. И́мате ли ка́рта?

Ма́йкъл Джо́нсън Не, ня́мам.

Служи́телка Заповя́дайте, това́ е ка́рта на Со́фия. Булева́рд «Ви́тоша» е бли́зо до хоте́л «Ше́ратон».

Ма́йкъл Джо́нсън И́ма ли трамва́й до булева́рд «Ви́тоша»?

Служи́телка Да, трамва́й но́мер едно́ и трамва́й но́мер се́дем.

Ма́йкъл Джо́нсън А какво́ е това́ тук?

Служи́телка	Това́ е голя́м търго́вски це́нтър с мно́го магази́ни. Ка́зва се ЦУМ.
Ма́йкъл Джо́нсън	Благодаря́ мно́го. И́мам о́ще еди́н въпро́с.
Служи́телка	Каже́те!
Ма́йкъл Джо́нсън	Кога́ и́ма автобу́с за Бо́ровец?
Служи́телка	В о́сем часа́.
Ма́йкъл Джо́нсън	Кога́ присти́га той в Бо́ровец?
Служи́телка	В Бо́ровец присти́га в де́сет часа́.
Ма́йкъл Джо́нсън	Благодаря́. Това́ е вси́чко. Дови́ждане!
Служи́телка	Дови́ждане. Лек ден!

служи́телка	*counter assistant* (woman), *clerk*
бли́зо	*near*
на	*of; at; on*
до	*to; near to*
голя́м	*big*
магази́н	*store, shop*
търго́вски це́нтър	*shopping mall*
мно́го	*a lot, very* (*much*)
о́ще еди́н	*one more*
въпро́с	*question*
каже́те!	*yes, I'm listening*
за	*for; to*

True or false?

Say which of the following statements are true and which are false and rewrite the false ones:

1. Булева́рд «Ви́тоша» е бли́зо.
2. Г-н Джо́нсън и́ма ка́рта на Со́фия.
3. Хоте́л «Ше́ратон» е бли́зо до булева́рд «Ви́тоша».
4. Ня́ма трамва́й до булева́рд «Ви́тоша».
5. Г-н Джо́нсън и́ма о́ще еди́н въпро́с.
6. И́ма автобу́с за Бо́ровец в о́сем часа́.
7. Той (the word for *bus*, remember, is masculine!) присти́га в Бо́ровец в де́вет часа́.

03 какъ́в сте? каква́ сте?

who are you and what is your job?

In this unit you will learn

- **how to ask people where they come from and what they do**
- **how to tell people where you come from and what you do**
- **how to give your nationality and marital status**

Dialogue

Nevena is now asking Mrs Collins, who has just arrived at the hotel and is wishing to register, some formal – and less formal – questions about herself and her family.

Неве́на	Откъде́ сте?
г-жа́ Ко́линс	От Ма́нчестър.
Неве́на	Така́, от А́нглия. По наро́дност сте англича́нка. Каква́ сте по профе́сия?
г-жа́ Ко́линс	Преводáчка.
Неве́на	Омъ̀жена ли сте?
г-жа́ Ко́линс	Да, омъ̀жена съм.
Неве́на	И́мате ли деца́?
г-жа́ Ко́линс	Да, и́мам едно́ дете́.
Неве́на	Мъжъ̀т Ви и дете́то Ви тук ли са?
г-жа́ Ко́линс	Мъжъ̀т ми е тук, но синъ̀т ми е в А́нглия.
Неве́на	Какъ̀в е мъжъ̀т Ви по профе́сия?
г-жа́ Ко́линс	Той е учи́тел.
Неве́на	За пъ̀рви път ли сте в Бълга́рия?
г-жа́ Ко́линс	Не, не съ̀м за пъ̀рви път в Бълга́рия. Позна́вам страна́та ви добре́.
Неве́на	Позна́вате ли Марк Де́йвис?
г-жа́ Ко́линс	Не. Какъ̀в е той?
Неве́на	Журнали́ст. Той съ̀що позна́ва Бълга́рия добре́.
г-жа́ Ко́линс	Англича́нин ли е?
Неве́на	Не, америка́нец. Же́нен е за бъ̀лгарка. Той и жена́ му Виоле́та са тук сега́.

Откъде́ сте?	*Where are you from?*
От Ма́нчестър.	*From Manchester.*
Така́, от А́нглия.	*Right, from England.*
По наро́дност сте англича́нка.	*By nationality you're English.*
Каква́ сте по профе́сия?	*What do you do for a job?* (asking a woman)
преводáчка	*a translator/ interpreter* (woman)
Омъ̀жена ли сте?	*Are you married?* (asking a woman)
Да, омъ̀жена съм.	*Yes, I am* (*married*).
И́мате ли деца́?	*Have you any children?*
Да, и́мам едно́ дете́.	*Yes, I have one child.*
Мъжъ̀т Ви и дете́то Ви тук ли са?	*Are your husband and your child here?*

Мъжът ми е тук, но синът ми е в А́нглия.	*My husband is here, but my son is in England.*
Какъв е мъжът Ви по профе́сия?	*What does your husband do for a job?*
Той е учи́тел.	*He's a teacher.*
За първи път ли сте в Бълга́рия?	*Are you in Bulgaria for the first time?*
Позна́вам страна́та ви добре́.	*I know your country well.*
Позна́вате ли Марк Де́йвис?	*Do you know Mark Davies?*
Какъв е той?	*What does he do for a job?*
Журнали́ст.	*(He's a) journalist.*
Той също позна́ва Бълга́рия добре́.	*He also knows Bulgaria well.*
Же́нен е за българка.	*He's married to a Bulgarian.*
Той и жена́ му Виоле́та са тук сега́.	*He and his wife Violeta are here now.*

Questions

1 Try to answer the questions

- **a** Откъде́ е г-жа́ Ко́линс?
- **b** Каква́ е г-жа́ Ко́линс по профе́сия?
- **c** Омъжена ли е г-жа́ Ко́линс?
- **d** Тя и́ма ли деца́?
- **e** Какъв е г-н Ко́линс по профе́сия?
- **f** Добре́ ли позна́ва г-жа́ Ко́линс Бълга́рия?

2 True or false?
Say which of the following statements are true and which are false. Rewrite the false ones:

- **a** Госпожа́ Ко́линс е от Ли́върпул.
- **b** Госпожа́ Ко́линс ня́ма деца́.
- **c** Господи́н Ко́линс е учи́тел.
- **d** Господи́н и госпожа́ Ко́линс и́мат еди́н син.
- **e** Госпожа́ Ко́линс е за първи път в Бълга́рия.
- **f** Госпожа́ Ко́линс не позна́ва Марк и Виоле́та Де́йвис.

i *Married* or *single?* же́нен/неже́нен and омъжена/неомъжена

In Bulgarian there are two different words for *married*. When referring to a man who is married, you say **той е же́нен** (from **жена́** *wife*, *woman* – lit. *he is wifed*). If he is single you say **той не é жéнен**. When referring to a woman who is married, you say **тя е омъжена** (lit. *she is husbanded*). If she is single you say **тя не é омъжена**.

The words **жéнен** and **омъжена** are also used when filling in forms asking for your marital status. Here, however, if you are unmarried, you should join up the words (as in English!) and put either **нежéнен** if you are a man or **неомъжена** if you are a woman. If you are divorced you will enter **развéден** or **развéдена** (lit. *separated*).

You will notice that the words have the appropriate feminine or masculine endings: **-а** for the woman and a consonant for the man. Thus, if you are a woman and are married, in official documents, for example, you will enter **омъжена**, and if you are a man and married **жéнен**. In everyday speech, however, you will find that a married woman will say of herself **жéнена съм**.

	For a man		For a woman
аз съм/не сѣм		аз съм/не сѣм	
ти си/не сѝ	**жéнен**	ти си/не сѝ	**омъжена**
той е/не é		тя е/не é	**(жéнена)**
Вѝе сте/не стé		Вѝе сте/не стé	

Remember that the **не** is not emphasized. As the stress marks show, the emphasis is placed on the forms of **съм**.

Still on the subject of masculine and feminine, you will notice that many naming words for women, especially for nationalities and professions, have **-ка** on the end. Often the **-ка** is simply added to the corresponding masculine noun:

студéнт *student* (male) студéнт**ка** *student* (female)
учѝтел *teacher* (male) учѝтел**ка** *teacher* (female)

Words ending in **-ец** or **-ин**, however, drop these letters before adding **-ка**:

българ**ин** *a Bulgarian* (male)	българ**ка** *a Bulgarian* (female)
америка́н**ец** *an American* (male)	америка́н**ка** *an American* (female)
кана́д**ец** *a Canadian* (male)	кана́д**ка** *a Canadian* (female)

How do you say it?

- Asking where someone is from and saying where you are from

Откъде́ си? От Ма́нчестър съм. *Where are you from? I'm from Manchester.*

Откъде́ сте? Аз съм от Гла́згоу. *Where are you from? I'm from Glasgow.*

- Asking someone what job they do and saying what job you do

For a man **Какъ́в си/сте по профе́сия?**

Аз съм учи́тел/Учи́тел съм. *I'm a teacher.*
Аз съм ле́кар/Ле́кар съм. *I'm a doctor.*
Аз съм преводáч/Преводáч съм. *I'm a translator/interpreter.*
Аз съм сервитьо́р/Сервитьо́р съм. *I'm a waiter.*

For a woman **Каква́ си/сте по профе́сия?**

Аз съм учи́телка/Учи́телка съм. *I'm a teacher.*
Аз съм ле́карка/Ле́карка съм. *I'm a doctor.*
Аз съм секретáрка/Секретáрка съм. *I'm a secretary.*

- Saying whether you are married or not

For a man

Же́нен ли си/сте? *Are you married?*
Да, же́нен съм. *Yes, I am married.*
Не, не съ́м же́нен. *No, I'm not married.*
Не, разве́ден съм. *No, I'm divorced.*

For a woman

Омъ́жена ли си/сте? *Are you married?*
Да, омъ́жена съм. *Yes, I am married.*
Не, не съ́м омъ́жена. *No, I am not married.*
Не, разве́дена съм. *No, I'm divorced.*

- Referring to your family

With definite article:*		*Without definite article*:*	
дете́то ми	*my child*	**ба́ба ми**	*my grandmother*
мъжъ́т ми	*my husband*	**бащá ми**	*my father*
синъ́т ми	*my son*	**брат ми**	*my brother*
		братовчéд(ка) ми	*my cousin*
		дъщеря́ ми	*my daughter*
		дя́до ми	*my grandfather*
		жена́ ми	*my wife*
		ма́йка ми	*my mother*
		сестра́ ми	*my sister*

*See Grammar sections 2 and 3 below.

Grammar

1 Какъ́в? каква́?

These are the masculine and feminine forms of the question word **какво́?** *what?* You already know **какво́** from **какво́ е това́?** *what is that?* where the neuter form is being used in a question. When you want to find out more about specific persons or things you have to use **какъ́в** for a masculine word, **каква́** for a feminine one and **какво́** for a neuter.

When you use **какъ́в** (or **каква́** or **какво́**) you are essentially asking what someone or something is like. However, depending on the situation, the simple question **Какъ́в е Ма́йкъл Джо́нсън?** may have at least three possible meanings:

What is Michael Johnson like?
What does Michael Johnson do for a job?
What is Michael Johnson's nationality?

Possible answers might be:

Той е висо́к и ху́бав.	*He is tall and handsome.*
Той е би́знесмен.	*He is a businessman.*
Той е англича́нин.	*He is an Englishman.*

That is why, in order to make the meaning clear, questions with **какъ́в** (or **каква́**) directed at persons, often have to be phrased more precisely. If you are interested in someone's profession you will ask:

(of a man)	Какъ́в сте **по профе́сия?**	*What do you **do for a job**?*
(of a woman)	Каква́ сте **по профе́сия?**	

If you are interested in their nationality, you will ask:

(of a man)	**Какъ́в сте по наро́дност?**	*What is your **nationality**?*
(of a woman)	**Каква́ сте по наро́дност?**	

2 -ът, -та, -то *the*

The difference between ***a*** *man* and ***the*** *man*, ***a*** *country* and ***the*** *country*, ***a*** *child* and ***the*** *child* is expressed in Bulgarian in the following way:

Masculine	мъж	becomes	мъж**ъ́т**
Feminine	страна́	becomes	страна́**та**
Neuter	дете́	becomes	дете́**то**

From this you can see that the Bulgarian equivalent of the English definite article *the* is added to the end of the word. And, since all naming words in Bulgarian have either a masculine, feminine or neuter ending, there are also masculine (**-ът**) pronounced **-ъ**, without the **т**, feminine (**-та**) and neuter (-**то**) forms of the definite article.

Most masculine naming words add -ът

Хоте́л**ът** е бли́зо.	*The hotel is nearby.*
Апартаме́нт**ът** е голя́м.	*The flat is big.*
Клу́б**ът** е до по́щата.	*The club is next to the post office.*

However, almost all nouns ending in -**тел** or **-ар** add **-ят** and all masculine nouns ending in **-й** first drop the **-й** and then add **-ят**:

учи́т**ел**	*teacher*	учи́тел**ят**	***the*** *teacher*
ле́к**ар**	*doctor*	ле́кар**ят**	***the*** *doctor*
музе́**й**	*museum*	музе́**ят**	***the*** *museum*
трамва́**й**	*tram*	трамва́**ят**	***the*** *tram*
троле́**й**	*trolleybus*	троле́**ят**	***the*** *trolleybus*
ча**й**	*tea*	ча́**ят**	***the*** *tea*

Feminine naming words add -та

Стáя**та** е свобо́дна.	*The room is free.*
Вода́**та** е ху́бава.	*The water is nice.*
В ба́нка**та** и́ма телефо́н.	*There is a telephone in the bank.*

Neuter naming words add -то

Дете́**то** е голя́мо.	*The child is big.*
Кафе́**то** е ху́баво.	*The coffee is nice.*
Свобо́дно ли е мя́сто**то**?	*Is the seat free?*

3 Ми and Ви (or ви) *My* and *your*

In the dialogue you met one of the ways of saying *my* and *your* in Bulgarian. These are short form possessive pronouns:

мъжъ́т **ми**	***my** husband*
мъжъ́т **Ви**	***your** husband* (polite)
дете́то **Ви**	***your** child* (polite)
синъ́т **ми**	***my** son*

You will notice that **ми**, the word for *my*, and **Ви** *your*, come after the naming word and that the naming word here has the definite article added.

It is very important to remember that, as an exception to the general rule, with most words for relatives the naming word has to be used without the definite article. You will find a list on p. 30.

You will learn other, longer and less conversational, ways of saying *my*, *your*, etc. in later units, but for the time being here is a full list of all the short form possessive pronouns used with the word **апартаме́нт** *flat*:

апартаме́нтът **ми**	***my** flat*	апартаме́нтът **ни**	***our** flat*
апартаме́нтът **ти**	***your** flat*	апартаме́нтът **ви/Ви**	***your** flat*
апартаме́нтът **му**	***his** flat*		
апартаме́нтът **ѝ**	***her** flat*	апартаме́нтът **им**	***their** flat*

Remember that **ѝ**, the little word for *her*, is *always* written with a grave accent so as to distinguish it from the word **и** meaning *and*. The stresses are indicated by an acute accent.

Exercises

1 Have another look at the dialogue, then rearrange the following words to form sentences:

a едно́, и́мам, дете́
b омъ́жена, сте, ли?
c преводá́чка, е, г-жá Кó́линс
d по наро́дност, г-жá Ко́линс, е, каквá?
e ли, за пъ́рви път, в Бъ́лгáрия, е, г-жá Ко́линс?
f г-жá Ко́линс, са, и, г-н Ко́линс, откъде́?
g добре́, странá́та ви, познá́вам

2 Match these questions and answers (often the gender will be a useful clue):

i От Ма́нчестър ли е г-жá Ко́линс?
ii Преводá́ч (*translator*) ли е г-н Ко́линс?

a Ирлá́ндка съм.
b Да. От Ирлá́ндия съм.

iii	Каква́ си по наро́дност?	**c**	Ле́кар съм.
iv	От Ирла́ндия (*Ireland*) ли сте?	**d**	Да, тя е от Ма́нчестър.
v	Какъ̀в сте по профе́сия?	**e**	Той е от Ва́рна.
vi	Откъде́ са Марк и Виоле́та Де́йвис?	**f**	Не, той не е́ прево́дач.
vii	И́мате ли деца́?	**g**	Той е от Са́нта Ба́рбара, а тя е от Со́фия.
viii	Откъде́ е Никола́й?	**h**	И́мам две деца́.

3 Complete the dialogues (**a**) to (**d**) below. Use **какъ̀в** or **каква́** to form the appropriate question and choose the correct gender form from the list of occupations and nationalities:

Model: Учи́телка ли сте?
Не, не съ́м учи́телка.
Каква́ сте по профе́сия?
Студе́нтка съм. (*I'm a student.*)

Ирла́ндец ли сте?
Не, не съ́м ирла́ндец.
Какъ̀в сте по наро́дност?
Шотла́ндец съм.

прево́дач	ле́кар	америка́нец	шотла́ндка
студе́нт	учи́телка	ирла́ндка	ирла́ндец
секрета́рка	шофьо́р (*driver*)	англича́нка	шотла́ндец

a Ле́карка ли сте?
Не, не ________
________ сте по профе́сия?
________ съм.

b Бъ́лгарка ли сте?
Не, не ________
________ сте по наро́дност?
________ съм.

c Сервитьо́р ли сте?
Не, не ________
________ сте по профе́сия?
________ съм.

d Англича́нин ли сте?
Не, не ________
________ сте по наро́дност?
________ съм.

4 Write out a short description of the following people, using the information given. Then read the answer in the Key out loud. This exercise will help you learn some words for the professions and also to practise using words for marital status.

Model: Г-н Ко́линс е учи́тел. Той е от Ма́нчестър. Той е же́нен (не е́ же́нен).

a Марк Де́йвис – журнали́ст – Са́нта Ба́рбара – же́нен
b Миле́на – худо́жничка (*artist*) – Со́фия – не омъ́жена
c А́ндрю – студе́нт – Гла́згоу – не же́нен
d г-жа́ Ко́линс – превода́чка – Ма́нчестър – омъ́жена
e На́дя – секрета́рка – Пло́вдив – не омъ́жена
f Ма́йкъл Джо́нсън – би́знесмен – Че́лмсфорд – же́нен
g г-н Анто́нов – дире́ктор (*director*) – Бурга́с – же́нен
h Никола́й – фотогра́ф (*photographer*) – Ва́рна – не же́нен

Now give your own name, say what you do for a job and where you come from, and indicate your marital status.

5 Complete with the appropriate masculine or feminine definite forms (**-ът** or **-та**):

a Журнали́ст... е от Са́нта Ба́рбара.
b Худо́жничка... е от Со́фия.
c Студе́нт... е от Гла́згоу.
d Превода́чка... е от Ма́нчестър.
e Секрета́рка... е от Пло́вдив.
f Би́знесмен... е от Че́лмсфорд.
g Дире́ктор... е от Бурга́с.
h Фотогра́ф... е от Ва́рна.

6 To practise the use of the alternative (**-ят**) form of the masculine definite article, read and then answer the questions:

a Джеймс Ми́лър е ле́кар. Той е шотла́ндец.
Какъв е ле́карят по наро́дност?

b Джордж Ко́линс е учи́тел. Той е англича́нин.
Какъв е учи́телят по наро́дност?

c Ча́ят е ху́бав. Той е от А́нглия.
Какъв е ча́ят? Откъде́ е той?

7 Mr Antonov introduces his wife to Michael Johnson and says: Запозна́йте се – жена́ ми! *Meet my wife!* (lit. *Get to know one another – my wife*). What would you say when introducing the following people to a new Bulgarian acquaintance? (Beware of the vanishing definite article with the words for certain relatives!):

a your husband
b your son
c your daughter
d your brother
e your sister

8 Answer the questions below following this model:

Как се ка́зва мъжът Ви/ти? Мъжът ми се ка́зва Ива́н.
Как се ка́зва ма́йка Ви/ти? Ма́йка ми се ка́зва Еле́на.

a Как се ка́зва синъ́т Ви/ти? (А́ндрю)
b Как се ка́зва дете́то Ви/ти? (Ви́ктор)
c Как се ка́зва ма́йка Ви/ти? (Ири́на)
d Как се ка́зва жена́ Ви/ти? (Мари́я)
e Как се ка́зва дъщеря́ Ви/ти? (Си́лвия)
f Как се ка́зва баща́ ти? (Пол)

9 Mrs Collins has taught her husband some expressions to use in restaurants. He is in Bulgaria for the first time and likes his coffee, soup and tea hot. Read the model and then practise with him. Don't forget that **кафе́** (*coffee*), **су́па** (*soup*), **чай** (*tea*), etc. should be referred to as **то**, **тя** and **той** respectively!

Model: **Сервитьо́р** Кафе́то Ви, господи́не!
г-н Ко́линс Но то е студе́но! (*But it's cold!*)

a **Сервитьо́р** Су́пата Ви, господи́не!
г-н Ко́линс ________

b **Сервитьо́р** Ча́ят Ви, господи́не!
г-н Ко́линс ________

Nor does Mrs Collins like her beer, wine, water or gin warm (то́пъл, то́пла, то́пло). Complete and read out the following:

c **Сервитьо́р** Би́рата Ви, госпо́жо!
г-жа́ Ко́линс ________
d **Сервитьо́р** Ви́ното Ви, госпо́жо!
г-жа́ Ко́линс ________
e **Сервитьо́р** Вода́та Ви, госпо́жо!
г-жа́ Ко́линс ________
f **Сервитьо́р** Джи́нът Ви, госпо́жо!
г-жа́ Ко́линс ________

10 If asked to show your passport, your reply would be: Заповя́дайте, това́ е паспо́ртът ми. How would you reply if asked to show your visa (ви́за), your reservation (резерва́ция) or your ticket (биле́т)?

11 Look at the map of Bulgaria overleaf. Then complete and write out the sentences.

a Това́ е ____ на Бълга́рия.
b На и́зток гра́ницата (*the border*) е ____
c На се́вер гра́ницата е река́. Река́та се ка́зва ____
d На юг са ____ и ____
e Сто́лицата (*the capital*) на Бълга́рия е град (*town*) ____

Do you understand?

In the lift

Nikolai and Milena meet in the lift on their way to see Nadya, the secretary. They work for the same advertising agency, but they don't yet know one another.

Никола́й	Здраве́йте!
Миле́на	До́бър ден! Позна́ваме ли се?
Никола́й	Не. Да се запозна́ем! Ка́звам се Никола́й Димитро́в. А Ви́е как се ка́звате?
Миле́на	Аз се ка́звам Миле́на Мари́нова.
Никола́й	Прия́тно ми е! (*They go into the office.*) Е́то и На́дя, секрета́рката. Здраве́й, На́дя!
На́дя	Здраве́йте! Мо́ля, запов́ядайте! Ви́е позна́вате ли се?
Никола́й	И да, и не. Миле́на, Ви́е каква́ сте?
На́дя	Миле́на е худо́жничка. Тя е худо́жничката на фи́рмата.
Никола́й	Разби́рам. Това́ е мно́го интере́сна профе́сия.
Миле́на	А Ви́е какъ́в сте?
Никола́й	Аз съм фотогра́ф.
Миле́на	Фотогра́фът съ́що е худо́жник.
На́дя	И́мате ли вре́ме за едно́ кафе́?
Миле́на	Да, разби́ра се.
Никола́й	Аз съ́що. За кафе́ ви́наги и́мам вре́ме!
На́дя	Мо́ля, запов́ядайте. Кафе́то е гото́во.

да се запозна́ем	*let's get acquainted*
е́то	*here is*
худо́жник	*artist*
фи́рма	*firm*
разби́рам	*I understand*
разби́ра се	*of course*
съ́що	*too, also*
ви́наги	*always*
гото́во	*ready*
Гъ́рция	*Greece*
Ду́нав	*Danube*
(на) за́пад	*(in/to) the west*
запозна́йте се ...	*meet...*
(на) и́зток	*(in/to) the east*
интере́сен, -сна, -сно	*interesting*
Македо́ния	*Macedonia*
наро́дност (f)	*nationality*
прия́тно ми е!	*pleased to meet you!*
Румъ́ния	*Romania*
(на) се́вер	*(in/to) the north*
Съ́рбия	*Serbia*
то́пъл (то́пла, то́пло)	*warm*
Ту́рция	*Turkey*
че́рен (че́рна, че́рно)	*black*
(на) юг	*(in/to) the south*

Questions

Decide which of these statements are false and write out correct versions.

1 Никола́й и Миле́на не се позна́ват.
2 Миле́на е секрета́рката на фи́рмата.
3 Миле́на и́ма интере́сна профе́сия.
4 Никола́й е фотогра́ф.
5 Никола́й и Миле́на ня́мат вре́ме за кафе́.

04

кóлко? кóлко е часъ́т?

how much? how many? what's the time?

In this unit you will learn

- how to ask people where they come from and what they do
- how to tell people where you come from and what you do
- how to give your nationality and marital status

Dialogue

The morning after Mr Johnson arrives at the hotel, Nevena, the ever-obliging receptionist, stops him in the foyer.

Неве́на До́бър ден, г-н Джо́нсън! И́мате писма́ днес.
г-н Джо́нсън Писма́? Ко́лко писма́?
Неве́на Три. Заповя́дайте! И́скате ли български ве́стници?
г-н Джо́нсън Съжаля́вам, но не разби́рам добре́ български.
Неве́на В хоте́ла ни́е и́маме ве́стници и списа́ния и на англи́йски ези́к.
г-н Джо́нсън Това́ е чуде́сно! Благодаря́!
Неве́на Извине́те, г-н Джо́нсън, и́мате ли о́ще ма́лко вре́ме?
г-н Джо́нсън А ко́лко е часъ́т? Часо́никът ми не рабо́ти.
Неве́на Часъ́т е едина́йсет и полови́на.
г-н Джо́нсън Да, и́мам о́коло пет мину́ти свобо́дно вре́ме. Въпро́си ли и́мате?
Неве́на Са́мо еди́н въпро́с. За ко́лко вре́ме сте в Бълга́рия?
г-н Джо́нсън За две се́дмици.
Неве́на Това́ пра́ви четирина́йсет но́щи в хоте́ла, нали́?
г-н Джо́нсън То́чно така́. Ко́лко е часъ́т сега́?
Неве́на Ве́че е двана́йсет без два́йсет и пет.
г-н Джо́нсън Благодаря́. И́мам сре́ща то́чно в двана́йсет часа́. Дови́ждане!

И́мате писма́ днес.	*You have some letters today.*
Ко́лко писма́?	*How many letters?*
И́скате ли български ве́стници?	*Do you want any Bulgarian newspapers?*
Не разби́рам добре́ български.	*I don't understand Bulgarian very well.*
Ни́е и́маме ве́стници и списа́ния и на англи́йски ези́к.	*We have newspapers and magazines in English too.*
Това́ е чуде́сно!	*That's wonderful/ marvellous!*
Извине́те.	*Excuse me.*
о́ще ма́лко	*a little more*
А ко́лко е часъ́т?	*But what's the time?*
Часо́никът ми не рабо́ти.	*My watch has stopped/ isn't working.*
Часъ́т е едина́йсет и полови́на.	*The time is half past eleven.*
И́мам о́коло пет мину́ти свобо́дно вре́ме.	*I have about five minutes' free time.*

Въпро́си ли и́мате?	*Do you have any questions?*
Са́мо еди́н въпро́с.	*Just one question.*
За ко́лко вре́ме сте в Бълга́рия?	*How long are you in Bulgaria for?*
За две се́дмици.	*For two weeks.*
Това́ пра́ви четирина́йсет но́щи в хоте́ла, нали́?	*That makes fourteen nights in the hotel, doesn't it?*
То́чно така́.	*Exactly so.*
Ве́че е двана́йсет без два́йсет и пет.	*It's already twenty-five to twelve.*
И́мам сре́ща то́чно в двана́йсет часа́.	*I have an appointment at twelve o'clock exactly/sharp.*

Questions

1 Try to answer the questions.

a Ко́лко писма́ и́ма г-н Джо́нсън?
b И́ска ли г-н Джо́нсън бъ́лгарски ве́стници?
c Разби́ра ли г-н Джо́нсън добре́ бъ́лгарски?
d Ко́лко свобо́дно вре́ме и́ма г-н Джо́нсън?
e За ко́лко вре́ме е той в Бълга́рия? (Don't forget to use **за**!)
f В ко́лко часа́ и́ма той сре́ща? (Here it is **в**!)

2 True or false?
Write out correct versions of the false statements.

a За г-н Джо́нсън и́ма три писма́.
b В хоте́ла ня́ма англи́йски ве́стници и списа́ния.
c Г-н Джо́нсън и́ска англи́йски ве́стници.
d Неве́на и́ма мно́го въпро́си.
e Часъ́т е двана́йсет и полови́на.
f Г-н Джо́нсън е в Бълга́рия за една́ се́дмица.

i Morning, noon and night

The Bulgarians have no real equivalent for *a.m.* and *p.m*. To avoid misunderstanding, especially when referring to opening times of shops or to bus or train times, they use the 24-hour clock. Alternatively, in situations not involving travel, immediately after giving the time they insert the word **сутринта́** *in the morning*, **следо́бед** *in the afternoon*, **вечерта́** *in the evening* and **през нощта́** *at night*. So, if your plane arrives at 9.30 p.m. you will say: **самоле́тът присти́га в два́йсет и еди́н часа́ и три́йсет мину́ти**, but if you are merely getting together with a friend in the evening, you will arrange to meet **в де́вет и полови́на вечерта́**.

Interestingly, where in English we would say *at one* (or *two*) *in the morning*, the Bulgarians say **в еди́н** (or **два**) **часа́ през нощта́**. For us the night would seem to end at midnight, while for the Bulgarians it goes on at least until two in the morning!

One further important thing to note is that the Bulgarian word **о́бед** means *lunch* or *lunchtime* as well as *noon* or *midday*. Noon for Bulgarians, however, is not really such a precise time. It is rather the general period between midday and two. So, if someone invites you for lunch (**на о́бед**) at midday (**по о́бед**), make sure you also agree on a precise time, or you could be in for a long wait for your meal!

How do you say it?

- Asking *How many?* and *How much?*

Ко́лко писма́ и́мате?	*How many letters do you have?*
Ко́лко вре́ме и́мате?	*How much time do you have?*

- Asking *For how long?*

За ко́лко вре́ме сте в Бълга́рия?	*How long are you in Bulgaria for?*

- Asking, and saying, what the time is

Ко́лко е часъ́т?	*What's the time?*
Часъ́т е то́чно двана́йсет.	*It is exactly twelve o'clock.*

- Begging someone's pardon

Извине́те! or **Извиня́вайте!**	*Excuse me!/I beg your pardon.*

- Seeking agreement or confirmation using нали́?

Ви́е сте в Со́фия за четирина́йсет дни, нали́?	*You are in Sofia for fourteen days, aren't you?*
Г-н Джо́нсън е в Со́фия за 14 дни, нали́?	*Mr Johnson is in Sofia for 14 days, isn't he?*

- Agreeing and approving

То́чно така́!	*That's right!/Exactly!/Precisely!*
Това́ е чуде́сно!	*That's wonderful!*

- Indicating the time of day

сутринта́	*in the morning*
следо́бед	*in the afternoon*
вечерта́	*in the evening*
през нощта́	*at night*

Grammar

1 Ко́лко? *How many? How much?*

Ко́лко is the question word for quantity:

Ко́лко писма́ и́ма за г-н Джо́нсън?	*How many letters are there for Mr Johnson?*
Ко́лко свобо́дно вре́ме и́ма той?	*How much free time has he got?*
За **ко́лко** дни е г-н Джо́нсън в Бълга́рия?	*How many days is Mr Johnson in Bulgaria for?*

When **ко́лко** refers to quantity, it is used to express both *how many?* (with naming words for concrete or countable things) and *how much?* (with abstract or uncountable things).

You also use **ко́лко** when asking questions about the time, such as *what's the time?* or *at what time?*

Ко́лко е часъ̀т?	*What's the time?*
В ко́лко часа́ е самоле́тът за Ло́ндон?	*What time is the plane for London?*
До ко́лко часа́ рабо́ти о́фисът?	*Until what time is the office open?*

мно́го	*many, much, a lot of*
ма́лко	*few, a few, a little, not many, not much*

Мно́го is also used as the equivalent of the English *very* or *very much*:

Г-жа́ Ко́линс разби́ра бъ́лгарски **мно́го добре́**.	*Mrs Collins understands Bulgarian very well.*
Хоте́лът е **мно́го ху́бав**.	*The hotel is very beautiful/nice.*
Благодаря́ **мно́го**.	*Thank you very much.*
Извиня́вайте **мно́го!**	*I am very sorry!*

2 Plural of nouns

The most common (but not the only) plural ending is **-и**. It occurs with both masculine and feminine nouns.

Masculine nouns

The plural ending **-и** is attached to masculine words in a number of ways:

a by simply adding **-и** to the singular:

автобу́с	автобу́с**и**	*buses*

ресторáнт	ресторáнт**и**	*restaurants*
учи́тел	учи́тел**и**	*teachers*
лéкар	лéкар**и**	*doctors*
тури́ст	тури́ст**и**	*tourists*
óфис	óфис**и**	*offices*

Note that all these masculine nouns, as well as the following ones, have more than one syllable! Most masculine nouns of only one syllable form their plurals differently. You will learn them in Unit 7.

b by adding **-и** and also changing the final consonant of the singular. One of the most frequent changes is **-к** to **-ц**:

вéстни**к**	вéстни**ци**	*newspapers*
ези́**к**	ези́**ци**	*languages, tongues*
худóжни**к**	худóжни**ци**	*artists*
часóвни**к**	часóвни**ци**	*watches, clocks*

c by adding **-и** and also dropping the vowel that comes before the final consonant of the singular. Certain combinations of vowel and consonant, such as **-ец** or **-ър**, favour this method, but there is no simple rule.

америкáн**ец**	америкáн**ци**	*Americans*	**-ец** (**е** is dropped)
чужден**éц**	чужден**ци́**	*foreigners*	
шотлáнд**ец**	шотлáнд**ци**	*Scots*	
компю́т**ър**	компю́т**ри**	*computers*	**-ър** (**ъ** is dropped)
ли́т**ър**	ли́т**ри**	*litres*	
мéт**ър**	мéт**ри**	*metres*	
ден	**дни**	*days*	(**е** is dropped)

d by substituting **-и** for the singular ending in **-й**.

музé**й**	музé**и**	*museums*
трамвá**й**	трамвá**и**	*trams*
тролé**й**	тролé**и**	*trolleybuses*

Feminine nouns

The plural of feminine nouns is always **-и**, which replaces the singular ending **-а** or **-я**:

сéдмиц**а**	сéдмиц**и**	*weeks*
англичáнк**а**	англичáнк**и**	*English women*
фóнокáрт**а**	фóнокáрт**и**	*phonecards*
резервáци**я**	резервáци**и**	*reservations*
дъщер**я́**	дъщер**и́**	*daughters*
стá**я**	стá**и**	*rooms*

The few feminine nouns which end in a consonant form their plural by adding **-и** to the singular. You have already come across **нощ**,

ве́чер and **су́трин**:

една́ нощ	мно́го но́щ**и**	*many nights*
една́ ве́чер	мно́го ве́чер**и**	*many evenings*
една́ су́трин	мно́го су́трин**и**	*many mornings*

Neuter nouns

The most common plural endings for neuter nouns are **-а** and **-я**. The choice is determined by the endings in the singular.

a nouns in -**о** replace the final **-о** by **-а**:

писм**о́**	писм**а́**	*letters*
семе́йств**о**	семе́йств**а**	*families*

Note that the stress sometimes moves to the final syllable:

ви́н**о**	вин**а́**	*wines*

b nouns in -**ие** replace the final **-е** by **-я**:

списа́н**ие**	списа́н**ия**	*magazines*
упражне́н**ие**	упражне́н**ия**	*exercises*

(More neuter plurals in Unit 8!)

3 Разби́рам *I understand* and и́скам *I want* (a-pattern verbs)

As with **и́мам** and **присти́гам**, the endings of these verbs contain the vowel **-а-**. We can refer to them as **а**-pattern verbs. They are also known as verbs of Conjugation 3. This is the most regular and the most common pattern, and also the easiest to learn:

аз	разби́р**ам**	*I understand*	ни́е разби́р**аме**	*we understand*
ти	разби́р**аш**	*you understand*	ви́е разби́р**ате**	*you understand*
той / тя / то	разби́р**а**	*he, she, it understands*	те разби́р**ат**	*they understand*

4 Пра́вя *I make, I do* and рабо́тя *I work* (и-pattern verbs)

аз	пра́в**я**/ рабо́т**я**	*I make/do, work*	ни́е пра́в**им**/ рабо́т**им**	*we make/do, work*
ти	пра́в**иш**/ рабо́т**иш**	*you make/do, work*	ви́е пра́в**ите**/ рабо́т**ите**	*you make/do, work*
той / тя / то	пра́в**и**/ рабо́т**и**	*he, she, it makes/ does, works*	те пра́в**ят**/ рабо́т**ят**	*they make/do, work*

As you can see, **прáвя** and **рабóтя** have **-и-** in all their endings except the forms for *I* and *they*. Verbs like **прáвя** and **рабóтя** belong to the **и**-pattern and are known as verbs of Conjugation 2.

Прáвя can mean both *I make* and *I do*. Here, too, Bulgarian conveniently has one word with a number of different meanings in English. Compare:

Две и две прáви чéтири.	*Two and two makes four.*
Каквó прáвиш?	*What are you doing?*

5 -а and -я: the short definite article

In Unit 3, you were introduced to the Bulgarian equivalent of the English definite article *the*. You learnt to add the endings **-ът** or **-ят** to masculine nouns. These forms, known as the full forms, are, however, only used when the noun is the subject in the sentence, determining the ending of the verb, as in the sentence: хотéл**ът** е мнóго хýбав *the hotel is very nice*:

Masculine nouns also have a short form of the definite article. This short form has to be used whenever the noun is not the subject in the sentence, after prepositions, for example (see в óфис**а** at the end of the Dialogue and в ресторáнт**а** on p. 11). The short forms of the definite article (with masculine nouns only, remember!) are **-а** or **-я**. Compare:

	Хотéл**ът** е блѝзо.	*The hotel is near.*
and	Аз съм **в хотéла**.	*I'm in the hotel.*
	Музé**ят** е на ýлица «Ивáн Вáзов».	*The museum is on Ivan Vazov Street.*
and	Ѝма мнóго турѝсти **в музéя**.	*There are a lot of tourists in the museum.*

street sign in Sofia

улица
ИВАН ВАЗОВ
21А→37

6 A note on pronunciation

The **-а** and **-я** of the short forms are not fully pronounced, but are reduced to the sounds **-ъ** and **-йъ** respectively.

Although in written Bulgarian a distinction is still made between the short and the long form, when speaking it is normal to ignore the final **т** of the full form and to pronounce the endings as if they were the short form. So, what you will hear for **трамва́ят** and **трамва́я** will be **трамва́йъ**, for **учи́телят** and **учи́теля** you will hear **учи́телйъ** and for **хоте́лът** and **хоте́ла**, **хоте́лъ**.

Only in formal speech, in news bulletins on the radio or television, for example, or when people feel they need to be 'ultra-correct' in their speech, will you hear the long form articulated in full with the final **-т** pronounced. As you listen to the different speakers on the recording, see if you can detect any difference. (For further pronunciation changes in everyday speech, look again at the Appendix.)

7 Numerals 11 to 100

11	едина́йсет	14	четирина́йсет	17	седемна́йсет
12	двана́йсет	15	петна́йсет	18	осемна́йсет
13	трина́йсет	16	шестна́йсет	19	деветна́йсет

The numbers from 11 to 19 are formed by the addition of **-найсет**, (the equivalent of the English *-teen*), to the numbers from 1 to 9. For 11 you add **-на́йсет** to the masculine **еди́н** and for 12 you add **-на́йсет** to **два** not to **две**.

20	два́йсет (два́десет)	25	два́йсет и пет
21	два́йсет и едно́/еди́н/една́	26	два́йсет и шест
22	два́йсет и две/два	27	два́йсет и се́дем
23	два́йсет и три	28	два́йсет и о́сем
24	два́йсет и че́тири	29	два́йсет и де́вет

From 20 upwards the numerals are formed on the principle of *twenty and one*, *twenty and two*, etc. with the word for *and* **и** being inserted between **два́йсет**, **три́йсет**, **чети́рисет**, etc. and **едно́**, **две**, **три**, etc. There are alternative more formal spellings and pronunciations – given in brackets – for some numbers. Be careful to distinguish between **двана́йсет** (12) and **два́йсет** (20) – all the teens are longer!

30	три́йсет (три́десет)	70	седемдесе́т
40	чети́рисет (чети́ридесет)	80	осемдесе́т
50	петдесе́т	90	деветдесе́т
60	шейсе́т (шестдесе́т)	100	сто

Remember that **едно́** has different forms for the three genders. Also that **две** has an alternative form **два**, as in **два часа́** *two o'clock*. (More about this in Unit 8.)

8 Telling the time

Ко́лко е часът?	*What is the time?*
Часът е...	*The time is...*

When telling the time in Bulgarian you begin with the hours and move on to the minutes. For times up to the half hour you give the hour first and add the minutes using the word **и**. As in English, the words for *hours* and *minutes* can be omitted:

Ко́лко е часът?

Едина́йсет часа́ **и** де́сет мину́ти. (*The time is*) *ten past eleven.*

or

(Часът е) едина́йсет **и** де́сет.

Ко́лко е часът?

Де́вет часа́ **и** два́йсет и пет мину́ти. (*The time is*) *twenty-five past nine.*

or

(Часът е) де́вет **и** два́йсет **и** пет.

For times after the half hour you give the number of the next hour first and take away the minutes from the next hour using the word **без** (*without* or *less*):

Ко́лко е часът?
(Часът е) се́дем **без** де́сет.

Ко́лко е часът?
(Часът е) три без пет.

Bulgarian has alternative forms for half past and the quarters:

Óсем **и полови́на**
or óсем **и три́йсет**

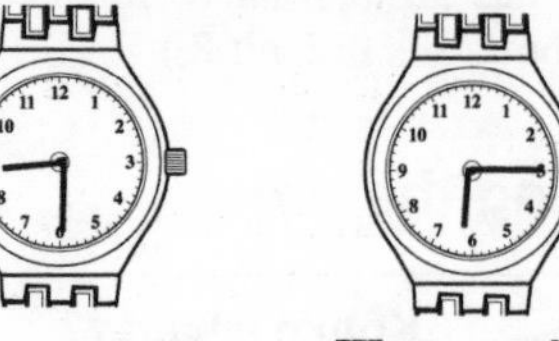

Шест **и чéтвърт**
or шест **и петна́йсет**

Пет **без чéтвърт**
or пет **без петна́йсет**

9 Нали́? *Isn't it so?*

In conversational Bulgarian you will often hear the word **нали́** tagged on the end of statements making them into questions seeking confirmation. In English there is no proper one-word equivalent for **нали́** and you have to repeat the verb in the negative to achieve the same effect. Bulgarians learning English have great difficulty with our different forms, but as you will see from the following examples, **нали́** is very easy for us to use.

Хотéлът е мно́го ху́бав, **нали́**?	*The hotel is very nice, **isn't it**?*
Ви́е не сте́ бъ́лгарка, **нали́?**	*You are not Bulgarian, **are you**?*
Ймате са́мо еди́н въпро́с, **нали́**?	*You do only have one question, **don't you**?*
Той не и́ска бъ́лгарски вéстници, **нали́**?	*He doesn't want Bulgarian newspapers, **does he**?*

Exercises

1 Make full sentences using the information on the bus departures and arrivals board below. Best use the 24-hour clock!

РАЗПИСА́НИЕ *(Timetable)*

За *(to)*	Замина́ва *(departs)*	Присти́га *(arrives)*
Мальо́вица	6.35	9.15
Ба́нкя	10.10	10.45
Са́моков	11.20	13.30
Бо́ровец	13.50	17.25

Model: Автобу́сът за ____ замина́ва в ____ часа́ и ____ мину́ти и присти́га в ____ часа́ и ____ мину́ти.

Now use the short version of the times omitting **часа́** and **мину́ти**.

2 Looking at the timetable above, answer the following questions, (the actual time is given in brackets):

Model: (Часъ́т е де́сет без пет.) След ко́лко мину́ти замина́ва автобу́сът за Ба́нкя? *In how many minutes does the bus leave for Bankya?*

● Автобу́сът за Ба́нкя замина́ва след петна́йсет мину́ти.

a (Часъ́т е едина́йсет и петна́йсет.) След ко́лко мину́ти замина́ва автобу́сът за Са́моков?
b (Часъ́т е еди́н и полови́на.) След ко́лко мину́ти замина́ва автобу́сът за Бо́ровец?
c (Часъ́т е шест и два́йсет и пет.) След ко́лко мину́ти замина́ва автобу́сът за Мальо́вица?

3 Answer these questions reading out the times on the clocks.

a В ко́лко часа́ замина́ва автобу́сът за Пло́вдив?

b Кога́ присти́га самоле́тът от Ло́ндон?

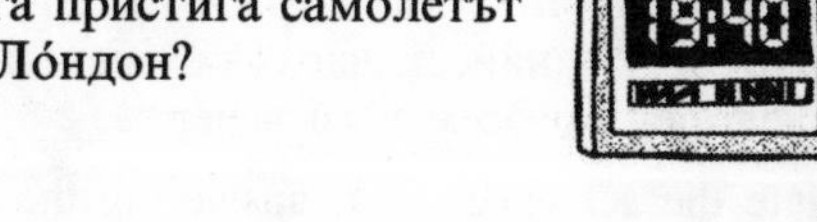

c Кога́ и́ма самоле́т за Ва́рна?

d Кога́ замина́ваш за Со́фия?

e В ко́лко часа́ е сре́щата на г-н Джо́нсън?

4 Answer the questions below presuming that:

a you are staying in Bulgaria for 12/15/20 days
b you are staying in the hotel for 3/13 nights
c you are staying in Varna for one/two weeks

i За кóлко дни сте в Бълга́рия?
ii За кóлко нóщи сте в хотéла?
iii За кóлко сéдмици сте във Ва́рна? (When **в** is used before words beginning with the letters **в** or **ф** it is extended to **във**.)

5 Read the notices below:

ЦЕНТРА́ЛНА ПО́ЩА Рабóтно врéме (*opening hours*) от (*from*) 7 до (*to*) 20.30 часа́	АПТÉКА (*Pharmacy*) Рабóтно врéме от 9 до 21 часа́	РЕСТОРА́НТ Рабóтно врéме от 18 до 23 часа́
ПОДА́РЪЦИ (*gifts*) су́трин от 8 до 12 часа́ следóбед от 16 до 20 часа́	СЛАДКА́РНИЦА (*patisserie, cakeshop*) су́трин от 10 до 13 часа́ следóбед от 14 до 19 часа́	

A more natural way to read the notices would be to use **рабóти** and a 12-hour clock, for example:

> Магази́нът за пода́ръци рабóти от óсем часа́ сутринта́ до двана́йсет часа́ на óбед и от чéтири часа́ следóбед до óсем часа́ вечерта́.

Now complete the sentences as if answering the question **До кóлко часа́ рабóти…?** using the 12-hour clock:

a Пóщата ____ от 7 часа́ сутринта́ до 8.30 часа́ ____.
b Аптéката рабóти от 9 ____ ____ до 9 ____ ____.
c Ресторáнтът рабóти ____ 6 ____ 11 часа́ ____.
d ____ рабóти ____ 10 часа́ ____ до еди́н часа́ на óбед и от 2 часа́ ____ до 7 часа́ ____.

6 To practise using **кóлко**, ask questions to which the following could be answers. Concentrate on the numbers involved and don’t forget to repeat the prepositions.

a В хотéла и́ма две америка́нки.
b Г-н Джóнсън е в Бълга́рия за две сéдмици.
c Брат ми присти́га след чéтири дни.

d Г-н и г-жá Кóлинс са в Сóфия от три дни.
e Автобу́сът заминáва в дéсет часá.
f Днес и́маш три писмá и две кáртички (*postcards*).
b Г-н Джóнсън и́ма две децá.

7 Do you take sugar (**зáхар**) and milk (**мля́ко**)? Read and then answer the questions:

Секретáрката Нáдя пи́е (*is drinking*) кафé с Николáй и Милéна. Нáдя пи́е кафéто с мáлко зáхар. Николáй и́ска кафé с мнóго зáхар, а Милéна и́ска кафé без зáхар. Те оби́чат (*like*) кафéто с мáлко мля́ко.

a Каквó прáви Нáдя?
b С кóлко зáхар пи́е кафéто Нáдя?
c С кóлко зáхар пи́е кафéто Николáй?
d Каквó кафé и́ска Милéна?
e Как оби́чат те кафéто – с мнóго или́ с мáлко мля́ко?
f Как оби́чате кафéто Ви́е?

Expressions to use

със зáхар *with sugar* (when **с** is used before a word beginning with **с** or **з** it is extended to **със** – remember what happened to **в** before **в** and **ф**?)

без зáхар, с мнóго зáхар, с мáлко зáхар, с мнóго мáлко зáхар *(with very little sugar)*

8 Continuing the milk and sugar theme, this exercise will help you practise different ways of saying the same thing. The short dialogues on the left below present identical situations as those on the right. Complete the right-hand column using the model and observing the change to the short definite form with **чай**:

Тури́стка	Чáят е със зáхар, нали́?	В чáя и́ма зáхар, нали́?
Сервитьóрка	Да, с мáлко зáхар.	Да, и́ма мáлко зáхар.
Тури́стка	Кафéто е със зáхар, нали́?	**a** ___________
Сервитьóрка	Да, с мáлко зáхар.	___________
Тури́стка	Кафéто е с мля́ко, нали́?	**b** ___________
Сервитьóрка	Да, с мáлко мля́ко.	___________
Тури́стка	Чáят е с мля́ко, нали́?	**c** ___________
Сервитьóрка	Да, с мáлко мля́ко.	___________

9 You can also use **нали́** in negative questions. Try it here, adapting the statements with **без** (*without*). Notice that the answer can be with **не** or **да**.

Тури́стка	Ча́ят е без мля́ко, нали́?	В ча́я ня́ма мля́ко, нали́?
Сервитьо́рка	Да, без мля́ко е.	Не, ня́ма/ Да, ня́ма.
Тури́стка	Кафе́то е без мля́ко, нали́?	**a** ________
Сервитьо́рка	Да, без мля́ко е.	________
Тури́стка	Кафе́то е без за́хар, нали́?	**b** ________
Сервитьо́рка	Да, без за́хар е.	________
Тури́стка	Ча́ят е без за́хар, нали́?	**c** ________
Сервитьо́рка	Да, без за́хар е.	________

10 Use the words in brackets in the plural:

a Г-н и г-жа́ Ко́линс и́скат стя́я с две ______ (легло́ *bed*).
b Г-н и г-жа́ Ко́линс са ______ (чуждене́ц).
c ______ ли са г-н и г-жа́ Ко́линс? (америка́нец).
d Ма́йкъл Джо́нсън не и́ска български ______ (ве́стник).
e Никола́й и́ма мно́го ______ (въпро́с).
f Ма́йкъл Джо́нсън разби́ра мно́го ______ (ези́к).
g В ЦУМ и́ма мно́го ______ (продава́чка *shop assistant* f).
h На булева́рд «Ви́тоша» и́ма спи́рка на ______ но́мер 1, 7 и 9 (трамва́й).
i В сладка́рницата и́ма мно́го ______ (чужденка́ *foreigner* f).

11 Finally, to practise using the full and short definite article, answer the following questions, using the words in brackets with the preposition **до**:

a Къде́ е хоте́лът? (рестора́нт)
b Къде́ е рестора́нтът? (хоте́л)
c Къде́ е теа́търът? (магази́н)
d Къде́ е магази́нът? (теа́тър *theatre*)
e Къде́ е музе́ят? (парк *park*)
f Къде́ е па́ркът? (музе́й)

Do you understand?

Dialogue

Mr Antonov has some good news for Nikolai.

г-н Анто́нов Заповя́дай, Никола́й. Седни́!

Никола́й	Благодаря́.
г-н Анто́нов	И́мам ху́бава новина́. Замина́ваш за А́нглия.
Никола́й	Но... аз не разби́рам англи́йски!
г-н Анто́нов	Ни́що. Във фи́рмата и́ма еди́н англича́нин, ко́йто разби́ра български.
Никола́й	Мно́го интере́сно! В кой град е фи́рмата?
г-н Анто́нов	В Че́лмсфорд.
Никола́й	Аз не зна́я къде́ е Че́лмсфорд.
г-н Анто́нов	Че́лмсфорд е ма́лък град бли́зо до Ло́ндон.
Никола́й	Мно́го фотогра́фи ли и́ма във фи́рмата?
г-н Анто́нов	Не, но и́ма мно́го компютри и моде́рна те́хника.
Никола́й	Чуде́сно! Кога́ замина́вам?
г-н Анто́нов	След три се́дмици.
Никола́й	За ко́лко дни?
г-н Анто́нов	За два́йсет дни. Ху́бава новина́, нали́?
Никола́й	Мно́го ху́бава новина́. Благодаря́ мно́го!

седни́!	*sit down!*
новина́	*news*
замина́вам, -ваш	*to leave/depart*
англи́йски	*English*
ни́що	*no matter, never mind*
кой град	*which town*
ма́лък, ма́лка, ма́лко	*small, little*
моде́рна те́хника	*the latest equipment*
след	*after*

True or false?

Write out correct versions of the false statements.

1 Никола́й замина́ва за Шотла́ндия.
2 Той разби́ра добре́ англи́йски.
3 Англича́нинът разби́ра български.
4 Фи́рмата е в Че́стърфийлд.
5 Фи́рмата е в ма́лък град бли́зо до Ло́ндон.
6 Никола́й не зна́е къде́ е Че́лмсфорд.
7 Във фи́рмата и́ма мно́го фотогра́фи.
8 Той замина́ва след де́сет дни.

гово́рите ли англи́йски?

do you speak English?

In this unit you will learn

- **how to ask people if they speak your language**
- **how to ask people what languages they speak**
- **how to say what languages you know**

Dialogue

Although you do not need a third person to introduce you to someone in Bulgaria, Nevena's natural Bulgarian curiosity enables the English hotel guests to get to know one another.

Невéна Г-н Джóнсън, знáете ли, че в хотéла úма и дрýги англичáни?

г-н Джóнсън Нúщо чýдно. Англичáни úма в мнóго странú по светá.

Невéна Но не мнóго англичáни говóрят бъ́лгарски! Вúе говóрите бъ́лгарски добрé, но г-жá Кóлинс говóри пó-добрé.

г-н Джóнсън Кой говóри пó-добрé?

Невéна Г-жá Кóлинс.

г-н Джóнсън Но коя́ е г-жá Кóлинс? Не знáя коя́ е тя.

Невéна Говóря за англичáнката, коя́то живéе в стáя нóмер дéсет.

г-н Джóнсън А Вúе говóрите ли англúйски, Невéна?

Невéна За съжалéние, не. Но знáя ня́колко дрýги езúка.

г-н Джóнсън Каквú езúци знáете?

Невéна Фрéнски, рýски и испáнски. Фрéнски е езúкът, кóйто говóря нáй-добрé.

г-н Джóнсън Мнóго бъ́лгари говóрят чýжди езúци.

Невéна Товá е вя́рно. А, éто г-н и г-жá Кóлинс! (*Calls out to them.*) Г-н Кóлинс, г-жá Кóлинс, извинéте за минýта!

г-жá Кóлинс Разбúра се, госпóжице. Здравéйте!

Невéна Мóля, запознáйте се. Товá е господúн Джóнсън, англúйски бúзнесмен, кóйто живéе в Чéлмсфорд.

г-жá Кóлинс Мнóго ми е прия́тно!

г-н Кóлинс (*Echoing Mrs Collins in Bulgarian.*) Прия́тно ми е!

Невéна (*Aside.*) Кóлко интерéсно! Англичáни, кóйто говóрят бъ́лгарски!

дрýги англичáни	*other English people*
Нúщо чýдно.	*Not surprising.*
по светá	*in the world*
Но не мнóго англичáни говóрят бъ́лгарски.	*But not many English people speak Bulgarian.*
Вúе говóрите бъ́лгарски добрé, но г-жá Кóлинс говóри пó-добрé.	*You speak Bulgarian well, but Mrs Collins speaks better.*

Кой говóри пó-добрé?	*Who speaks better?*
Но коя́ е г-жá Кóлинс?	*But who is Mrs Collins?*
Не знáя.	*I don't know.*
Говóря за англичáнката, коя́то живéе в стáя нóмер дéсет.	*I'm speaking about the English woman who is staying in room number ten.*
А Ви́е говóрите ли англи́йски?	*And do you speak English?*
за съжалéние	*unfortunately*
Но знáя ня́колко дрýги ези́ка.	*But I know several other languages.*
Каквѝ ези́ци знáете?	*What languages do you know?*
френски	*French*
рýски	*Russian*
испáнски	*Spanish*
Фрéнски е ези́кът, кóйто говóря нáй-добрé.	*French is the language I speak best.*
Мнóго българи говóрят чýжди ези́ци.	*A lot of Bulgarians speak foreign languages.*
Товá е вя́рно.	*That's true.*
извинéте за минýта	*excuse me, just a minute*
англи́йски би́знесмен, кóйто живéе в Чéлмсфорд	*an English businessman who lives in Chelmsford*
Кóлко интерéсно!	*How interesting!*
Англичáни, който говóрят бъ́лгарски!	*English people who speak Bulgarian!*

Questions

1 Try to answer the questions.

- **a** Къдé и́ма англичáни?
- **b** Какъ́в чужд ези́к говóри г-жá Кóлинс мнóго добрé?
- **c** Коя́ е г-жá Кóлинс?
- **d** Кóлко ези́ка знáе Невéна?
- **e** Каквѝ ези́ци говóри Невéна?
- **f** Къдé живéе г-н Джóнсън?

2 True or false?
Write out correct versions of the false statements.

- **a** Мнóго англичáни говóрят бъ́лгарски.
- **b** Г-жá Кóлинс е америкáнката, коя́то живéе в стáя нóмер дéсет.
- **c** Г-жá Кóлинс говóри бъ́лгарски мнóго добрé.
- **d** Невéна не знáе англи́йски.

e Тя говóри рýски нáй-добрé.
f Мáлко бъ́лгари говóрят чýжди езúци.

Does anyone speak English?

You should already be able to cope using your Bulgarian in a number of different situations. However, you will be reassured to know that English is now quite widely spoken in Bulgaria, especially by the younger generation in the larger towns. You will usually find English-speakers on the reception desks of big hotels, in money-changing bureaux, in tourist and airline offices and also in the more prestigious places for eating out. With shop-assistants, tram and bus drivers and policemen, however, although you might still venture a timid **говóрите ли англи́йски?** you would probably do best to resort to your Bulgarian straightaway.

Big or small? When to use capital letters

Bulgarian uses far fewer capital letters than English. The names of nationalities and the national languages all begin with small letters. You will therefore find, for example, **американец, американка (американски)**; **англичанин, англичанка (англи́йски)**; **испанец, испанка (испански** – *Spanish*); **италианец, италианка (италиански** – *Italian*); **немец, немкиня (немски** – *German*), and **францу́зин, французо́йка (френски** – *French*).

Names of places begin with capital letters, but when the place name consists of more than one word, the second often begins with a small letter: **Златни пясъци** (*Golden Sands*), **Слънчев бряг** (*Sunny Beach*) and **Черно море** (*the Black Sea*).

Adjectives formed from the names of places also begin with small letters: Лóндон: **лóндонски**, Сóфия: **софи́йски**, Вáрна: **вáрненски**.

Giving your phone number

In Bulgarian, as in English, there is no single pattern for writing or reading out the individual digits in phone numbers. Some speakers group the digits in pairs, others in threes, depending on the amount of digits in the number. However, the need for ever-increasing strings of numbers, coupled with the widespread use of mobile phones (**мобилен телефóн, мóбифон** or **GSM** – the last written using English letters and pronounced **джиесéм**), means that the simplest way to give your phone number is by reading out the individual digits, one by one.

When you answer the phone, it's best to follow the Bulgarian practice and, without giving your name, say '**А́ло!**' or '**Да, мо́ля?**' or just '**Да?**' and wait for the person making the call to open the conversation.

When making a call yourself, be prepared to respond to an answerphone (**телефо́нен секрета́р** or just **секрета́р** for short). The standard message goes something like this: '**Тук е телефо́нният секрета́р на...** [the name of the person]. **Мо́ля, оставе́те съобще́ние след сигна́ла.**' ('*This is the answerphone of... Please leave your message after the beep.*')

ФОТО
СТУДИО ИНДЕР
БЛ.111 ВХ.Б ЕТ.2
ТЕЛ. 847 89 47

Abbreviations used in this sign are: БЛ. = блок (*block*), ВХ. = вход (*entrance*), ЕТ. = ета́ж (*floor*) and ТЕЛ. = телефо́н (*telephone*).

How do you say it?

- Asking whether a person speaks a foreign language

Гово́рите ли англи́йски?	*Do you speak English?*
Зна́ете ли фре́нски?	*Do you speak (know) French?*
Какъ́в (чужд) ези́к гово́рите/зна́ете?	*What (foreign) language do you speak/know?*
Какви́ (чу́жди) ези́ци гово́рите?	*What (foreign) languages do you speak?*

- Answering whether, and how well, you speak a language

Гово́ря добре́ фре́нски.	*I speak French well.*
Разби́рам испа́нски, но не гово́ря добре́.	*I understand Spanish but I don't speak it well.*
Зна́я ма́лко ру́ски.	*I know a little Russian.*

Не разби́рам бъ́лгарски.	*I don't understand Bulgarian.*
Говóря фрéнски нáй-добрé.	*I speak French best.*

- Responding to what you hear

Товá е вя́рно!	*That's true!*
Ни́що чу́дно!	*That's hardly surprising.*

- Expressing interest, agreement or regret

Кóлко интерéсно!	*How interesting!*
разби́ра се	*of course/naturally*
за съжалéние	*unfortunately/sadly*

Grammar

1 Some plurals

Nationalities and masculine nouns ending in -(н)ин

This is one of the endings that form names of nationalities or inhabitants of a place. The plural of such names is once again **-и**, but it is not added to the singular. Instead, the **-н** of the singular is dropped:

англичáнин	*Englishman*	англичáни	*Englishmen*
бъ́лгарин	*Bulgarian*	бъ́лгари	*Bulgarians*
грáжданин	*citizen*	грáждани	*citizens*
лондончáнин	*Londoner*	лондончáни	*Londoners*

Plural of adjectives and other defining words

In the plural, no matter what the gender of the noun they describe, all adjectives in Bulgarian end in **-и**. Compare:

чужд ези́к	*a foreign language*	чу́жд**и** ези́ци	*foreign languages*
чу́жда странá	*a foreign country*	чу́жд**и** страни́	*foreign countries*
чу́ждо списáние	*a foreign magazine*	чу́жд**и** списáния	*foreign magazines*

Similarly, you will find the **-и** ending in **какви́** (*what*), the plural form of **какъ́в**, **каквá**, **каквó**:

Какъ́в ези́к говóрите?	*What language do you speak?*
Какв**и́** ези́ци говóрите?	*What languages do you speak?*

Adjectives which end in **-ски** in the masculine singular remain the same in the plural:

английски вéстник	*an English newspaper*
американски бизнесмен	*an American businessman*
български курóрт	*a Bulgarian resort*
рýски грáжданин	*a Russian citizen*
английски вéстници	*English newspapers*
американски бизнесмени	*American businessmen*
български курóрти	*Bulgarian resorts/spas*
рýски грáждани	*Russian citizens*

2 Друг/дрýги *Another/other*

друг, дрýга, дрýго	*another*
дрýги	*other*
нéщо дрýго	*something else*

3 Special masculine plural after numbers

In the dialogue you came across two plurals of **език** *language*, one ending in **-и** and the other in **-а**:

Каквú **езúци** знáете?	*What languages do you know?*
Знáя няколко **езúка**.	*I know several languages.*

The first is the regular plural, (remember the change of **-к** to **-ц**!). The second is the plural form used after any number or after the word **някoлко** *several*. This plural form only occurs in masculine nouns and always ends in **-а** or **-я**. Examples:

Невéна знáе **три езúка**.	*Nevena knows three languages.*
Дéсет билéта, мóля.	*Ten tickets, please.*
В Гáброво úма **някoлко музéя.**	*In Gabrovo there are several museums.*

You must also use this special numerical masculine plural in questions after **кóлко** *how many*:

Кóлко езúка знáе Невéна?	*How many languages does Nevena know?*
Кóлко билéта úскате, мóля?	*How many tickets do you want, please?*
Кóлко музéя úма в Гáброво?	*How many museums are there in Gabrovo?*

4 Говóря *I speak*

This is an **и**-pattern, Conjugation 2 verb:

аз	говóря	*I speak*	нúе	говóр**им**	*we speak*
ти	говóр**иш**	*you speak*	вúе	говóр**ите**	*you speak*
той / тя / то	говóр**и**	*he/she/it speaks*	те	говóрят	*they speak*

5 Знáя *I know*, живéя *I live*

These verbs contain the vowel **-е-** in most of their present tense endings. They are examples of Conjugation 1, **е**-pattern verbs. Notice that once again the final vowel is the same in the *I* form and in the *they* form:

аз	знáя/живéя	нúе	знá**ем**/живé**ем**
ти	знá**еш**/живé**еш**	вúе	знá**ете**/живé**ете**
той / тя / то	знá**е**/живé**е**	те	знáят/живéят

6 The present tense: patterns and meanings

To summarize, Bulgarian verbs have three patterns or conjugations:

Conjugation 1 verbs follow the **е**-pattern
Conjugation 2 verbs follow the **и**-pattern
Conjugation 3 verbs follow the **а**-pattern

The present tense in Bulgarian corresponds in meaning to two distinct tense forms in English. **Невéна говóри фрéнски** might mean, depending on the context, either *Nevena speaks French* or *Nevena is speaking French*. Similarly, **аз ýча бъ́лгарски** might mean either *I learn Bulgarian* or *I am learning Bulgarian*.

From now on in the vocabulary you will find all verbs given with the endings of both the *I* and the *you* forms (1st and 2nd singular). This will help you to identify the correct conjugation pattern. The endings of the *you* form will always be preceded by the letter to which the endings for the other forms need to be added:

Conjugation 1 живéя, -éеш; пúя, -úеш (*I drink*)
Conjugation 2 говóря, -риш; мúсля, -лиш (*I think*); ýча, -чиш (*I learn*)*
Conjugation 3 дáвам, -ваш (*I give*); запóчвам, -ваш; разбúрам, -раш
*After **ж**, **ч** and **ш** the **-я** in all the *I* and *they* forms changes to **-а**.

And pronunciation too...

The **-я**, **-ят** and **-а**, **-ат** endings of the *I* and *they* forms of Conjugation 1 and 2 verbs are pronounced **-йъ**, **-йът** and **-ъ**, **-ът**.

7 Кой? *Who?*

The question word for *who* in Bulgarian is **кой**. It stands in place of a noun and you use it to ask for the subject of a sentence no matter whether the subject is masculine, feminine, neuter or even plural.

Ма́йкъл Джо́нсън живе́е в Че́лмсфорд.
Кой живе́е в Че́лмсфорд? *Who lives in Chelmsford?*
Г-жа́ Ко́линс гово́ри бъ́лгарски по́-добре́.
Кой гово́ри бъ́лгарски по́-добре́? *Who speaks Bulgarian better?*
Мно́го бъ́лгари гово́рят чу́жди ези́ци.
Кой гово́ри чу́жди ези́ци? *Who speaks foreign languages?*

8 Кой? коя́? кое́? and кои́? *Which?*

Кой also means *which* when used before a noun and then it has a different form for each of the three genders and for the plural:

Masculine
Кой? В кой град е фи́рмата? *Which town is the firm in?*
Кой ези́к гово́рите на́й-добре́? *Which language do you speak best?*

Feminine
Коя́? В коя́ ста́я сте? *Which room are you in?*

Neuter
Кое́? Кое́ списа́ние и́скате? *Which magazine do you want?*

Plural
Кои́? Кои́ ези́ци зна́ете? *Which languages do you know?*

When a feminine, neuter or plural noun (or pronoun) is mentioned in the question itself, the correct alternative form of **кой** has to be used, no matter whether it means *who* or *which*:

Коя́ е г-жа́ Ко́линс? *Which one is Mrs Collins?*
Кое́ е това́ дете́? *Who is that child?*
Кои́ са те? *Who are they?* or *Which are they?*

9 Госпожа́та, коя́то... *The woman who...*

In expressions like these, the words *who* and *which* relate to the last person or thing mentioned. They are called relative pronouns. In Bulgarian, you have to concentrate not on the distinction between persons and things, but rather on whether the preceding noun is masculine, feminine, neuter or plural. In the singular, you have to use **ко́йто** (кой+то) for masculine, **коя́то** (коя́+то) for feminine and **коéто** (коé+то) for neuter nouns. The plural form is **които** (кой+то). All the forms must be preceded by a comma:

Masculine

Господи́нът, ко́йто гово́ри български, е би́знесмен.	*The man who speaks/who is speaking Bulgarian is a businessman.*

Feminine

Госпожа́та, коя́то и́ма въпро́с, у́чи български.	*The woman who has a question is learning Bulgarian.*

Neuter

Дете́то, кое́то гово́ри, е синъ́т на г-н Анто́нов.	*The child who is speaking is Mr Antonov's son.*

Plural

Г-н и г-жа́ Ко́линс са англича́ни, които живе́ят в Ма́нчестър.	*Mr and Mrs Collins are English people living/ who live/in Manchester.*

Note that in English you can sometimes omit the words *who* and *which*. In Bulgarian the relative pronoun can *never* be omitted.

10 Аз зна́я, че... *I know that...*

Че is the Bulgarian equivalent of *that*. It is used as the connecting word (conjunction) after certain verbs and, unlike *that*, can never be omitted. It must always be preceded by a comma:

Аз зна́я, **че** Со́фия е сто́лицата на Бълга́рия.	*I know (that) Sofia is the capital of Bulgaria.*
Зна́ете ли, **че** мно́го българи гово́рят англи́йски?	*Do you know (that) many Bulgarians speak English?*

11 Comparison of doing *well, better* or *best of all*

In Bulgarian, when you want to compare the way in which something is done, you change the adverb, in this case **добре́** (*well*), by adding **по́-** and **на́й-** on the front. You add **по́-** when comparing the way in which two things are done and **на́й-** when you want to compare more than two. The **по́-** and **на́й-** are pronounced with an emphasis and in the book we will add a stress mark to remind you of this. Examples:

Г-н Джóнсън говóри български **добрé**, но г-жá Кóлинс говóри **пó-добрé**.	*Mr Johnson speaks Bulgarian **well**, but Mrs Collins speaks **better**.*
Невéна знáе няколко езúка, но знáе фрéнски **нáй-добрé**.	*Nevena knows several languages, but knows French **best of all**.*

In the same way, the adverbs **блúзо** *near* and **бързо** *quickly*, *fast* become:

пó-блúзо	*nearer*	**нáй-блúзо**	*nearest* (of all)
пó-бързо	*more quickly*	**нáй-бързо**	*quickest* (of all)

In Bulgarian, you use **от** in comparisons much as you use *than* in English:

Г-жá Кóлинс говóри български **пó-добрé от** г-н Джóнсън.	*Mrs Collins speaks Bulgarian **better than** Mr Johnson.*
Г-жá Кóлинс говóри **пó-бързо от** г-н Джóнсън.	*Mrs Collins speaks **more quickly than** Mr Johnson.*

Exercises

1 Turn the following sentences into questions requiring the answer 'yes' or 'no' by making the words in bold type the focus of your questions. Remember to put the verb immediately after the question word **ли**.

Model: Г-жá Кóлинс е **англичáнка. Англичáнка ли** е г-жá Кóлинс? Да.

a В хотéла úма **мнóго англичáни**.
b **Мнóго българи** говóрят англúйски.
c Г-н Антóнов и Николáй са **българи**.
d Във фúрмата рабóтят **българи и англичáни**.
e Г-н и г-жá Кóлинс са **англичáни**.

2 The following questions may be useful when you want to ask for something else, or something different, using the Bulgarian equivalent of *another* or *other*. Use **друг**, **дрýга**, **дрýго** or **дрýги** as apprropriate:

a Úмате ли _______ въпрóси?
b Каквó _______ вúно úмате?
c Къдé úма _______ бáнка?
d Каквú _______ езúци говóрите?

e Ѝма ли _______ банкомát (*cashpoint, ATM*) до хотéла?
f Каквѝ _______ цигáри (*cigarettes*) ѝмате?
g Когá ѝма _______ автобýс за Мальóвица?
h Ѝмате ли _______ детé?
i Знáете ли къдé ѝма _______ аптéка?
j Ѝмате ли _______ свобóдни местá?

3 A tourist, map in hand, stops a passer-by and asks which of two places on the map is closer:

i Тук на кáртата ѝма два хотéла. Кой (хотéл) е пó-блѝзо?

How would you ask about:

a ресторáнт
b град
c курóрт
d къмпинг (*campsite*)
e мотéл (*motel*)

When asking the same question about places which are feminine, remember, you have to use **коя́**:

ii На кáртата ѝма две туристѝчески агéнции. Коя́ (агéнция) е пó-блѝзо?

How would you ask the same question about:

a аптéка
b бензиностáнция (*petrol station*)
c спѝрка

4 Use **кой** or **коя́** as appropriate:

a ____ град е нáй-блѝзо до курóрта «Злáтни пя́съци»?
b ____ трамвáй е нáй-блѝзо до ýлица «Ракóвски»?
c ____ спѝрка е нáй-блѝзо до гáрата (*railway station*)?
d ____ магазѝн е нáй-блѝзо до хотéл «Шéратон»?
e ____ туристѝческа агéнция е нáй-блѝзо до спѝрката?
f ____ сýпермаркет (*supermarket*) е нáй-блѝзо до пóщата?

5 Ask questions with **кóлко**, remembering to put the subject at the end of the question, as in the model: Г-н и г-жá Кóлинс ѝскат два чáя. Кóлко чáя ѝскат г-н и г-жá Кóлинс?

a Невéна говóри три чýжди езѝка.
b Те ѝскат дéсет билéта.
c Сервитьóрът сервѝра (*serves*) три джѝна.
d Мáйкъл Джóнсън знáе ня́колко чýжди езѝка.

6 In this exercise you need to change a word from the normal masculine plural form to the special numerical plural. (The two forms are often used very near to one another.)

Турúст	Извинéте, úма ли магазúни до гáрата?
Грáжданин	Да, до гáрата úма някoлко магазúна.

Compose similar questions and answers to the above model using:

a хотéл
b ресторáнт
c музéй
d óфис

7 Choose the correct combinations to make sentences:

(*a*)

Познáвам { мъжá, / женáта, / англичáни, / семéйството, }

коéто живée в стáя нóмер дéсет.
кóйто пристúга от Лóндон.
кoятo говóри хýбаво български.
кoйто живéят в Бългáрия.

(*b*)

Познáваш ли { българина, / англичáни, / шотлáндци, / българката, }

коятo е омъжена за англичáнин?
кoйто не пúят уиски?
кóйто заминáва за Áнглия?
кoйто са жéнени за българки?

8 This exercise draws your attention to the fact that what looks like the same masculine form may have two distinct meanings. For instance, **хотéла** can be either *the hotel*, in the non-subject form, or, when used after numerals, *hotels*.

Товá е хотéлът.
but Éто хотéла. *Here's the hotel.*
Éто два хотéла. *Here are two hotels.*

Using the examples as a model, practise pointing to one or two of the following:

a трамвáй
b тролéй
c автобýс
d къмпинг
e компютър
f банкомáт

You will see from the example that after **éто** you need to add the short definite article to the noun.

9 Michael Johnson writes down his home address and shows it to Nevena saying: **Éто адрéса ми.**

What would you say while showing or pointing to the following?

a your ticket
b your passport
c your husband
d your son
e your luggage (**багáж**)

10 This exercise will help you practise checking whether, when your correspondent answers the phone with **'А́ло!'** or **'Да, мóля?'**, you have got the right number. Read the short dialogue **На телефóна** (*On the telephone*) out loud:

Извинéте, 947 54 26 ли е? (дéвет, чéтири, сéдем, пет, чéтири, две, шест)
Да, кажéте! (*Yes, can I help you?)*

Now repeat, using the following numbers: 0888 32 18 91; 0898 15 67 32; 789 02 66.

Do you understand?

Dialogue

Milena goes into the office and sees Nikolai who is busy reading.

Милéна Здравéй, Николáй. Каквó прáвиш?
Николáй У́ча английски. Ти знáеш ли английски?
Милéна Да, но не мнóго добрé. Ми́сля, че е мнóго трýден ези́к.
Николáй И аз такá ми́сля. И́мам нýжда от учи́тел. Познáваш ли учи́тели по англи́йски?
Милéна Да, познáвам ня́колко учи́теля по англи́йски, които живéят бли́зо.
Николáй Чудéсно. И́мам нýжда и от учéбници по англи́йски.
Милéна Аз и́мам два мнóго хýбави учéбника, също и интерéсни англи́йски списáния.
Николáй Мнóго добрé, но и́мам тóлкова мáлко врéме! Ми́сля, че съм вéче стар за чýжди ези́ци...
Милéна Глýпости! На кóлко годи́ни си?
Николáй На двáйсет и шест.
Милéна Е да, вя́рно, мнóго си стар...

трýден, трýдна	*difficult*
такá	*likewise/just so*
и́мам нýжда от	*I need*
учéбник, -ици	*textbook*
тóлкова	*so* (much/little)
вéче	*already*
стар	*old*
глýпости! (pl)	*nonsense!*
на кóлко годи́ни си?	*how old are you?*

True or false?

Write out correct versions of the false statements.

1 Николáй ýчи фрéнски.
2 Николáй úма нýжда от учúтел.
3 Милéна не познáва учúтели по англúйски.
4 Милéна ня́ма учéбници по англúйски.
5 Николáй ня́ма нýжда от учéбници.
6 Николáй мúсли, че е вéче стар за чýжди езúци.
7 Николáй е на трúйсет и шест годúни.

09 йскате ли да...?

would you like to...?

In this unit you will learn

- **how to say *would you like to...?* and *may I...?***
- **how to answer to *would you like to...?* and *may I...?***
- **how to say you *must* or *have to* do something**

Dialogue

Michael Johnson is keeping his appointment with Boyan Antonov at the advertising agency.

г-н Джо́нсън	(*Knocking on the office door and going in.*) До́бър ден! Мо́же ли? Ка́звам се Ма́йкъл Джо́нсън.
На́дя	О, г-н Джо́нсън, добре́ дошли́! Мо́ля, заповя́дайте.
г-н Джо́нсън	Благодаря́. Тук ли е г-н Анто́нов? Аз и́мам сре́ща с не́го.
На́дя	Да, разби́ра се. Г-н Анто́нов Ви оча́ква.
г-н Джо́нсън	(*At the door into the director's office.*) Мо́же ли?
г-н Анто́нов	Заповя́дайте, г-н Джо́нсън. Добре́ дошли́! Ра́двам се да се запозна́я с Вас.
г-н Джо́нсън	Аз съ́що.
г-н Анто́нов	Как се чу́вствате в Со́фия? Надя́вам се, че сте дово́лен от хоте́ла.
г-н Джо́нсън	Да, вси́чко е наре́д.
г-н Анто́нов	Йскате ли да обя́дваме за́едно?
г-н Джо́нсън	Разби́ра се, ня́мам ни́що проти́в. Мо́же ли пъ́рво да оти́дем в ба́нката? Тря́бва да обменя́ пари́.
г-н Анто́нов	Ня́ма пробле́ми. Ба́нката не е дале́че, а рестора́нтът е до не́я.
г-н Джо́нсън	Извиня́вайте, г-н Анто́нов, мо́же ли да гово́рите по́-ба́вно?
г-н Анто́нов	Мо́же, разби́ра се. Ра́двам се, че ня́маме ну́жда от прево́да́ч. Ви́е гово́рите бъ́лгарски мно́го добре́.
г-н Джо́нсън	Но аз и́скам да разби́рам бъ́лгарски о́ще по́-добре́ и да гово́ря по́-добре́ от г-жа́ Ко́линс.

Мо́же ли?	*May I* (come in)*?*
О, г-н Джо́нсън, добре́ дошли́!	*Oh, Mr Johnson, welcome!*
Мо́ля, заповя́дайте.	*Please, do come in.*
Г-н Анто́нов Ви оча́ква.	*Mr Antonov is expecting you.*
Ра́двам се да се запозна́я с Вас.	*Pleased to/meet you/ make your acquaintance.*
Аз съ́що.	*So am I/Me too.*
Как се чу́вствате в Со́фия?	*How are you feeling in Sofia?*
Надя́вам се, че сте дово́лен от хоте́ла.	*I hope you are happy with the hotel.*
Да, вси́чко е наре́д.	*Yes, everything is fine.*

Йскате ли да обя́двамe зáедно?	*Would you like to have lunch together?*
Разби́ра се, ня́мам ни́що проти́в.	*Certainly, why not.*
Мóже ли първо да оти́дем в бáнката?	*Could we* (possibly) *go to the bank first?*
Тря́бва да обменя́ пари́.	*I have to change some money.*
ня́ма проблéми	*no problem*
Бáнката не е далéче, а ресторáнтът е до нéя.	*The bank is not far and the restaurant is next to it.*
мóже ли да говóрите пó-бáвно?	*Could you* (please) *speak more slowly?*
Мóже, разби́ра се.	*I can, of course.*
Рáдвам се, че ня́маме нýжда от преводáч.	*I am glad we do not need an interpreter.*
Но аз йскам да разби́рам бъ́лгарски óще пó-добрé!	*But I want to understand Bulgarian even better.*

Questions

1 Try to answer the questions.

a Кой и́ма срéща с г-н Антóнов?
b Кой очáква г-н Джóнсън?
c Йма ли г-н Джóнсън проблéми в Сóфия?
d Къдé и́ска да оти́де първо г-н Джóнсън?
e Кой тря́бва да обмени́ пари́?
f Как тря́бва да говóри г-н Антóнов?

2 True or false?

a Г-н Джóнсън не é довóлен от хотéла.
b Г-н Антóнов и́ска да обя́два зáедно с г-н Джóнсън.
c Бáнката и ресторáнтът са далéче от óфиса.
d Г-н Джóнсън тря́бва да говóри пó-бáвно.
e Г-н Антóнов и г-н Джóнсън и́мат нýжда от преводáч.
f Г-н Джóнсън и́ска да разби́ра бъ́лгарски пó-добрé.

i Responding to words of welcome

Мóля, you will remember, is the set response to **благодаря́**. The Bulgarians also have set formal responses to the traditional words of welcome **Добрé дошъ́л!**, **Добрé дошлá!** and **Добрé дошли́!** These responses are **Добрé завáрил!**, **Добрé завáрила!** and **Добрé завáрили!** (lit. *Well met!*). Once again, notice, you use differing forms for the masculine, feminine and plural. Both the words of welcome, and the responses, which are often immediately preceded or followed by **благодаря́**, are used particularly when someone has arrived safely after a long journey. If you cannot manage the full responses, nowadays **благодаря́** will also suffice.

Knocking and entering

In the Dialogue at the beginning of this unit you will have noticed Mr Johnson knocked at the door to Nadya's office and immediately went in. In the English-speaking world, this would have been considered rude. Being in Bulgaria, however, he was right not to wait, for it is normal, especially in offices, to knock and enter immediately. When knocking and entering you would do well simultaneously to give out a **Мо́же ли?** in the hope that, if you are a stranger, someone will eventually respond with a **Да, мо́ля?** and invite you to state your business.

Changing money

Sooner or later (probably sooner rather than later), you will need to change some money. This is not difficult in Bulgaria, certainly not in the bigger towns and the main tourist resorts. You will find all manner of agencies, from the larger hotels and state and private banks to numerous small 'change' bureaux, all keen to take your **валу́та** (*currency*) banknotes in exchange for the local Bulgarian *lev*. The 'change' bureaux are indicated by notices such as **ОБМЕ́ННО БЮРО́**, **ОБМЯ́НА НА ВАЛУ́ТА** or simply **CHANGE**. Travellers' cheques can only be exchanged in banks. All the banks and agencies will present you with a certificate of exchange, which you should check carefully before you leave against the sum paid out to you.

ОБМЕННО БЮРО

ВСИЧКИ СВЕТОВНИ ВАЛУТИ И МОНЕТИ

ALL WORLD CURRENCIES AND COINS

ВАЛУТА	БАНКНОТИ	
	КУПУВА	ПРОДАВА
EUR	1,94	1,95
USD	1,68	1,69
GBP	2,69	2,74
CHF	1,28	1,30
CYP	3,20	3,26
JPY	1,43	1,48
CAD	1,19	1,23
AUD	1,06	1,09

ТЕЛЕФОНИ ЗА ВРЪЗКА: 088/504125

Д.П.: ТЕЛ.: 91 50 441

Before changing any money, make sure you know the exchange rates. These can differ considerably from dealer to dealer, but are clearly displayed. The boards list, from left to right, the currency to be exchanged, then the rate at which the bureau buys and sells for levs. Commission is not usually charged, but, like everything else, it's worth checking!

How do you say it?

- Saying *Welcome!*

To a man:	**Добре́ дошъ̀л!**
To a woman:	**Добре́ дошла́!**
To more than one person (and polite):	**Добре́ дошли́!**

- Attracting attention

Мо́же ли?	*May I? Excuse me, but...*

- Requesting politely

Мо́же ли да говоря́ с Вас?	*May I have a word with you?*
Мо́же ли да оти́дем в ба́нката?	*Could we (possibly) go to the bank?*
Мо́же ли да гово́рите по́-ба́вно?	*Could you (please) speak more slowly?*

- Asking *May I..?/Can I..?* and responding to the same request

Мо́же ли да обменя́ пари́ тук?	*Can I change (some) money here?*
Да, мо́же.	*Yes, you can.*
Не, не мо́же.	*No, you can't.*

- Saying *I'm pleased to/that..., I'm glad...*

Ра́двам се да се запозна́я с Вас!	*Pleased to meet you.*
Ра́двам се, че всѝчко е наре́д!	*I'm pleased/glad everything is all right.*

- Expressing satisfaction with the state of affairs

Всѝчко е наре́д!	*Everything is fine!*
Ня́ма пробле́м(и)!	*No problem(s)!*

- Agreeing with a proposal

Ня́мам ни́що проти́в!	*Why not?/I don't mind if I do!*

- Saying *I need/don't need*

Ѝмам ну́жда от учи́тел.	*I need a teacher.*
Ня́мам ну́жда от преводa̍ч.	*I don't need an interpreter.*

Grammar

1 Йскам да *I want to*

Verbs like **искам** *I want* and **трябва** *I must* need another verb to complete their meaning. When two (or more) verbs are combined in Bulgarian the second verb is introduced by **да**. (Do not confuse it with **да** meaning *yes*!) The **да** form of the Bulgarian verb corresponds to the English infinitive with or without *to*. An essential difference from English, however, is that the **да** form has personal endings just like a main verb.

The personal endings of the main verb and the **да** form may agree or be different, depending on the meaning:

(*a*) When the two verbs share the same subject, both agree with that subject. The following examples go through all the persons:

Йскам да **говоря** български по́-добре́.	*I want to speak Bulgarian better.*
Йскаш ли да **учиш** английски?	*Do you want to study English?*
Миле́на **иска** да **оти́де** в А́нглия.	*Milena wants to go to England.*
Ни́е **и́скаме** да **обмени́м** пари́.	*We want to change some money.*
Йскате ли да **оти́дете** в ба́нката?	*Do you want to go to the bank?*
Миле́на и Никола́й **и́скат** да **пи́ят** кафе́.	*Milena and Nikolai want to drink coffee.*

(*b*) When the two verbs have different subjects each agrees with its own subject (although the subject word may be omitted!). In the dialogue Mr Antonov asks:

Йск**ате** ли да обя́дв**аме** за́едно?

This literally means *Do **you** want that **we** have lunch together?* Now compare the two – with the same subject and with different subjects:

Йск**ам** да обя́дв**ам** с тях.	*I want to have lunch with them.*
Те и́ск**ат** да обя́дв**ам** с тях.	*They want me to have lunch with them.*
Той и́ск**а** да обя́дв**а** с тях.	*He wants to have lunch with them.*
Той и́ск**а** да обя́дв**аш** с тях.	*He wants you to have lunch with them.*

So, to make sure you clearly express who wants to do what with whom you have to choose the endings of the **да** form very carefully. One letter can make all the difference between who gets a meal and who doesn't!

2 Тря́бва да... *Must* or *have to...*

You use **тря́бва да** + verb for both *must* and *have to*. As with **мо́же ли да...?** below, **тря́бва да**... itself stays the same for all persons. The verb that follows changes to fit the subject, which is not always expressed. Again, therefore, you have to be very careful to listen for the ending of the verb to work out the correct meaning:

(аз)	тря́бва да оти́д**а** в Пло́вдив.	***I*** *have to go to Plovdiv.*
(ти)	тря́бва да оти́д**еш** в по́щата.	***You*** *must go to the post office.*
Миле́на	тря́бва да се запозна́**е** с г-н Джо́нсън.	***Milena*** *must get to know Mr Johnson.*
(ни́е)	тря́бва да оти́д**ем** в ба́нката.	***We*** *have to go to the bank.*
(ви́е, Ви́е)	тря́бва да обмени́**те** пари́.	***You*** *must change some money.*
(те)	тря́бва да оти́д**ат** в по́щата.	***They*** *have to go to the post office.*

3 Мо́же ли...? *May I...? Could you...?*

Мо́же ли...? is a commonly used phrase which never changes its form. It is used to attract attention, to ask whether something is possible or permitted, or to make a polite request. (**Мо́же** is, in fact, the *it* form of the verb meaning *can* or *be able*.)

Мо́же ли on its own

Мо́же ли is used on its own to attract attention or to ask *Is it all right?* (for me to do this, that or the other), or *Could you?* (do this, that or the other for me). For instance, you say **Мо́же ли?** on its own:

(*a*) at the door when you want permission to go in
(*b*) when people are in your way and you want to get past
(*c*) when you need to interrupt someone

In a restaurant you use **мо́же ли** on its own just to attract the waiter's attention, or you may add another word to make your meaning clear:

Мо́же ли меню́то?	*Could you bring (pass etc.) the menu?*

Similarly, at table, if you want someone to pass something, the milk, for example, you would say:

Мо́же ли мля́кото?	*Could you pass (bring etc.) the milk?*

Мо́же ли да...? *May I...?*

This is used to ask if something is possible or permitted. **Мо́же ли да** + main verb is used to formulate full questions. When the main verb involves the speaker (*I* or *we*), **Мо́же ли да...?** can be used to ask for permission, in which case the answer will be **Мо́же,** or **Да, мо́же** and, if you are unlucky, **Не мо́же**, or **Не, не мо́же**.

Мо́же ли да говоря́ с г-н Анто́нов?	*Can I speak to Mr Antonov?*
Не, сега́ не мо́же.	*No, it isn't possible now.*
Мо́же ли да оти́дем в ба́нката?	*Could we (possibly) go to the bank?*
Мо́же, разби́ра се.	*We could, of course.*
Мо́же ли да се́днем до вас?	*Can we sit next to you?*
Разби́ра се, заповя́дайте!	*Certainly, go ahead!*

Мо́же ли да гово́рите по́-ба́вно? *Could you please speak more slowly?*

When the main verb is addressed to someone else, in the 2nd person singular or plural, **Мо́же ли да...?** is used to make a polite request:

Мо́же ли да гово́риш по́-ба́вно?	*Would you please speak more slowly?*
Мо́же ли да се оба́дите по́-къ́сно?	*Could you please ring/ call later?*

4 A bit more about verbs

Note that some verbs can only be used in the present tense when preceded by a **да**. You will learn more about these verbs in Unit 12, but from now on when listed in the vocabulary they will all be preceded by (**да**).

5 И́мам сре́ща с не́го *I've a meeting with him*

As in English, personal pronouns have different forms when they are not used as subjects, for instance after prepositions. Compare: *I have a meeting **with him*** (**аз и́мам сре́ща с не́го**), and ***he** has a meeting **with me*** (**той и́ма сре́ща с ме́не**). Both subject and non-subject (full) forms are given below side by side for comparison:

И́скате ли да обя́двате с ме́не?	*Would you like to have lunch with me?*
Г-н Джо́нсън и́ма сре́ща с не́го.	*Mr Johnson has a meeting with him.*
Това́ е ба́нката, а рестора́нтът е до не́я.	*That is the bank and the restaurant is next to it.*

И́ма три́ писма́ за Вас.	*There are three letters for you.*
На́дя пи́е кафе́ с тях.	*Nadya is drinking coffee with them.*

Subject forms		**Non-subject (full) forms**	
Singular	аз	с ме́не	*with me*
	ти	от те́бе	*from you*
	той	с не́го	*with him*
	тя	от не́я	*from her*
	то	до не́го	*next to it*
Plural	ни́е	до нас	*near us*
	ви́е (Ви́е)	с вас (Вас)	*with you*
	те	от тях	*from them*

NB You'll find more on non-subject forms in Units 7 and 11.

6 Getting to know one another

Verbs that are accompanied by the 'satellite' word **се** are known as reflexive verbs. One of the uses of a reflexive verb is to express the meaning *each other* or *one another*.

Sometimes the same verb can be used with and without **се** with different meanings. Compare the non-reflexive *without* **се**:

Неве́на и́ска да запозна́е г-н Джо́нсън със семе́йство Ко́линс.	*Nevena wants to introduce Mr Johnson to the Collins family.*
Г-н Джо́нсън разби́ра бъ̀лгарски.	*Mr Johnson understands Bulgarian.*

Now the same verbs used *with* **се**:

Никола́й и Миле́на и́скат да се запозна́ят.	*Nikolai and Milena want to meet (one another).*
Г-н Анто́нов и г-н Джо́нсън се разби́рат без превода́ч.	*Mr Antonov and Mr Johnson understand one another without an interpreter.*

A number of reflexive verbs, usually denoting feelings or emotions, never appear without **се**: **надя́вам се** *I hope*, **ра́двам се** *I am glad*. (There's more about reflexives in Unit 20.)

7 Where to place 'се'

Strict rules govern the position of **се**. Most importantly, it can never be the very first word in a sentence. Like a satellite it remains close to its verb, but:

(**a**) it comes before the verb if there are other words in first position such as pronouns, adverbs, question words or even little words like **да** in a **да** form or the negative **не**

(**b**) it follows the verb if the verb is the first word in the sentence:

Before the verb	**After the verb**
Той се надя́ва, че г-н Джо́нсън е дово́лен. *He hopes Mr Johnson is pleased.*	Надя́вам се, че сте дово́лен. *I hope you are pleased.*
Как се чу́вствате? *How do you feel?* Не се́ чу́вствам добре́. *I don't feel well.*	Чу́вствам се добре́. *I feel well.*

(The Appendix has a table to help you with word order.)

Exercises

1 Form short dialogues following the model:

- Ймате ли резерва́ция?
- – Не. Тря́бва ли да и́мам резерва́ция?
- Да, тря́бва.

Use **ви́за/биле́т/бо́рдна ка́рта** (*boarding pass/card*) instead of **резерва́ция**.

2 Using the model: Йскате ли да оти́дем на рестора́нт? ask someone to go:

a to the opera
b to a concert
c to a patisserie
d to a disco (**дискоте́ка**)
e to the theatre
f on an excursion (**екску́рзия**)
g skiing (**на ски**)
h to the beach (**плаж**)

Logo of the National Palace of Culture in Sofia, Национа́лен Дворе́ц на Култу́рата (НДК, pronounced 'еН-Де-Ка́')

3 You fear you have misheard an important telephone message. On the basis of the following questions and answers, see if you can write out the original message in just one sentence.

Кой тря́бва да оти́де в А́нглия? – Никола́й.
В кой град тря́бва да оти́де Никола́й? – в Че́лмсфорд.

Когá трябва да отúде Николáй в Чéлмсфорд? – След три сéдмици.

4 Which of the **мóже ли?** questions might you use in the following situations. In some of them, a variety of questions may be appropriate.

i	at the information desk	**a**	Мóже ли?
ii	looking for a place in a restaurant	**b**	Мóже ли да говóря с Милéна?
iii	in a crowded bus	**c**	Мóже ли товá?
iv	at table	**d**	Мóже ли да сéдна до Вас?
v	pointing at something in a shop	**e**	Мóже ли да обменя́ парú тук?
vi	asking for Milena on the phone	**f**	Мóже ли солтá? (*the salt*)
vii	at the bank		
viii	entering a room	**g**	Мóже ли еднá кáрта на Сóфия?
ix	attracting the attention of a waiter		

5 By using pronouns instead of the names and the nouns in the next two exercises you will be able to practise using the non-subject forms.

a Познáваш ли Невéна? Ńмам писмó от ____.
b Познáваш ли Марк? Ńмам срéща с ____.
c Познáваш ли г-н и г-жá Кóлинс? Ńма билéти за ____.

6 You are giving directions using a well-known place as a reference point. Complete with the appropriate personal pronoun:

a Знáете къдé е бáрът (*bar*), налú? Сладкáрницата е до ____.
b Знáете къдé е сладкáрницата, налú? Дискотéката е до ____.
c Знáете къдé е дискотéката, налú? Бюрó «Информáция» е до ____.
d Знáете къдé е бюрó «Информáция», налú? Пóщата е до ____.
e Знáете къдé е пóщата, налú? Музéят е до ____.
f Знáете къдé е музéят, налú? Магазúнът е до ____.

7 Introduce yourself and ask for the things listed below.

Model: Кáзвам се ____. Ńмате ли **стáя** за мéне?

писмá / факс / вéстници / билéти / мáса (*table*)

8 Read the following text and make it into a conversation between Nikolai, Mr Antonov and Nadya. It will help you practise using verbs in the *I* form.

Никола́й и́ска да гово́ри с г-н Анто́нов. Г-н Анто́нов съжаля́ва, но сега́ ня́ма вре́ме за не́го. Той и́ма сре́ща с г-н Джо́нсън. На́дя пи́та (*asks*) и́ма ли г-н Анто́нов ну́жда от не́я. Г-н Анто́нов ми́сли, че те ня́мат ну́жда от преводა́ч. Той пи́та На́дя мо́же ли да напра́ви (*make*) кафе́ за тях. На́дя ня́ма ни́що проти́в.

9 This exercise will help you ask for things you might need in a hotel. Prefacing your answer by И́мам ну́жда от, use the words listed below to reply to the question: От какво́ и́мате ну́жда?

a юти́я

b чадъ́р

c коли́чка

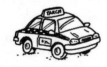

d такси́

e коса́ч

f пари́

10 Now for a few useful reflexives. Complete the following sentences without forgetting to alter the position of **се**. Here is a model to guide you:

Ра́двам се да се запозна́я с Вас! – И аз **се ра́двам**.

a Надя́вам се да оти́да във Ва́рна. – И аз ______
b Ра́двам се, че замина́ваш за А́нглия. – И аз ______
c Чу́вствам се добре́. – И аз ______

Do you understand?

Dialogue

(*The telephone rings.*)

На́дя	Да, мо́ля?
Клие́нт	А́ло, мо́же ли да гово́ря с дире́ктора г-н Анто́нов?
На́дя	Съжаля́вам, г-н Анто́нов е зае́т в моме́нта. Мо́же ли да се оба́дите по́-къ́сно?
Клие́нт	Кога́ да се оба́дя?
На́дя	По́-къ́сно следо́бед, мо́ля.
Клие́нт	Благодаря́. Дочу́ване.
Никола́й	Дире́кторът с г-н Джо́нсън ли е?
На́дя	Да. Тря́бва да се запозна́еш с не́го.
Никола́й	Да, тря́бва, разби́ра се. Но сега́ г-н Джо́нсън и дире́кторът са зае́ти. Миле́на, ти зае́та ли си след ра́бота? И́скаш ли да оти́дем на те́нис?
Миле́на	Добра́ иде́я, но пъ́рво тря́бва да гово́ря с брат ми. Той и́ска да оти́де с ме́не на конце́рт.
Никола́й	Мо́же всички за́едно да оти́дем на конце́рт.
Миле́на	Така́ е на́й-добре́. На́дя, мо́же ли да се оба́дя по телефо́на?
На́дя	Мо́же, разби́ра се. И аз тря́бва да се оба́дя след те́бе. И́скам да оти́да с вас на конце́рт.

клие́нт	*client, customer*
(да) се оба́дя, -диш	*to ring, call*
а́ло	*hello* (on the phone)
зае́т	*busy*
в моме́нта	*at the moment*
по́-къ́сно	*later*
дочу́ване	*goodbye* (on the phone)
сега́	*now*
те́нис	*tennis*
иде́я	*idea*

Questions

1 Кой и́ска да гово́ри с дире́ктора?
2 Свобо́ден ли е г-н Анто́нов сега́?
3 Кога́ тря́бва да се оба́ди клие́нтът?
4 Къде́ и́ска да оти́де Никола́й след ра́бота?
5 Къде́ и́ска да оти́де бра́тът на Миле́на с не́я?
6 И́ска ли На́дя да оти́де с Никола́й и Миле́на?

ко́лко стру́ва...?

how much is...?

In this unit you will learn

- **how to point out and ask for things**
- **how to ask *how much does it cost?***
- **how to shop at Bulgarian open-air fruit markets**

Dialogue

Mr and Mrs Collins go to the market to buy fresh fruit and vegetables. They have consulted Nevena for advice about where to shop.

г-жа́ Ко́линс Неве́на, покаже́те ни, мо́ля, къде́ и́ма магази́н за плодове́ и зеленчу́ци.

Неве́на На́й-добре́ е да оти́дете на паза́ра. Плодове́те и зеленчу́ците там не са́ е́втини, но са на́й-пре́сни. Паза́рът не е́ дале́че.

At the market, Mr and Mrs Collins become so carried away that they speak to each other in Bulgarian.

г-жа́ Ко́линс Виж, Джордж, та́зи жена́ прода́ва ху́бави зеленчу́ци. Да ку́пим дома́ти от не́я.

г-н Ко́линс Зеленчу́ци? Дома́ти? А-ха́...

Продава́чка Запове́дайте, мо́ля, вземе́те си!

г-н Ко́линс Какви́ са те́зи зеленчу́ци?

Продава́чка Това́ са ти́译квички, господи́не. Да Ви дам ли?

г-н Ко́линс Не, благодаря́. Жена́ ми не оби́ча ти́квички.

Продава́чка В Бълга́рия ня́ма мно́го мъже́, които пазару́ват!

г-н Ко́линс Мо́ля? Не разби́рам.

г-жа́ Ко́линс Жена́та и́ска да ка́же, че мъже́те в Бълга́рия не оби́чат да пазару́ват.

г-н Ко́линс О, аз ня́мам ни́що проти́в да пазару́вам! Да́йте ми, мо́ля, еди́н килогра́м дома́ти. Жена́ ми оби́ча дома́ти.

г-жа́ Ко́линс Ко́лко стру́ват дома́тите?

Продава́чка Че́тири ле́ва.

г-жа́ Ко́линс А пъпешите?

Продава́чка Шест ле́ва и петдесе́т стоти́нки за килогра́м.

г-жа́ Ко́линс Претегле́те ми то́зи пъпеш, ако́ оби́чате.

Продава́чка Гото́во! Пъпешът е два килогра́ма и полови́на.

г-жа́ Ко́линс Какви́ дру́ги плодове́ и́мате?

Продава́чка И́маме я́бълки, пра́скови и гро́зде.

г-жа́ Ко́линс Да́йте ми еди́н килогра́м от те́зи я́бълки и полови́н килогра́м бя́ло гро́зде.

Продава́чка Вси́чко три́йсет и о́сем ле́ва и шейсе́т стоти́нки, мо́ля.

г-жа́ Ко́линс Джордж, плати́, ако́ оби́чаш. (*Popping a grape into her mouth.*) Ммм, гро́здето е мно́го сла́дко. Джордж, купи́ о́ще еди́н килогра́м.

г-н Кóлинс Добрé, добрé. Добрé, че ѝма óще* мъжé, който пазарýват с удовóлствие...

*To express 'still', Mr. Collins should have said **óще** before **ѝма**.

Покажéте ни, мóля къдé ѝма магазѝн за плодовé и зеленчýци.	*Please show us where there is a greengrocer's.*
Нáй-добрé е да отѝдете на пазáра.	*You'd do best to go to the market.*
Плодовéте и зеленчýците там не сá éвтини.	*The fruit and vegetables are not cheap there.*
нáй-прéсни	*freshest*
пазáрът не é далéче	*the market is not far*
Виж, Джордж, тáзи женá продáва хýбави зеленчýци.	*Look, George, this woman is selling nice vegetables.*
Да кýпим домáти от нéя.	*Let's buy some tomatoes from her.*
Вземéте си!	*Help yourself!*
тéзи	*these*
тѝквички	*courgettes/zucchinis*
Да Ви дам ли?	*Shall I give you some?*
Женá ми не обѝча тѝквички.	*My wife doesn't like courgettes.*
В България нямa мнóго мъжé, който пазарýват!	*In Bulgaria, there aren't many men who do the shopping.*
Женáта ѝска да кáже, че мъжéте в Бългáрия не обѝчат да пазарýват.	*What the woman means is that men in Bulgaria don't like shopping.*
О, аз нямам нѝщо протѝв да пазарýвам.	*Oh, I don't mind shopping.*
Дáйте ми, мóля, едѝн килогрáм домáти.	*Please give me one kilogram of tomatoes.*
Кóлко стрýват домáтите?	*How much are the tomatoes?*
чéтири лéва	*four levs*
А пъпешите?	*And the melons?*
Шест лéва и петдесéт стотѝнки за килогрáм.	*Six levs and fifty stotinkas a kilogram.*
Претеглéте ми тóзи пъпеш, акó обѝчате.	*Weigh this melon for me, if you please.*
Готóво! Пъпешът е два килогрáма и половѝна.	*There you go! The melon is $2^1/2$ kilograms.*
Каквѝ дрýги плодовé ѝмате?	*What other fruit do you have?*
Ѝмаме ябълки, прáскови и грóзде.	*We have apples, peaches and grapes.*

еди́н килогра́м от те́зи я́бълки	*one kilogram of these apples*
полови́н килогра́м	*half a kilogram of*
бя́ло гро́зде	*white grapes*
плати́, ако́ оби́чаш	*pay, (if you) please*
Гро́здето е мно́го сла́дко.	*The grapes are very sweet.*
Купи́ о́ще еди́н килогра́м.	*Buy another kilogram.*
Добре́, че о́ще* и́ма	*It's a good thing that there still*
мъже́, кои́то	*are men who gladly*
пазару́ват с удово́лствие ...	*do the shopping ...*

*See the note to the **Dialogue**

Questions

1 Try to answer the questions.

- **a** Къде́ е на́й-добре́ да оти́дат г-н и г-жа́ Ко́линс за плодове́ и зеленчу́ци?
- **b** Какви́ са плодове́те и зеленчу́ците на паза́ра?
- **c** Какво́ не оби́ча г-жа́ Ко́линс?
- **d** Ко́лко килогра́ма дома́ти и́ска г-н Ко́линс?
- **e** Какви́ плодове́ прода́ва жена́та?
- **f** Ко́лко стру́ва вси́чко?

2 True or false?

- **a** Г-н и г-жа́ Ко́линс и́скат Неве́на да им пока́же сладка́рницата.
- **b** Г-н Ко́линс и́ска да ку́пи ти́квички.
- **c** Г-н Ко́линс е еди́н от те́зи мъже́, кои́то оби́чат да пазару́ват.
- **d** Г-жа́ Ко́линс и́ска да ѝ прете́глят еди́н пъпеш.
- **e** Г-жа́ Ко́линс и́ска еди́н килогра́м пра́скови.
- **f** Гро́здето е мно́го сла́дко и г-жа́ Ко́линс и́ска да ку́пи о́ще.

i More about money

Since the early 1880s, shortly after the liberation of Bulgaria from the Ottoman Empire, the basic Bulgarian currency unit has been the **лев** (*lev*, lit. *lion*, after the rampant lion that is the official emblem of free Bulgaria). The sub-unit (one hundred to every lev) is the **стоти́нка** (*stotinka*, from **сто** meaning *hundred*).

In English, the plural of 'lev' should rightly be 'levs'. The temptation, however, is to say 'leva' or 'levas', influenced by the masculine counting form **два ле́ва**, **три ле́ва** etc., which is far more frequently heard than the straight singular **лев**. Similarly, the plural of 'stotinka' in English should be 'stotinkas', but you will most likely be tempted to say 'stotinki', influenced by the Bulgarian feminine plural **стоти́нки**.

The Bulgarian national coat of arms: *STRENGTH THROUGH UNITY*

The Bulgarian for 'one dollar' – whether US or Canadian – is **еди́н до́лар**, so you say **сто до́лара** (only one **л** remember!) The pound sterling has a feminine and masculine form: **една́ англи́йска ли́ра** or **еди́н брита́нски па́унд**, so 'one hundred pounds' would be either **сто англи́йски ли́ри** or **сто брита́нски па́унда**. The 'euro', now universally listed on currency exchange boards (see Unit 6), is neuter and has no plural: **едно́ е́вро**, **сто е́вро** etc.

In everyday conversation, you will often hear **ле́вче** or **едно́ ле́вче** used instead of **еди́н лев**. This is the affectionate, diminutive form. There are coins for 1, 2, 5, 10, 20 and 50 stotinkas, and also for one lev(che). Notes come in denominations of 1, 2, 5, 10, 20, 50 and 100 levs.

Buying fruit

The best place to buy fruit is at one of the many open-air markets. Here you will find a great variety of seasonal fruit and vegetables being offered for sale by individual stallholders, all eager that you should leave your money with them. It is normal practice almost everywhere for you to select your own fruit. Sometimes the stall-holder will even offer you something to taste.

Fruit and vegetables are sold by the kilogram – not by the pound – and even cucumbers and melons are usually sold by weight. When buying quantities less than a kilogram, the weight is usually calculated in grams or fractions of a kilogram. So if you want half a kilogram of tomatoes you say **Полови́н килогра́м дома́ти, мо́ля**. And if you want less than a pound, of cheese, say, you say **три́ста гра́ма си́рене, мо́ля**. (Not that Bulgarians ever buy in such small quantities!)

Bulgaria is a Mediterranean-type country and a 'bridge to the East', but you will not be expected to haggle over the prices of fruit and vegetables. Although not always marked up, the prices you will be given when you ask **Ко́лко стру́ва?** (or **Ко́лко стру́ват?**) will be firm. As with waiters, the arithmetic of stallholders can be unreliable, and overcharging is not unknown. So do tot up the various items yourself, preferably in Bulgarian and out loud!

In Bulgaria, courgettes (or zucchinis if you prefer) are more like small marrows. They are light in colour and larger than the ones we are used to.

How do you say it?

- Asking someone to give you/show you something

Да́йте ми, мо́ля, де́сет биле́та!	*Please give me ten tickets.*
Покаже́те ми, мо́ля, това́ списа́ние!	*Please show me this magazine.*

- Asking how much something costs

Ко́лко стру́ва пъпешът?	*How much is the melon?*
Ко́лко стру́ват я́бълките?	*How much do the apples cost?*

- Making suggestions

Да оти́дем на паза́ра!	*Let's go to the market.*
Да ку́пим дома́ти от та́зи жена́!	*Let's buy some tomatoes from this woman.*

- Giving advice

На́й-добре́ е да оти́дете на паза́ра!	*You'd do best to go to the market.*

- Expressing your likes and dislikes

Оби́чам гро́зде.	*I like grapes.*
Оби́чам да пазару́вам.	*I like shopping.*
Не оби́чам пра́скови.	*I don't like peaches.*
Не оби́чам да у́ча.	*I don't like studying.*

Grammar

1 More masculine plurals

Masculine nouns of one syllable have a plural ending all of their own. If they end in a consonant they add **-ове** to the singular. If they end in **-й** they add **-еве**. Some nouns keep the stress on the first syllable, while in others the stress jumps either to the middle or to the final syllable:

клуб	–	клу́б**ове**	*clubs*			
ключ	–	клю́ч**ове**	*keys*	плод	–	плод**ове́** *fruit*
плик	–	пли́к**ове**	*envelopes*	брой	–	бро́**еве** *numbers; copies*
сок	–	со́к**ове**	*juices*			
нож	–	нож**о́ве**	*knives*			
град	–	град**ове́**	*towns*			

Note that це́нтър (*centre*), although more than one syllable, has the plural це́нтр**ове**.

Only very few masculine nouns of one syllable form their plurals differently. Two common examples are:

брат – бра́тя *brothers* мъж – мъже́ *men/husbands*

2 Using *the* with plural nouns: adding -те and -та

The Bulgarian equivalent of *the* is added to the end of the word, as we saw earlier:

Singular		with *the*	
пъпеш	*a melon*	пъпеш**ът**	*the melon*
Plural		with *the*	
пъпеши	*melons*	пъпеши**те**	*the melons*

There are two alternative plural forms of *the*: **-те** and **-та**. Which you need depends entirely on the final letters of the plural form. Gender plays no part whatsoever. Once again, however, you will notice an element of rhyme or vowel harmony.

(*a*) **-те** is added to plurals in **-и** or **-е**:

зеленчу́к: зеленчу́**ци**	–	зеленчу́ци**те**	*the vegetables*
плод: плодо**ве́**	–	плодове́**те**	*the fruit*
пра́скова: пра́скови	–	пра́скови**те**	*the peaches*
я́бълка: я́бълки	–	я́бълки**те**	*the apples*

(*b*) **-та** is added to plurals in **-а** and **-я**:

ви́но: вин**а́**	–	вин**а́та**	*the wines* (note the stress change!)
се́ло: сел**а́**	–	сел**а́та**	*the villages* (stress change here too!

дете́: деца́	–	**деца́та**	*the children*
писмо́: писма́	–	**писма́та**	*the letters*
брат: бра́тя	–	**бра́тята**	*the brothers*

(There are more neuter plurals in Unit 8.)

3 Telling people what to do

Да́йте ми, мо́ля!	*Please give me.*
Вземе́те си, мо́ля!	*Please help yourself.* (lit. *take to yourself*)
Покаже́те ми, мо́ля!	*Please show me.*

These are all commands or requests in the polite plural. You have already come across a number of similar forms (all ending in **-те**) **заповя́дайте! здраве́йте!** and **каже́те!** These forms are known as imperatives. There is a singular imperative, for situations when you would need to use the singular **ти** form, and a plural imperative, for situations when you would use **Ви́е** or **ви́е**.

The endings of the imperative are either **-й (-йте)** or **-и́ (-е́те)**.

(*a*) In **а**-pattern verbs and verbs with an *I* form ending in two vowels you replace the present tense endings of the *I* form with **-й** or **-йте**:

Present tense	Imperative singular	Imperative plural	
парки́рам (*I park*)	не парки́рай!	не парки́райте!	*don't park*
ра́двам се	ра́двай се!	ра́двайте се!	*be happy*
игра́я	игра́й!	игра́йте!	*play*
пи́я	пи́й!	пи́йте!	*drink*

(*b*) In most **е**- and **и**-pattern verbs the ending of the *I* form of the present tense is replaced by **-и́** in the singular and **-е́те** in the plural:

Present tense	Imperative singular	Imperative plural	
(да) пока́жа	покажи́!	покаже́те!	*show*
(да) се́дна	седни́!	седне́те!	*sit down*
(да) ку́пя	купи́!	купе́те!	*buy*
(да) платя́	плати́!	плате́те!	*pay*

Note that in these verbs the stress is on the final syllable in the singular and on the penultimate syllable in the plural.

Some common irregular imperatives:

Present		Singular	Plural	
(да)	ви́дя	виж!	ви́жте!	*look*
(да)	дам	дай!	да́йте!	*give*
(да)	ям	яж!	я́жте!	*eat*
(да)	до́йда	ела́!	ела́те!	*come*

4 (Да) дам *I give*

This verb follows the **е**-pattern, but the *I* form is irregular. In the present tense **дам** only occurs after **да**. The examples below are therefore accompanied by **тря́бва**:

аз	тря́бва да дам	*I must give*	ни́е тря́бва да даде́м	*we must give*
ти	тря́бва да даде́ш	*you must give*	ви́е тря́бва да даде́те	*you must give*
той / тя / то	тря́бва да даде́	*he, she, it must give*	те тря́бва да дада́т	*they must give*

5 Да́йте ми! покаже́те ми! *Give me, show me*

When using verbs like *give* and *show* you usually need to mention both what you give or show (the direct object), and the person to whom the thing is given or shown (the indirect object).

Да́йте **ми**, мо́ля, еди́н килогра́м гро́зде!	*Please give **me** a kilogram of grapes.*
Покаже́те **ми**, мо́ля, та́зи ка́ртичка!	*Please show **me** this postcard.*
Претегле́те **ми**, мо́ля, то́зи пъ́пеш!	*Please weigh this melon for **me**.*

In English, you often need two words (a preposition like *to* or *for* and a naming word or a pronoun like *me*) to express the indirect object: *Give it **to me*** or *Weigh it **for me***. Bulgarian, however, usually manages without a preposition. Happily, the forms of the most common indirect object pronouns (the so-called 'short forms') are the same as those used to express possession (see Unit 3). Here is a list of those short indirect object pronouns with the subject forms in brackets:

(аз)	**ми**	*to me*	(нúе)	**ни**	*to us*
(ти)	**ти**	*to you*	(вúе)	**ви**	*to you*
(той)	**му**	*to him*			
(тя)	**й**	*to her*	(те)	**им**	*to them*
(то)	**му**	*to it*			

6 Where to put the indirect object pronoun

Like the reflexive pronoun **се**, the short indirect object pronoun usually comes immediately before the verb:

Йскам да **ти** покáжа Сóфия. — *I want to show **you** Sofia.*
Мóже ли да **ни** покáжете пазáра? — *Could you show **us** the market?*

(Watch the stress of **покáжете**. This is the *you* form, *not* the imperative!)

If the verb is the first word in the sentence, the pronoun comes immediately after the verb:

Покажéте **ни** менюто, мóля. — *Please show us the menu.*
Дáйте **ми** менúто, мóля. — *Please give me the menu.*

7 Да *Let's!* and *shall we?*

Да can be used with the *we* form to express the English *let's!* or *shall we?*:

Да отúдем на пазáра! — *Let's go to the market!*
Да кýпим пъпеша! — *Let's buy the melon!*
Да платúм! — *Let's pay!*

If we add **ли** and turn these examples into questions, the affirmative answer will involve two different usages of **да**:

Да отúдем ли на пазáра? — *Shall we go to the market?*
Да, да отúдем! — *Yes, let's!*
Да кýпим ли пъпеш? — *Shall we buy a melon?*
Да, да кýпим! — *Yes, let's!*

8 Тóзи, тáзи, товá and тéзи: *this, these*

In situations where in English you use *this* or *these* – when pointing to or referring to something or someone nearby – in Bulgarian you have to select one of four slightly different forms:

Masculine	**то́зи** голя́м магази́н	*this large shop*
Feminine	**та́зи** ста́ра жена́	*this old woman*
Neuter	**това́** ху́баво дете́	*this beautiful child*
Plural	**те́зи** мла́ди мъже́	*these young men*

9 Е́втин, по́-е́втин *Cheap, cheaper*

To say that something is cheaper, bigger or more beautiful, for example (i.e. to make the comparative form of the adjective), all you do is place **по́-** on the front, as you did with the adverbs in Unit 5. The adjectives, however, have to be changed according to gender, depending on what noun they go with. So you say:

То́зи пъпеш е е́втин/ **по́**-е́втин.	*This melon is cheap/cheaper.*
Та́зи ка́ртичка е ху́бава/ **по́**-ху́бава.	*This card is beautiful/ more beautiful.*
Това́ ви́но е сла́дко/ **по́**-сла́дко.	*This wine is sweet/sweeter.*
Те́зи кра́ставици са е́втини/ **по́**-е́втини.	*These cucumbers are cheap/ cheaper.*

As with the adverbs, the **по́-** is emphasized and we will again add a stress mark to remind you of this.

If you want to compare one thing (or person) with another, you use **от** in place of the English *than*, just as you did with the adverbs:

Я́бълките са по́-е́втини **от** пра́сковите.	*The apples are cheaper than the peaches.*
Неве́на е по́-ху́бава **от** На́дя.	*Nevena is more beautiful than Nadya.*

When there is a preposition before the noun, you have to use **отко́лкото** instead of **от**:

В Бълга́рия зеленчу́ците са по́-евти́ни **отко́лкото в** А́нглия.	*In Bulgaria the vegetables are cheaper than in England.*
На паза́ра плодове́те са по́-пре́сни **отко́лкото в** магази́ните.	*At the market the fruit is fresher than in the shops.*

Exercises

1 Select from the regular and numerical plural forms in the box (all masculines!) to complete these sentences:

a Ѝмате ли ____ .	
b Нáдя ѝска да кýпи два ____ .	плѝка, плѝкове
c Два ____, мóля.	
d Обѝчаш ли ____?	банáна, банáни (*banana*)
e Да ви дам ли два ____?	
f Г-жá Кóлинс обѝча ____ .	пъпеша, пъпеши
g Мóля, дáйте ни ____!	
h Éто тук ѝма някoлко ____ .	нóжа, ножóве
i Г-н Джóнсън ѝска да отѝде в нѝколко бъ́лгарски ____ .	
j Рýсе и Тъ́рново са ____ в Българ́ия.	грáда, градовé

2 Public notices are often instructions, sometimes given in the singular, sometimes in the plural. You would do well to note – and observe! – the following common instructions:

Which of the notices would you expect to find:

Бутнѝ! *Push.* **Дръпнѝ!** *Pull.* **Не пѝпай!** *Don't touch!*
Платéте на кáсата! *Pay at the cash desk.*
Пазéте чистотá! *No litter* (lit. *Observe cleanliness*).
Не газéте тревáта! *Keep off the grass!*

a in a shop or bank
b in a park
c on doors into a shop
d near live electricity cables

3 Ask the appropriate questions using the phrases given below and choosing between **павилиóн** (*kiosk*), **телефóн**, **аптéка** and **бáнка**.

Model: Мóже ли да ми кáжете къдé ѝма павилиóн? Трябва да кýпя билéти.

a Тря́бва да се обáдя на мъжá ми.
b Тря́бва да обменя́ парѝ.

c Тря́бва да ку́пя аспири́н.
d Тря́бва да ку́пя ве́стници.

4 Imagine you are in a pharmacy/drugstore. Ask for the items listed below using Мо́же ли да ми пока́жете and either:

a то́зи, b та́зи, c това́ or **d те́зи**

ка́рта
чадъ́р
крем (*cream*)
списа́ние
ножо́ве
ча́ша (*glass/cup*)
списа́ния
кре́мове
ча́ши
лека́рство (*medicine*)

5 You've now moved to the open-air market. Ask for the items below using the model: Ко́лко стру́ват дома́тите? Да́йте ми еди́н килогра́м дома́ти:

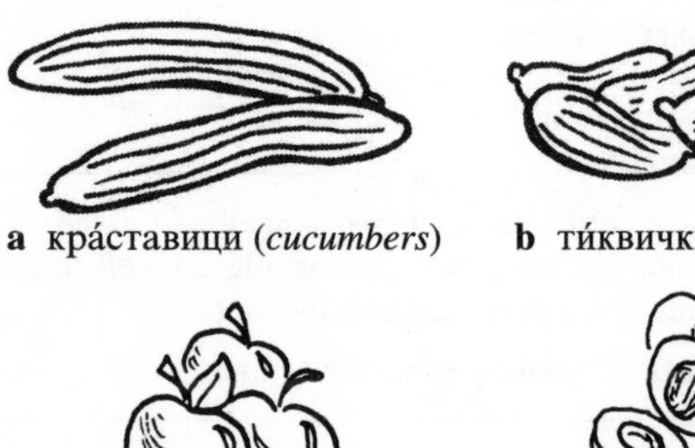

a кра́ставици (*cucumbers*) **b** ти́score

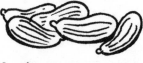

c я́бълки **d** пра́скови

6 Give affirmative answers to these questions following the model: Да ку́пим ли крем? Да, да ку́пим!

a Да оти́дем ли на Ви́тоша?
b Да оти́дем ли на те́нис?
c Да плати́м ли сега́?
d Да се оба́дим ли на Никола́й?

7 To practise saying what you do and do not like doing, and also to make sure you have not forgotten how to use the construction with **да**, answer the following questions:

a Оби́чате ли да пъту́вате (*travel*)?
Да, мно́го оби́чам ______.
b Оби́чаш ли да игра́еш (*play*) на компю́тър?
Не, не оби́чам ______.

c Оби́чате ли да пазару́вате? Не, не оби́чам ______.
d Оби́чате ли да ка́рате ски (*to go skiing*)?
Да, мно́го оби́чам ______.
e Оби́чаш ли да чете́ш?
Да, мно́го оби́чам ______.

8 First read aloud these polite (plural) forms of a number of common instructions. Then use their familiar, singular forms, as if you were talking to a child or a good friend:

a Купе́те мля́ко, мо́ля!
b Ела́те, мо́ля!
c Седне́те, мо́ля!
d Ви́жте, мо́ля!
e Каже́те, мо́ля!
f Да́йте, мо́ля!

9 Try rearranging the words below to make proper sentences:

a ли, да дам, Ви, солта́...?
b пока́жете, ста́ята, мо́же ли, да, ни...?
c ни, да́йте, мо́ля, ключа́!
d това́, покаже́те, списа́ние, ми, мо́ля...!
e да, мо́же ли, пъ́пеш, ми, даде́те, то́зи...?

10 Practise some comparisons by making complete sentences out of the words below. With the exception of (*d*) you have to use the definite forms throughout.

Model: Пъ́пеш/бана́н/голя́м
Пъ́пешът е по́-голя́м от бана́на.

a Я́бълки/пра́скови/е́втини
b Дома́ти/ти́квички/пре́сни
c Пъ́пеш/гро́зде/сла́дък
d На́дя/Неве́на/зае́та
e Кра́ставици/ти́квички/голе́ми

Do you understand?

Dialogue

Mrs. Collins is at the post office (**в по́щата**).

г-жа́ Ко́линс Мо́же ли една́ ка́ртичка от Со́фия, мо́ля?
Продава́чка Коя́ да Ви дам?
г-жа́ Ко́линс Та́зи с фонта́ните и Наро́дния теа́тър.
Продава́чка Та́зи ли?
г-жа́ Ко́линс Не, не та́зи. До не́я и́ма о́ще една́. Да́йте ми също ка́ртичката с Университе́та.

Продава́чка Не́що дру́го?
г-жа́ Ко́линс Да, и́скам и де́сет биле́та за трамва́й.
Продава́чка Ня́маме биле́ти. Да Ви дам ли пли́кове и ма́рки?
г-жа́ Ко́линс А, да – два пли́ка и две ма́рки за Аме́рика. Покаже́те ми, мо́ля, и та́зи ка́рта на Со́фия.
Продава́чка Ето, ви́жте. Това́ е но́ва ка́рта на Со́фия.
г-жа́ Ко́линс Ко́лко стру́ва?
Продава́чка Ка́ртата стру́ва три ле́ва.
г-жа́ Ко́линс Ко́лко тря́бва да Ви дам вси́чко?
Продава́чка Ка́ртичките са лев и два́йсет, пли́ковете и ма́рките са два и де́сет. Плюс ка́ртата, това́ пра́ви шест ле́ва и три́йсет стоти́нки.

фонта́н	*fountain*
Наро́дният теа́тър	*The National Theatre*
също	*also*
ма́рка	*stamp*
(да) пока́жа, -жеш	*to show*
нов	*new*
плюс	*plus*
си́рене	*white cheese (feta)*

True or false?

1 Наро́дният теа́тър е в Со́фия.
2 В по́щата и́ма ня́колко ка́ртички с Наро́дния теа́тър.
3 Г-жа́ Ко́линс не и́ска ни́що дру́го.
4 Г-жа́ Ко́линс и́ска шест пли́ка и шест ма́рки.
5 Ка́ртичките стру́ват два ле́ва и де́сет стоти́нки.
6 Г-жа́ Ко́линс тря́бва да даде́ шест ле́ва и три́йсет стоти́нки.

The Ivan Vazov National Theatre

08

какво́ ми препоръ́чвате?

what can you recommend?

In this unit you will learn

- **how to order a meal in a restaurant**
- **how to say what Bulgarian dishes you prefer**
- **how to recommend dishes to someone else**

Dialogue

Mr Antonov and Mr Johnson, his guest from England, are about to order a meal.

г-н Анто́нов Какво́ да пору́чаме?
г-н Джо́нсън Мо́же ли да ви́дя меню́то?
г-н Анто́нов Запове́дайте! (*Opening the menu and pointing.*) Е́то, това́ са су́пите и сала́тите. Това́ са бъ́лгарските специалите́ти.
г-н Джо́нсън Какво́ ми препору́чвате?
г-н Анто́нов Шо́пската сала́та е типи́чно бъ́лгарска. Тя е с дома́ти, кра́ставици и си́рене.
г-н Джо́нсън Добре́, една́ шо́пска сала́та за ме́не.
г-н Анто́нов И́скате ли тарато́р?
г-н Джо́нсън Какво́ е тарато́р?
г-н Анто́нов Това́ е су́па от ки́село мля́ко и кра́ставици. Серви́ра се студе́на. Мно́го е вку́сна.
г-н Джо́нсън Не, благодаря́. Предпочи́там то́пла су́па. (*Reading and pointing.*) Е́то та́зи – пи́лешка су́па.
г-н Анто́нов Препору́чвам Ви тога́ва то́зи бъ́лгарски специалите́т – пъ́лнени чу́шки.
г-н Джо́нсън Добре́, да взе́мем пъ́лнени чу́шки.
г-н Анто́нов (*To the waiter.*) Мо́же ли...?
Сервитьо́р Запове́дайте, мо́ля.
г-н Анто́нов Две шо́пски сала́ти, една́ пи́лешка су́па, еди́н тарато́р и два пъ́ти пъ́лнени чу́шки.
Сервитьо́р Ко́лко хляб?
г-н Анто́нов Че́тири бе́ли хле́бчета, мо́ля.
Сервитьо́р Не́що за пи́ене?
г-н Анто́нов А, да. Да взе́мем ли бути́лка ви́но, г-н Джо́нсън?
г-н Джо́нсън Не, благодаря́. Аз оби́чам бъ́лгарските вина́, но на о́бед не пи́я алкохо́л. И́мате ли пло́дови со́кове?
Сервитьо́р Не, за съжале́ние. Са́мо ко́ла, лимона́да и гази́рана вода́.
г-н Джо́нсън За ме́не една́ гази́рана вода́, ако́ оби́чате.
Сервитьо́р А за Вас, господи́не? Бя́лото ви́но е мно́го ху́баво.
г-н Анто́нов Добре́, тога́ва за ме́не ча́ша бя́ло ви́но, мо́ля.
Сервитьо́р Не́що дру́го?
г-н Анто́нов Не, благодаря́.

Какво́ да поръ́чаме?	*What shall we order?*
Мо́же ли да ви́дя меню́то?	*Can I see the menu?*
Е́то, това́ са су́пите и сала́тите.	*Look, here are the soups and the salads.*
Това́ са бъ́лгарските специалите́ти.	*These are the Bulgarian specialities.*
Какво́ ми препоръ́чвате?	*What can you recommend* (*me*)*?*
Шо́пската сала́та е типи́чно бъ́лгарска.	*The 'shopska' salad is typically Bulgarian.*
тарато́р	*tarator* (Bulgarian cold summer soup)
Това́ е су́па от ки́село мля́ко и кра́ставици.	*It is a soup made of yoghurt and cucumbers.*
Серви́ра се студе́на.	*It is served cold.*
Мно́го е вку́сна.	*It is delicious.*
Предпочи́там то́пла су́па.	*I prefer a hot soup.*
Е́то та́зи – пи́лешка су́па.	*This one here – chicken soup.*
Препоръ́чвам Ви тога́ва то́зи бъ́лгарски специалите́т.	*Then I recommend you this Bulgarian speciality.*
пъ́лнени чу́шки	*stuffed peppers*
два пъ́ти	*twice*
Ко́лко хляб?	*How much bread?*
че́тири бе́ли хле́бчета	*four white bread rolls*
Не́що за пи́ене?	*Anything to drink?*
Да взе́мем ли бути́лка ви́но?	*Shall we take a bottle of wine?*
На о́бед не пи́я алкохо́л.	*I don't drink alcohol at lunchtime.*
И́мате ли пло́дови со́кове?	*Have you any fruit juices?*
гази́рана вода́	*soda water*
ако́ оби́чате	*if you please*
Бя́лото ви́но е мно́го ху́баво.	*The white wine is very good.*
Тога́ва за ме́не ча́ша бя́ло ви́но.	*A glass of white wine for me, then.*
Не́що дру́го?	*Anything else?*

Questions

1 Try to answer these questions.

- **a** Какво́ и́ска да ви́ди г-н Джо́нсън?
- **b** Какво́ препоръ́чва г-н Анто́нов?
- **c** Какво́ е тарато́р?
- **d** Какво́ предпочи́та г-н Джо́нсън?
- **e** Какво́ и́ска г-н Джо́нсън за пи́ене?
- **f** Кой поръ́чва ча́ша ви́но?

2 True or false?

- **a** Шо́пската сала́та е с ки́село мля́ко и кра́ставици.
- **b** Тарато́рът се серви́ра студе́н.
- **c** Пъ́лнените чу́шки са бъ́лгарски специалите́т.
- **d** Г-н Анто́нов и г-н Джо́нсън не поръ́чват хляб.
- **e** Г-н Джо́нсън и́ска не́що за пи́ене, но не алкохо́л.
- **f** На о́бед г-н Анто́нов пи́е са́мо лимона́да.

i Food and eating out

Bulgarians enjoy eating out. They go as much for the company as for the food, which is often served warm rather than hot. They eat lots of bread – not just with their soup course – and spend a long time over their meals, especially in the evenings. The more popular, smaller restaurants often get very busy, noisy and full of cigarette smoke, so go early. And if the weather is good, try and find a table outside. For the more popular establishments, it's best to make a reservation (**резерва́ция**). Service can be slow, so allow plenty of time for your meal and enjoy the company and the atmosphere!

If you go out in a group, you may be asked on entering **Ко́лко ду́ши сте?** *How many (people) are you?* and **Имате ли резерва́ция?** *Do you have a reservation?*

All restaurants serve alcohol – at any time of the day or night. Non-smoking sections are the exception rather than the rule. Specifically vegetarian restaurants are few and far between, but you can usually make up a very decent vegetarian meal from the standard dishes on offer.

Restaurants in hotels with restaurants (**хоте́л-рестора́нт**) – mainly at holiday resorts - are generally open to non-residents, unless they have been pre-booked for a closed function. They offer a wide choice of dishes, many of them 'international', with menus in more than one language. Some of these restaurants are quite formal, with waiters in black ties.

In the larger towns there are plenty of eating places to choose from. Most of the well-known Western food chains are represented. There are innumerable Italian restaurants, both large and small, serving traditional pizza and pasta dishes. Look for the sign **Пицари́я**. If you are wanting a Chinese restaurant, look for **Кита́йски рестора́нт**. There are plenty of these too, and they generally offer good value for money.

For a quick bite, look for the notice **Бърза заку́ска** or **Закусва́лня**. There are myriad informal snack bars, very functional, self-service establishments, often with limited seating. Pop in for a sandwich, maybe toasted, a Bulgarian **ба́ничка** (*pasty*), a cup of coffee or a **ко́ла** – usually Coca-Cola or Pepsi. Many of these establishments have foreign names, usually English. There are also many small eating places offering dishes such as grilled chicken to take away (**пи́ле на грил за вкъщи**). Some sell Middle Eastern food and have appropriate Middle Eastern names.

If you want something similarly cheap – but more Bulgarian – and are not bothered about decor, look for a notice with the word **ска́ра** (*grill*), preferably **би́ра-ска́ра**. Once the Bulgarian equivalent of the English fish and chip shop, these **би́ра-ска́ра** establishments are regrettably becoming increasingly rare, certainly in the large urban centres. They serve beer, freshly grilled meatballs (**кюфте́та**) and delicious, spicy grilled sausages (**кеба́пчета**). Order any number and eat with beer, bread and a piquant red sauce made of tomatoes, red peppers and chopped onions. Grilled meat dishes are also popular in more fashionable, up-market establishments.

There are many small street bars – look for **Бар** or **Кафе́** – with tables out on the pavement in the summer. Here you can find soft drinks, a variety of alcoholic drinks, coffee, hot chocolate, tea etc. Although traditionally in Bulgaria you only drank tea (without milk) when you were unwell, you can find all kinds of tea, including tea made from a variety of different herbs. Remember, though, that if you do want a traditional 'cuppa', **че́рен чай** (*black tea*), you will probably be presented with a cup or, more likely, a glass of hot water, some sugar and a tea bag. You will be expected to brew up yourself at the table. And if you want milk, you will have to ask for it!

How do you say it?

- Asking *What can you recommend?* and recommending something yourself

Какво́ ми препоръ́чваш?	*What can you recommend* (*me*)*?*
Препоръ́чвам ти та́зи су́па.	*I recommend you this soup.*
Препоръ́чвам ви/Ви това́ ви́но.	*I recommend you this wine.*

- Asking for someone's preference and expressing your own

Ви́е какво́ предпочи́тате?	*What do you prefer?*
Предпочи́там то́пла су́па.	*I prefer hot soup.*

- Saying *once*, *twice*, etc.

еди́н път	*once* (lit. *one time*)
два пъ́ти	*twice*
три пъ́ти	*three times*
че́тири пъ́ти, etc.	*four times*

- Asking for something to eat or drink

Не́що за я́дене, мо́ля!	*Something to eat, please.*
Не́що за пи́ене, мо́ля!	*Something to drink, please.*

- Saying *please* in a more formal way

ако́ оби́чате	*if you please*

- Saying a *glass of..., a cup of..., a bottle of...*

ча́ша ви́но	*a glass of wine*
ча́ша кафе́	*a cup of coffee*
бути́лка ви́но	*a bottle of wine*

Grammar

1 *The* with adjectives

When an adjective is added to a noun used with the definite article, the definite article moves from the noun to the adjective:

Feminine	сала́т**та** *the salad*	becomes	шо́пска**та** сала́та *the 'shopska' salad*
Neuter	ви́но**то** *the wine*	becomes	черве́но**то** ви́но *the red wine*
Plural	су́пи**те** *the soups*	becomes	то́пли**те** су́пи *the hot soups*

If you use more than one adjective, you only put the definite article on the end of the first adjective:

специалите́т**ите** *the specialities*	becomes	ху́бав**ите** бъ́лгарски специалите́ти *the lovely Bulgarian specialities*

As you can see, the definite article added to adjectives is the same as the definite article added to nouns of the same gender. Only with masculine nouns is there any change. (You will learn about this in Unit 9.)

2 More neuter plurals

Many neuter nouns ending in **-(ч)е** form their plural by adding **-та**:

едно́ хле́бче	че́тири хле́бчета	*four bread rolls*
едно́ кафе́	три кафе́та	*three coffees*
едно́ парче́	две парче́та	*two pieces*
едно́ ле́вче	мно́го ле́вчета	*many one-lev coins/notes*

Some words adopted from other languages, words like **интервю́**, **меню́**, **такси́** and **у́иски**, which are considered neuter nouns, also take this plural ending:

мно́го интервю́та	*many interviews*
ня́колко меню́та	*several menus*
мно́го такси́та	*many taxis*
ня́колко у́искита	*several whiskies*

Be careful not to confuse these plurals with singular feminine nouns used with the definite article – they both end in **-та**!

When neuter plurals like **меню́та** and **парче́та** are used with the definite article, they end in a double **-тата**, and the resulting 'rhyme' creates the distinctive Bulgarian 'machine-gun' effect:

хле́бче**тата**	*the bread rolls*	меню́**тата**	*the menus*
кафе́**тата**	*the coffees*	такси́**тата**	*the taxis*
парче́**тата**	*the pieces*	у́иски**тата**	*the whiskies*

3 Два *and* две: two times two

You have already briefly come across these two forms of the numeral for two in Unit 4. **Два**, as in **два часа́**, remember, goes with masculine nouns denoting things and animals (but not persons). **Две** goes with neuter and feminine nouns.

Masculine		Feminine	Neuter
два тарато́ра	but	две сала́ти	две парче́та
два со́ка		две ма́рки	две писма́
два пли́ка		две ча́ши	две такси́та
два килогра́ма		две ста́и	две места́

4 Два́ма *two* and три́ма *three*: persons

You have to use special forms of certain numerals with masculine nouns for people. These forms exist for the numerals from *two* to *six*, but you will probably only come across **два́ма** *two* and **три́ма** *three*. These numerals are used with the normal plural of the noun, not with the special counting form:

два́ма англича́ни и три́ма америка́нци	*two Englishmen and three Americans*

два́ма ду́ши *two people* (lit. *two souls*)

5 Бя́ло and бе́ли, я and е: fickle vowels

Depending on stress and the vowels that occur in the following syllable, you will find that the vowels **я** and **е** may alternate. Happily, the rules governing these alternations are well-defined. The changes are confusing, though, and you would do well to learn the rules, perhaps putting a slip of paper between these pages, so you can find them easily.

я́ is used either	(*a*)	if it is stressed and the vowel in the following syllable is **а**, **о**, **у** or **ъ**;
or	(*b*)	if it is stressed and occurs in the final syllable.
е is used either	(*a*)	if it is stressed and the vowels **е** or **и** occur in the following syllable;
or	(*b*)	if it is unstressed.

So you will find:

бял, бя́ла, бя́ло *white*	but	**бе́ли**
мя́сто *place*	but	**места́** (note the stress change!)
свят *world*	but	по **света́** *around the world*

6 Плод, пло́дов сок *Fruit, fruit juice*

By adding **-ов** (**-ова**, **-ово**, **-ови**) to a noun you can often form an adjective with the meaning *made of...* If the noun is feminine or neuter, you first have to remove the final vowel:

плод:	пло́д**ов** сок	*fruit juice*
	пло́д**ова** то́рта	*fruit gateau*
	пло́д**ово** мля́ко	*fruit-flavoured milk*
	пло́д**ови** то́рти	*fruit gateaux* or *pieces of fruit gateau*
гро́зде:	гро́зд**ова** раки́я	*grape brandy*
сли́ва:	сли́в**ова** раки́я	*plum brandy*
портока́л:	портока́л**ов** сок	*orange juice*
я́бълка:	я́бълк**ов** сок	*apple juice*

Exercises

1 The Bulgarian verbs for *order* **(да) поръ́чам**, *recommend* **препоръ́чвам** and *prefer* **предпочи́там** sound very much alike. Practise them using the following words in place of the words in bold:

Model: Сервитьо́рът препоръ́чва **бя́ло ви́но**, но аз предпочи́там **черве́но**. Да поръ́чаме **черве́но ви́но!**

a пи́лзенска (*Pilsner*) би́ра, бъ́лгарска би́ра
b гро́здова раки́я, сли́вова раки́я
c пи́лешка су́па, зеленчу́кова (*vegetable*) су́па

2 In a restaurant, which of the Bulgarian words for *order*, *recommend* and *prefer* would you use to complete these sentences?

a Коя́ су́па ми ____ -ате?
b Г-н Анто́нов и́ска да ____ -а бути́лка ви́но.
c Кое́ ви́но ____ -ате, черве́ното или́ бя́лото?
d Г-н Анто́нов ____ -а пъ́лнените чу́шки.
e Да ____ -ме то́зи бъ́лгарски специалите́т!
f Г-н Джо́нсън ____ -а пло́дов сок, а не ви́но.
g Йскате ли да ____ -ате шо́пска сала́та?

3 Here are the ingredients for tarator soup:

ки́село мля́ко
една́ кра́ставица
че́сън (*garlic*)
сол
о́лио (*vegetable oil*)
о́рехи (*walnuts*)

Now answer the question: Каквó и́ма в таратóра?

4 Read the following list of drinks and cakes out loud:

не́с(кафе) = *instant* (*coffee*)
кафе́ еспре́со = *espresso*
че́рен чай
ме́нтов чай
би́лков чай
пло́дова то́рта
шокола́дова (*chocolate*) то́рта
о́рехова то́рта
портока́лов сок
гро́здов сок
я́бълков сок
сок от я́годи (*strawberries*)

Now, using **и́ма**, say what is on offer in the way of:

a coffee
b tea
c cakes
d fruit juices

Words you might need to know are: **би́лка** *herb*, **ме́нта** *peppermint* and **о́рех** *walnut*.

5 So as to fix in your mind the correct use of the different Bulgarian words for *two*, use **два**, **две** or **два́ма** as appropriate. Here you can again see the special plural form of masculine nouns used after numbers – but not after **два́ма** and **три́ма**.

a Да́йте ми ____ парче́та пи́ца (*pizza*) и ____ о́рехови то́рти.
b Да поръ́чаме ____ гро́здови со́ка и ____ сала́ти.
c Там и́ма ____ свобо́дни места́.

d ____ деца́ игра́ят те́нис. (Remember the singular of деца́ is дете́.)
e Да ку́пим ____ пли́ка и ____ ма́рки.
f Да́йте ни ____ лимо́нови сладоле́да (*lemon ice-creams*), мо́ля.
g В ста́ята и́ма ____ бъ́лгарски студе́нти.
h И́скаш ли да поръ́чаме ____ тарато́ра?
i В хоте́ла и́ма ____ англича́нки.
j Ни́е сме са́мо ____ ду́ши. *(There are only two of us.)*
k И́маме ну́жда от ____ ча́ши.
l До га́рата и́ма ____ магази́на.

6 Choose a soup and another item from the list below and order:

a just for yourself
b another combination for yourself and a companion
c a third combination for your family of four

Меню́
зеленчу́кова су́па
вегетариа́нска (*vegetarian*) су́па
омле́т (*omelette*) със си́рене
пи́ца с кашкава́л (*yellow cheese*)
омле́т с шу́нка (*ham*)
кюфте́та (*meatballs*)

7 You go into a **Бъ́рза заку́ска** (*snack bar*) with a group of friends. Complete the dialogue below, acting as the customer:

Продава́чка	Какво́ оби́чате, мо́ля? (*What would you like?*)
Клие́нт	(Ask what sandwiches they have.)
Продава́чка	И́маме са́ндвичи с шу́нка и с кашкава́л.
Клие́нт	(Ask for two sandwiches with ham and one with cheese.)
Продава́чка	Дру́го? (*Anything else?*)
Клие́нт	(Ask for one orange juice, two cokes and three coffees.)

8 Now you want two coffees, two bread rolls and two meatballs. Ask how much they are in two ways, with and without the numeral.

i **a** Ко́лко стру́ват две ____? (кеба́пчета, кеба́пчетата)
b Ко́лко стру́ват ____?

ii a Ко́лко стру́ват две ____? (хле́бчета, хле́бчетата)
b Ко́лко стру́ват ____?
iii a Ко́лко стру́ват две ____? (кюфте́та, кюфте́тата)
b Ко́лко стру́ват ____?

9 In a Sofia restaurant your dining partner praises the food – all except the chicken soup and the Bulgarian yoghurt. You agree. Using the words in brackets, follow the model to give your reaction in more precise terms.

Your partner Сала́тата е мно́го вку́сна!
You Да, шо́пската сала́та е мно́го вку́сна!

This will help you remember that the definite article moves from the noun to the defining word!

a Су́пата е мно́го вку́сна! (вегетериа́нска)
b Чу́шките са мно́го вку́сни! (пъ́лнени)
c Гро́здето е мно́го вку́сно! (бя́ло)
d Су́пата не е мно́го вку́сна! (пи́лешка)
e Я́бълките са мно́го вку́сни! (черве́ни)
f То́ртата е мно́го вку́сна! (пло́дова)
g Хле́бчетата са мно́го вку́сни! (бе́ли)
h Мля́кото не е мно́го вку́сно! (бъ́лгарско, ки́село)

10 Now, using the model Препоръ́чвам Ви черве́ното ви́но, recommend your companion the following:

a бя́ло ви́но
b сли́вова раки́я
c вегетариа́нска су́па
d шокола́дова то́рта
e бъ́лгарски специалите́ти
f пи́лзенска би́ра

Do you understand?

Dialogue

Nadya and Milena meet in front of the office early one morning.

На́дя Здраве́й, Миле́на. О́ще е ра́но за ра́бота. Да оти́дем в сладка́рницата.
Миле́на Не е ли затво́рена?
На́дя Ко́лко е часъ́т?
Миле́на О́сем и полови́на.
На́дя Тря́бва да е отво́рена ве́че.
(*Inside.*)
Сервитьо́рка Какво́ оби́чате, мо́ля?
На́дя Какво́ и́ма за заку́ска?

Сервитьо́рка	Са́ндвичи, ки́фли, ба́нички.
Миле́на	Не́що сла́дко?
Сервитьо́рка	И́ма кекс, и́ма също пло́дова то́рта.
На́дя	За ме́не еди́н са́ндвич и парче́ то́рта.
Миле́на	За ме́не същото.
Сервитьо́рка	Зна́чи два са́ндвича и две парче́та то́рта. Дру́го?
На́дя	И две кафе́та.
Сервитьо́рка	Нес или́ еспре́со?
Миле́на	Еспре́со, мо́ля. И́мате ли портока́лов сок?
Сервитьо́рка	Не, са́мо я́бълков.
Миле́на	Добре́, два я́бълкови со́ка, ако́ оби́чате.

(*The waitress comes back with the order.*)

На́дя	Мо́же ли да плати́м веднa̍га?
Сервитьо́рка	Разби́ра се. Е́то, това́ е сме́тката.

ра́но	*early*
сла́дък, сла́дка	*sweet*
затво́рен	*closed*
отво́рен	*open*
заку́ска	*breakfast, snack*
ки́фла	*bun*
ба́ничка	*cheese roll, pasty*
не́що сла́дко	*something sweet*
кекс	*(sponge) cake*
са́мо	*only*
(да) платя́, -ти́ш	*to pay*
ведна́га	*immediately*
сме́тка	*bill*
зна́чи	*so/that is to say*

Questions

1 Ко́лко е часъ́т?
2 Ра́но ли е за ра́бота?
3 Затво́рена ли е сладка́рницата?
4 Какво́ и́ма за заку́ска?
5 Какво́ поръ́чват На́дя и Миле́на за я́дене?
6 Какво́ поръ́чват те за пи́ене?

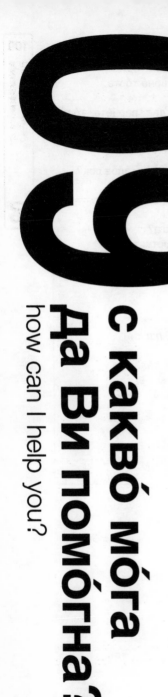

09 с какво мога да Ви помогна?

how can I help you?

In this unit you will learn

- **how to ask for help**
- **how to offer assistance**
- **how to describe things and people**

Dialogue

Mrs Collins uses her superior knowledge of Bulgarian to assist Nevena to help two young Americans.

Неве́на А́ло, мо́же ли да гово́ря с г-жá Ко́линс?

г-жá Ко́линс Да, на телефо́на. С какво́ мо́га да Ви помо́гна, Неве́на?

Неве́на Две момче́та от Аме́рика ня́мат пари́ и и́мат ну́жда от превода́ч. Мо́жете ли да им помо́гнете? Те са го́сти на на́шия хоте́л.

г-жá Ко́линс Къде́ са сегá момче́тата?

Неве́на На лети́щето. Мо́жете ли да оти́дете на лети́щето?

г-жá Ко́линс Ми́сля, че мо́га. Какъв е пробле́мът?

Неве́на Митнича́рите не мо́гат да наме́рят бага́жа на момче́тата. Ня́ма го в ми́тницата.

г-жá Ко́линс Мно́го неприя́тно! Надя́вам се да мо́га да помо́гна!

(*At the airport.*)

г-жá Ко́линс До́бър ден! Аз съм превода́чката.

Митнича́р Не мо́жем да наме́рим бага́жа на те́зи момче́та. Ку́фарите и ча́нтите, който но́сят, не са́ те́хни.

г-жá Ко́линс Разби́рам. Товá е бага́жът на ня́кой друг.

Митнича́р То́чно такá. Мо́ля, пи́тайте ко́лко ча́нти и ко́лко ку́фара и́мат.

г-жá Ко́линс Джон ка́зва, че и́ма еди́н ку́фар и две ча́нти. Кен и́ма два ку́фара.

Митнича́р Как изгле́ждат ча́нтите и ку́фарите им?

г-жá Ко́линс Джон ка́зва, че ча́нтите му са си́ни. Една́та ча́нта е голя́ма, а дру́гата – ма́лка. Ку́фарът му е че́рен. Кен ка́зва, че не́говите ку́фари са също че́рни, но не са́ голе́ми.

Митнича́р Ела́те да ви пока́жа ня́колко ку́фара и ча́нти. Пи́тайте мо́гат ли да наме́рят тук сво́я бага́ж.

(*Mrs Collins translates, then continues.*)

г-жá Ко́линс Да, че́рните ку́фари са на Кен, а ма́лката си́ня ча́нта е на Джон. Дру́гата ча́нта на Джон я ня́ма. Дру́гият че́рен ку́фар също го ня́ма.

Митнича́р Ви́жте, о́нзи висо́к мъж но́си голя́ма си́ня ча́нта и еди́н че́рен ку́фар!

Пътник (*Coming up to the others.*) Извине́те, мо́жете ли да ми ка́жете къде́ е ми́тницата? Товá не е́ мо́ят бага́ж.

Митничáр Мúсля, че сегá всúчко е нарéд! Благодарś, госпóжо Кóлинс.
г-жá Кóлинс Нśма защó.

Да, на телефóна.	*Yes, speaking.*
С каквó мóга да Ви помóгна?	*How can I help you?*
две момчéта	*two boys*
Мóжете ли да им помóгнете?	*Can you help them?*
гóсти на нáшия хотéл	*residents at our hotel*
на летúщето	*at the airport*
Мóжете ли да отúдете на летúщето?	*Could you get out to the airport?*
Мúсля, че мóга.	*I think I can.*
Митничáрите не мóгат да намéрят багáжа на момчéтата.	*The customs men can't find the boys' luggage.*
Нśма го в мúтницата.	*It's not at the customs.*
Мнóго неприśтно!	*Very unpleasant!*
Надśвам се да мóга да помóгна.	*I hope to be able to help.*
Не мóжем да намéрим...	*We can't find...*
Кýфарите и чáнтите, който нóсят, не сá тéхни.	*The suitcases and bags which they're carrying aren't theirs.*
Товá е багáжът на нśкой друг.	*This is someone else's luggage.*
пúтайте	*ask*
Джон кáзва, че úма едúн кýфар и две чáнти.	*John says that he has one suitcase and two bags.*
Как изглéждат чáнтите и кýфарите им?	*What do their bags and suitcases look like?*
Чáнтите му са сúни.	*His bags are blue.*
Еднáта чáнта е голśма, а дрýгата – мáлка.	*One of the bags is big and the other small.*
чéрен	*black*
Нéговите кýфари са също чéрни, но не сá голéми.	*His suitcases are black, too, but they are not big.*
Елáте да ви покáжа нśколко кýфара и чáнти.	*Come and let me show you several suitcases and bags.*
Пúтайте мóгат ли да намéрят тук свóя багáж.	*Ask if they can find their luggage here.*
Чéрните кýфари са на Кен.	*The black suitcases are Ken's.*
Дрýгата чáнта на Джон я нśма.	*John's other bag is missing.*

Дру́гият че́рен ку́фар също го ня́ма.	*The other black suitcase is missing, too.*
О́нзи висо́к мъж но́си голя́ма си́ня ча́нта и еди́н че́рен ку́фар.	*That tall man is carrying a big blue bag and a black suitcase.*
пътник	*passenger, traveller*
ми́тница	*customs*
Това́ не е́ мо́ят бага́ж.	*This is not my luggage.*
Ня́ма защо́.	*You're welcome/Don't mention it.*

Questions

1 Try to answer the questions

- **a** Кой и́ска да гово́ри с г-жа́ Ко́линс?
- **b** Къде́ са момче́тата сега́?
- **c** Откъде́ са момче́тата?
- **d** От какво́ и́мат ну́жда те?
- **e** Какво́ не мо́гат да наме́рят митнича́рите?
- **f** Ко́лко ку́фара и́ма Кен?
- **g** Какво́ но́си висо́кият мъж?

2 True or false?

- **a** Момче́тата са в хоте́ла.
- **b** Г-жа́ Ко́линс не мо́же да оти́де на лети́щето.
- **c** Г-жа́ Ко́линс мо́же да им помо́гне.
- **d** Ку́фарите и ча́нтите, който но́сят момче́тата, са на ня́кой друг.
- **e** Ку́фарите на Кен са голе́ми.
- **f** Висо́кият мъж не мо́же да наме́ри сво́я бага́ж.

i Getting about in town

For travel within the larger towns you will find well-developed networks of trams, buses, trolleybuses and minibuses. Movement is slow in the centre and – especially in the rush hours – not always a pleasant experience. Services are, however, frequent and still relatively cheap. The only underground in Bulgaria is a single line in Sofia running from the Obelya district in the northwest into the centre of town. There are plans to extend the line out to the southeast.

In Sofia there are no conductors on buses, trams or trolleybuses. Best buy your tickets in advance in strips, rather than individually. It's cheaper! Do this at one of the many small street kiosks with their minuscule, low-down windows through which, if you are lucky, you will just be able to see the assistant's hands and the tickets. The kiosks display signs **ГРА́ДСКИ ТРАНСПО́РТ – БИЛЕ́ТИ И КА́РТИ**, and the tickets are all one price for bus, tram and trolleybus.

You get on by any door. Once on, and in rush hours, you may have to push a bit. Make sure you punch a ticket as soon as possible in one of the small machines fixed to the side of the vehicle. The driver will not want to see your ticket. Ticket inspectors will, though. Dressed in plain clothes, armed with passes and usually in groups, they make collective raids to deter ticket dodgers. To be caught without a punched ticket inevitably leads to altercation and most probably a fine. Most locals have season tickets.

If you want to move about more quickly, take a taxi or a minibus. There are plenty of both. Taxis all have meters registering distance and time. Seat belts are fitted and should be worn, but the driver will probably suggest you ignore them or merely lay them across your lap. The minibuses (**маршру́тни такси́та**, or, more colloquially, **маршру́тки**) ply predetermined routes, but pick up and set down on request anywhere along the route. There is a single fixed fare for any distance. So, far cheaper than taxis, but almost three times the cost of the normal tram ticket. Good for longer distances, bad for short.

ГРАДСКИ ТРАНСПОРТ
БИЛЕТИ и КАРТИ

How do you say it?

- Asking for and offering help

Мо́жете ли да ми помо́гнете?	*Can you help me?*
С какво́ мо́га да Ви помо́гна?	*How can I help you?*
Мо́га ли да Ви помо́гна с не́що?	*Can I help you with anything?*

- Saying that *something* or *somebody* is missing

(Къде́ е ку́фарът?)	
Ня́ма го./Ку́фарът го ня́ма.	*It's missing./ The case is missing.*
(Къде́ е г-н Анто́нов?)	
Ня́ма го./Г-н Анто́нов го ня́ма.	*He's not in./ Mr Antonov is not in.*
(Там ли е г-жа́ Ко́линс?)	
Ня́ма я./Г-жа́ Ко́линс я ня́ма.	*She's not in./ Mrs Collins is not in.*

- Saying *one (of the...)*

Masculine	
Еди́ният ку́фар го ня́ма.	*One (of the) case(s) is missing.*
Feminine	
Една́та ча́нта е голя́ма.	*One (of the) bag(s) is large.*
Neuter	
Едно́то момче́ е тук.	*One (of the) boy(s) is here.*

- Responding to unpleasant news

Мно́го неприя́тно!	*Very unpleasant.*

- Responding to being thanked

Ня́ма защо́.	*You're welcome./ Don't mention it.*

Grammar

1 Мо́га да *I can, I am able to*

The Bulgarian verb expressing ability or a particular skill to do things is **мо́га** *I can/I am able to/I am in a position to*. **Мо́га** belongs to the **е**-pattern. The *he/she/it* form **мо́же** with its distinct usage will be familiar to you from Unit 6. In addition to the change of personal endings, there is a change of **г** to **ж** in all forms containing **е** in the ending:

Мо́га requires a **да** form of the following main verb:

(аз)	мо́га	(ние́)	мо́жем
(ти)	мо́жеш	(вие́)	мо́жете
(той) (тя) (то)	мо́же	(те)	мо́гат

(Аз) мо́га да ка́рам ски.	*I know how to ski.*
(Ти) мо́жеш да гово́риш англи́йски.	*You can speak English.*
Митнича́рите не мо́гат да наме́рят бага́жа.	*The customs officers cannot find the luggage.*

2 -ият and -ия: *the* with masculine adjectives

(**a**) To make a masculine adjective definite, you add **-ият** to the simple masculine form (or **-ия** if the phrase is not the subject in the sentence):

висо́к мъж	*a tall man*	висо́к**ия(т)** мъж	***the*** *tall man*
млад мъж	*a young man*	мла́д**ия(т)** мъж	***the*** *young man*

(**b**) If the adjective ends in **-ски**, you only need to add **-ят** or **-я**:

англи́йски – англи́йски**я(т)** ре́чник
български – българск**ия(т)** ре́чник

(**c**) If the adjective loses **ъ** or **е** from its ending in the feminine, neuter and plural, then it does so in the definite form as well (see Appendix, p. 294):

добър (добра́, добро́, добри́)
добри́я(т) българин *the kind Bulgarian*

че́рен (че́рна, че́рно, че́рни)
че́рния(т) чадъ́р *the black umbrella*

(**d**) If there is **я** in the basic form, it will naturally be affected by the rules governing the change of **я** to **е** before **и** (see Unit 8):

бял – бе́лия(т)
голя́м – голе́мия(т)

(**e**) If you use more than one adjective, you only add **-ият** or **-ия** to the first adjective:

висо́к**ият** млад мъж	*the tall young man*
голе́м**ият** че́рен ку́фар	*the large black case*

3 *My, your, his, her,* etc.

When you say **мъжъ́т ми** *my husband*, **ку́фарът Ви** *your suitcase* or **бага́жът им** *their luggage*, you are using a noun in the definite form followed by a short possessive pronoun (see Unit 3). It is also possible to express the same meaning, but with a different emphasis, by a full possessive adjective which comes before the noun and bears the definite article. Like all adjectives, the full possessive adjectives have different endings depending on whether they are used with masculine, feminine, neuter or plural words. Here are examples used with the Bulgarian for *my* and *your*:

ку́фарът ми/ти	becomes	мо́ят/тво́ят ку́фар	*my/your case*
ча́нтата ми/ти	becomes	мо́ята/тво́ята ча́нта	*my/your bag*
дете́то ми/ти	becomes	мо́ето/тво́ето дете́	*my/your child*
деца́та ми/ти	becomes	мо́ите/тво́ите деца́	*my/your children*

4 Бага́жът ми or мо́ят бага́ж?

Normally you can use the short possessive pronoun, as explained in Unit 3. However, for purposes of contrast, when the ownership is being emphasized, as in the sentence *this bag is* ***mine****, not yours*, for example, you must use the *full* possessive adjective with the definite article.

Мо́ите ку́фари са голе́ми.	***My*** *cases are big.*
Тво́ите са ма́лки.	***Yours*** *are small.*
Тво́ят син е в А́нглия.	***Your*** *son is in England.*
Мо́ят син е в Бълга́рия.	***My*** *son is in Bulgaria.*
Това́ не е́ мо́ят бага́ж.	*This is not* ***my*** *luggage.* (i.e. it belongs to someone else)
Това́ тво́ята ча́нта ли е?	*Is this* ***your*** *bag?* (i.e. not someone else's?)

5 Ча́нтата е мо́я *The bag is mine*

The possessive adjective can sometimes be used without the definite article to render the English independent possessives like *mine*, *yours*, *his*, *hers*, etc. Usually this happens when there is no word following the possessive word as in:

Тво́я ли е та́зи ча́нта?	*Is this bag yours?*
Да, ча́нтата е мо́я.	*Yes, the bag is mine.*
Твой ли е то́зи бага́ж?	*Is this luggage yours?*
Не, не е́ мой.	*No, it isn't mine.*

Твóе ли е товá детé?	*Is this child yours?*
Да, мóе е.	*Yes, it is mine.*
Твóи ли са тéзи кýфари?	*Are these suitcases yours?*
Да, мóи са.	*Yes, they are mine.*

Each subject pronoun has a different full possessive adjective. Turn now to the Appendix and you will find a very useful list of all the possessive forms. Look at the list when you do the exercises.

6 Свой, свóя, свóе and свóи *John's own* or *someone else's?*

When in English you say *John is carrying his bag* or *they are looking for their luggage*, it is not clear whether John is carrying his own or somebody else's bag and whether they are looking for their own or someone else's luggage. In Bulgarian, to avoid this ambiguity, you use a special form: **свой, свóя(т)** (**свóята**, **свóето**, **свóите**) no matter whether it is *his*, *her* or *their own*.

Here are the different forms, definite and indefinite:

Subject pronoun	Masculine	Feminine	Neuter	Plural
той/то/тя/те	свóя(т)	свóята	свóето	свóите
	свой	свóя	свóе	свóи

And here are some examples – the gender forms agree with the word that follows:

Джон не мóже да намéри свóя багáж/свóята чáнта/свóите кýфари.	*John cannot find his luggage/his bag/his cases.* (i.e. his own)

But

Митничáрят не мóже да намéри нéговия багáж.	*The customs officer cannot find his luggage.* (i.e. John's, not the customs officer's luggage!)
Англичáнката нóси свóя бáгаж/свóята чáнта/свóите кýфари.	*The English woman is carrying her* (own) *luggage/bag/cases.*

But

Г-жá Кóлинс нóси нéйния багáж.	*Mrs Collins is carrying her luggage.* (i.e. not her own)
Джон и Кен тъ́рсят свóя багáж/свóята чáнта/свóите кýфари.	*John and Ken are looking for their luggage/bag/cases.* (i.e. their own)

But

Митнича́рите тъ́рсят те́хния бага́ж.	*The customs officers are looking for their luggage.* (i.e. John and Ken's)

Here is a summary of the different ways you can express possession. Remember that the full possessive forms are used for stronger emphasis or contrast.

Та́зи ча́нта е на Джон.	*This bag is **John's**.*
Та́зи ча́нта е не́гова.	*This bag is **his**.*
Това́ е ча́нтата на Джон.	*This is **John's** bag.*
Това́ е не́говата ча́нта.	*This is **his** bag.*
Това́ е ча́нтата му.	*This is **his** bag.*

7 Ня́ма го *He isn't here*

With **ня́ма** you don't use **той**, **тя**, **то**, **те** but rather **го**, **я**, **го** and **ги** for the person(s) absent or the thing(s) missing. These are short object pronouns, the Bulgarian non-subject equivalents for *him*, *her*, *it*, *them*. (You will learn more about them in Unit 11.)

Къде́ е бага́жът? Ня́ма **го**.	*Where is the luggage? It's missing.*
Къде́ е ча́нтата? Ня́ма **я**.	*Where is the bag? It's missing.*
Къде́ са ку́фарите? Ня́ма **ги**.	*Where are the cases? They're missing.*

Oddly enough, you have to use the short object pronoun even if you also name the person or thing, so you get a repetition:

Ча́нтата я ня́ма.	*The bag is missing.*
Момче́то го ня́ма.	*The boy is not here.*
Ку́фарите ги ня́ма.	*The suitcases are missing.*
Бага́жът им го ня́ма.	*Their luggage is missing.*

8 Помогне́те ми! *Give me a hand!*

The Bulgarian verb **(да) помо́гна** is used more like the English phrase *to give help to* rather than just *to help*. So you need to use the indirect object pronouns as explained in Unit 7:

Мо́жете ли да **ми** помо́гнете?	*Can you help **me**?* (as if you were saying *Can you give help **to me**?*)

Exercises

1 Look again at the Dialogue and then rearrange the words below to make sentences:

- a Ви, мо́га, да, помо́гна, какво́, с..?
- b от, и́мат, момче́тата, Аме́рика, ну́жда, преводáч, от
- c не, бага́жа, момче́тата, митнича́рите, мо́гат, на, да наме́рят
- d бага́ж, не, това́, мо́ят, е
- e си́ня, на, ма́лката, е, ча́нта, Джон

2 Answer the following questions as appropriate to your own skills and abilities:

- a Мо́жете ли да игра́ете те́нис?

- b Мо́жеш ли да ка́раш ски?

- c Мо́жете ли да плу́вате?

- d Мо́жете ли да ка́рате кола́?

e Мо́жеш ли да игра́еш на ка́рти?

3 Read the following short dialogue:

You	Извине́те, мо́жете ли да ми пока́жете къде́ е спи́рката на трамва́й но́мер четирина́йсет?
Passer-by	Съжаля́вам, не мо́га. Аз съ́що съм тури́ст.

Now use the same pattern to ask to be shown the way to:

a the chemist's
b the customs
c the Sheraton Hotel
d the stop for trolleybus No. 2
e the Central Railway Station

4 Match the questions with the answers on the right:

i	Кой пъ́пеш и́скате, голе́мия или́ ма́лкия?	**a**	Не, ни́ският.
ii	Кой е Ва́шият ку́фар?	**b**	Англи́йския.
iii	Висо́кият мъж ли е англича́нин?	**c**	Че́рния.
iv	Кой ве́стник и́скате?	**d**	Си́ният.
v	Кой чадъ́р да Ви дам?	**e**	Ма́лкия.

5 Repeat the dialogue below substituting the word in bold with different words from the box. Make sure you change the defining words (all underlined) according to gender.

Your friend	<u>Тво́ята</u> **ча́нта** ли е това́?
You	Не, <u>та́зи</u> **ча́нта** не е́ <u>мо́я</u>. <u>Мо́ята</u> **ча́нта** е <u>по́-голя́ма</u>.

ку́фар	*suitcase*
портмоне́	*purse, wallet*
чадъ́р	*umbrella*
па́пка	*folder*
писа́лка	*pen*
моли́в	*pencil*
беле́жник	*diary*
химика́лка	*ball-point pen*

6 Disaster has struck: you have lost your wallet, your luggage, your umbrella, your diary, your folder and your money. Making up separate sentences for each item, tell a policeman that they are missing. You may find the words in Ex. **5**. useful. And don't forget that the word for *money* **пари́** is always plural!

7 Read the story below about a tourist who has lost his way in Sofia. First answer the questions to test your understanding, then turn the story into a dialogue between a tourist and a policeman.

Тури́ст пи́та еди́н полица́й (*policeman*) мо́же ли да му помо́гне. Тури́стът не мо́же да наме́ри своя́ хоте́л. Полица́ят пи́та как се ка́зва не́говият хоте́л. Тури́стът отгова́ря (*answers*), че не зна́е и́мето на хоте́ла. Той зна́е са́мо, че хоте́лът е бли́зо до спи́рката на троле́й но́мер едно́ и троле́й но́мер пет. Полица́ят пи́та зна́е ли господи́нът на коя́ у́лица е хоте́лът. Тури́стът отгова́ря, че не зна́е у́лицата, но зна́е, че хоте́лът е бли́зо до Университе́та. Полица́ят ка́зва, че и́ма два хоте́ла бли́зо до Университе́та. Еди́ният се ка́зва «Со́фия», дру́гият се ка́зва «Се́рдика». Тури́стът сега́ ве́че зна́е и́мето на хоте́ла. Не́говият хоте́л се ка́зва «Се́рдика». Той благодари́ на полица́я.

- **a** Какво́ не мо́же да наме́ри тури́стът?
- **b** Зна́е ли тури́стът и́мето на хоте́ла?
- **c** Къде́ е хоте́лът?
- **d** Ко́лко хоте́ла и́ма до Университе́та?
- **e** Как се ка́зва не́говият хоте́л?

8 Complete the answers in the following dialogue using **го**, **я** or **ги** as appropriate:

На телефо́на:

- **a** Извине́те, там ли е Неве́на?
  Ня́ма ______ .
- **b** Извине́те, там ли е г-н Джо́нсън?
  Ня́ма ______ .
- **c** Извине́те, там ли е дире́кторът?
  Ня́ма ______ .
- **d** Извине́те, там ли са Никола́й и Миле́на?
  Ня́ма ______ .
- **e** Извине́те, там ли е секретá́рката?
  Ня́ма ______ .

Do you understand?

Dialogue

Milena goes into a café and sees that there are two free seats at the table where Mr and Mrs Collins are having coffee.

Милéна	Извинéте, мóже ли да сéдна до Вас?
г-жá Кóлинс	Разби́ра се, заповя́дайте! Местáта са свобóдни.
Милéна	(*To the waitress.*) Еднó кафé и еди́н сладолéд, мóля. (*To Mr and Mrs Collins.*) Днес е мнóго тóпло, нали́?
г-жá Кóлинс	Да, наистина. Врéмето е хýбаво за тури́сти.
Милéна	На почи́вка ли сте в България?
г-жá Кóлинс	Да, и́скаме да оти́дем с мъжá ми на Злáтни пя́съци, но първо и́маме мáлко рáбота в Сóфия.
Милéна	Ви́е говóрите мнóго добрé български.
г-жá Кóлинс	Благодаря́, аз тря́бва да говóря добрé български, защóто българският ези́к е мóята профéсия.
Милéна	Разби́рам. Си́гурно сте преводáчка.
г-жá Кóлинс	Тóчно такá.
Милéна	Да се запознáем! Кáзвам се Милéна Мари́нова.
г-жá Кóлинс	Прия́тно ми е, Виктóрия Кóлинс.
г-н Кóлинс	Аз съм Джордж Кóлинс.
Милéна	Ви́е си́гурно сте англичáни.
г-жá Кóлинс	Да, англичáни сме.
Милéна	Еди́н мой колéга заминáва скóро за Áнглия. И аз мнóго и́скам да оти́да ня́кой ден.
г-жá Кóлинс	Пожелáвам Ви скóро да мóжете да оти́дете.
Милéна	Надя́вам се. Мóга ли да ви помóгна с нéщо, докатó сте в Сóфия?
г-жá Кóлинс	Ми́сля, че мóжете. Тря́бва да оти́дем в Централна пóща, а не знáем къдé е.

(да) сéдна, -неш	*to sit*
наистина	*indeed*
врéме	*weather*
на почи́вка	*on holiday*
отговáрям, -ряш	*to answer*

защóто	*because*
сúгурно сте преводáчка	*you must be an interpreter*
докатó	*while*

True or false?

1 До г-н и г-жá Кóлинс ня́ма свобóдни местá.
2 Врéмето е мнóго тóпло.
3 Г-н и г-жá Кóлинс са на почúвка в България.
4 Г-н и г-жá Кóлинс ня́мат рáбота в Сóфия.
5 Г-жá Кóлинс говóри добрé бъ́лгарски, защóто е преводáчка.
6 Милéна заминáва скóро за Áнглия.
7 Г-н и г-жá Кóлинс знáят къдé е Централна пóща.

какво́ ще бъ́де вре́мето?

what's the weather going to be like?

In this unit you will learn

- **how to discuss the weather**
- **how to offer your opinion**
- **how to talk about future events**

Dialogue

Nikolai and Nadya make plans for two outings and keep an eye on the weather.

Никола́й (*Nikolai rushes into the office.*) На́дя, здраве́й! Мо́жеш ли да ми помо́гнеш? Тря́бва да организи́рам екску́рзия до Ви́тоша за г-н Анто́нов и за на́шия го́ст от А́нглия.

На́дя По́-споко́йно, Никола́й! Говори́ по́-ба́вно. Защо́ бъ́рзаш то́лкова?

Никола́й Защо́то тря́бва да поръ́чам такси́ и да запа́зя ма́са в рестора́нта за у́тре.

На́дя Ня́ма пробле́ми. На́й-ва́жно е вре́мето да бъ́де ху́баво.

Никола́й Вя́рно. И́маш ли ве́стник с прогно́за за вре́мето?

На́дя Не, но мо́жем да чу́ем прогно́зата по ра́диото.

(*Some time later they are listening to the radio.*)

Ра́дио У́тре вре́мето ще бъ́де преди́мно слъ́нчево, но ветрови́то. По висо́ките планини́ ще и́ма разкъ́сана о́блачност с преваля́вания на места́. Температу́ри: между́ осемна́йсет и два́йсет и два гра́дуса.

Никола́й Жа́лко, вре́мето на Ви́тоша ня́ма да е мно́го ху́баво. На Ви́тоша си́гурно ще вали́ дъжд. И си́гурно г-н Джо́нсън не но́си туристи́чески обу́вки.

На́дя Ни́що, не е́ фата́лно. Предла́гам да оти́дете на юг – в Ме́лник. Там вре́мето си́гурно ще е ху́баво. На Ви́тоша мо́же да оти́дете в съ́бота.

Никола́й Добра́ иде́я, но какво́ ще е вре́мето в съ́бота?

На́дя Споре́д прогно́зата в кра́я на се́дмицата ня́ма да вали́ и ще бъ́де по́-то́пло.

Никола́й Ше́фът ще се съгласи́ ли с но́вия план?

На́дя Ще се съгласи́. Аз ще гово́ря с не́го. В Ме́лник е изключи́телно краси́во.

Никола́й Да, зна́я. На́дя, предла́гам и ти да до́йдеш. Съгла́сна ли си?

На́дя Съгла́сна съм. Ще до́йда с удово́лствие!

да организи́рам екску́рзия до Ви́тоша	*to organize an outing to Mount Vitosha*
По́-споко́йно!	*Take it easy!*
Защо́ бъ́рзаш то́лкова?	*What's the hurry?*

да поръ́чам такси́ и да запа́зя ма́са	*to order a taxi and reserve a table*
у́тре	*tomorrow*
На́й-ва́жно е вре́мето да бъ́де ху́баво.	*The main thing is for the weather to be fine.*
прогно́за за вре́мето	*weather forecast*
Мо́жем да чу́ем прогно́зата по ра́диото.	*We can hear the forecast on the radio.*
Вре́мето ще бъ́де предимно слъ́нчево.	*The weather will be mainly sunny.*
ветрови́то	*windy*
По висо́ките планини́ ще и́ма разкъ́сана о́блачност с превал́явания на места́.	*Over the high mountains there will be broken cloud with showers in places.*
температу́ри между́ осемна́йсет и два́йсет и два гра́дуса	*temperatures between 18° and 22° Centigrade*
Жа́лко.	*What a pity.*
Вре́мето на Ви́тоша ня́ма да е мно́го ху́баво.	*The weather on Mount Vitosha isn't going to be very good.*
Си́гурно ще вали́ дъжд.	*It will most probably rain.*
Си́гурно г-н Джо́нсън не но́си туристи́чески обу́вки.	*Mr Johnson probably doesn't have walking shoes with him.*
не е́ фата́лно	*it isn't fatal*
Предла́гам да оти́дете на юг.	*I suggest you go south.*
Там вре́мето си́гурно ще е ху́баво.	*The weather is sure to be good there.*
в съ́бота	*on Saturday*
Какво́ ще е вре́мето?	*What is the weather going to be like?*
споре́д прогно́зата	*according to the forecast*
в кра́я на се́дмицата	*at the weekend*
ня́ма да вали́	*it isn't going to rain*
Ше́фът ще се съглася́ ли с но́вия план?	*Will the boss agree to the new plan?*
Аз ще говоря́ с не́го.	*I'll speak to him.*
изключи́телно краси́во	*exceptionally beautiful*
Предла́гам и ти да до́йдеш.	*I suggest you come too.*
Съгла́сна ли си?	*Do you agree?*
Съгла́сна съм!	*I agree!*
Ще до́йда с удово́лствие!	*I'd love to come!* (lit. *I'll come with pleasure!*)

Questions

1 Try to answer the questions.

- **a** Защо́ бъ́рза Никола́й?
- **b** Как мо́гат Никола́й и На́дя да разбера́т (*find out*) прогно́зата?
- **c** Какво́ ще бъ́де вре́мето на Ви́тоша у́тре?
- **d** Какво́ предла́га На́дя?
- **e** Каква́ е прогно́зата за кра́я на се́дмицата?
- **f** Кой ще гово́ри с ше́фа?

2 True or false?

- **a** Никола́й тря́бва да организи́ра екску́рзия до Ви́тоша за г-н Джо́нсън и г-н Анто́нов.
- **b** Той тря́бва да ку́пи биле́ти за автобу́с за у́тре.
- **c** Във ве́стника и́ма прогно́за за вре́мето, но На́дя ня́ма ве́стник.
- **d** У́тре вре́мето на Ви́тоша ще бъ́де ху́баво.
- **e** Г-н Джо́нсън си́гурно но́си туристи́чески обу́вки.
- **f** Ше́фът ня́ма да се съгласи́ да оти́де в Ме́лник.

i Relying on the weather

Bulgaria has a continental climate – hot summers and cold winters. The extremes of temperatures are, however, tempered by the Black Sea in the east and the Aegean to the south. At the Black Sea resorts, even in the summer there is usually a slight breeze and the temperatures are bearable. In the winter, you will find the coldest weather to the north of the Balkan Mountains which stretch from the west to the east of the country. In the Thracian Plain to the south of the Balkan range, and in the valleys leading down towards Greece, the winters are milder.

In the spring and autumn the weather is less reliable. Particularly in March and April, and sometimes into May, you can expect a good deal of rain, so do take an umbrella. In the higher mountains, of course, rain at these times usually means snow, and snow in Bulgaria means skiing. In the Rila and Pirin Mountains to the south of Sofia and also on Mount Vitosha, which majestically rises to nearly 2,300 metres, just half an hour's drive from the centre of the capital city, you can often ski into May.

Getting out of town

Everywhere in Bulgaria there are mountains. The accessibility of the mountains is, of course, wonderful, but do go prepared for rapid changes of weather, especially in the spring and autumn. It can be sunny and warm in the valleys and snowing hard higher up.

The distances in Bulgaria are not great, and it is well worth hiring a car to get out of town. (Book well in advance!) There are some very good roads – as well as many very bad ones. Do remember though, Bulgarian driving patterns are rather like the climate, a mixture of continental and Mediterranean. Remember too that Bulgarian traffic police make on-the-spot fines and are particularly hot on speeding and unauthorized overtaking.

The rail network is small and trains are slow, so, unless you hire a car, you may prefer the increasingly large selection of cross-country minibuses and long-distance coaches. You'll have to book in advance, and do take your passport with you. In fact, it's best to take your passport wherever you go – just in case!

How do you say it?

- Asking *what will the weather be like?*

  Какво́ ще бъ́де вре́мето? *What's the weather going to be?*

- Describing the weather

То́пло е. *It's warm.*

Студе́но е. *It's cold.*

Слъ́нчево е. *It's sunny.*

О́блачно е. *It's cloudy.*

Ветрови́то е. *It's windy.*

Вали́ дъжд. *It's raining.*

Вали́ сняг. *It's snowing.*

- Evaluating a situation

Ху́баво е/Не е́ ху́баво.	*It's fine/bad.*
Интере́сно е/Не е́ интере́сно.	*It's interesting/not interesting.*
Ва́жно е/Не е́ ва́жно.	*It's important/not important.*
Не е́ фата́лно.	*It's not fatal.*

- Making a suggestion

Предла́гам да оти́дем на Ви́тоша.	*I suggest we go to Mount Vitosha.*
Предла́гам да оти́дете в Ме́лник.	*I suggest you go to Melnik.*

- Agreeing or disagreeing

For a man

Съгла́сен съм.	*I agree.*
Не съ́м съгла́сен.	*I disagree.*

For a woman

Съгла́сна съм.	*I agree.*
Не съ́м съгла́сна.	*I disagree.*

- Expressing regret

Жа́лко!	*What a pity!*

Grammar

1 Слъ́нчево е *It's sunny*

When describing the weather in Bulgarian you do not need an equivalent of the English *it*:

Слъ́нчево е.	*It is sunny.*
Я́сно е.	*It is clear.*

As you see, you use the neuter form of the corresponding adjective and put **е** after the 'weather' word. You follow the same pattern for sentences describing the situation in more general terms:

Тъ́мно е.	*It is dark.*
Ра́но е.	*It is early.*
Къ́сно е.	*It is late.*

You can also begin with the actual word for *weather*:

Вре́мето е мно́го ло́шо днес.	*The weather is very bad today.*
Вре́мето днес е я́сно.	*It is clear today.*

Very often weather sentences begin with a reference to where and when it is warm, cold, dark, etc. In such cases the verb **е** comes before the neuter adjective:

В Мéлник вúнаги е тóпло.	*In Melnik it is always warm.*
През зúмата е студéно.	*In winter it is cold.*
В стáята е тъ́мно.	*It is dark in the room.*

2 Валú (дъжд) *It's raining*

For descriptions of the weather involving precipitation Bulgarian uses the *it* form of an old verb meaning *fall*: **валú**. Depending on the context, **валú** can mean *it is raining* or *it is snowing*. To be more specific you add the word for *rain* or *snow*:

Валú **дъжд**.	*It is raining.*
Валú **сняг**.	*It is snowing.*

3 Чудéсно е, че... *It is wonderful that...*

Some evaluating expressions like *it is wonderful* or *it is important* are linked to further statements. If the linking word in English is *that*, in Bulgarian you use **че**:

Чудéсно е, **че** сте тук!	*It's wonderful (that) you are here.*
Жáлко е, **че** нямаме врéме.	*It's a pity (that) we have no time.*

In English, you often omit *that*. In Bulgarian, you can *never* leave out **че**.

If the linking word is *to*, followed by a verb, you need a **да** form of the following verb:

Вáжно е **да пристúгнем** наврéме.	*It's important for us to get there on time.*
Приятно е **да пъту́ваш** с колá.	*It's pleasant to travel by car.*

Note that the verb **е** always comes second no matter what other word is used in first position:

Не **é** вярно, че...	*It is not true that...*
Мнóго **е** приятно да...	*It is very pleasant to...*

4 (Аз) Ще дóйда *I will come* (future tense)

It is very easy to refer to future events in Bulgarian. You merely insert **ще** in front of the verbal forms for the present tense. With (**да**) **дóйда**, therefore, you say:

(аз)	**ще** до́йда	*I'll come*	(ни́е)	**ще** до́йдем	*we'll come*
(ти)	**ще** до́йдеш	*you'll come*	(ви́е)	**ще** до́йдете	*you'll come*
(той)/(тя)/(то)	**ще** до́йде	*he/she/it will come*	(те)	**ще** до́йдат	*they'll come*

To say *I will not*, *you will not*, etc. instead of **ще** you insert **ня́ма** followed by **да**:

(аз)	**ня́ма да** до́йда	*I won't come*
(ти)	**ня́ма да** до́йдеш	*you won't come*
(той)	**ня́ма да** до́йде	*he won't come*
(ни́е)	**ня́ма да** до́йдем	*we won't come*
(ви́е)	**ня́ма да** до́йдете	*you won't come*
(те)	**ня́ма да** до́йдат	*they won't come*

5 Аз ще съм and аз ще бъда *I will be*

You have two verb forms to choose from to express *I will be* or *I am going to be*, etc. The form with **бъда**, etc. tends to be more formal:

(аз)	ще съм/ ще бъда	*I will be*	(ни́е)	ще сме/ ще бъдем	*we will be*
(ти)	ще си/ ще бъдеш	*you will be*	(ви́е)	ще сте/ ще бъдете	*you will be*
(той)/(тя)/(то)	ще е/ ще бъде	*he, she, it will be*	(те)	ще са/ ще бъдат	*they will be*

Аз ще съм/бъда в Пло́вдив у́тре.	*I will be in Plovdiv tomorrow.*
Той ще е/бъде на екску́рзия в съ́бота.	*He will be going on an excursion on Saturday.*

To say *I will not*, etc. you simply replace **ще** with **ня́ма да**:

Ня́ма да съм/бъда в Со́фия.	Ня́ма да сме/бъдем свобо́дни.
Ня́ма да си/бъдеш свобо́ден.	Ня́ма да сте/бъдете във фи́рмата.
Ня́ма да е/бъде на те́нис.	Ня́ма да са/бъдат в Пло́вдив.

6 In what manner?

A great number of words that tell us *how* or *in what manner* something is done (adverbs) can be formed from adjectives. In English, you often add **-ly** to adjectives to form adverbs. In Bulgarian, many adverbs look exactly like the neuter form of an adjective because they end in **-о**:

Adverbs

Той гово́ри мно́го бъ́рзо.	*He speaks very quickly.*
Тря́бва да гово́риш по́-споко́йно.	*You must speak more calmly.*
Ле́сно ще наме́рим такси́.	*We'll find a taxi easily.*

Adjectives

Такси́то е мно́го бъ́рзо.	*The taxi is very quick.*
Оби́чам споко́йно море́.	*I like a calm sea.*
Това́ е ле́сно упражне́ние.	*This is an easy exercise.*

Adverbs are also used to make adjectives more specific as in:

Вре́мето ще бъ́де **преди́мно** слъ́нчево.	*The weather will be predominantly sunny.*
Ме́лник е **изключи́телно** краси́во градче́.	*Melnik is an exceptionally beautiful little town.*

7 На́й- for *biggest* and *best*

To say that something or someone is *the biggest* or *the best* or *the most beautiful*, (i.e. to make the superlative form of the adjective), you place **на́й-** on the front of the adjective, and, usually, the definite article on the end.

На́й-голе́ми**ят** пъ́пеш е тук.	*The biggest melon is here.*
Та́зи англича́нка е **на́й**-ху́бава**та**.	*This English woman is the most beautiful one.*
Това́ е **на́й**-сла́дко**то** ви́но.	*This is the sweetest wine.*
На́й-е́втини**те** кра́ставици са на паза́ра.	*The cheapest cucumbers are at the market.*

But, as in English, you can sometimes use the superlative without the definite article:

Вре́мето е **на́й**-то́пло в Ме́лник.	*The weather is hottest in Melnik.*

Exercises

1 To practise talking about the weather, first read the following short dialogue:

– Днес е слъ́нчево, но ветрови́то. У́тре ще бъ́де ли съ́що слъ́нчево и ветрови́то?
• Не, у́тре ня́ма да бъ́де слъ́нчево и ветрови́то.

Now complete these dialogues following the same pattern:

a Днес е о́блачно и мра́чно (*dull*). ________________?
Не, ________________.
b Днес е мъгли́во (*foggy*). ________________?
Не, ________________.
c Днес е то́пло и слъ́нчево. ________________?
Не, ________________.
d Днес е студе́но и вла́жно (*damp*). ________________?
Не, ________________.
e Днес е дъждо́вно (*rainy*). ________________?
Не, ________________.

2 Agree or disagree with the following comments, using the model:

– Интере́сно е.
• Наи́стина, мно́го е интере́сно. (*Indeed, it is very interesting*)
• Не съм съгла́сен/съгла́сна. Изо́бщо не е́ интере́сно. (*I don't agree. It isn't interesting at all.*)

a Горе́що е. (*It's hot.*)
b Къ́сно е. (*It's late.*)
c Заба́вно е. (*It's amusing.*)
d Удо́бно е. (*It's convenient, comfortable.*)
e Ле́сно е. (*It's easy.*)

3 Choose a good reason for the statements below from the list on the right:

i Г-н Джо́нсън ня́ма да оти́де на екску́рзия, ___
ii Ня́ма да оти́да на Ви́тоша, ___
iii Тря́бва да поръ́чаме такси́, ___
iv В Бълга́рия и́ма мно́го тури́сти, ___
v Кита́йският (*Chinese*) рестора́нт е затво́рен, ___

a защо́то е къ́сно и ня́ма трамва́и.
b защо́то е мно́го ра́но.
c защо́то ля́тото (*the summer*) е дъ́лго и то́пло.
d защо́то ня́ма удо́бни обу́вки.
e защо́то ще вали́ дъжд.

4 You turn on the radio and hear the following weather forecast:

У́тре в ця́лата (*the whole*) страна́ ще бъ́де я́сно и горе́що. По Черномо́рието (*Black Sea Coast*) ще и́ма слаб (*light*) до уме́рен (*moderate*) и́зточен (*from the east*) вя́тър. Температу́рата на въ̀здуха (*air*): между́ два́йсет и о́сем и три́йсет и два гра́дуса, а на мо́рската вода́ (*the sea water*) – о́коло два́йсет и три гра́дуса.

Now, using full sentences, try to answer the following questions.

a О́блачно ли ще бъ́де у́тре?
b Ще и́ма ли си́лен (*strong*) вя́тър по Черномо́рието?
c Ко́лко горе́що ще бъ́де?
d Каква́ ще бъ́де температу́рата на море́то?

5 Imagine you are Nikolai and complete this conversation:

Миле́на Ще до́йдеш ли днес с нас на те́нис, Никола́й?
Никола́й (*I won't come because I haven't got time.*)
Миле́на Жа́лко. Кога́ ще и́маш вре́ме?
Никола́й (*Tomorrow.*)
Миле́на Къде́ предла́гаш да оти́дем у́тре?
Никола́й (*I suggest we go on an outing. Do you agree?*)
Миле́на Какво́ ще бъ́де вре́мето?
Никола́й (*The weather will be sunny and warm.*)
Миле́на Добре́, съгла́сна съм. Но все пак (*all the same*) ще взе́ма я́ке (*jacket*).
Никола́й (*Good. I'll take my jacket too.*)

6 Use **бъ́рзо** *quickly*, **ле́сно** *easily*, **тру́дно** *with difficulty/not easily* or **по́-ти́хо** *more quietly* to complete these sentences:

a Г-н Анто́нов ще се съгласи́ ______.
b ______ ще наме́рим га́рата.
c ______ ще наме́рим бага́жа.
d Шшш! Говори́ ______!

Do you understand?

Dialogue

Milena succumbs to gentle GSM* persuasion and agrees to go to Melnik.

Никола́й Здраве́й, Миле́на!
Миле́на Ти ли си, Никола́й? Защо́ не си на екску́рзия?

(*Bulgarian mobile phone, remember?)

Никола́й Вре́мето е ло́шо.
Миле́на Не изгле́жда ло́шо. Слъ̀нчево е.
Никола́й Да, но и́ма си́лен вя́тър и на Ви́тоша вали́.
Миле́на Вя́рно, там ви́наги е по́-студе́но.
Никола́й Да, защо́то е висо́ко. Затова́ и́скаме да оти́дем в Ме́лник у́тре.
Миле́на В Ме́лник е чуде́сно. Си́гурно ще бъ́де то́пло, защо́то е на юг.
Никола́й Но все пак ще взе́мем я́кета. И́скаш ли да до́йдеш и ти, Миле́на?
Миле́на Възмо́жно ли е?
Никола́й Разби́ра се, че е възмо́жно. На́дя също ще до́йде. Ще бъ́де по́-интере́сно с две ху́бави моми́чета. [Note that although моми́че means *girl*, the word itself is neuter!]
Миле́на Добре́, съгла́сна съм. Кога́ замина́вате?
Никола́й В се́дем и полови́на.
Миле́на Сери́озно? Но това́ е ужа́сно ра́но!
Никола́й Шегу́вам се, защо́то зна́я, че не оби́чаш да ста́ваш ра́но. Сре́щата ни е в де́вет и полови́на пред хоте́ла на г-н Джо́нсън.

все пак	*all the same*
изгле́ждам, -даш	*to look, seem*
си́лен, си́лна	*strong*
затова́	*that is why*
я́ке	*jacket*
възмо́жно	*possible*
сери́озно?	*are you serious?*
ужа́сно	*terribly*
шегу́вам, -ваш се	*to joke*
ста́вам, -ваш	*to get up*
пред	*in front of*

True or false?

1 Никола́й не е́ на екску́рзия, защо́то вре́мето на Ви́тоша е ло́шо.
2 На Ви́тоша ви́наги е по́-то́пло.
3 Ме́лник е на и́зток.
4 Миле́на е съгла́сна да оти́де в Ме́лник.
5 Миле́на оби́ча да ста́ва ра́но.
6 Сре́щата на Никола́й с г-н Джо́нсън е пред хоте́ла му.

план за слéдващата сéдмица

In this unit you will learn

- how to refer to the days of the week
- some time expressions
- how to give the date
- some more numbers

Dialogue

Mr Johnson firms up plans for his second week in Bulgaria.

г-н Антóнов (*Looking at his diary.*) Днес е четвъртък, четиринáйсети май. Вéче е четвъртият ден от Вáшия престóй. Остáват óще дéсет дни. Трябва да напрáвим план за слéдващата сéдмица.

г-н Джóнсън В понедéлник йскам да отида в Бóровец, за да разглéдам хотéлите. Женá ми и синът ми йскат да дóйдат през зимата на ски в Бългáрия.

г-н Антóнов Йскате ли някой да Ви придружи?

г-н Джóнсън Не, благодаря. Ще наéма колá и ще отида сам.

г-н Антóнов Добрé, кáкто предпочитате. Във втóрник преди óбед сме покáнени на излóжба на плакáти. След товá е запланýван óбед с худóжника, кóйто организира излóжбата. Следóбед трябва да отговóрим на фирмата, от коятo ще кýпим компютри. Ймам еднá молбá към Вас – да ни дадéте съвéт за нáй-изгóдните цени.

г-н Джóнсън Разбира се. Ще отидем ли слéдващата сéдмица в Плóвдив?

г-н Антóнов Да. Плóвдивският панаир запóчва на двáйсети май, в сряда. Ще отидем на първия ден, за да имаме врéме да разглéдаме всичко.

г-н Джóнсън Когá ще бъдат прéговорите?

г-н Антóнов На втóрия и трéтия ден. Трябва да поръчаме някои брошýри и машини за фирмата. Разчитаме на Вáшата пóмощ.

г-н Джóнсън Разбира се, аз съм тук, за да помóгна на фирмата Ви.

г-н Антóнов За съжалéние, на двáйсет и втóри май трябва да се върна в Сóфия. На тóзи ден трябва да посрéщна делегáцията, коятo пристига от Япóния. Николáй ще бъде с Вас до края на сéдмицата.

г-н Джóнсън Тогáва ще обясня на Николáй кой продýкти са нáй-подходящи и кой са нáй-съврéменните машини.

г-н Антóнов Отлично, товá ще е изключително полéзно за нас. Нáдя, обади се на Николáй. Питай го свобóден ли е. Кажи му за плáновете на г-н Джóнсън. Обясни му защó разчитаме на нéго за слéдващия пéтък.

г-н Джóнсън Извинéте, Бояне, когá ще се върнем от Плóвдив?

г-н Антонов А, да! С Николай ще се върнете в събота, а в неделя сте поканени у нас на гости.

г-н Джонсън Благодаря. Втората ми седмица в България изглежда доста интересна!

Днес е четвъртък, четиринайсети май.	*Today is Thursday May 14.*
четвъртият ден от Вашия престой	*the fourth day of your stay*
Остават още десет дни.	*There are still ten days left.*
Трябва да направим план за следващата седмица.	*We must make a plan for the coming week.*
в понеделник...	*on Monday...*
за да разгледам хотелите	(*in order*) *to take a look at the hotels*
Искате ли някой да Ви придружи?	*Would you like someone to accompany you?*
Ще наема кола.	*I'll hire a car.*
както	*as*
Във вторник преди обед сме поканени на изложба на плакати.	*On Tuesday, before lunch we are invited to a poster exhibition.*
След това е запланувван обед.	*After that a lunch has been planned.*
който организира...	*who is organizing...*
Имам една молба към Вас.	*I have a favour to ask of you.*
съвет за най-изгодните цени	*advice concerning the most favourable prices*
Пловдивският панаир започва на двайсети май.	*The Plovdiv Trade Fair begins on May 20.*
в сряда	*on Wednesday*
на първия ден	*on the first day*
да разгледаме всичко	*to look round everything*
Кога ще бъдат преговорите?	*When will the talks be?*
на втория и третия ден	*on the second and third day*
някои брошури и машини	*certain brochures and machines*
Разчитаме на Вашата помощ.	*We are relying on your help.*
за да	(*in order*) *to*
На двайсет и втори май трябва да се върна в София.	*On May 22 I must return to Sofia.*
На този ден трябва да посрещна делегацията, която пристига от Япония.	*That day I must meet the delegation arriving from Japan.*
до края на седмицата	*until the end of the week*

Ще обясня́ на Никола́й кой продýкти са на́й-подходя́щи.	*I'll explain to Nikolai which products are the most suitable.*
кой са на́й-съврéменните маши́ни	*which are the most up-to-date machines*
отли́чно	*excellent*
полéзно	*useful*
Пи́тай го свобóден ли е.	*Ask him whether he is free.*
Кажи́ му за пла́новете на г-н Джóнсън.	*Tell him about Mr Johnson's plans.*
Обясни́ му защó разчи́таме на нéго за слéдващия пéтък.	*Explain to him why we are counting on him for next Friday.*
В недéля сте покáнени у нас на гóсти.	*On Sunday you are invited to our place.*
дóста	*pretty (very), quite*

Questions

1 Try to answer the questions.

- **a** За когá трябва да напра́вят план г-н Антóнов и г-н Джóнсън?
- **b** Защó г-н Джóнсън и́ска да оти́де в Бóровец?
- **c** Когá са покáнени на излóжба г-н Джóнсън и г-н Антóнов?
- **d** Защó ще оти́дат на панаи́ра на пъ́рвия ден?
- **e** Когá трябва да се въ́рне в Сóфия г-н Антóнов?

2 True or false?

- **a** Г-н Джóнсън и́ска ня́кой да го придружи́ до Бóровец.
- **b** Панаи́рът в Плóвдив запóчва на два́йсети май.
- **c** Прéговорите ще бъ́дат на пъ́рвия и втóрия ден.
- **d** Г-н Антóнов ще посрéщне делегáция, коя́то присти́га от Фрáнция.
- **e** Ма́йкъл Джóнсън и Николáй ще се въ́рнат от Плóвдив в съ́бота.

i Of high days and holidays

Although Bulgaria is on the south-eastern fringe of Europe and, for nearly five centuries, was within the Ottoman Empire, the people share with us most of the traditional feast days in the Christian calendar. They belong, however, to the Eastern Orthodox branch of Christianity and occasionally there are differences of emphasis. They place less importance on Christmas and more on Easter, for example, and sometimes the dates of Easter in Bulgaria and in Western Europe and America do not coincide.

The Bulgarian Orthodox service on the Saturday night before Easter Sunday is a very beautiful occasion with candles, rich vestments and wonderful singing.

The Bulgarians also have a number of special days in their calendar that are to do with nationality, their cultural identity and the political experiences of their recent past rather than with religion. March 3 (**трéти март**), for example, is Bulgaria's day of national liberation and is a public holiday. Bulgarians then celebrate the end of the Russo-Turkish War of 1877–8 and their liberation from the Ottoman Empire.

May 24 (**двáйсет и четвърти май**) is a very old holiday. It has a cultural significance for all the Slav peoples and has survived numerous changes of regime. It is dedicated to Saints Cyril and Methodius, the so-called 'apostles of the Slavs' whom the Bulgarians regard very much as their own. This holiday, which is probably Bulgaria's most popular 'high day', celebrates the achievements of Bulgarian education and culture through the ages and has traditionally seen street parades, singing, dancing and other public festivities.

How do you say it?

- Giving the date

Днес е шéсти юни.	*Today is June 6.*

- Saying *on* with a date

на петнáйсети май	*on May 15*

- Saying *on* with days of the week

в понедéлник	*on Monday*
във втóрник	*on Tuesday*
в сря́да	*on Wednesday*
в четвъ́ртък	*on Thursday*
в пéтък	*on Friday*
в съ́бота	*on Saturday*
в недéля	*on Sunday*

- Asking for advice/a favour

Мóля, дáйте ми съвéт.	*Please give me some advice.*
Какъ́в съвéт ще ми дадéте?	*What advice would you give me?*
Ймам еднá молбá към Вас.	*I have a favour to ask of you.*

- Saying *rely on*

Разчи́тайте на ме́не!	*Rely (count) on me.*
Разчи́там на не́го.	*I am relying on him.*

- Stating your purpose

Ще оти́дем ра́но, за да и́маме вре́ме.	*We'll go early so as to have time.*
Обади́ се на Никола́й, за да го пи́таш кога́ ще до́йде.	*Get in touch with/ ring Nikolai (in order) to ask him when he'll be coming.*

- Inviting someone home

Ела́(те) у нас на го́сти.	*Come to our place.*

Grammar

1 Пъ́рви, вто́ри, тре́ти *First, second, third*

The numerals indicating order (ordinals) are used as adjectives:

Masculine	**Feminine**	**Neuter**
пъ́рви *first*	пъ́рва	пъ́рво
вто́ри *second*	вто́ра	вто́ро
тре́ти *third*	тре́та	тре́то
четвъ́рти *fourth*	четвъ́рта	четвъ́рто

From *fifth* on, you obtain the masculine forms by adding **-и** to the number. For feminine and neuter words you replace **-и** with **-а** or **-о** as above. Note the occasional shift of stress.

(пет)	пе́ти	*fifth*		единáйсети	*eleventh*
(шест)	ше́сти	*sixth*		дванáйсети	*twelfth*
(се́дем)	се́дми	*seventh*	(with loss of **е** before **м**)	тринáйсети	*thirteenth*
(о́сем)	о́сми	*eighth*		четиринáйсети	*fourteenth*
(де́вет)	деве́ти	*ninth*		петнáйсети	*fifteenth*
(де́сет)	десе́ти	*tenth*		шестнáйсети	*sixteenth*

Note that the **-на́йсети**, **-на́йсета**, **-на́йсето** endings are pronounced **-на́йсти**, **-на́йста** and **-на́йсто**.

For numbers consisting of more than one word you add **-и** (**-а**, **-о**) only to the last part of the number:

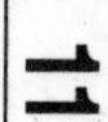

двáйсет и първ**и**	*twenty-first*
двáйсет и втóр**и**	*twenty-second*
двáйсет и трéт**и**	*twenty-third*

Like all other adjectives, the ordinal numerals also have definite forms:

втóрата сéдмица	*the second week*
четвъ́ртият ден	*the fourth day*

(You will find a full list of all the numerals in the Appendix on p. 290.)

2 Първи януáри *January 1*

To give the date in Bulgarian you say **днес е** *today is* followed by the day and the masculine ordinal numeral (an adjective, remember!) in the indefinite form:

(днес е) втóрник, трéти февруáри	*(today is) Tuesday 3 February*

Here are some dates together with the names of all the months. Certain of the dates are particularly important in the Bulgarian calendar. The significance of some of them was explained in the information section:

пъ́рви	**януáри**	*1 January*	(1.I.)
óсми	**февруáри**	*8 February*	(8.II.)
трéти	**март**	*3 March*	(3.III.)
двáйсет и шéсти	**апри́л**	*26 April*	(26.IV.)
двáйсет и четвъ́рти	**май**	*24 May*	(24.V.)
втóри	**юни**	*2 June*	(2.VI.)
сéдми	**юли**	*7 July*	(7.VII.)
четиринáйсети	**áвгуст**	*14 August*	(14.VIII.)
девéти	**септéмври**	*9 September*	(9.IX.)
три́йсети	**октóмври**	*30 October*	(30.X.)
десéти	**ноéмври**	*10 November*	(10.XI.)
двáйсет и пéти	**декéмври**	*25 December*	(25.XII.)

The names of the months are spelt with a small letter. When you write the number of the month in figures, you normally use Roman numerals, as in the brackets.

3 101 and above

101	сто и еднó	300	три́ста
110	сто и дéсет	400	чéтиристотин
123	сто двáйсет и три	500	пéтстотин
200	двéста	600	шéстстотин

700	се́демстотин	1 000	хиля́да
800	о́семстотин	2 000	две хи́ляди
900	де́ветстотин	1 000 000	еди́н милио́н

(Note the change of stress in **хиля́да** and **две хи́ляди**!)

4 През две хи́ляди и четвъ́рта годи́на *In 2004*

For English *in* with the year you use the preposition **през**. The year is given in thousands (**хиля́да** *thousand* or **две хи́ляди** *two thousand*), followed by the hundreds and the tens. Only the last element of the number is an ordinal, the feminine form agreeing with **годи́на**:

Роде́н съм **през хиля́да деветсто́тин осемдесе́т и вто́ра годи́на**.	*I was born in 1982.* (In Bulgarian you have to say *I* ***am*** *born.*)

Note that **и** comes before the final numeral (see Unit 4).

5 *When*: prepositions in time expressions

Here are some of the most common prepositions used with time expressions. Try to learn the expressions as whole phrases:

в сря́да	*on Wednesday*
до десе́ти ное́мври	*before/until November 10*
за две се́дмици	*for 2 weeks* (looking to the future)
от една́ се́дмица	*for a week** (looking to the past)
на о́сми март	*on March 8*
от сря́да **до** пе́тък	*from Wednesday till Friday*
преди́ о́бед	*before lunch*
преди́ три дни	*three days ago*
през деня́	*during the day*
през есента́	*in autumn*
през нощта́	*at night*
през пролетта́	*in spring*
през (ме́сец) януа́ри	*in January*
след една́ се́дмица	*a week later/in a week*

*Note that with expressions like от една́ се́дмица when they answer the question *How long have you been here for?* Bulgarian uses the present tense:

От ко́лко вре́ме сте в Бълга́рия?	*How long have you been in Bulgaria for?*
В Бълга́рия съм **от** една́ се́дмица.	*I've been in Bulgaria for a week.*

6 Го and я *Him* and *her*

The most frequent substitute for things or persons when they are not subjects are the short object pronouns. (After prepositions, nouns are replaced by full form pronouns – see Unit 6.)

Кой търси бага́жа?	*Who is looking for the luggage?*
Митнича́рите **го** търсят.	*The customs officers are looking for it.*
Кой но́си ча́нтата?	*Who is carrying the bag?*
Висо́кият мъж **я** но́си.	*The tall man is carrying it.*

As you can see, the short object pronouns usually precede the verb, but if the verb comes first in the sentence, they come second:

Пи́тайте **ги** мо́гат ли да наме́рят сво́я бага́ж.	*Ask them if they can find their luggage.*

Like other short pronoun forms, they are normally unstressed, unless preceded by **не**.

Here are all the short object pronouns (subject forms in brackets):

(аз)	**ме**	*me*	(ни́е)	**ни**	*us*
(ти)	**те**	*you*	(ви́е)	**ви/Ви**	*you*
(той)	**го**	*him/it*			
(тя)	**я**	*her/it*	(те)	**ги**	*them*
(то)	**го**	*it*			

(You'll find the short indirect object pronouns in Unit 7 and parallel lists in the Appendix.)

7 Ще обясня́ на Никола́й *I'll explain to Nikolai*

In Unit 7, you learned what pronouns to use with verbs that require an indirect object – the person to whom or for whom something is done. If, however, you want to use the person's name or a noun, you need to introduce it by the preposition **на** (which in most cases corresponds to the English *to*). Here are examples with some of the most common verbs that require an indirect object in Bulgarian: (да) дам, (да) помо́гна, (да) обясня́ and (да) ка́жа:

Той ще даде́ съве́т **на момче́то**.	*He will give the boy some advice.*
Г-жа́ Ко́линс мо́же да помо́гне **на момче́тата**.	*Mrs Collins can help (give help to) the boys.*
Ма́йкъл Джо́нсън ще обясни́ сво́ите пла́нове **на Никола́й**.	*Michael Johnson will explain his plans to Nikolai.*

Николáй ще кáже **на Миле́на** за нóвия план.	*Nikolai will tell Milena about the new plan.*

8 Ще му обясня́ *I'll explain to him*

Compare the examples in the last section with their alternatives where the short indirect object pronouns replace **на** + noun and move to the left of the verb:

Той ще **му дадé** съвéт.	*He'll give him some advice.*
Г-жá Кóлинс мóже да **им помóгне**.	*Mrs Collins can help them.*
Мáйкъл Джóнсън ще **му обясни́** свóите плáнове.	*Michael Johnson will explain his plans to him.*
Николáй ще **й кáже** за нóвия план.	*Nikolai will tell her about the new plan.*

When **на** is used with the full non-subject pronoun as an alternative to the short pronoun to the left of the verb, this highlights a contrast. Compare:

Ще се обáдя **на нéя** (не на нéго!).	*I'll ring her (not him).*
with Ще **й** се обáдя.	
Ще помóгна **и на тéбе** (не сáмо на тях!).	*I'll help you too (not just them).*
with Ще **ти** помóгна.	

(Look at the list of full non-subject pronouns in Unit 6.)

9 Ни́е сме покáнени *We are invited*

Some verbal forms can be used with the verb *to be* as in *we are* or *we have been* ***invited***. In such sentences you are not interested in who does the inviting but who is or has been invited. That is why they are called passive sentences. Such **-ed** forms of the verb are known as passive participles and are used as adjectives. In Bulgarian, you form the passive participle of most verbs by replacing the personal endings of the past form by **-ен**:

(да) покáн**я** becomes покáн**ен**	
аз съм покáнен	*I am invited*

This is the masculine form to which you can then add the feminine, neuter or plural endings: **тя е покáнена, то е покáнено, ни́е сме покáнени**.

А-pattern verbs add **-ан**, so запланýвам *to plan* becomes **запланýван** (**-а**, **-о**, **-и**) *planned*:

Конферéнцията **е запланýвана** за сéдми септéмври.	*The conference is planned for September 7.*

A small number of verbs add **-ян** or **-т**. You will find some of them among the participles listed in the Appendix.

Exercises

1 Read this notice found just inside the entrance to a department store:

ПА́РТЕР (*ground floor*):	подáръци и козмéтика (*cosmetics*)
I ЕТА́Ж (*floor*):	всѝчко за детéто
II ЕТА́Ж:	обýвки
III ЕТА́Ж:	мъ̀жка и дáмска конфéкция (*men's and ladies' ready-made clothes*)
IV ЕТА́Ж:	килѝми (*carpets*)
V ЕТА́Ж:	ресторáнт, тоалéтна

Now answer Каквó ѝма:

a	на пáртера?	**d**	на трéтия етáж?
b	на пъ̀рвия етáж?	**e**	на четвъ̀ртия етáж?
c	на втóрия етáж?	**f**	на пéтия етáж?

2 Still looking at the notice, say on which floor they sell the indicated items. На кой етáж продáват:

a	маратóнки? (*trainers, athletic shoes*)	**c**	я́кета?
b	парфю́ми? (*perfumes*)	**d**	шампоáни? (*shampoos*)

3 Try using some object pronouns by replacing the names and filling the spaces with the Bulgarian for *him, her,* etc.

Обадѝ се:
- **a** на Марк и __ поканѝ (*invite*) у нас на гóсти.
- **b** на Невéна и __ поканѝ у нас на гóсти.
- **c** на Николáй и __ поканѝ у нас на гóсти.
- **d** на г-н и г-жá Антóнови и __ поканѝ у нас на гóсти.

4 You are looking at your diary and making plans for the days ahead. Following the model complete the sentences with the appropriate days of the week or time expressions:

Днес е понедéлник. След три дни ще бъ̀де четвъ̀ртък. Ще кýпя билéт (for за) четвъ̀ртък.

a Днес е четвъ̀ртък. След два дни ще бъ̀де ____ Ще запáзя мáса (for) ____ .
b Днес е недéля. След пет дни ще бъ̀де ____ Ще отѝда на излóжбата (on) ____ .
c Днес е втóрник. Ýтре ще бъ̀де ____ Ще кýпя билéт (for tomorrow).

5 Look carefully at this page from a brochure, then answer the questions below in Bulgarian. For the rounded, long-hand letters look back at p. xii.

БЕЛГРАД

ЕДИН ПРИЯТЕН УИКЕНД

ДАТИ НА ЗАМИНАВАНЕ	ЦЕНА
април – 26	*193 лв.*
май – 31	*193 лв.*
август – 2	*193 лв.*
септември – 6	*193 лв.*
октомври – 11	*193 лв.*

1 ДЕН – Отпътуване в 6,00 ч. по маршрут София - Белград. Пристигане в Белград в ранния следобед. Настаняване. Кратка почивка. Панорамна обиколка на Белград с екскурзовод на български език. Свободно време. По предварителна заявка – вечеря в бохемския квартал «Скадарлия». Нощувка.
2 ДЕН – Закуска. Целодневна екскурзия до Нови Сад с екскурзовод на български език. Разглеждане на Старата Патриаршия и Катедралата; посещение на манастира Ново Хопово; разглеждане на средновековната крепост Петроварадин. Свободно време. Връщане в Белград. По желание – разходка с корабче по р.Дунав и р.Сава. Нощувка.
3 ДЕН – Закуска. Отпътуване за България. Пристигане в София в късния следобед.

ЦЕНАТА ВКЛЮЧВА
- транспорт с луксозен автобус*** (климатик, видеосистема, мини бар - безплатни топли напитки);
- 2 нощувки със закуски в хотел*** в центъра на Белград;
- панорамна обиколка на Белград с екскурзовод на български език;
- целодневна екскурзия до Нови Сад с екскурзовод на български език;
- застраховка.

ЦЕНАТА НЕ ВКЛЮЧВА
- вечеря в бохемския квартал «Скадарлия»;
- разходка с корабче по р.Дунав и р. Сава;
- входни такси и билети за музеи.

ОТСТЪПКИ
- ученици и студенти: 8 лв.;
- деца до 12 г., настанени в стаята на двамата си родители: 18 лв.;
- пенсионери: 8 лв.

a How does the agency describe the trip to Belgrade?
b What is the means of transport?
c Where will the participants be staying?
d Reckoning on two nights away, what will the return dates be for the different departures?
e What trips does the price include?
f What language will the guide use?
g Does the price include entrance tickets to museums?

6 Read the following page from Nadya's diary for the week ahead. This exercise will help you practise talking about future events:

Понеде́лник	Да помо́гна на Никола́й с докуме́нтите (*documents*).
Вто́рник	Да ка́жа на ше́фа за да́тата (*the date*) на изло́жбата. (Two different meanings of **на** here, notice!)
Сря́да	Да отгово́ря на писмо́то на худо́жника. (Here too!)
Четвъ́ртък	Да изпра́тя пока́ни (*send invitations*) на вси́чки, който рабо́тят във фи́рмата.
Пе́тък	Да се оба́дя на коле́гата в Пло́вдив.
Съ́бота	Да ку́пя пода́рък на сина́ на Анто́нови. (And here...)
Неде́ля	Да пока́жа на Миле́на но́вите плака́ти.

Now answer Какво́ ще пра́ви На́дя?

a в понеде́лник?
b във вто́рник?
c в сря́да?
d в четвъ́ртък?
e в пе́тък?
f в съ́бота?
g в неде́ля?

Now, instead of using the days of the week, use dates starting from Monday, May 18, to ask Nadya **Какво́ ще пра́виш на...?**

Do you understand?

Dialogue

Ken changes his air ticket – with a little help from his friends.

Невéна Добрó ýтро, г-жá Кóлинс! Заминáвате ли вéче?

г-жá Кóлинс Да, отúваме във Вáрна. Предú да замúнем úмам еднá молбá. Акó úма писмá за нас, мóля да ни ги изпрáтите в хотéл «Одéса». Ще бъ́дем там до четвъ́рти юни.

Невéна Разбúра се. Разчúтайте на мéне. На добъ́р път и приятно прекáрване! (*She sees Ken obviously anxious to speak to Mrs Collins.*) Вúжте, Кен úска да Ви кáже нéщо.

г-жá Кóлинс (*After having exchanged a few words with Ken.*) Невéна, Кен úска да въ́рне свóя билéт на авиокомпáнията. Той ня́ма да мóже да пътýва на двáйсет и втóри юли. Úска да отúде в Копрúвщица, за да вúди фолклóрния фестивáл.

Невéна Добрé. Ще се опúтам да помóгна и на нéго. Úмам приятелка в тáзи авиокомпáния. Едúн момéнт, ще úскам съвéт от нéя. (*After speaking on the phone.*) Всúчки билéти от двáйсет и втóри юли до дванáйсети áвгуст са продáдени. Úма билéти за сря́да, тринáйсети áвгуст.

г-жá Кóлинс Мóля, запазéте едúн билéт за тринáйсети áвгуст.

Невéна (*Finishes conversation and rings off.*) Кажéте на Кен, че мóже да отúде в агéнцията в понедéлник и да въ́рне билéта на приятелката ми. Тя говóри англúйски.

г-жá Кóлинс Благодаря́ Ви за помощтá!

Кен Благодаря́, Невéна!

Невéна Ня́ма защó. Аз съм тук, за да помáгам на гóстите на хотéла.

(да) замúна, -неш	*to leave*
(да) изпрáтя, -тиш	*to send*
На добъ́р път!	*Have a good/safe journey!*
Приятно прекáрване!	*Have a good time!*
авиокомпáния	*airline*
фолклóрен фестивáл	*folk festival*

(да) опитам, -таш	*to try*
продаден	*sold*
помощ (f)	*help*
продавам, -ваш	*to sell*
(да) поканя, -ниш	*to invite*
маратонки	*trainers, athletic shoes*
парфюм	*perfume*
шампоан	*shampoo*

True or false?

1 Ако има писма за г-н и г-жа Колинс, Невена ще им ги изпрати във Варна.
2 Г-н и г-жа Колинс ще бъдат във Варна до четвърти юли.
3 Кен иска да върне своя билет.
4 Кен може да пътува на двайсет и втори юли.
5 Всички билети от двайсет и втори юли до дванайсети август са продадени.
6 Кен трябва да отиде в агенцията във вторник.

почáкай, не поръ́чвай óще!

wait, don't order yet!

In this unit you will learn

- how to use negative imperatives to tell people not to do things
- how to choose between two verbs describing the same situation
- how to talk about being on time
- how to select a table in a restaurant

Dialogue

Nadya and Milena are looking for a table in a café.

Милéна	Нáдя, елá! Тук и́ма свобóдна мáса.
Нáдя	Не оби́чам да ся́дам до вратáта.
Милéна	Хáйде да сéднем до прозóреца тогáва.
Нáдя	Добрé, каквó ще поръ́чаме?
Милéна	Не поръ́чвай óще. Николáй тря́бва да дóйде след мáлко. Да го почáкаме.
Нáдя	Ня́мам ни́що проти́в, но той ви́наги закъсня́ва.
Милéна	Такá ли? Надя́вам се, че днес ня́ма да закъснéе. Нóся му два англи́йски учéбника.
Нáдя	Той ня́ма да дóйде за учéбниците, а за да те ви́ди.
Милéна	Каквó и́скаш да кáжеш?
Нáдя	Не ви́ждаш ли, че те харéсва?
Милéна	О, не зня́я, мóже би... Все еднó, не оби́чам да чáкам.

(*Milena gets up.*)

Нáдя	Къдé оти́ваш?
Милéна	Оти́вам да се обáдя на Николáй по телефóна и да го попи́там защó не и́два.
Нáдя	Недéй да оти́ваш! Почáкай óще мáлко. Си́гурна съм, че ще дóйде. Éто го, и́два.
Николáй	Здравéйте, моми́чета. Извинéте за закъснéнието. Отдáвна ли ме чáкате?
Нáдя	Не, сáмо от две минýти.
Милéна	(*Significantly.*) Кáкто кáзва Нáдя, ти ви́наги си тóчен...
Николáй	Ха-ха! Нáдя и́ма чýвство за хýмор.
Нáдя	Хáйде, ня́ма ли да сéднеш?
Николáй	Ще сéдна, разби́ра се. Оби́чам да ся́дам до хýбави моми́чета!

Не оби́чам да ся́дам до вратáта.	*I don't like sitting by the door.*
Хáйде да сéднем до прозóреца тогáва.	*Come on, let's sit by the window then.*
Не поръ́чвай óще.	*Don't order yet.*
Николáй тря́бва да дóйде след мáлко.	*Nikolai should be coming soon.*
Да го почáкаме.	*Let's wait for him.*
той ви́наги закъсня́ва	*he's always late*

днес ня́ма да закъсне́е	*today he won't be late*
Нóся му два англи́йски учéбника.	*I have two English textbooks for him.*
Той ня́ма да дóйде за учéбниците.	*He won't be coming for the textbooks.*
за да те ви́ди	(*in order*) *to see you*
Какво́ и́скаш да кáжеш?	*What do you mean?*
Не ви́ждаш ли, че те харéсва?	*Can't you see he likes you?*
мóже би	*maybe*
Все еднó, не оби́чам да чáкам.	*All the same, I don't like waiting.*
Къдé оти́ваш?	*Where are you going?*
Оти́вам да се обáдя на Николáй.	*I'm going to phone Nikolai.*
да го попи́там защó не и́два	*to ask him why he isn't coming*
Недéй да оти́ваш.	*Don't go.*
Почáкай óще мáлко.	*Wait a bit longer.*
Си́гурна съм, че ще дóйде.	*I'm sure he'll come.*
Извинéте за закъснéнието.	*Sorry I'm late.*
Отдáвна ли ме чáкате?	*Have you been waiting long for me?*
Кáкто кáзва Нáдя, ти ви́наги си тóчен ...	*As Nadya says, you are always punctual …*
Ха-ха!	*Ha-ha!*
чу́вство за ху́мор	*sense of humour*
ня́ма ли да сéднеш?	*Won't you sit down?*
Ще сéдна.	*I will sit down.*

Questions

1 Try to answer the questions.

- **a** Какво́ не оби́ча Нáдя?
- **b** Защó Милéна кáзва на Нáдя да не порѣчва óще?
- **c** Защó спорéд Нáдя ще дóйде Николáй?
- **d** Защó Милéна и́ска да се обáди на Николáй?
- **e** И́ма ли Милéна моби́лен телефóн (GSM)?
- **f** Къдé оби́ча да ся́да Николáй?

2 True or false?

- **a** Николáй тря́бва да дóйде след полови́н час.
- **b** Нáдя кáзва, че Николáй ви́наги е тóчен.
- **c** Николáй харéсва Милéна.
- **d** Милéна ня́ма ни́що проти́в да чáка.
- **e** Нáдя е си́гурна, че Николáй ще дóйде.

How do you say it?

- Saying *Don't* (do something)

Не оти́вай! Не оти́вайте!	*Don't go.*
Неде́й да ча́каш! **Неде́йте да ча́кате!**	*Don't wait.*

- Saying *Come on!* and *Come on, let's…!*

Ха́йде!	*Come on!*
Ха́йде да се́днем!	*Come on, let's sit down!*

- Asking someone to wait

Поча́кай/поча́кайте ма́лко!	*Wait a minute.*

- Excusing yourself for being late

Извине́те за закъсне́нието.	*Forgive me for being late.*
Извиня́вайте за закъсне́нието.	*I am sorry for the delay.*

- Asking someone to be more explicit

Какво́ и́скаш да ка́жеш?	*What do you mean?*

- Saying *Maybe*

Мо́же би ще до́йда.	*Maybe/Perhaps I'll come.*

Grammar

1 Verb twinning

If you look carefully at the dialogue you will notice that it contains a number of verbs which differ slightly in Bulgarian, but which are translated in a similar way in English. Here, with a couple added, is a list of these 'twinned' verbs in alphabetical order with the significant differences highlighted:

A	**B**	
ви́**ж**дам	(да) ви́**дя**	*to see*
закъсня́**ва**м	(да) закъс**не́**я	*to be late*
йд**ва**м	(да) до́йда	*to come*
ка́з**ва**м	(да) ка́жа	*to say*
пом**а́га**м	(да) помо́**гна**	*to help*
поръ́ч**ва**м	(да) поръ́чам	*to order*
прод**а́ва**м	(да) прод**а́**м	*to sell*
ся́дам	(да) се́д**на**	*to sit*
харе́с**ва**м	(да) харе́сам	*to like*
ча́кам	(да) **по**ча́кам	*to wait*

In Bulgarian, an action can be seen from two different points of view, or *aspects*: either as incomplete and still going on (column A), or as momentary and complete (column B). We refer to verbs in column A as imperfective and those in column B as perfective verbs. In fact, you can think of most Bulgarian verbs as having a 'twin' with which it forms an 'aspectual pair', and when you come across a new verb you should try and learn it together with its twin.

In the English–Bulgarian vocabulary we have, where appropriate, given both verbs.

Formally, the verbs in a pair may differ in one of four main ways:

(**a**) Imperfective verbs (A) often have the suffix **-ва-**, as in закъсня́**вам**, кáз**вам** and поръ́ч**вам**
(**b**) Perfective verbs (B) often have the suffix **-на-**, as in сéд**на**, запóч**на** and стá**на** (*to get up*)
(**c**) Perfective verbs frequently have extra letters (a prefix) added on the front as in **на**прáвя, **по**пи́там and **по**чáкам
(**d**) There may be some other internal alternation of letters, often a change of vowel or consonant, as in разб**и́**рам – (да) разб**е**рá, затв**á**рям – (да) затв**ó**ря (*to close*), оти́**в**ам – (да) оти́**д**а (*to go*) and ви́**жд**ам – (да) ви́**д**я (*to see*).

Some verbs such as **обя́двам**, **организи́рам**, **парки́рам** and **пъту́вам** have the same form for both imperfective and perfective. They are identical twins!

Occasionally, two very different verbs form an imperfective/perfective pair, **и́двам** and **(да) дóйда**, for example. In the Dialogue, remember, you came across Éто го, **и́два** and Николáй тря́бва да **дóйде** след мáлко.

2 Imperfective and perfective – which to use when

Which of a pair with the present tense?

In the present tense you always use an imperfective verb because the action is still going on:

Къдé оти́ваш?	*Where are you going?*
Каквó кáзва той?	*What is he saying?*
Ви́ждаш ли табéлката?	*Can you see the notice?*

You also use an imperfective verb when making generalizations:

Г-н Джóнсън оби́ча хýбаво ви́но.	*Mr Johnson loves good wine.*

Николáй ви́наги закъсня́ва. *Nikolai is always late.*

You normally cannot use perfective verbs to describe actions in the present tense. The only exception is when you envisage a completed action that is not really taking place yet – it is still potential. This happens:

(**a**) when you say that you *want to*, *have to* or *can* do something using verbs like **и́скам (да), тря́бва (да), мóже (да)**:

И́скам **да порь́чам** салáта. *I want to order a salad.*
Тря́бва **да оти́да** в бáнката. *I have to go to the bank.*
Мóже ли **да сéдна** до Вас? *May I sit next to you?*

(**b**) after words such as **когáто** (*when*) and **акó** (*if*) indicating that an action will only take place if certain conditions are fulfilled, as in **когáто дóйде** (*when he comes*) and **акó дóйде** (*if he comes*).

(**c**) after **за да** (*in order to*) or just **да** on its own, when there is a sense of purpose or a need to 'get something done'. Here again there is an emphasis on the completion of an action:

Той и́два, за да те ви́ди. *He is coming* (*in order*) *to see you.*

Оти́вам да се обáдя. *I am going off to phone.*

Which of a pair with the future tense?

You will usually need to use the perfective twin when talking about future events:

Ще сéдна до прозóреца. *I'll take a seat by the window.*
У́тре **ня́ма да закъснéя**. *Tomorrow I won't be late.*
Ще напрáвя кáкто ми кáзвате. *I'll do what you tell me.*
Ще Ви донесá менюто. *I'll bring you the menu.*

In all these examples you are concerned with one specific occasion and concentrating on getting something done.

Sometimes, however, when you are not concerned with one specific occasion or not concentrating on getting something done, you use the imperfective twin:

(**a**) Ви́наги **ще стáвам** рáно. *I'll always get up early.*
(**b**) **Ще чáкам** до 11 часá. *I'll wait until 11 o'clock.*

Here you are referring either ***(a)*** to something you are going to do regularly in the future, or ***(b)*** to something that is going to go on for some time.

3 With да and without

The verbs that have been listed with **(да)** are all perfective verbs. They were listed in this way so as to indicate that perfective verbs cannot be used without a 'prop' such as **да** (or **когáто** or **акó**) in the present tense.

You should note, however, that **да** is not used exclusively with perfective verbs. In generalizations when there is no concentration on the need to complete an action or achieve a result, it can also be used with imperfectives. Thus you can say **обúчам да помáгам** *I like to help* and **не обúчам да ся́дам до прозóреца** *I don't like sitting by the window*. In both cases you are making generalizations.

4 Do and don't

If you look back at Unit 7 where – among other things – you learnt how to give instructions, you will see that almost all the verbs were used in their perfective forms: **вземéте си!**, **дáйте ми!**, **претеглéте ми тóзи пъ́пеш!** etc. In fact, you almost always use the perfective twin in positive instructions, when you are telling someone to do something specific on a particular occasion:

Седнéте до прозóреца!	*Sit by the window.*
Затворú вратáта!	*Close the door.*
Направú кафé!	*Make some coffee.*

Contrariwise, you use the imperfective twin in negative instructions, when you want to stop someone from doing something, no matter whether it is on a specific occasion or as a general rule:

Не ся́дайте до прозóреца!	*Don't sit by the window.*
Не затвáряйте вратáта!	*Don't close the door.*
Не правú кафé!	*Don't make any coffee.*

Almost the only time you use the imperfective twin in positive instructions is when you issue a general prohibition valid not just on one particular occasion. You will find the following notice on doors, for example:

Затвáряйте вратáта!	*Close the door.* (i.e. always)

You will also find that Bulgarians use the imperfective **Извиня́вайте мнóго!** in preference to the perfective **Извинéте!** for *Excuse me!* when they want to be especially polite or insistent.

5 Недéй(те) да *Don't*!

Instead of using **не** with the special command (imperative) forms of the verb, you can tell someone not to do something by using **недéй да** or **недéйте да**:

Недéй да спи́раш тук!	*Don't stop here.*
Недéйте да спи́рате тук!	
Недéй да закъсня́ваш!	*Don't be late.*
Недéйте да закъсня́вате!	

You can see that this is followed by the normal present tense endings of the *you* form of the verb, in the singular or plural as the occasion demands. The verb must be in the imperfective, remember, because it is a negative command. You will also have noticed that in Bulgarian, imperative forms are usually followed by an exclamation mark, thereby emphasizing the urgency of the situation.

(Don't forget that there is a list of imperatives in the Appendix and that positive command forms are explained in Unit 7.)

6 Оби́чам and харéсвам *To love* and *to like*

Both **оби́чам** and **харéсвам** may be translated as *I like*:

Оби́чам класи́ческа му́зика.	*I like/love classical music.*
Харéсвам тáзи му́зика.	*I like/love this music.*
Оби́чам сладолéд.	*I like/love ice-cream.* (i.e. all ice-cream)
Харéсвам тóзи сладолéд.	*I like/love this ice-cream.*

As you can see from these examples, however, **харéсвам** is normally used with individual, specified things, while **оби́чам** is used for more general statements. But when you use **оби́чам** with people it always means *I love*:

Оби́чам товá momи́че.	*I love that girl.*
Оби́чам те!	*I love you!*

When **харéсвам** is used with people it simply means *I like*, nothing more exciting, alas!

Do remember, though, that when you want to say you like doing something, you have to use **оби́чам да**, as in **оби́чам** (or more likely **не оби́чам**) **да чáкам**.

Exercises

1 In the short dialogue below you will find the 'twin' verbs for *to leave*: **остáвям** (**а-/я**-pattern and imperfective) and **(да) остáвя** (**и**-pattern and perfective). First work out which is which and note how they are used.

В теáтъра

Николáй Акó ѝскаш, оставѝ чáнтата на гардерóба (*cloakroom*).

Милéна Нямa да я остáвя.

Николáй Защó?

Милéна Виж табéлката (*notice*): Не остáвяйте цéнности на гардерóба! (*Valuables left at your own risk*)

Николáй В такъ̀в слýчай (*in that case*), недéй да я остáвяш. Оставѝ сáмо чадъ̀ра.

Now complete the following sentences with the appropriate verb for *to leave*:

a ________ тáзи тéжка (*heavy*) чáнта вкъ̀щи (*at home*)!
b Сѝгурно ще валѝ. Нямa да ________ чадъ̀ра вкъ̀щи.
c Недéй да ________ вратáта отвóрена.

2 Here are some common Bulgarian notices with their English equivalents:

a

НЕ ПИПАЙ!
ОПАСНО
ЗА ЖИВОТА

DO NOT TOUCH!
DANGER OF DEATH!

b

НЕ Е ВХОД

NO ENTRY

c

ПАЗЕТЕ
ЧИСТОТА!

NO LITTER

d

НЕ ПУШЕТЕ
в леглото!

NO SMOKING IN BED!

e

OFFICIAL PARKING ONLY

f

NO SMOKING!

Now see if you can match the notices with these negative imperatives which have been translated literally:

i Не вли́зайте!	*Don't go in.*
ii Не пи́пай!	*Don't touch.*
iii Не парки́рай!	*Don't park.*
iv Не пуше́те!	*Don't smoke.*
v Не хвѐрляйте отпа́дъци!	*Don't throw litter.*

3 Try to memorize these time words which usually go with imperfective verbs:

ви́наги	*always*	**обикнове́но**	*usually*
че́сто	*often*	**ря́дко**	*rarely*

Now look for them in the following sentences which you should complete choosing the imperfective verb and the right personal ending. (For once the perfective verbs have been given without **да**!)

a Г-н Ко́линс че́сто (пома́гам/помо́гна) на сво́ята жена́.
b Ни́е ви́наги (ста́вам/ста́на) ра́но.
c Обикнове́но На́дя (и́двам/до́йда) на ра́бота в о́сем и полови́на.
d Ма́йкъл Джо́нсън ря́дко (порѐчвам/порѐчам) ви́но за обя́д.

4 Here Nevena is talking to another receptionist and enviously watching a very smart American lady enter the restaurant. Nevena is describing what she sees using imperfective verbs. Try to complete her story choosing the correct form of the perfective verb after **и́скам да**..., **ха́йде да**..., **за да**... and **ще**.

Невéна Ви́ждам, че еднá америкáнка вли́за в ресторáнта. Йскам да (*see*) с когó* и́ма срéща – хáйде да (*go in*). Éто, ся́да на мáсата до прозóреца. Хáйде и ни́е да (*sit*) в ресторáнта. Сегá тя разглéжда (*look at*) меню́то и изби́ра нéщо за я́дене. Дай меню́то, и ни́е ще (*choose*) нéщо. О, и́два еди́н мъж при нéя. А тя къдé оти́ва? Почáкай мáлко, ще (*I'll go*) пó-бли́зо, за да (*look at*) блу́зата *(blouse)* ѝ. Виж, мъжъ́т поръ́чва два джи́на. Йскам да (*you order*) и за мéне еди́н джи́н.

(*See Unit 13, Grammar section 5.)

5 Read the passage below, following Nadya's thoughts when she fails to make a meeting with Milena.

Милéна **ще дóйде**, **ще ви́ди**, че не съм там и **ще влéзе** в сладкáрницата. **Ще ви́ди** свобóдна мáса и **ще сéдне**. **Ще изберé** (*choose*) нéщо за заку́ска и веднáга **ще поръ́ча**. Сервитьóрката **ще донéсе** кафé и сáндвич сáмо за нéя. **Ня́ма да ме почáка** дори́ (*even*) пет мину́ти! **Ще плати́**, **ще стáне** (*get up*) и **ще оти́де** в ЦУМ – без мéне!

Now imagine you are observing Milena and, beginning with **Éто**, recount what you see, turning all the verbs into the present. You will need to replace each perfective verb with its imperfective twin.

6 **Оби́чам** or **харéсвам?** Choose one of the verbs to complete the sentences.

- **a** Невéна ______ да говóри с чужденци́.
- **b** Николáй ______ Милéна.
- **c** Г-н Кóлинс ______ да игрáе голф (*golf*).
- **d** Нáдя ______ тáзи излóжба.
- **e** Г-жá Кóлинс ______ кафé без зáхар.
- **f** Ви́е си́гурно ще ______ тóзи град. (Use the perfective: **(да) харéсам**)
- **g** Те ______ бъ́лгарските специалитéти.
- **h** Не ______ да чáкам.
- **i** Мáйкъл Джóнсън ______ бъ́лгарско ви́но.
- **j** Милéна ще ______ тóзи нов при́нтер. (Again you need **(да) харéсам**)
- **k** Николáй не ______ тóзи учéбник.

Do you understand?

Dialogue

Michael Johnson has a hard time on his own in out-of-season Borovets.

Полицáй Мóля, не паркѝрайте тук. Опáсно е. Вѝжте табéлката.

г-н Джóнсън Вѝждам я, но не я́ разбѝрам. Аз съм чужденéц. Каквó знáчи «Внимáние! Пáдащи предмéти»?

Полицáй Товá знáчи, че хотéлът е в ремóнт и поня́кога пáдат тéжки предмéти. Мóже нéщо да пáдне връхý колáта Ви.

г-н Джóнсън Такá ли?. Къдé мóже да паркѝрам? Тъ́рся ресторáнт, но не вѝждам пáркинг наóколо.

Полицáй Пáркингът е зад хотéла. Ще вѝдите табéлката. В кой ресторáнт отѝвате?

г-н Джóнсън Не зня́я. Кажéте ми кой ресторáнт е нáй-добъ́р.

Полицáй Не Вѝ препоръ́чвам тóзи голя́м ресторáнт. Отидéте в мáлкия ресторáнт до лѝфта. Сегá ня́ма мнóго турѝсти и мѝсля, че ня́ма да чáкате дъ́лго.

г-н Джóнсън Благодаря́ за съвéта. Ще напрáвя кáкто ми кáзвате.

(*Later, in the small restaurant by the ski lift, Mr Johnson is about to take a seat at a corner table.*)

Сервитьóр Извиня́вайте мнóго, господѝне, но не ся́дайте на тáзи мáса, акó обѝчате. Мáсата в ъ́гъла е запáзена.

г-н Джóнсън Съжаля́вам, грéшката е мóя. Днес изглéжда прáвя всѝчко не кáкто тря́бва.

Сервитьóр Мóля, заповя́дайте, седнéте до прозóреца. Ѝма чудéсен ѝзглед към планинáта. Сегá ще Ви донесá менѝото. Ще дóйда за поръ́чката Ви след катó изберéте.

г-н Джóнсън Мóля, недéйте да бъ́рзате. Аз избѝрам мнóго бáвно, защóто не разбѝрам всѝчко.

Сервитьóр Тогáва ѝдвам веднáга. Ще Ви помóгна да изберéте.

г-н Джóнсън Благодаря́ мнóго. Запóчвам да харéсвам Бóровец.

опáсно	*dangerous*
внимáние!	*danger!; attention!*
пáдащи предмéти	*falling objects*
поня́кога	*sometimes*
пáдам, -даш	*to fall*
тéжък, тéжка	*heavy*
(да) пáдна, -неш	*to fall*
такá ли?	*really? is that so?*
пáркинг	*car park*
наóколо	*nearby*
зад	*behind*
лифт	*ski/chairlift*
ъ́гъл	*corner*
запáзен	*reserved*
грéшка	*mistake*
и́зглед	*view*
планинá	*mountain(s)*
(да) донесá, -сéш	*to bring*
поръ́чка	*order*
изби́рам, -раш	*to choose*
(да) изберá, -рéш	*to choose*
абонамéнт	*subscription*
вли́зам, -заш	*to enter*
вход	*entrance*
живóт	*life*
забранéно	*forbidden, not allowed*
отпáдък, -ъци	*litter, rubbish*
пу́ша, -шиш	*to smoke*
пу́шене	*smoking*
ря́дко	*rarely*
служéбен, -бна	*official, for staff only*
(да) стáна, -неш	*to get up*
хвъ́рлям, -ляш	*to throw*
чистотá	*cleanliness*

Questions

1 Защó г-н Джóнсън не тря́бва да парки́ра до табéлката?
2 Къдé е пáркингът?
3 Защó полицáят препоръ́чва мáлкия ресторáнт?
4 Защó не мóже г-н Джóнсън да сéдне на мáсата в ъ́гъла?
5 Как г-н Джóнсън кáзва на сервитьóра да не бъ́рза?
6 Защó сервитьóрът ще помóгне на г-н Джóнсън да избере́ нéщо за я́дене?

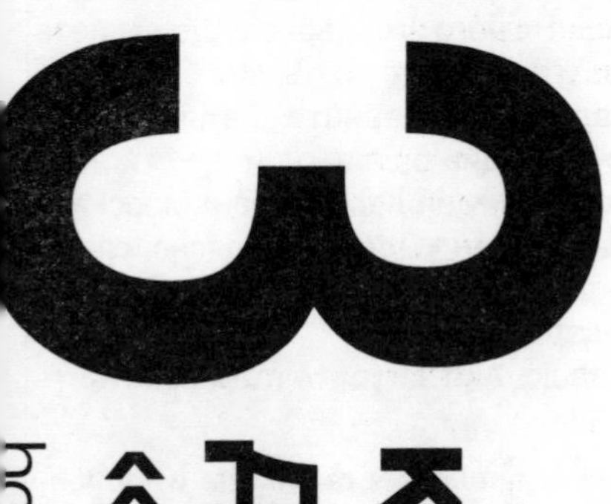

13 Как да стигнем до хотел «Одéса»?

how can we get to the Odessa Hotel?

In this unit you will learn

- **how to ask the way**
- **how to give and understand directions**
- **how to talk about events in the past**

Dialogue

Mr and Mrs Collins have just arrived in Varna. Mr Collins stops the car so Mrs Collins can ask a policeman the way.

г-жа́ Ко́линс Извине́те, мо́жете ли да ни ка́жете как да сти́гнем до хоте́л «Оде́са»?

Полица́й Хоте́л «Оде́са» е бли́зо до це́нтъра. Ка́райте напра́во и ще сти́гнете до еди́н площа́д. На не́го и́ма цъ́рква. Ще зави́ете наля́во и ще ка́рате до пъ́рвия светофа́р. На светофа́ра зави́йте надя́сно. Ще пресече́те еди́н булева́рд и ще сти́гнете до вхо́да на еди́н парк. Това́ е Мо́рската гради́на. Хоте́л «Оде́са» е вдя́сно, срещу́ Мо́рската гради́на.

г-жа́ Ко́линс Благодаря́ мно́го.

Полица́й Ня́ма защо́. Ако́ загу́бите пътя попи́тайте пак.

(*Mr and Mrs Collins do lose their way and it is rather late when they eventually arrive at the hotel.*)

г-жа́ Ко́линс До́бър ве́чер. И́маме запа́зена стя́ в то́зи хоте́л.

Администра́торка До́бър ве́чер. И́мето, мо́ля?

г-жа́ Ко́линс Джордж и Викто́рия Ко́линс.

Администра́торка Да, и́ма стя́ за вас. Добре́ дошли́! Не ви́ оча́квахме то́лкова късно. И́махте ли пробле́ми по пътя?

г-жа́ Ко́линс Не, пъту́ването бе́ше прия́тно. Пробле́мите запо́чнаха, кога́то присти́гнахме във Ва́рна, защо́то ня́махме ка́рта на града́.

Администра́торка Кога́ присти́гнахте?

г-жа́ Ко́линс Присти́гнахме преди́ о́коло два ча́са, към се́дем часа́. Бе́ше о́ще све́тло.

Администра́торка Не пи́тахте ли за пътя?

г-жа́ Ко́линс Да, попи́тахме еди́н полица́й. Ка́рахме напра́во, но не сти́гнахме до площа́да с цъ́рквата. У́лицата бе́ше в ремо́нт и и́маше отклоне́ние. На сле́дващата у́лица зави́хме наля́во и загу́бихме пътя.

Администра́торка Защо́ не попи́тахте пак?

г-жа́ Ко́линс В това́ вре́ме запо́чна да вали́ и ня́маше хо́ра по у́лиците. Ня́маше кого́ да попи́таме.

Администра́торка	Как наме́рихте пътя?
г-жа́ Ко́линс	Еди́н шофьо́р на такси́ ни помо́гна да наме́рим пътя.
Администра́торка	Си́гурно сте уморе́ни и гла́дни. Ресторáнтът о́ще е отво́рен.
г-жа́ Ко́линс	О, да. Уми́раме за ча́ша чай.
Администра́торка	Заповя́дайте, ресторáнтът е на па́ртера вля́во.
г-жа́ Ко́линс	Благодаря́ мно́го. Къде́ мо́жем да оста́вим бага́жа?
Администра́торка	Ста́ята ви е на четвъ́ртия ета́ж, коридо́рът вдя́сно. Прия́тна почи́вка! Ле́ка нощ!

The city crest of Varna

администра́торка	*receptionist*
как да сти́гнем (до)	*how we can get to*
ка́райте напра́во	*drive straight ahead*
ще сти́гнете до еди́н площа́д	*you'll get to a square*
църква	*church*
Ще зави́ете наля́во	*you* (will) *turn left*
светофа́р	*traffic lights*
надя́сно	*to the right*
Ще пресече́те	*you* (will) *cross*
вхо́д	*entrance*
вдя́сно	*on the right*
ако́ загу́бите пътя...	*if you lose the way...*
И́махте ли пробле́ми по пътя?	*Did you have any problems on the way?*
пъту́ването бе́ше прия́тно	*the journey was pleasant*
Пробле́мите запо́чнаха, кога́то присти́гнахме във Ва́рна.	*The problems started when we arrived in Varna.*

ня́махме	*we didn't have*
преди́ о́коло два ча́са	*about two hours ago*
към се́дем часа́	*at about 7 o'clock*
бе́ше о́ще све́тло	*it was still light*
Не пи́тахте ли за пътя?	*Didn't you ask the way?*
попи́тахме еди́н полица́й	*we asked a policeman*
ка́рахме напра́во	*we drove straight ahead*
не сти́гнахме до площа́да с църквата	*we didn't get to the square with the church*
у́лицата бе́ше в ремо́нт	*the road was under repair*
и́маше отклоне́ние	*there was a diversion*
зави́хме наля́во	*we turned left*
загу́бихме пътя	*we lost the way*
запо́чна да вали́	*it started raining*
ня́маше хо́ра по у́лиците	*there weren't any people out in the streets*
Как наме́рихте пътя?	*How did you find the way?*
Еди́н шофьо́р на такси́ ни помо́гна.	*A taxi driver helped us.*
Си́гурно сте уморе́ни и гла́дни.	*You must be tired and hungry.*
Уми́раме за ча́ша чай.	*We are dying for a cup of tea.*
вля́во	*on the left*
Ле́ка нощ!	*Good night!*

Questions

1 Imagine you are Mrs Collins: see if you can answer the questions she and her husband are asked on arrival at the hotel.

- **a** Към ко́лко часа́ присти́гнахте?
- **b** Как бе́ше пъту́ването ви?
- **c** Защо́ и́махте пробле́ми?
- **d** Кога́ запо́чнаха пробле́мите ви?
- **e** Тъмно ли бе́ше, кога́то присти́гнахте?
- **f** Защо́ не сти́гнахте до площа́да с църквата?

2 True or false?

- **a** Г-н и г-жа́ Ко́линс ще зави́ят наля́во и ще сти́гнат до една́ църква.
- **b** Хоте́л «Оде́са» е вля́во, зад Мо́рската гради́на.
- **c** Г-н и г-жа́ Ко́линс присти́гнаха във Ва́рна към шест и полови́на.

d Еди́н шофьо́р на такси́ им помо́гна да наме́рят пътя.
e Ресторáнтът е в коридóра вдя́сно.

How do you say it?

- Asking the way

Как да сти́гна до га́рата?	*How do I get to the station?*
В коя́ посо́ка е по́щата?	*In which direction is the post office?*
Мо́жете ли да ми пока́жете пътя за...?	*Can you show me the way to...?*

- Giving directions

Ка́райте напра́во./Върве́те напра́во.	*Drive straight on./Go straight on.*
Зави́йте наля́во.	*Turn **to** the left.*
Зави́йте надя́сно.	*Turn **to** the right.*
Върне́те се.	*Go back.*

- Saying ***On** the left/**on** the right*

Тре́тата врата́ вля́во.	*The third door **on** the left.*
Коридо́рът вдя́сно.	*The corridor **on** the right.*
Фоайе́то е вдя́сно/вля́во от асансьо́ра.	*The foyer is **on** the right/**on** the left of the lift.*

- Giving approximate times

Присти́гнахме преди́ о́коло полови́н час.	*We arrived about half an hour ago.*
Сти́гнахме Ва́рна за о́коло шест ча́са.	*We reached Varna in about six hours.*
По́щата е на о́коло пет мину́ти.	*The post office is about five minutes away.*
Запо́чна да вали́ към три часа́.	*It started to rain towards three o'clock.*
Никола́й ще до́йде към едина́йсет часа́.	*Nikolai will come towards eleven o'clock.*

- Saying *I am tired* and *Good night*

Уморе́н съм/уморе́на съм.	*I am tired.*
Уморе́ни сме.	*We are tired.*
Ле́ка нощ!	*Good night!*

Grammar

1 Past tense

Verbs describing past events also have special endings. In the following sentences, which take you from the *I* form to the *they* form, these endings (**-х**, -, -, **-хме**, **-хте**, **-ха**) and the preceding vowel have been highlighted. You will see that in the *you* (familiar) and *he/she/it* forms there is no special ending added to the vowel.

Ку́п**их** но́ва програ́ма за компю́търа.	*I bought a new computer program.*
Ти пи́т**а** ли къде́ е площа́дът?	*Did you ask where the square is?*
Тя помо́гн**а** на Джон и Кен.	*She helped John and Ken.*
Присти́гн**ахме** във Ва́рна към се́дем часа́.	*We arrived in Varna about 7 o'clock.*
Сти́гн**ахте** ли до площа́да?	*Did you get to the square?*
Деца́та игр**а́ха** до къ́сно.	*The children played until late.*

The endings are the same for all three verb patterns, but they are added to a variety of vowels and this makes forming the past tense in Bulgarian a little tricky. You will, however, be able to take things gradually, learning in this and the following units which vowels go with which groups of verbs. To make things easier we will move from the regular to the less regular forms.

(**a**) Verbs that add past endings to **-а-**
With all **а**-pattern verbs (Conjugation 3) like **пи́там**, **ка́рам** *to drive*, (да) **разгле́дам** *to look at* you replace the **-м** of the *I* form with the special past endings. So пи́та-**м** becomes:

(аз)	пи́т**ах**	*I asked*	(ни́е)	пи́т**ахме**	*we asked*
(ти)	пи́т**а**	*you asked*	(ви́е)	пи́т**ахте**	*you asked*
(той) (тя) (то)	пи́т**а**	*he/she/it asked*	(те)	пи́т**аха**	*they asked*

You will notice that there is no difference between the past той **пи́та** and the present той **пи́та**. You therefore have to rely on the context to tell you whether it means *he asked*, *he asks* or *he is asking*.

You form the past tense of some **е**-pattern verbs in the same way: **(да) сти́гна**, **(да) присти́гна**, **(да) запо́чна**, **(да) помо́гна**, for example. You can recognize this group by the presence of **-на** in the dictionary form.

Сти́г**нах** до хоте́ла. — *I reached the hotel.*
Вче́ра Никола́й запо́ч**на** да у́чи англи́йски. — *Yesterday Nikolai began to study English.*
Помо́г**нахме** на момче́тата. — *We helped the boys.*
Присти́г**наха** къ́сно във Ва́рна. — *They arrived late in Varna.*

(**b**) Verbs adding past endings to **-и-**
Most **и**-pattern verbs (Conjugation 2) have the vowel **-и-** before the past endings: **(да) загу́бя** *to lose*, **(да) ку́пя**, **(да) наме́ря**, **(да) напра́вя** as well as **пра́вя**, **рабо́тя**, **тъ́рся**, etc.

(аз)	ку́п**их**	*I bought*	(ни́е)	ку́п**ихме**	*we bought*
(ти)	ку́п**и**	*you bought*	(ви́е)	ку́п**ихте**	*you bought*
(той) (тя) (то)	ку́п**и**	*he/she/it bought*	(те)	ку́п**иха**	*they bought*

Тъ́рсих г-н Анто́нов, но не го **наме́рих**. — *I looked for Mr Antonov but didn't find him.*
На́дя **напра́ви** кафе́ за вси́чки. — *Nadya made coffee for everyone.*
Какво́ **загу́бихте**? — *What did you lose?*

(**c**) For the past tense forms of **е**-pattern verbs in **-и́я** and **-а́я** like **(да) зави́я** *to turn*, **пи́я** *to drink*, **игра́я** *to play* you simply replace the **-я** of the first person *I* form by the appropriate past endings. The resulting forms look just like the ones in (*a*) and (*b*) above:

Та́зи су́трин **пих** мля́ко. — *This morning I drank some milk.*
Кола́та **зави́** надя́сно. — *The car turned to the right.*
Деца́та **игра́ха** до къ́сно. — *The children played until late.*

2 И́мах *I had* and ня́мах *I didn't have*

When describing past situations, the verbs **и́мам** and **ня́мам** have slightly different forms:

(аз)	и́мах/ня́мах	*I had/ didn't have*	(ни́е)	и́махме/ня́махме	*we had/ didn't have*
(ти)	и́ма**ше**/ня́ма**ше**	*you had/ didn't have*	(ви́е)	и́махте/ня́махте	*you had/ didn't have*
(той) (тя) (то)	и́ма**ше**/ня́ма**ше**	*he she it had/ didn't have*	(те)	и́маха/ня́маха	*they had/ didn't have*

(You will find out more about these forms in Unit 17.)

3 Аз бях *I was*

(аз)	**бях**	*I was*	(нúе)	**бя́хме**	*we were*
(ти)	**бéше**	*you were*	(вúе)	**бя́хте**	*you were*
(той) (тя) (то)	**бéше**	*he/she/it was*	(те)	**бя́ха**	*they were*

4 When and how to use the past forms

The verb endings for the past are used when you want to describe an action that was fully completed in the past. You can use them either with the perfective or with the imperfective twin, but they tend to be used more with the perfective. There are other ways of describing past actions and you will learn about them in later units.

When describing past actions using two and more verbs linked by **да**, you should remember that only the first (main) verb needs the past endings. The verb(s) after **да** remain in the present tense:

Запóчна **да валú**.	*It started to rain.*
Едúн полицáй ни помóгна **да намéрим** пътя.	*A policeman helped us find the way.*
В Лóндон úмах възмóжност **да вúдя** катедрáлата «Светú Пáвел».	*In London, I had a chance to see St Paul's.*

5 Кой or когó *Who* or *whom*

Когó *whom* is a form of **кой** *who* and you should use it in the non-subject position:

Subject position			**Non-subject position**	
Кой пúта?	*Who asked?*	but	**Когó** пúтахте?	*Whom did you ask?*
Кой помóгна?	*Who helped?*	but	**На кóго** помóгнахте?	*Whom did you help?*
			Ня́маше когó да пúтаме.	*There was nobody (whom) we could ask.*

6 Едúн/еднá/еднó An alternative for *a* or *a certain*

Very often **едúн/еднá/еднó** (see Unit 2) doesn't mean *one* in a counting sense. Instead it can be an equivalent of the English *a* or *a certain* as in:

Ще сти́гнете до **еди́н** площа́д. *You'll come to **a** square.*
Еди́н шофьо́р на такси́ ни помо́гна. *A taxi driver helped us.*

You will also find the plural form **едни́** meaning *some* or *certain*:

Едни́ па́ркинги са по́-ма́лки, а дру́ги са по́-голе́ми. *Some/certain car parks are smaller and others are larger.*

7 (Да) пресека́ у́лицата *(To cross the street)*: к changes to ч

Verbs with a **-к-** immediately before the ending of the *I* and the *they* forms change the **-к-** to **-ч-** in all the other persons:

(аз)	ще пресе**ка́**	*I will cross*	(ни́е)	ще пресе**чѐм**	*we will cross*
(ти)	ще пресе**чѐш**	*you will cross*	(ви́е)	ще пресе**чѐте**	*you will cross*
(той) (тя) (то)	ще пресе**чѐ**	*he/she/it will cross*	(те)	ще пресе**ка́т**	*they will cross*

Exercises

1 Match the following questions and answers:

i На ко́лко мину́ти е га́рата?
ii Напра́во ли е къ́мпинг «Оа́зис»?
iii Към ко́лко часа́ да до́йдем?
iv Кого́ тъ́рсите?
v В та́зи посо́ка ли е цъ́рквата «Света́ (*Saint*) Со́фия»?
vi Къдѐ е отклоне́нието за магистра́лата (*motorway*)?

a Ела́те към се́дем часа́.
b За отклоне́нието завѝйте надя́сно на тре́тата у́лица.
c Тъ́рся секрета́рката на фи́рмата.
d Не, Света́ Со́фия е в обра́тната (*opposite*) посо́ка.
e Га́рата е на о́коло де́сет мину́ти.
f Не, за къ́мпинг «Оа́зис» тря́бва да завѝете наля́во.

2 To what questions might the following be answers? The important bits are highlighted!

a Запо́чна да валѝ **към 6 часа́**.
b Загу́бихме пътя, **защо́то бе́ше тъ́мно**.

c Ба́нката е **вля́во от катедра́лата** (*the cathedral*).
d Пи́тахме **еди́н мъж** къде́ е магистра́лата.
e **Едно́ момче́** ни помо́гна да наме́рим пътя.
f **На тре́тата у́лица** зави́хме надя́сно.

3 This exercise will help you use some key verbs in the past tense. Complete the answers following the model.

Model: И́скате ли да Ви **обясня́** къде́ живе́е г-н Анто́нов?
Той ве́че ми **обясни́**.

a И́скате ли да **обя́дваме** за́едно?
Аз ве́че ______
b Да **ку́пя** ли биле́ти за «Травиа́та»?
На́дя ве́че ______
c Кога́ **ще зами́нат** г-н и г-жа́ Ко́линс?
Те ве́че ______
d Да **напра́вя** ли кафе́?
Неве́на ве́че ______
e Кога́ **ще запо́чне** конце́ртът?
Той ве́че ______
f Да **пи́там** ли къде́ е магистра́лата?
Ни́е ве́че ______
g Да **поръ́чам** ли такси́?
Аз ве́че ______
h **Ще изпра́тиш** ли и́-мейл в Че́лмсфорд?
Никола́й ве́че ______

4 A friendly policeman tells you how to get to the museum by car:

Върне́те се по съ́щата у́лица. Ще сти́гнете еди́н булева́рд. Зави́йте надя́сно и ка́райте напра́во. Като́ сти́гнете площа́да, парки́райте на па́ркинга и пи́тайте пак (*again*). Музе́ят не е дале́че от площа́да.

You successfully follow his instructions. Now tell your friend how you got there. You will need to put the verbs into the past and change them to the *I* form.

5 Look at the map opposite and tell a stranger how to get from the museum to the chemist's.

6 You too need to get to the chemist's. Having checked the instructions you gave in Ex. **5** (in the Key!), say how you and your companion drove there.

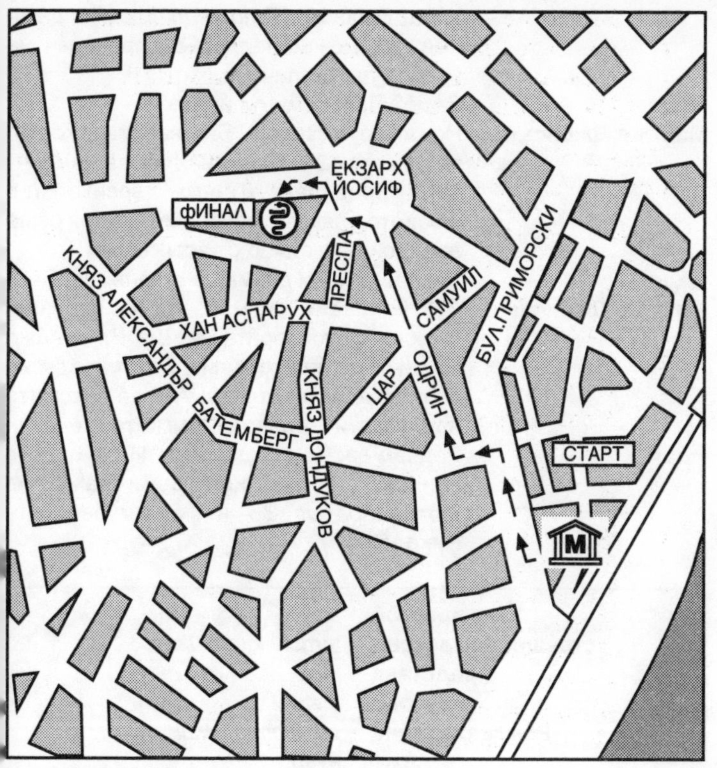

Do you understand?

Dialogue

На́дя Дово́лен ли сте от престо́я в Пло́вдив?

Ма́йкъл Джо́нсън Мно́го съм дово́лен. За ме́не бе́ше стра́шно интере́сно. Ня́мах предста́ва от българската исто́рия.

На́дя И́махте ли вре́ме да разгле́дате ста́рия град?

Ма́йкъл Джо́нсън Да, бях в на́й-интере́сните ста́ри къщи, разгле́дах Ри́мската стена́, ста́рия теа́тър и църквата «Свети́ Константи́н и Еле́на».

На́дя Ху́баво ли бе́ше вре́мето?

Ма́йкъл Джо́нсън Да, вре́мето бе́ше мно́го прия́тно. Не бе́ше мно́го горе́що.

На́дя И́маше ли мно́го хо́ра?

Ма́йкъл Джо́нсън О, да. На панаи́ра бе́ше пъ́лно с хо́ра от

	ця́ла Евро́па. (*Tongue in cheek.*) Да́же и́мах възмо́жност да бъ́да превода́ч на една́ гру́па англича́ни.
На́дя	Защо́? Пробле́ми ли и́махa?
Ма́йкъл Джо́нсън	Не, ни́що серио́зно. Бях накли́зо, кога́то те присти́гнаха. Помо́гнах им да наме́рят сво́я преводаа́ч. Те го тъ́рсиха във фоайе́то вля́во от реце́пцията, а той бе́ше във фоайе́то вля́во от асансьо́ра.
На́дя	Напра́вихте ли сни́мки в ста́рия град?
Ма́йкъл Джо́нсън	Да, напра́вих сни́мки. За съжале́ние, загу́бих фо́тоапара́та си! Ще Ви пока́жа ка́ртичките, ко́йто ку́пих. Е́то тук, вдя́сно от площа́да, е хоте́лът. А това́ е къ́щата на Ламарти́н, вля́во е Ри́мската стена́.
На́дя	Ра́двам се, че сте дово́лен. И ще бъ́дете о́ще по́-дово́лен, кога́то Ви ка́жа, че фо́тоапара́тът Ви не е́ загу́бен – у Никола́й е!

престо́й	*stay*
стра́шно интере́сно	*terribly interesting*
предста́ва	*idea*
исто́рия	*history*
Ри́мската стена́	*the Roman Wall*
да́же	*even*
възмо́жност (f)	*opportunity, chance*
гру́па	*group*
накли́зо	*nearby*
реце́пция	*reception*
сни́мка	*photo*
фо́тоапара́т	*camera*
къ́ща	*house*
Ламарти́н	*Lamartine* (French poet)
загу́бен	*lost*
у	*with*

Questions

To practise narration in the first person, imagine you have shared Michael Johnson's experience in Plovdiv and answer instead of him:

1 От какво́ ня́махте предста́ва, преди́ да оти́дете в Пло́вдив?
2 Какво́ разгле́дахте в ста́рия град?
3 Защо́ бе́ше прия́тно вре́мето?
4 Каква́ възмо́жност и́махте, кога́то присти́гна гру́па англича́ни?
5 Къде́ тъ́рсиха англича́ните сво́я преводa̍ч?
6 Защо́ ще пока́жете на На́дя ка́ртички, а не сни́мки?

Plovdiv Trade Fair logo

поздравя́вам те!

congratulations!

In this unit you will learn

- **how to congratulate people on special occasions**
- **how to name items and places in the home**

Dialogue

It is Sunday, May 24, the traditional day of Saints Cyril and Methodius. Nikolai meets Michael Johnson to take him to Mr Antonov's house.

Ма́йкъл Джо́нсън Никола́й, какъв пода́рък се но́си на домаки́нята, кога́то се хо́ди на го́сти в Бълга́рия?

Никола́й Обикнове́но се но́сят цветя́ или́ бонбо́ни.

Ма́йкъл Джо́нсън Ела́те да ку́пим цветя́ за г-жа́ Анто́нова. (*At the florist's.*) Ви́ждам, че мно́го хо́ра купу́ват цветя́ днес.

Никола́й Да, защо́то е пра́зник.

Ма́йкъл Джо́нсън Какъв пра́зник?

Никола́й Днес се празну́ва Ки́рил и Мето́дий*, деня́т на българската култу́ра.

Ма́йкъл Джо́нсън Те́зи ро́зи ми харе́сват. Ще ку́пя буке́т ро́зи.

(*At the Antonovs' Mrs Antonov opens the door helped by Sashko, their 7-year-old son.*)

Зла́тка Анто́нова Добре́ дошли́! Заповя́дайте. Какви́ краси́ви цветя́!

Са́шко А за ме́не и́ма ли не́що?

Зла́тка Анто́нова Са́шко!

Ма́йкъл Джо́нсън Мо́же би и́ма не́що и за те́бе, но първо тря́бва да ми ка́жеш какво́ се ка́зва, кога́то и́скаш да поздрави́ш ня́кого.

Са́шко Мо́жеш да ми ка́жеш „Чести́т рожде́н ден!"

Зла́тка Анто́нова Са́шко, но днес не е́ тво́ят рожде́н ден!

Са́шко Да, но на рожде́н ден се получа́ват пода́ръци.

(*After some conferring with Nikolai, Michael Johnson gives Sashko a bar of chocolate and a set of coloured pencils.*)

Ма́йкъл Джо́нсън Ти си учени́к, нали́? Чести́т пра́зник! Поздравя́вам те по слу́чай пра́зника Ки́рил и Мето́дий!*

*In current Bulgarian the saint names 'Кирил и Методий' are always preceded by 'Свети' (*saint, holy*).

Са́шко	Благодаря́ мно́го. И аз те поздравя́вам, че ми доне́се шокола́д. И моли́вите ми харе́сват.
Зла́тка Анто́нова	Са́шко, мно́го гово́риш. Иди́ и донеси́ ва́зата от спа́лнята. Внима́вай да не я счу́пиш!
Боя́н Анто́нов	Зла́тке, покани́ го́стите в хо́ла.
Никола́й	Ко́лко краси́во е наредéна ма́сата! Са́шко ли я нареди́?
Зла́тка Анто́нова	Да, той нареди́ ви́лиците, ножо́вете и салфе́тките. Той оби́ча да пома́га.
Са́шко	Ма́мо, доне́сох ва́зата. Мо́же ли да донеса́ и ви́ното за го́стите?
Зла́тка Анто́нова	Не, баща́ ти ще го донесе́. Боя́не, мо́ля те донеси́ ви́ното от ку́хнята.

(*Boyan Antonov returns with the wine and pours it out.*)

Боя́н Анто́нов	Да запо́чваме! Наздра́ве! Чести́т пра́зник!
Ма́йкъл Джо́нсън	Чести́т пра́зник! Наздра́ве!
Зла́тка Анто́нова	Заповя́дайте, докато́ е то́пла ба́ницата. Надя́вам се, че ще ви харе́са.

Какъв пода́рък се но́си на домаки́нята кога́то се хо́ди на го́сти?	*What kind of present does one take to the lady of the house when one goes visiting?*
Обикнове́но се но́сят цветя́ или́ бонбо́ни.	*Usually one takes flowers or chocolates.*
мно́го хо́ра купу́ват цветя́	*a lot of people are buying flowers*
пра́зник	*a special day, festival, holiday*
Днес се празну́ва ... деня́т на	*Today we are celebrating the day of...*
Те́зи ро́зи ми харе́сват.	*I like these roses.*
буке́т	*bunch*
какво́ се ка́зва кога́то и́скаш да поздрави́ш ня́кого	*what one says when you want to congratulate someone*
Чести́т рожде́н ден!	*Happy birthday!*
На рожде́н ден се получа́ват пода́ръци.	*On one's birthday one gets presents.*
Чести́т пра́зник!	*Congratulations!*
Поздравя́вам те по слу́чай...	*I congratulate you on the occasion of...*

че ми доне́се шокола́д	*that you brought me a bar of chocolate.*
Моли́вите ми харе́сват.	*I like the pencils.*
Иди́ и донеси́ ва́зата.	*Go and bring the vase.*
спа́лня	*bedroom*
Внима́вай да не я счу́пиш!	*Watch you don't break it!*
нареде́н	*arranged*
Покани́ го́стите в хо́ла.	*Ask our guests into the living-room.*
Той нареди́ ви́лиците, ножо́вете и салфе́тките.	*He arranged the forks, knives and serviettes.*
Той оби́ча да пома́га.	*He likes to help.*
Доне́сох ва́зата.	*I've brought the vase.*
ку́хня	*kitchen*
Да запо́чваме!	*Let's begin!*
Наздра́ве!	*Cheers!/Your good health!*
докато́ е то́пла ба́ницата	*while the banitsa cheese pasty is still warm*
ще ви харе́са	*you will like it*

Questions

1 Try to answer the questions.

- **a** Какво́ се но́си на домаки́нята, кога́то се хо́ди на го́сти в Бълга́рия?
- **b** Какво́ се празну́ва днес?
- **c** Защо́ Ма́йкъл Джо́нсън не мо́же да ка́же на Са́шко „Чести́т рожде́н ден“?
- **d** За какво́ благодари́ Са́шко на Ма́йкъл Джо́нсън?
- **e** Кога́ се получа́ват пода́ръци?
- **f** Откъде́ ще донесе́ ви́ното Боя́н Анто́нов?

2 True or false?

- **a** Ни́кой (*nobody*) не купу́ва цветя́ днес.
- **b** Ма́йкъл Джо́нсън купу́ва буке́т ро́зи, защо́то ро́зите му харе́сват.
- **c** На Са́шко му харе́сват моли́вите.
- **d** Зла́тка Анто́нова ще пока́ни го́стите в ку́хнята.
- **e** Са́шко не оби́ча да пома́га.
- **f** Зла́тка Анто́нова се надя́ва, че ба́ницата ще им харе́са.

How do you say it?

- Offering general congratulations on any festive occasion

Чести́то!/Чести́т пра́зник!	*Congratulations!*

- Congratulating someone on an achievement

Поздравя́вам те/Ви с успе́ха!	*Congratulations on your success!*
Поздравле́ния!	*Congratulations!*

- Offering good wishes on specific occasions

Поздравя́вам те/ Ви с рожде́ния ден!	*Many happy returns of the day!*
Чести́т рожде́н ден!	*Happy birthday!*
Ве́села/Чести́та Ко́леда!	*Merry/Happy Christmas!*
Чести́та Но́ва Годи́на! (ЧНГ*)	*Happy New Year!*

*This abbreviation is mainly found on New Year cards.

За мно́го годи́ни!	*Many happy returns!* (lit. *for many more years.* Also used on other festive occasions such as New Year)
Жела́я ти/Ви мно́го здра́ве!	*I wish you good health!*

- Wishing someone *Good health* (on drinking!)

Наздра́ве!	*Cheers!*

- Giving a warning

Внима́вай(те)!	*Watch out!*
Внима́вай да не па́днеш!	*Mind you don't fall.*

- Saying *on the occasion of...*

По слу́чай тре́ти март...	*On the occasion of the March 3 holiday...*

Grammar

1 Какво́ се пра́ви? *What do people do?*

There are two ways to generalize. You can either use the *you* singular form as in English, but leaving out **ти**:

Кога́то и́скаш да поздрави́ш ня́кого, кажи́ «Чести́то!».	*When you want to congratulate someone, say 'Congratulations!'.*

Or, with most verbs, you can put **се** in front of the *it* form making the verb reflexive:

Какво́ **се пра́ви** на Ко́леда в Бълга́рия?	*What do people do (is done) for Christmas in Bulgaria?*
Какво́ **се ка́зва** на Ко́леда?	*What do people say (is said) at Christmas?*
Какво́ **се но́си** на домаки́нята, кога́то **се хо́ди** на го́сти?	*What does one take (is taken) to the lady of the house when one goes visiting?*
Как **се ка́зва** „Happy birthday" на бъ́лгарски?	*How does one say 'Happy birthday' (is 'Happy birthday' said) in Bulgarian?*

Note that although there is no separate word for *one* in Bulgarian, this form with **се** is, in fact, the Bulgarian equivalent. And remember too, that **какво́** is a singular word and is followed by a singular verb.

As you can see from the alternative translation given above in brackets, and also from the little homily Ези́кът се у́чи, кога́то се гово́ри *Language is learned when it is spoken*, there is more of an emphasis here on what is done and not so much on the person who does it. (Look back too to the True or false? section in Unit 8 and you will find the sentence: **Тарато́рът се серви́ра студе́н** *The tarator soup is served cold.*)

The **се** may also be used with the *they* form of certain verbs, again when you want to emphasize what is done and not the person who does it.

Обикнове́но **се но́сят** цветя́ или́ бонбо́ни.	*Usually people take flowers or chocolates (flowers or chocolates are taken).*
На рожде́н ден **се получа́ват** пода́ръци.	*On one's birthday one receives presents (presents are received).*

(This is another way of expressing the passive which you came across in Unit 11 and about which you can discover more in the Appendix.)

You will find this generalizing form used widely in public notices and instructions:

Тук не се́ пу́ши!	*No smoking.*
Тук се прода́ват биле́ти.	*Tickets sold here.*
Тук не се́ парки́ра.	*No parking.*

Most of these constructions with **се** have no subject: they are impersonal constructions.

тук
се продават
билети за
ГРАДСКИЯ
ТРАНСПОРТ

2 Another way of saying *I like*

In Unit 12 you learnt the verbs **обичам** and **харе́свам/(да) харе́сам**. You can use **харе́свам** and **(да) харе́сам** in a slightly different way, focusing not so much on your liking – or disliking – something, but rather on the effect something – or someone – has on you. So, instead of saying you like something, you are, in effect, saying it 'appeals' to you. You can therefore say:

Either Аз харе́свам те́зи ро́зи *or* Те́зи ро́зи ми харе́сват (*I like these roses*).

Either Ма́йкъл Джо́нсън харе́са ро́зите *or* Ро́зите харе́саха на Ма́йкъл Джо́нсън (*Michael Johnson liked the roses*).

Either Той харе́са ро́зите *or* Ро́зите му харе́саха (*He liked the roses*).

In fact, the more usual form is the second one with the indirect object pronouns (cf. Unit 7) as in:

Надя́вам се, че ба́ницата ще ви харе́са.	*I hope you will like the banitsa.*
Ба́ницата харе́са на го́стите.	*The guests liked the banitsa.*
Ба́ницата им харе́са.	*They liked the banitsa.*

You will notice that when you use a person's name or a noun (instead of a pronoun) you have to use **на**.

3 Present and past forms of *to buy*, *to bring/carry* and *to see*

When you want to say that something is happening at the moment or happens often, you need to use the imperfective verb. So, in the following examples, you can see the imperfective verbs **купу́вам**, **но́ся** and **ви́ждам** used in the present:

Миле́на **но́си** два учѐбника на Никола́й.	*Milena is taking two textbooks to Nikolai.*

Мно́го хо́ра **купу́ват** цветя́ днес.	*A lot of people are buying flowers today.*
Ма́йкъл Джо́нсън не **ви́жда** табе́лката.	*Michael Johnson does not see the notice.*

To say the same things in the past, you need to choose the perfective equivalents of the verbs **(да) ку́пя, (да) донеса́** and **(да) ви́дя**:

Миле́на **доне́се** два учёбника на Никола́й.	*Milena took two textbooks to Nikolai.*
Мно́го хо́ра **ку́пиха** цветя́ днес.	*A lot of people bought flowers today.*
Ма́йкъл Джо́нсън не **видя́** табе́лката.	*Michael Johnson did not see the notice.*

хо́ра *(people)* is the plural of **чове́к** (*person*).

4 Some more about past endings

(a) Verbs adding past endings to -я́-

These are **е**-pattern verbs in **-е́я** (**пе́я** *to sing*, **живе́я** *to live*):

живя́х	*I lived/used to live*	живя́хме	*we lived, used to live*
живя́	*you lived*	живя́хте	*you lived*
живя́	*he/she/ it lived*	живя́ха	*they lived*

A small group of **и**-pattern verbs also belong here, especially ones with stress on the final syllable like **вървя́** *to walk* and **стоя́** *to stay/stand*. Although not with final stress, **(да) ви́дя** adds the past ending to **-я́-**:

видя́х	*I saw*	видя́хме	*we saw*
видя́	*you saw*	видя́хте	*you saw*
видя́	*he/she/it saw*	видя́ха	*they saw*

(b) Past tense of (да) до́йда ***to come*****, (да) донеса́** ***to bring***

Verbs of the **е**-pattern with **д, з, к, с** or **т** before their present endings have **-о-** in front of all their past endings, except in the 2nd and 3rd singular:

(аз)	дойдо́х	доне́сох	(ни́е)	дойдо́хме	доне́сохме
(ти)	дойде́	доне́се	(ви́е)	дойдо́хте	доне́сохте
(той) (тя) (то)	дойде́	доне́се	(те)	дойдо́ха	доне́соха

Note the different stress in the past. Other similar verbs you already know are: **(да) оти́да** *to go* and **(да) пресека́** *to cross*. Remember the change from **к** to **ч** (Unit 13)!

5 Хо́дя and оти́вам *To go*

Usually you use the same verb to say that something is happening at the moment or happens often. **Хо́дя** and **оти́вам**, however, are special. You can only use **хо́дя** when you go somewhere often, while **оти́вам** can only be used when you are going somewhere from here, now, this very moment:

Все́ки ден хо́дя на ра́бота.	*Every day I go to work.*
Вся́ко ля́то хо́дя на морé.	*Every summer I go to the seaside.*
Вся́ка неде́ля хо́дя на цъ́рква.	*Every Sunday I go to church.*

And the answer to: Къдé оти́ваш? *Where are you going?* is

Оти́вам на ра́бота.	*I am going to work.* (Now!)
Оти́вам на морé.	*I am going to the seaside.* (Now!)
Оти́вам на цъ́рква.	*I am going to church.* (Now!)

Only **оти́вам** has a perfective counterpart:

Тря́бва веднa ́га да **оти́да** на ра́бота.	*I have to go to work immediately.*

6 Къдé and ня́къде *Where* and *somewhere*

All question words can be made into indefinite pronouns by adding **ня́-**:

как	*how*	**ня́**как	*somehow*
какъ̀в	*what sort of*	**ня́**какъв	*some sort of*
кога́	*when*	**ня́**кога	*sometime*
ко́лко	*how many*	**ня́**колко	*some, a few, several*
къдé	*where*	**ня́**къде	*somewhere*

Ня́кой *somebody* or *someone* is formed in a similar way. It has the non-subject form **ня́кого**.

7 Зла́тка and Зла́тке: a special address form for names

You may just remember from way back in Unit 2, when addressing someone using their name or title, you often need to use special forms of address, as in:

господи́не! госпо́жо! госпо́жице!

Some names of people have similar special forms, usually involving the change or addition of a single letter:

Masculine names ending in consonants add **-e**:

(Боя́н) Боя́не! (Ива́н) Ива́не!

Most feminine names don't have a special form, but certain names ending in **-ка** change to **-ке**:

(Зла́тка) Зла́тке! (Ра́дка) Ра́дке!

Exercises

1 Using the model: Поздравя́вам Ви с рожде́ния ден. Чести́то!, congratulate a Bulgarian on:

- a getting a new job
- b moving to a new flat (use **апартаме́нт**)
- c getting married (use **сва́тба** *wedding*)
- d some special achievement (use **успе́х** *success*)
- e a festive occasion (use **пра́зник**)

Don't forget to use definite nouns!

2 Read the sentences below and then alter them, following the model: Полу́чихме пока́на за конце́рт/Пока́нени сме на конце́рт (*We have received an invitation for a concert/We've been invited to a concert*). Note the different use of **за** and **на**.

This exercise will help you practise using the right gender of the passive participles and the right form of **съм**.

- a Миле́на полу́чи пока́на за о́пера.
- b Полу́чих пока́на за сва́тба.
- c Ма́йкъл Джо́нсън полу́чи пока́на за изло́жба.
- d Те полу́чиха пока́на за па́рти (*party*).
- e Полу́чихте ли пока́на за кокте́йла (*the cocktail party*)?

3 Ask questions about the words in bold using the question words **къде́, какво́** and **кога́**.

- a Валу́та се обме́ня **на ка́са 14**.
- b **Цига́ри и алкохо́л** на малоле́тни (*juveniles, young people*) не се́ прода́ват.
- c Резерва́ции се пра́вят **все́ки ден от 9 до 11 часа́**.

d С то́зи трамва́й се оти́ва **до поли́цията**.
e Отту́к (*from here*) се ви́жда **хоте́л «Роди́на»**.
f Отту́к се ви́ждат **ЦУМ и хоте́л «Ше́ратон»**.

ТУК
се продават
фонокарти

Тук се продава
sim карта
Prima!

4 Now for some irregular verbs! First read aloud this dialogue between two couples sightseeing in Sofia. Then change the dialogue to indicate that only you and a friend are talking. (The forms in bold will remind you which bits need altering.)

– Видя́**хте** ли катедра́лата «Свети́ Алекса́ндър Не́вски»?
• Да, видя́**хме** я.
– Харе́са ли **ви**?
• Мно́го **ни** харе́са.
– Разгле́да**хте** ли кри́птата (*the crypt*)?
• Да, разгле́да**хме** и не́я. Пред кри́птата се прода́ваха ико́ни. Ку́пи**хме** една́ ма́лка ико́на (*icon*).
– Мо́же ли да я ви́д**им**?
• Разби́ра се. Е́то я. Харе́сва ли **ви**?
– **Ни́**е не разби́р**аме** от ико́ни, но та́зи **ни** харе́сва.

5 This exercise will help you practise saying *I like*. Give a full answer to the following short questions.

Model: Харе́сва ли ти шампа́нското (*champagne*)? Да, шампа́нското мно́го ми харе́сва.

a Харе́сва ли Ви то́зи компа́ктдиск (*CD*) с бъ́лгарска му́зика?

- **b** Харе́сва ли Ви тарато́рът?
- **c** Харе́сва ли Ви ба́ницата?
- **d** Харе́сват ли ти те́зи цветя́?
- **e** Харе́сва ли Ви бъ́лгарското ви́но?
- **f** Харе́сват ли ти пъ́лнените чу́шки?
- **g** Харе́сват ли Ви бонбо́ните?
- **h** Харе́сва ли Ви шо́пската сала́та?

6 First read the following sentences out loud in which people are taking things somewhere. Then read the sentences again as if the various errands were completed yesterday.

Model: Аз но́ся те́жкия ку́фар. Вче́ра доне́сох те́жкия ку́фар.

- **a** Ма́йкъл Джо́нсън и Никола́й но́сят ро́зи за Зла́тка Анто́нова.
- **b** Миле́на но́си еди́н уче́бник за Никола́й.
- **c** Ни́е но́сим брошу́ри от панаи́ра в Пло́вдив.
- **d** Но́сите ли пода́рък за сво́ите прия́тели?
- **e** Ма́йкъл Джо́нсън но́си шокола́д за Са́шко.
- **f** Г-н Анто́нов и синъ́т му но́сят две бути́лки ви́но от ку́хнята.

Do you understand?

Dialogue

John and a girl, whom even Nevena doesn't know, approach Nevena's desk with an open box of chocolates.

Е́ли Здраве́йте, аз съм Е́ли. Заповя́дайте, вземе́те си бонбо́ни.

Неве́на О, англи́йски бонбо́ни. Благодаря́! По какъ́в слу́чай?

Джон Неве́на, ни́е се оже́нихме.

Неве́на Какву́ изнена́да! Чести́то!

Джон Благодаря́.

Неве́на Джон, Ви́е ве́че гово́рите ма́лко бъ́лгарски.

Джон Да, запо́чнах да у́ча.

Неве́на Кога́ бе́ше сва́тбата?

Е́ли Вче́ра. Празну́вахме в рестора́нт «Берли́н». И́маше мно́го хо́ра и полу́чихме мно́го пода́ръци.

Неве́на Отда́вна ли се позна́вате?

Е́ли Запозна́хме се ми́налата зи́ма в Бо́ровец. Аз

празну́вах там рожде́ния си ден, а Джон бе́ше там като́ тури́ст. След това́ той дойде́ в Со́фия на го́сти у роди́телите ми.

Неве́на Мно́го романти́чно! Пожела́вам ви мно́го щя́стие! Сега́ какво́ ще пра́вите?

Е́ли Пъ́рво ще оти́дем на море́. По́сле ще оти́дем на фолкло́рния фестива́л в Копри́вщица. Пока́нихме и Кен с нас.

Неве́на Да, Кен ми ка́за, че ви́е три́мата ще оти́дете в Копри́вщица. (*After a pause.*) Ще си взе́ма о́ще еди́н бонбо́н по слу́чай ра́достната новина́. Ча́кайте ма́лко, сега́ ще до́йда. (*Returning with a bottle of brandy.*) И́мам тук ма́лко коня́к. Наздра́ве!

Джон и Е́ли Благодаря́. Наздра́ве!

(да) се оже́ня, -ниш	*to get married*
изнена́да	*surprise*
(да) полу́ча, -чиш	*to receive*
ми́налата зи́ма	*last winter*
роди́тел	*parent*
романти́чно	*romantic*
пожела́вам, -ваш	*to wish*
щя́стие	*happiness*
по́сле	*after that, then*
ви́е три́мата	*the three of you*
ра́достен, -тна	*joyful, happy*
коня́к	*brandy*

Questions

1 Къде́ празну́ваха Джон и Е́ли сва́тбата?
2 По какъ́в слу́чай предла́га Е́ли бонбо́ни на Неве́на?
3 Къде́ и кога́ се запозна́ха Е́ли и Джон?
4 Какво́ им пожела́ва Неве́на?
5 Какво́ ка́зват Е́ли и Джон, кога́то запо́чват да пи́ят коня́к?

15 бях на лéкар

I went to see the doctor

In this unit you will learn

- **how to talk about feeling ill and getting better**
- **how to describe feelings**

Dialogue

Nadya and Milena are coming to the end of their coffee break.

На́дя Йскаш ли о́ще кекс?
Миле́на Не, благодаря́.
На́дя Не ти́ ли харе́са?
Миле́на Мно́го ми харе́са, но не ми́ се яде́.
На́дя Ти ви́наги внима́ваш какво́ яде́ш, гри́жиш се за килогра́мите си. Пак ли си на дие́та?
Миле́на Не, не е́ това́. Не се́ чу́вствам добре́.
На́дя Какво́ ти е?
Миле́на Ло́шо ми е. От вче́ра ме боли́ стома́хът.
На́дя Защо́ не оти́деш на ле́кар?
Миле́на Бях на ле́кар та́зи су́трин. Страху́вах се, че и́мам апендиси́т. Сла́ва бо́гу, не е́ апендиси́т. Ле́карят ка́за, че си́гурно е ня́какъв лек грип.
На́дя Отиди́ си вкъщи, ако́ не си́ добре́.
Миле́на Ня́ма ну́жда, ни́що дру́го не ме́ боли́. Ня́мам хре́ма или́ ка́шлица. Ка́кто ти ка́зах, и́мам бо́лки в стома́ха и непреќъснато ми се пи́е вода́.
На́дя За стома́х пий ме́нтов чай – мно́го пома́га. Сега́ ще ти напра́вя.
Миле́на Неде́й, ня́ма ну́жда. Не ми́ се пи́е чай след кафе́то.
На́дя Студе́но ли ти е?
Миле́на Не, не ми́ е студе́но, ня́мам температу́ра. Не се́ безпоко́й, ще ми ми́не.
На́дя Да, щом ня́маш температу́ра, ско́ро ще ти ми́не. Спо́мням си, ми́налата годи́на по това́ вре́ме и́мах стра́шен грип с висо́ка температу́ра и си́лна ка́шлица. Не можа́х да се опра́вя цял ме́сец. Тря́бваше да взи́мам антибио́тик.
Миле́на Аз не оби́чам да взи́мам антибио́тици.
На́дя И аз не оби́чам, но чове́к тря́бва ви́наги да се гри́жи за здра́вето си.
Миле́на Пра́ва си.

Не ти́ ли харе́са?	*Didn't you like it?*
Не ми́ се яде́.	*I don't feel like eating.*
Гри́жиш се за килогра́мите си.	*You're worrying about your weight.*
на дие́та	*on a diet*
Не се́ чу́вствам добре́.	*I don't feel well.*
Какво́ ти е?	*What is the matter with you?*

Ло́шо ми е.	*I'm not well.*
От вче́ра ме боли́ стома́хът.	*I've had stomachache since yesterday.*
на ле́кар	*to the doctor's*
Страху́вах се, че и́мам апендиси́т.	*I was afraid I had appendicitis.*
Сла́ва бо́гу!	*Thank heavens!*
ня́какъв лек грип	*a kind of mild flu*
Отиди́ си вкъщи.	*Go home.*
ако́ не си́ добре́	*if you are not (feeling) well*
ни́що дру́го не ме́ боли́	*nothing else is hurting*
хре́ма	*cold* (in the head)
ка́шлица	*cough*
И́мам бо́лки в стома́ха.	*I have stomach pains.*
Непрекъ́снато ми се пи́е вода́.	*I feel like drinking water all the time.*
Не ми́ се пи́е чай.	*I don't feel like drinking tea.*
Студе́но ли ти е?	*Are you cold?*
Не се́ безпоко́й.	*Don't worry.*
Ще ми ми́не.	*It will pass./I'll be fine.*
щом ня́маш температу́ра	*since you don't have a temperature*
ско́ро	*soon*
спо́мням си	*I remember*
ми́налата годи́на по това́ вре́ме	*last year at the same time*
Не можа́х да се опра́вя цял ме́сец.	*It took me a whole month to get over it.*
Тря́бваше да взи́мам антибио́тик.	*I had to take antibiotics.*
Чове́к тря́бва ви́наги да се гри́жи за здра́вето си.	*One always has to look after one's health.*

Questions

1 Try to answer the questions.

- **a** Защо́ Миле́на не и́ска по́вече (*more*) кекс?
- **b** Какво́ ѝ е?
- **c** Какво́ ѝ се пи́е?
- **d** Кога́ и́маше На́дя грип с висо́ка температу́ра?
- **e** За какво́ тря́бва да се гри́жи чове́к?

2 True or false?

a Милéна не йска кекс, защóто се грижи за килогрáмите си.
b Кéксът не ѝ харéса.
c Милéна йма бóлки в стомáха от вчéра.
d Тя йма хрéма и кáшлица.
e Мйналата годйна Нáдя не можá да се опрáви от грип цял мéсец.

How do you say it?

- Asking someone how they feel

Как се чýвстваш?/чýвствате?	*How do you feel?*

- Asking someone what is the matter with them

Каквó ти/Ви е?	*What is the matter with you?*
Каквó те/Ви болй?	*What is hurting?*

- Complaining of ill health

Не сé чýвствам добрé.	*I don't feel well.*
Чýвствам се зле.	*I feel unwell.*
Лóшо ми е.	*I'm not well.*
Ймам бóлки в стомáха.	*I have stomach pains.*

- Saying you'll get better

Ще ми мйне.	*It'll pass.*
Ще се опрáвя.	*I'll get better.*

- Telling someone not to worry

Не сé безпокóй!	*Don't worry!*

- Saying that you do or don't feel like doing something

Пйе ми се водá.	*I feel like a drink of water.*
Не мй се пйе чай.	*I don't feel like tea.*
Ядé ми се нéщо слáдко.	*I feel like something sweet.*
Не мй се рабóти.	*I don't feel like working.*

Grammar

1 Каквó ти е? *What's the matter with you?*

To ask someone how they feel, physically or mentally, or what the matter with them is, you say **Каквó ти е?** or **Каквó Ви е?** You will notice that the indirect object pronouns (Unit 7) are used to refer to the person affected. Similarly, to tell someone how you feel, you describe your state (in the neuter!) e.g. студе́но *cold* and then refer to yourself using the indirect object pronoun **ми**:

Студе́но **ми** е.	*I am cold.*

These expressions are related to the weather descriptions you came across in Unit 10. Here are some examples for all persons:

Ло́шо ми е.	*I'm not well./I'm sick/poorly.*
Горе́що ли ти/Ви е?	*Are you hot?*
Ло́шо ѝ е.	*She is sick/poorly, not well.*
Студе́но му е.	*He is cold.*
Интере́сно ни е.	*It is interesting for us./ We find it interesting.*
Ску́чно им е.	*They are bored.*

In the negative, **не** is placed first, the word coming immediately after **не** is stressed, and the word expressing the feeling is placed after the verb:

Не ми́ е ло́шо.	*I'm not unwell/sick/poorly.*
Не ти́ ли е горе́що?	*Aren't you hot?*
Не му́ е студе́но.	*He is not (feeling) cold.*

You can also use the alternative ways to indicate the person affected (Unit 11):

на + name

На На́дя ѝ е ло́шо.	*Nadya is not feeling well.*

на + noun

На секрета́рката ѝ е ло́шо.	*The secretary is not feeling well.*

на + full pronoun

На не́я ѝ е ло́шо.	*She's not feeling well.*

You will have noticed that you still need to keep the indirect object pronoun. Here are some more examples:

На Никола́й/на не́го му е студе́но.	*Nikolai/He is cold.*
На го́стите/на тях им е ску́чно.	*The guests/They are bored.*

2 Боли́ ме *It hurts*

If you want to say that some particular part (or parts) of your body hurts (or hurt) you use **боли́** – or **боля́т** – with the short object pronoun **ме** (there's a full list in Unit 11):

Боли́ **ме** главáта (*or* Главáта **ме** боли́).	*My head hurts/ I have a headache.*
Болят **ме** очи́те (*or* Очи́те **ме** болят).	*My eyes hurt.*

It is as though you were saying *My head hurts me* or *My eyes hurt me*. And the doctor might ask you **Каквó Ви боли́?** (or **Каквó те боли́?** if he knows you well) *What is hurting you?*

Note that many parts of the body, especially those that come in pairs, have irregular plural forms:

коля́но	– колена́	*knee*	– *knees*
крак	– крака́	*foot/leg*	– *feet/legs*
окó	– очи́	*eye*	– *eyes*
ръка́	– ръце́	*hand/arm*	– *hands/arms*
ухó	– уши́	*ear*	– *ears*
зъб	– зъби	*tooth*	– *teeth*

In the following examples people, other than you, are in pain, and **ме** is replaced by the appropriate short object pronouns:

Боли́ ли те гърлото?	*Does your throat hurt?*
Боли́ го ухóто.	*His ear hurts/He has earache.*
Боли́ я кракът.	*Her leg hurts.*
Болят ли те уши́те?	*Are your ears hurting?*
Болят го ръце́те.	*His hands/arms hurt.*
Болят я зъбите.	*Her teeth hurt.*
Болят ги крака́та.	*Their feet hurt.*

3 Яде́ ми се *I'm hungry*

Another very useful way of saying how you feel is to use the *it* form of the verb with **се** (cf. Unit 14). You merely insert the indirect object pronoun between the verb and **се**:

Яде́ **ми** се.	*I'm hungry.*
Пи́е **ми** се.	*I'm thirsty.*
Спи **ми** се.	*I'm sleepy.*

If you don't feel like doing something, put **не** first and the verb last:

Не **ми́** се яде́.	*I'm not hungry.*
Не **ми́** се пи́е.	*I'm not thirsty.*
Не **ми́** се спи.	*I'm not sleepy.*

This construction can be extended:

Ядé **ми** се сладолéд.	*I feel like an ice-cream.*
Пи́е **ми** се водá.	*I feel like a drink of water.*

If you use a person's name you still have to use the pronoun:

На Сáшко не **мý** се спи.	*Sashko isn't sleepy.*
На Милéна не **ѝ** се ядé сладолéд.	*Milena doesn't feel like an ice-cream.*

You can use this pattern with almost any verb to express your wish to do (or not do) something:

Хóди **ми** се на морé.	*I feel like going to the seaside.*
Не **ми́** се хóди на рáбота.	*I don't feel like going to work.*
Не **ми́** се рабóти.	*I don't feel like working.*

4 Some awkward past tense forms

Past tense of *to say/tell* кáзвам/да кáжа – кáзах

In the present tense you have to use the imperfective **кáзвам**, but in the past you change to the perfective **(да) кáжа**:

Чýваш ли каквó ти **кáзвам**?	***Do you hear*** *what* ***I'm telling*** *you?*
Чу ли каквó ти **кáзах**?	***Did you hear*** *what* ***I told*** *you?*

(Да) кáжа belongs to a small group of **е**-pattern verbs that change their last consonant from the present to the past, in this case **ж** to **з**. (For other changes and other examples see the Appendix, and also **мóга** with the change from **г** to **ж** below.) Compare the forms of **(да) кáжа**:

	Present		**Past**	
(трябва да)	кáжа	*I must say*	кáзах	*I said*
(трябва да)	кáжеш	*you must say*	кáза	*you said*
(трябва да)	кáже	*he/she must say*	кáза	*he/she said*
(трябва да)	кáжем	*we must say*	кáзахме	*we said*
(трябва да)	кáжете	*you must say*	кáзахте	*you said*
(трябва да)	кáжат	*they must say*	кáзаха	*they said*

Past tense of *can* мóга – можáх

Не можáхме да спим цялa нощ.	*We couldn't sleep all night.*
Тя не можá да ядé мнóго от кéкса.	*She wasn't able to eat much of the cake.*

Не можа́х да се опра́вя цял ме́сец.	*It took me a whole month to get over it.*

можа́х	*I was able*	можа́хме	*we were able*
можа́	*you were able*	можа́хте	*you were able*
можа́	*he/she was able*	можа́ха	*they were able*

Past tense of *must/had to* тря́бва – тря́бваше

Тря́бва has only one past form – **тря́бваше** – for all persons singular and plural:

Тря́бваше да взи́мам антибио́тик.	*I had to take an antibiotic.*
Тря́бваше да ста́не ра́но.	*He/she had to get up early.*
Тря́бваше да ча́каме/ча́кат дъ́лго.	*We/they had to wait a long time.*

Depending on the context, тря́бваше can also mean *should have* or *ought to have* (but didn't), so тря́бваше да взи́мам антибио́тик could mean *I ought to have* (or *should have*) *taken an antibiotic* (but didn't).

5 Possessive and reflexive pronoun си

(**a**) This is another difficult little word, not to be confused with the **си** in ти си. It belongs to the group of short possessive pronouns you first came across in Unit 3 and is a short form of **свой** (**свóя**, **свóе**, **свóи**) *his/her/their own* (cf. Unit 9). In fact, it can be used to replace any possessive adjective (мой, твой, не́гов etc.) with any person, masculine or feminine, singular or plural. Unlike the possessive adjective, however, it is placed after the word it refers to.

Note also that the definite article moves from the possessive adjective to the noun:

Ча́кам сво́**я** прия́тел = Ча́кам прия́тел**я си**.	*I am waiting for my friend.*
Ви́наги се гри́жиш за сво́е**то** здра́ве = Ви́наги се гри́жиш за здра́ве**то си**.	*You are always worrying about your health.*
Тя се гри́жи за сво́и**те** килогра́ми = тя се гри́жи за килогра́ми**те си**.	*She is worrying about her weight* (lit. *kilograms*).

(**b**) **Си** can also be used as an equivalent of *myself, yourself, himself, herself, itself, ourselves, yourselves* and *themselves:*

Ку́пих **си** модéрна блу́за.	*I bought* ***myself*** *a fashionable blouse.*
Невéна **си** ку́пи дъ́лга рóкля.	*Nevena bought* ***herself*** *a long dress.*
Николáй **си** ку́пи нóво ви́део.	*Nikolai bought* ***himself*** *a new video.*

(**c**) Some verbs you always have to use with **си**:

Почи́вам **си**.	*I am taking a rest.*
Спóмням **си**.	*I remember.*

To other verbs **си** adds a personalized, intimate sense of doing something for oneself. There is a difference, for example, between **оти́вам** *I am going* and **оти́вам си** *I am going home.* In the Dialogue, when Nadya suggests Milena goes home, she says: отиди́ **си** вкъщи.

(**d**) Like many other short grammatical words, **си** never appears as the first word in a sentence and is *always* stressed after **не**.

Exercises

1 Match the following questions and answers:

i	Каквó ти се пи́е?	**a**	Яде́ ми се ки́село мля́ко.
ii	Гъ́рло (*throat*) ли те боли́?	**b**	Лóшо ми е.
iii	Каквó те боли́?	**c**	Пи́е ми се би́ра.
iv	Ѝмаш ли хрéма?	**d**	Студéно ми е.
v	Каквó ти се яде́?	**e**	Боли́ ме кракъ́т.
vi	Каквó ти е?	**f**	Не, ня́мам хрéма, но и́мам висóка температу́ра.
vii	Как се чу́встваш?	**g**	Не, боля́т ме уши́те.

2 You are interpreting for a Bulgarian doctor working with English-speaking tourists. Give a full negative answer to the doctor's questions using the model:

Боли́ ли го ухóто? Не, не гó боли́ ухóто.

Watch the word order!

a
- **i** Боля́т ли го очи́те?
- **ii** Боли́ ли я зъб?
- **iii** Боля́т ли ги кракáта?
- **iv** Боли́ ли го коля́ното?
- **v** Боли́ ли я ръкáта?

Now give a full negative answer to the questions:

b **i** Хóди ли ти се на плаж?
ii Пúе ли Ви се чай?
iii Говóри ли ти се български?
iv Ýчи ли ти се?
v Рабóти ли ти се на компютър?

3 Now your friend is unwell. Complete your role in the dialogue:

– Не сé чýвствам добрé.
• (*Ask your friend what is the matter with him.*)
– Болú ме кръстът (*small of the back*).
• (*Ask him what the doctor said to him.*)
– Лéкарят ми кáза да си почúвам.
• (*Ask whether he's feeling sleepy.*)
– Не, не мú се спи.
• (*Ask him whether he is bored.*)
– Да, мнóго ми е скýчно.
• (*Tell him not to worry and reassure him that he'll soon be OK again.*)
– Да, и аз се надявам, че скóро ще ми мúне.

4 Now you've been to the doctor's and are answering your friend's questions. Using the model:

Каквó ти кáза лéкарят? Лéкарят ми кáза, че úмам алéргия (*allergy*).

And, at the risk of giving your friend a heart attack, say that:

a you have flu
b you have appendicitis
c you have a high temperature
d you have a cold in the head
e you have hepatitis (хепатúт)

5 Using the past of **мóга** fill in the answers. Follow the pattern:

Видяхте ли фолклóрния концéрт? Не **можáхме** да го **вúдим,** защóто закъсняхме.

a Джон **отúде** ли на гóсти?
______, защóто го болéше главáта. (cf. Unit 17)
b **Донéсе** ли чáнтата?
______, защóто ме болéше кръстът.
c Те **разглéдаха** ли курóрта?
______, защóто ги боляха кракáта.
d **Прáтихте** (*send*) ли писмóто?
______, защóто нямахме мáрки.

e **Я́де** ли от бъ́лгарските специалите́ти?
______, защо́то и́мах бо́лки в стома́ха.

6 In this exercise you can practise saying *came* and *went*. Read out the sentences, filling in the answers according to the model:

Защо́ не дойдо́хте с нас на екску́рзия?
Тря́бваше да посре́щнем прия́телите си. Оти́дохме да посре́щнем прия́телите си.

a Защо́ не дойде́ с нас на екску́рзия?
Тря́бваше да си ку́пя марато́нки. ______.

b Защо́ не дойдо́хте с нас на плаж?
Тря́бваше да си почи́нем (*have a rest*). ______.

c Защо́ не дойде́ с нас на вече́ря (*dinner, supper*)?
Тря́бваше да си ку́пя лека́рства. ______.

d Защо́ не дойде́ с нас на го́сти?
Тря́бваше да посре́щна дъщеря́ си. ______.

e Защо́ не дойде́ с ме́не на Ви́тоша?
Тря́бваше да оти́да на ле́кар. ______.

f Защо́ не дойдо́хте с ме́не на ски?
Тря́бваше да пра́тим писмо́ на роди́телите си. ______.

Do you understand?

Dialogue

Mr and Mrs Collins are at the doctor's in Varna. As usual, Mrs Collins prefers to do the talking.

г-жа́ Ко́линс До́бър ден, до́ктор Стоя́нов.
Ле́кар До́бър ден. Кaже́те. Зле ли се чу́вствате?
г-жа́ Ко́линс Не, не аз. Мъжъ́т ми не се́ чу́вства добре́.
Ле́кар Какво́ му е?
г-жа́ Ко́линс И́ма си́лно главобо́лие и все му е студе́но.
г-н Ко́линс Да, мно́го ми е студе́но, а навъ́н е то́лкова то́пло.
Ле́кар И́мате ли температу́ра?
г-жа́ Ко́линс Температу́рата му не е́ мно́го висо́ка – 37.1 [три́десет и се́дем и едно́.]
Ле́кар Боли́ ли го гъ́рло?
г-жа́ Ко́линс Не, ни́то го боли́ гъ́рло, ни́то и́ма хре́ма.
Ле́кар Ви́ждам, че ко́жата на ръце́те и крака́та му е до́ста черве́на.
г-жа́ Ко́линс О, да. Той мно́го оби́ча да стои́ на слъ́нце. Вче́ра цял ден бе́ше на пла́жа.
Ле́кар На ко́лко годи́ни сте г-н Ко́линс?

г-н Кóлинс На шейсéт и две.
Лéкар Ймахте ли шáпка на главáта си, когáто бяхте на плáжа?
г-н Кóлинс Не.
г-жá Кóлинс Кáзах му, че слънцето е мнóго сѝлно, но не можáх да го накáрам да слóжи шáпка.
Лéкар Страхýвам се, че ще трябва да стойте на сянка няколко дни. От слънцето Ви е лóшо.
г-жá Кóлинс Чýваш ли, Джордж? Трябваше да ми вярваш катó ти кáзвах, че слънцето тук е сѝлно дорѝ през май!

дóктор	*doctor* (only when addressing)
стоя́, стойш	*to stay*
зле	*unwell*
главобóлие	*headache*
все	*all the time*
навъ́н	*outside*
нѝто..., нѝто...	*neither..., nor...*
кóжа	*skin*
шáпка	*hat*
главá	*head*
слъ́нце	*sun*
(да) накáрам, -раш	*to make* (somebody do something)
(да) слóжа, -жиш	*to put on*
вя́рвам, -ваш	*to believe*
(да) си почѝна, -неш	*to have a rest*
спя, спиш	*to sleep*
чýвам, -ваш	*to hear*
катó	*when*

a pharmacy sign in Sofia.

Questions

1 Кой не сé чýвства добрé?
2 Каквó му е на г-н Кóлинс?
3 Защó е червéна кóжата на г-н Кóлинс?
4 Каквó трябваше да слóжи на главáта си г-н Кóлинс?
5 Каквó трябва да напрáви той сегá?

16

ако́ бях на тво́е мя́сто

if I had been in your place

In this unit you will learn

- **how to talk about things that might have happened but didn't (i.e. hypothetical situations)**
- **how to talk about giving presents**
- **how to form the past tense of some awkward verbs**

Dialogue

Following Michael Johnson's return to London, there is a short discussion over a cup of coffee back in the Sofia office.

Боя́н Анто́нов Никола́й, кажи́ как ми́на после́дният ден с Ма́йкъл Джо́нсън.

Никола́й Вси́чко ми́на норма́лно. Сутринта́ оти́дох да го взе́ма от хоте́ла. Плати́хме сме́тката. Моми́чето на реце́пцията поръ̀ча такси́ за два без петна́йсет. Г-н Джо́нсън ка́за, че е мно́го дово́лен от хоте́ла. Осо́бено от това́ моми́че – ми́сля че се ка́зва Неве́на. И́скаше да ѝ подари́ не́що за спо́мен. Стра́шни са те́зи англича́ни! Ако́ бях аз, щях да забра́вя дори́ да ка́жа дови́ждане. Но г-н Джо́нсън и́маше еди́н беле́жник и ѝ го подари́. Тя мно́го го харе́са.

На́дя И аз ако́ бях, и аз щях да го харе́сам!

Ми́лена Ако́ бях аз, ня́маше да го прие́ма!

Боя́н Анто́нов Моми́чета, сти́га глу́пости! Продължа́вай, Никола́й.

Никола́й По́сле оти́дохме в магази́на за пода́ръци. Избра́хме една́ сре́бърна гри́вна за жена́ му.

Боя́н Анто́нов Да́де ли му пода́ръка за жена́ му от мо́ята жена́?

Никола́й Разби́ра се, да́дох му го.

Боя́н Анто́нов Той пока́за ли ти програ́мата за тво́я престо́й в Че́лмсфорд?

Никола́й Не ми́ я пока́за. Ка́за, че ще ми я пра́ти с факс.

Боя́н Анто́нов Ще те посре́щне ли в Ло́ндон?

Никола́й Да, ще до́йде на Хийтроу да ме посре́щне.

Боя́н Анто́нов И ни́е щя́хме да го посре́щнем, но той не и́скаше. Иде́ята му бе́ше да хо́ди нався́къде сам, за да гово́ри по́вече български.

Никола́й О, щях да забра́вя на́й-ва́жното – це́лия ден гово́рихме на английски. Той ка́за, че напре́двам, но аз о́ще и́мам чу́вството, че ни́що не знам.

На́дя Сти́га, Никола́й! Ако́ бях на тво́е мя́сто, изо́бщо ня́маше да се безпокоя́.

Боя́н Анто́нов Мо́ля ви, по́сле ще гово́рите. И́скам да разбера́ – ти изпра́ти ли Ма́йкъл до лети́щето?

Никола́й	Да, да, изпра́тих го. Сла́ва бо́гу, не закъсня́хме за самоле́та!
Боя́н Анто́нов	Е, на́й-по́сле разбра́х, това́, кое́то и́сках да зна́я...
На́дя	И́скате ли о́ще кафе́, господи́н Анто́нов?
Боя́н Анто́нов	Не, благодаря́. Не и́скам по́вече.

Кажи́ как ми́на после́дният ден.	*Tell me how the final day went.*
нормáлно	*OK, normally*
да го взе́ма	*to take him*
осо́бено	*especially*
да ѝ подари́ не́що за спо́мен	*to give her something as a memento*
Стра́шни са те́зи англича́ни!	*Incredible, these English!*
Ако́ бях аз, щях да забра́вя дори́ да ка́жа дови́ждане.	*If it had been me, I'd have forgotten even to say goodbye.*
И аз ако́ бях, и аз щях да го харе́сам!	*And if it had been me, I'd have liked it too!*
Ако́ бях аз, ня́маше да го прие́ма!	*If it had been me, I wouldn't have accepted it.*
Сти́га глу́пости!	*Enough of that nonsense!*
Продължа́вай!	*Go on!*
Избра́хме една́ сре́бърна гри́вна.	*We chose a silver bracelet.*
Да́де ли му пода́ръка?	*Did you give him the present?*
Той пока́за ли ти програ́мата?	*Did he show you the programme?*
Ка́за, че ще ми я пра́ти.	*He said he'd send it to me.*
Ще те посре́щне ли...?	*Will he be meeting you...?*
И ни́е щя́хме да го посре́щнем.	*And we too were intending to meet him.*
нався́къде	*everywhere*
по́вече	*more*
Щях да забра́вя на́й-ва́жното.	*I nearly forgot the most important thing.*
Той ка́за, че напре́двам.	*He said I was making progress.*
Сти́га...!	*Stop it...!*
Ако́ бях на тво́е мя́сто...	*If I had been in your place...*
ня́маше да се безпокоя́	*I wouldn't have worried*
на́й-по́сле разбра́х	*at last I have found out*
о́ще кафе́	*some more coffee*
Не и́скам по́вече.	*I don't want any more.*

Questions

1 Nikolai has been asked these questions. What should he answer?

- **a** Какво́ пра́вихте после́дния ден с Ма́йкъл Джо́нсън в хоте́ла?
- **b** Какво́ подари́ Ма́йкъл Джо́нсън на Неве́на?
- **c** Какъ́в пода́рък избра́хте за г-жа́ Джо́нсън?
- **d** Да́де ли на Ма́йкъл Джо́нсън пода́ръка от г-жа́ Анто́нова?
- **e** По и́мейла ли ще ти пра́ти той програ́мата?
- **f** На какъ́в ези́к гово́рихте це́лия ден?

2 True or false?

- **a** Неве́на мно́го харе́са беле́жника, ко́йто Ма́йкъл Джо́нсън ѝ подари́.
- **b** На́дя на не́йно мя́сто съ́що щя́ше да го харе́са.
- **c** Ма́йкъл Джо́нсън избра́ една́ сре́бърна гри́вна за дъщеря́ си.
- **d** Той пока́за на Никола́й програ́мата за не́говия престо́й в Че́лмсфорд.
- **e** Ако́ На́дя бе́ше на не́гово мя́сто, тя щя́ше да се безпоко́й.
- **f** Боя́н Анто́нов не можа́ да разбере́ това́, ко́ето и́скаше да зна́е.

How do you say it?

- Saying *If I were you*

Ако́ бях на тво́е мя́сто.	*If I had been in your place.*
Ако́ бях аз.	*If it had been me.*

- Saying that you nearly forgot

Щях да забра́вя.	*I nearly forgot* (*that reminds me*).

- Telling someone to stop doing something

Сти́га!	*Stop it!*
Доста́тъчно!	*Enough!*

- Saying *At last* and *Thank heavens!*

На́й-по́сле!	*At last!*
Сла́ва бо́гу!	*Thank heavens!* (lit: *Praise to God!*)

- Asking for and declining more

Йскам óще мáлко. *I would like a little more.*
Не йскам пóвече, благодарй. *I don't want any more, thank you.*

- Saying you would not have done something

Нямаше да отйда без тéбе. *I would not have gone without you.*

Grammar

1 Past tense of (да) дам – дáдох

You will remember from Unit 7 that in all forms other than the *I* form of **(да) дам** there is a **-д-** before the present tense endings **(да) дадéш, (да) дадé,** etc. As explained in Unit 14, the past endings are therefore added to **-о-**:

(аз)	дáдох	*I gave*	(нйе)	дáдо**хме**	*we gave*
(ти)	дáде	*you gave*	(вйе)	дáдо**хте**	*you gave*
(той) / (тя) / (то)	дáде	*he/she/it gave*	(те)	дáдо**ха**	*they gave*

Remember: (**a**) in the *you* singular and *he*, *she*, *it* forms an **-е** replaces the **-о**; (**b**) in the *he*, *she*, *it* form it is only the position of the stress that distinguishes between the present (да) дадé and the past дáде.

2 Past tense of (да) разберá and (да) изберá – разбрáх and избрáх

These verbs belong to a small group of **е**-pattern verbs which have **-ер-** in the present tense. So, too, does **(да) съберá** *to gather*. These verbs all drop the vowel **-е-** before **-р-** in the past tense:

(аз)	разбрáх	*I (have) understood*	(нйе)	разбрáхме	*we (have) understood*
(ти)	разбрá	*you (have) understood*	(вйе)	разбрáхте	*you (have) understood*
(той) / (тя) / (то)	разбрá	*he/she/it (has) understood*	(те)	разбрáха	*they (have) understood*

3 Past tense of и́скам – и́сках

И́скам has the same past endings as **и́мам** and **съм**:

(аз)	иска**х**	*I wanted*	(ни́е)	и́ска**хме**	*we wanted*
(ти)	и́ска**ше**	*you wanted*	(ви́е)	и́ска**хте**	*you wanted*
(той) (тя) (то)	и́ска**ше**	*he/she/it wanted*	(те)	и́ска**ха**	*they wanted*

So far you have come across two patterns of past forms: with and without **-ше** in the *you* singular and *he*, *she*, *it* forms. We have been concentrating on the one without **-ше** which is used to describe a sequence of completed actions. Verbs like **и́скам**, **и́мам** and **съм**, however, stand for *states* rather than actions. That is why they are used in a past tense form with **-ше** which is used for describing incomplete actions. (You will find more on how to use the past forms with **-ше** with other verbs too in Unit 17.)

4 Pronoun word order with giving, sending and showing verbs

With verbs of giving, like **(да) дам** and **(да) подаря́**, sending, **(да) пра́тя**, and showing **(да) пока́жа**, you usually need to mention both the thing that is given (or shown or sent) – the direct object – and the 'beneficiary' – the indirect object – of whatever has been given, shown or sent. (Look back to Unit 7!) When you use the short pronouns as direct and indirect objects, pay attention to the word order. Look at the following sentences taken from the dialogue:

Г-н Джо́нсън и́маше еди́н беле́жник и **ѝ го** подари́. (i.e. на не́я, беле́жника)	*Mr Johnson had a diary and gave it to her.*
Тя не **ми я** пока́за. (i.e. на ме́не, програ́мата)	*She did not show it to me.*
Той ще **ми я** пра́ти. (i.e. на ме́не, програ́мата)	*He will send it to me.*
Да́дох **му го**. (i.e. на г-н Джо́нсън, пода́ръка)	*I gave it to him.*

What you need to remember here is:

(a) most importantly, that the indirect object pronouns always come before the direct object ones

(b) when the verb is not the first word in the sentence, then both short pronouns come immediately before the verb

(c) when the verb does come first in the sentence, they both come immediately after the verb (cf. the last example).

5 Щях да *I was going to (but I didn't)*

To express things you wanted or intended to do, but didn't, you need to use the past forms of **ще**, which, in fact, comes from **ща**, an old verb meaning *to want*:

щях	*I intended*	щя́хме	*we intended*
щéше	*you intended*	щя́хте	*you intended*
щéше	*he/she intended*	щя́ха	*they intended*

Аз щях да дóйда, но не можáх.	*I was going to come, but I couldn't.*
Той щéше да дóйде, но не можá.	*He was going to come, but couldn't.*

You also use this construction to refer to things that nearly happened (but didn't quite!):

Щях да закъснéя, но взех таксú.	*I would have been late, but I took a taxi.*
Той щéше да отúде без тéбе.	*He was about to go without you.*

In either case **щях** is followed by **да** and a verb in the present tense in the same person as the main verb.

6 Щях да забрáвя *I nearly forgot/that reminds me*

One of the most common occurrences of **щях** is in the phrase **щях да забрáвя** meaning *I nearly forgot* (but didn't quite!). Here are all the forms:

щях да забрáвя	*I nearly forgot*
щéше да забрáвиш	*you nearly forgot*
щéше да забрáви	*he/she nearly forgot*
щя́хме да забрáвим	*we nearly forgot*
щя́хте да забрáвите	*you nearly forgot*
щя́ха да забрáвят	*they nearly forgot*

When used with the *I* form **щях да забрáвя** is probably best translated as *that reminds me*.

7 Ня́маше да / (*you, he, she, it, we, etc*) *would not have*

You will remember from Unit 10 that the negative form of **ще** is **ня́ма да**, which stays the same for all persons. Its past form **ня́маше да**, which also stays the same for all persons, is used as the negative of **щях**:

Аз ня́маше да отúда без тéбе.	*I would not have gone without you.*
Нúе ня́маше да отúдем без тéбе.	*We would not have gone without you.*

8 Акó... щях *I would have done it, if...*

Щях is often used with **акó** *if* to introduce conditions under which something would have taken place, had the conditions been fulfilled (which they weren't!) These are a type of so-called 'conditional' sentences and you will find out more about them in Unit 20. There are a number of examples in the dialogue:

Акó бях аз, щях да забрáвя да кáжа дорú довúждане.	*If it had been me, I'd have forgotten even to say goodbye.*
И аз акó бях, и аз щях да го харéсам.	*And if it had been me, I'd have liked it too.*

Sometimes the *if* element, **акó**, may only be implied:

И нúе щя́хме да го посрéщнем (**implied**: акó той úскаше), но той не úскаше.	*And we too were intending to meet him* (**implied**: *if he had wanted*), *but he didn't want us to.*

The negative form is again with **ня́маше да**:

Акó бях аз, ня́маше да го приéма.	*If it had been me, I wouldn't have accepted it.*
Акó бях на твóе мя́сто, ня́маше да се безпокоя́.	*If I had been in your place, I wouldn't have worried.*

9 Пóвече and óще *more*

Bulgarian has two different words for *more*: **пóвече** and **óще**. It is not always easy to choose the right one, but if you remember the following simple rules, it will help.

(a) По́вече is to **мно́го** what *more* is to *much* or *many*. It is the irregular comparative of **мно́го**. It is used when you make comparisons and want to say that one person, for example, knows more words (or has more money!) than another:

Ма́йкъл зна́е **мно́го** бъ́лгарски ду́ми.	*Michael knows a lot of Bulgarian words.*
Викто́рия зна́е **по́вече** (бъ́лгарски ду́ми).	*Victoria knows more (Bulgarian words).*
Той и́ма **мно́го** пари́; аз и́мам **по́вече**.	*He has a lot of money; I have more.*

(b) По́вече is also used when you have had enough of something and don't want any more. It tends to be used with negatives and therefore has to do with not going beyond a limit that has already been reached:

Йскате ли о́ще би́ра? Не, не и́скам **по́вече.**	*Would you like some more beer? No, I don't want any more.*

(c) You use **о́ще** – and this is the difficult one! – when you are thinking of adding to what is (or **was**, if you are asking for **another** glass of beer!) already there:

Йскате ли о́ще би́ра? Да, и́скам **о́ще** ма́лко.	*Would you like some more beer? Yes, I'd like a bit more.* (i.e. in addition)

10 Indirect (reported) speech

When you repeat something someone else has said, a question asked or an answer given, you are creating what is called 'indirect' or 'reported speech', forming 'indirect' questions and answers. This usually occurs after an introduction such as *she asked* or *she said*. In English, the tense of the verbs used in indirect speech is changed. (You will see this in the examples given below, all of which are based on dialogues you have already studied.) In Bulgarian, in most instances, you can use the original verb tense of the question and answer. All you need to do is change the person of the speaker, from the *I* form to the *he* form, for example.

Ма́йкъл Джо́нсън

Мно́го съм дово́лен от хоте́ла. — *I am very pleased with the hotel.*

Никола́й

Ма́йкъл Джо́нсън ка́за, че **е** мно́го дово́лен от хоте́ла. — *Michael Johnson said (that) he **was** very pleased with the hotel.*

Мáйкъл Джóнсън
Ще ти прáтя прогрáмата. — *I'll send you the programme.*

Николáй
Мáйкъл Джóнсън кáза, че **ще ми прáти** прогрáмата. — *Michael Johnson said (that) he he **would send me** the programme.*

Боя́н Антóнов (to Nadya)
Свобóден ли е Николáй? — *Is Nikolai free?*

Нáдя (to Nikolai)
Шéфът попи́та свобóден ли **си**. — *The boss asked if you **were** free.*

In questions like the last one, using **ли**, you can replace **ли** with **дали́** (*whether*). Note the change of word order:

Нáдя
Шéфът попи́та **дали́ си** свобóден. — *The boss asked **whether** you **were** free.*

Exercises

1 This, and the following two exercises, will help you to practise talking about things that might have happened – but didn't. Read out loud the two sentences in which John and Eli explain what they would have done if they hadn't had more pressing things to attend to:

Джон и Éли Йскаме да оти́дем на екскýрзия.
Акó ня́махме дрýга рáбота, щя́хме да оти́дем на екскýрзия.

Now read the following sentences out loud and following the model say what you would have done. Use **щя́хме да** or **щя́х да**.

a Йскахме да оти́дем на плаж. Акó ня́махме вáжна срéща ______.
b Йсках да оти́да на Ви́тоша. Акó ня́мах дрýга рáбота ______.
c Йскахме да оти́дем на тéнис. Акó ня́махме дрýга рáбота ______.
d Йсках да оти́да на гóсти. Акó ня́мах вáжна срéща ______.
e Йсках да оти́да на ски. Акó ня́мах дрýга рáбота ______

2 What would you buy from Bulgaria as a present? Using the words provided, write out sentences in answer to the question below:

Ако́ и́скахте да ку́пите пода́рък от Бълга́рия, какъ́в пода́рък щя́хте да ку́пите?

кути́я (*box*) **бонбо́ни**	**календа́р**
бути́лка (*bottle*) **ви́но**	**плака́т**
кути́я с луксо́зни (*deluxe*) **пли́кове**	**кни́га**

3 In the following sentences you are being asked what you would have done, had you been in the position of the speaker. Read the model out loud, then answer the questions first using **да**, then using **не**.

Model: Ако́ бе́ше на мо́е мя́сто, ще́ше ли да оти́деш на лети́щето?
Да, ако́ бях на тво́е мя́сто, щях да оти́да на лети́щето.
Не, ако́ бях на тво́е мя́сто, ня́маше да оти́да на лети́щето.

a Ако́ бе́ше на мо́е мя́сто, ще́ше ли да прие́меш пока́ната?
b Ако́ бе́ше на мо́е мя́сто, ще́ше ли да ку́пиш цветя́?
c Ако́ бе́ше на мо́е мя́сто, ще́ше ли да изпра́тиш моми́чето?

d Ако́ бя́хте на мо́е мя́сто, щя́хте ли да донесе́те пода́рък?

e Ако́ бя́хте на на́ше мя́сто, щя́хте ли да посре́щнете америка́неца?

4 The next two exercises will help you to practise and then to choose correctly between **о́ще** and **по́вече**. The first exercise will also help you practise using the past tense of **(да) дам**. So, following the model, complete the sentences altering or replacing the words in bold as necessary:

Model: **Да́дох** две ка́ртички от Ри́лския манасти́р (*monastery*) на Кен. Той **и́скаше** о́ще, но аз **ня́мах** по́вече.

a Неве́на ______ на Джон и Е́ли. Те ______.
b Ни́е ______ на тури́стите. Те ______.
c Г-н и г-жа́ Ко́линс ______ на сво́я прия́тел. Той ______.

5 Choose **о́ще** or **по́вече** in the sentences below, remembering that **о́ще** has the sense of *in addition* or *another* while **по́вече** tends to be used with negatives and in comparisons.

a Йскаш ли ______ кекс?
b ______ две би́ри, мо́ля.
c Ня́маме ______ вре́ме да ча́каме.
d Миле́на и́ма ______ англи́йски кни́ги от Никола́й.
e Г-жа́ Ко́линс полу́чи две писма́ от А́нглия и ______ едно́ писмо́ от Аме́рика.
f Благодаря́, не и́скам ______ ви́но.
g И́маме ______ пет мину́ти до замина́ването (*departure*) на самоле́та.

6 This exercise will help you practise the awkward irregular past forms of **(да) дам**, **(да) избера́** and **(да) разбера́**. First read the little story out loud.

Г-жа́ Анто́нова и́скаше да даде́ на Ма́йкъл Джо́нсън **ма́лък пода́рък.** Тя разбра́ от не́го, **че жена́ му мно́го оби́ча криста́лни** (*crystal*) **ва́зи**. Вче́ра сутринта́ тя оти́де **в магази́н за пода́ръци.** Йскаше да избере́ **на́й-краси́вата криста́лна ва́за**. Тя не ку́пи криста́лна ва́за, **защо́то криста́лните ва́зи бя́ха ужа́сно скъ́пи** (*expensive*). Г-жа́ Анто́нова избра́ **една́ краси́ва ико́на**. По́сле тя да́де пода́ръка за г-жа́ Джо́нсън **на Никола́й**.

Now change the story into a dialogue between yourself and a friend. To do this turn every sentence into a question. Your friend has the answers in the story. When asking questions, concentrate on the sections in heavy type and use **какво́, къде́, защо́** or **на кого́**.

7 Using the questions and statements in the first of these sentence pairs, complete the second, making the necessary alterations for indirect speech. Try to think of two possible versions for the **ли** question in (**b**).

a Къде́ и́ма магази́н за плодове́ и зеленчу́ци?
Г-н и г-жа́ Ко́линс пи́таха ______.

b Ймате ли свобо́дно вре́ме?
Неве́на попи́та г-н Джо́нсън ______.

c Кога́ Ма́йкъл Джо́нсън ще изпра́ти програ́мата?
Боя́н Анто́нов попи́та ______.

d Йма́м сре́ща в два часа́.
Миле́на ка́за, че ______.

e Ще зами́нем за Ва́рна на два́йсет и о́сми май.
Джон и Е́ли ка́заха, че ______.

f Благодаря́, не и́скам по́вече кафе́.
Ше́фът ка́за, че ______.

Do you understand?

Dialogue

Nikolai and Milena accept an offer to exhibit in England.

Никола́й Миле́на, видя́ ли плака́та, ко́йто ни подари́ Ма́йкъл Джо́нсън?

Миле́на Да, На́дя ми го пока́за.

Никола́й Мно́го е интере́сен, нали́? Той ка́за, че ще ни изпра́ти о́ще рекла́ми.

Миле́на Мо́же да ги даде́ на те́бе да ги донесе́ш.

Никола́й Зна́еш ли какво́? Той ми предло́жи да напра́вим изло́жба с на́ши плака́ти в А́нглия.

Миле́на Да, разбра́х от На́дя. Ти какво́ му отгово́ри?

Никола́й Ка́зах, че ще поми́слим. Ти на мо́е мя́сто ще́ше ли да се съгласи́ш ведна́га?

Миле́на Разби́ра се, на тво́е мя́сто ведна́га щях да прие́ма. Това́ е чуде́сна възмо́жност.

Никола́й О́ще не е́ къ́сно. Аз ве́че избра́х на́й-ху́бавите от мо́ите плака́ти. Ако́ и́скаш, донеси́ от тво́ите и аз ще му ги дам, като́ зами́на.

Миле́на Кога́ да ти ги донеса́?

Никола́й Аз мо́га да до́йда у вас и да ги взе́ма. Щях да забра́вя – ще ми даде́ш ли и англи́йските писа́ния, които и́маш?

Миле́на Ако́ зна́ех, че ги и́скаш, щях да ти ги донеса́.

Никола́й Предпочи́там да те изпра́тя до вас. Мо́же ли?

Миле́на Защо́ не? Ако́ ня́мах дру́га ра́бота, щях да те пока́ня на го́сти.

Никола́й Ни́що. Ще ме пока́ниш, кога́то и́маш по́вече свобо́дно вре́ме.

(да) изпра́тя, -тиш	*to send; accompany*
рекла́ма	*advertisement*
(да) предло́жа, -жиш	*to offer*
(да) поми́сля, -лиш	*to think* (something) *over*
до вас	*home*
криста́лен, -лна	*crystal*
луксо́зен, -зна	*deluxe*
скъп	*expensive, dear*

Questions

1 Какво́ о́ще ще изпра́ти Ма́йкъл Джо́нсън?
2 На кого́ мо́же да даде́ рекла́мите Ма́йкъл Джо́нсън?
3 От кого́ разбра́ Миле́на за чуде́сната възмо́жност?
4 Какво́ ще́ше да напра́ви Миле́на, ако́ бе́ше на мя́стото на Никола́й?
5 Какво́ ще́ше да напра́ви Миле́на ако́ зна́еше, че той и́ска писа́нията?
6 Какво́ предпочи́та Никола́й?

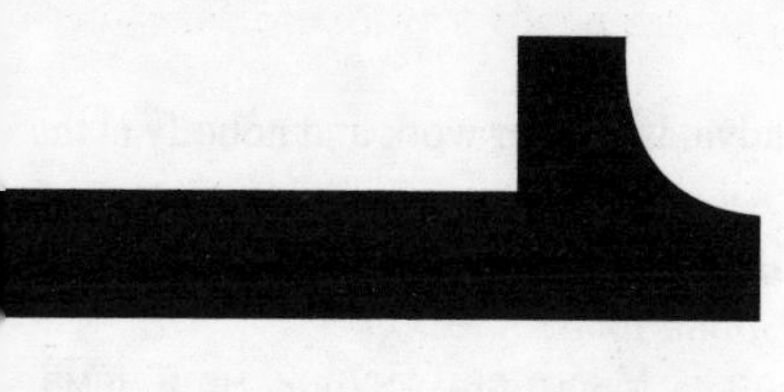

какво́ пра́веше тя?

what was she doing?

In this unit you will learn

- **how to talk about things breaking down/not working**
- **how to ask for help if something is wrong in your hotel room**
- **how to ask for help if you have trouble with your car**
- **how to refer to past events**

Dialogue

Boyan Antonov's secretary, Nadya, is late for work and nobody at the office knows why.

Боя́н Анто́нов Защо́ я ня́ма о́ще На́дя? Преди́ ви́наги и́дваше навре́ме. Бо́лна ли е?

Никола́й Не, не е́ бо́лна. Мно́го съм учу́ден, че я ня́ма, защо́то та́зи су́трин я видя́х от трамва́я. Оти́ваше на ра́бота с кола́та си.

Боя́н Анто́нов Миле́на, ти зна́еш ли защо́ я ня́ма?

Миле́на Ня́мам предста́ва. Аз съ́що я видя́х на у́лицата отдале́че, но не бе́ше с кола́.

Боя́н Анто́нов Какво́ пра́веше?

Миле́на Гово́реше с еди́н полица́й пред бо́лницата. Не мо́жех да чу́я какво́ гово́рят. Полица́ят ѝ пока́зваше зна́ка СПИ́РАНЕТО ЗАБРАНЕ́НО.

Никола́й Я́сно защо́ я ня́ма. Си́гурно и́ма неприя́тности с поли́цията.

Боя́н Анто́нов Ко́лко пъ́ти ѝ ка́звах да не парки́ра пред бо́лницата! Сега́ ще тря́бва да плати́ гло́ба.

(*A little later Nadya comes in.*)

На́дя Здраве́йте. Извиня́вайте за закъсне́нието, но и́мах неприя́тности с кола́та. Опи́твах мно́го пъ́ти да се оба́дя по телефо́на, но бе́ше зае́то.

Миле́на Да, аз гово́рех преди́ ма́лко. Кажи́ какво́ се слу́чи.

На́дя Оти́вах на ра́бота с кола́та, но пред бо́лницата мото́рът спря́ и не мо́жеше да запа́ли. Ня́мах предста́ва какво́ му е. От ня́колко дни мото́рът не рабо́теше добре́, но аз продължа́вах да ка́рам кола́та. Не мо́жех да напра́вя ни́що дру́го осве́н да оста́вя кола́та там.

Миле́на Аз те видя́х. Гово́реше с еди́н полица́й.

На́дя О, ужа́сен бе́ше, нали́? Ка́зах му, че кола́та и́ма повре́да, а той все ми пока́зваше зна́ка.

Боя́н Анто́нов Какво́ ста́на по́сле?

На́дя За щя́стие, видя́х еди́н позна́т. Той стое́ше на ъ́гъла до бо́лницата. Купу́ваше си ве́стник. Той наме́ри повре́дата ведна́га.

Никола́й Какво́ ѝ бе́ше на кола́та?

На́дя (*Evasively.*) Ни́що осо́бено. Повре́дата не бе́ше в мото́ра.

Миле́на	Защо́ не ни ка́жеш каква́ бе́ше повре́дата по́-то́чно?
На́дя	Е, добре́. Ня́маше бензи́н... За ща́стие, мо́ят позна́т и́маше ту́ба с бензи́н в бага́жника. (*General mirth.*)
Боя́н Анто́нов	Сле́дващия път ще бъ́де мото́рът. По́-добре́ иди́ ведна́га на серви́з!

Преди́ ви́наги и́дваше навре́ме.	*Before, she always used to come on time.*
Бо́лна ли е?	*Is she ill?*
Мно́го съм учу́ден.	*I'm very surprised.*
Оти́ваше на ра́бота.	*She was going to work.*
Ня́мам предста́ва.	*I have no idea.*
отдале́че	*from afar*
Какво́ пра́веше?	*What was she doing?*
Гово́реше с еди́н полица́й пред бо́лницата.	*She was talking to a policeman in front of the hospital.*
Не мо́жех да чу́я.	*I wasn't able to hear.*
Полица́ят ѝ пока́зваше зна́ка СПИ́РАНЕТО ЗАБРАНЕ́НО.	*The policeman was pointing out the NO STOPPING sign to her.*
я́сно защо́	*it's obvious why*
И́ма неприя́тности с...	*she is having trouble with...*
Ко́лко пъ́ти ѝ ка́звах...	*The times I've told her...*
гло́ба	*a fine*
опи́твах	*I tried* (kept trying)
аз гово́рех	*I was speaking*
какво́ се слу́чи	*what happened*
мото́рът спря́	*the engine stopped*
не мо́жеше да запа́ли	*wouldn't start*
от ня́колко дни	*for the past few days*
не рабо́теше добре́	*hasn't been working properly*
не мо́жех да напра́вя ни́що дру́го осве́н...	*all I could do was...*
ужа́сен бе́ше	*he was awful*
кола́та и́ма повре́да	*the car has broken down*
все ми пока́зваше зна́ка	*he kept pointing to the sign*
Какво́ ста́на по́сле?	*What happened next?*
за щъ́стие	*fortunately*
позна́т	*acquaintance*
той стое́ше на ъ́гъла	*he was standing on the corner*
Купу́ваше си ве́стник.	*He was buying himself* (cf. Unit 15) *a newspaper.*

повре́дата	*the fault*
ни́що осо́бено	*nothing special/nothing much*
бензи́н	*petrol*
ту́ба	*canister*
бага́жник	*boot/trunk*
сле́дващия път	*next time*
иди́ ведна́га на серви́з!	*go to a garage/service station immediately*

Questions

1 Try to answer the questions.

Answer pretending to be the person to whom the question is addressed.

- **a** Миле́на, бо́лна ли е На́дя?
- **b** Никола́й, защо́ си учу́ден, че На́дя о́ще не е́ на ра́бота?
- **c** Никола́й, какво́ пра́веше На́дя, кога́то я видя́?
- **d** Г-н Анто́нов, къде́ не тря́бваше да парки́ра На́дя?
- **e** На́дя, какво́ се слу́чи с кола́та?
- **f** На́дя, ти какво́ ка́за на полиця́я?

2 True or false?

- **a** Полица́ят пока́зваше на На́дя къде́ е серви́зът.
- **b** На́дя зна́еше добре́ какво́ му е на мото́ра.
- **c** Тря́бваше На́дя да оста́ви кола́та пред бо́лницата.
- **d** На́дя видя́ еди́н позна́т, ко́йто си купу́ваше ве́стник.
- **e** Не́йният позна́т не можа́ да наме́ри повре́дата.
- **f** Кола́та и́маше серио́зна повре́да.

How do you say it?

- Saying that something has gone wrong

Ду́шът не рабо́ти.	*The shower is not working.*
Кола́та и́ма повре́да.	*The car has broken down.*
Повре́дата е в мото́ра.	*The fault is in the engine.*
Асансьо́рът е повре́ден.	*The lift is out of order.*
И́мам неприя́тности с кола́та.	*I'm having trouble with the car.*

- Asking *What happened* or *What is the matter?*

Какво́ ста́на?	*What happened?*

Какво̀ се слу̀чи?	*What happened?*
Какво̀ ѝма?	*What's the matter?*
Какво̀ ста̀ва?	*What's up? What's going on?*

- Answering *Nothing special*

Нѝщо осо̀бено.	*Nothing special.*

- Expressing ignorance or surprise

Ня̀мам предста̀ва.	*I've no idea.*
Мно̀го съм учу̀ден.	*I'm very surprised.*

- Saying *Fortunately*

за щàстие	*fortunately/luckily*

(cf. **за съжалѐние** *unfortunately* Unit 5)

Grammar

1 The past imperfect

You will find below examples of phrases describing not completed actions in the past but actions that are seen as going on at a given past moment. Usually, these are background actions accompanying the description of a past event. In all such cases you need to use a set of past forms known as the past imperfect.

Какво̀ пра̀веше тя? *What was she doing?*

Examples based on the dialogue:

На̀дя отѝваше на ра̀бота.	*Nadya was going to work.*
Тя гово̀реше с едѝн полица̀й.	*She was talking to a policeman.*
Полица̀ят ѝ пока̀зваше зна̀ка.	*The policeman was showing her the sign.*

Here the reference to another past event (which happened when this one was going on) is only implied, but it can also be mentioned either:

- in phrases like **в това̀ врѐме** *just then*, **по същото врѐме** *at the same time* and **през ця̀лото врѐме** *all that time*
- or in accompanying phrases introduced by **кога̀то** *when*, that describe another action with the 'ordinary' past tense:

През ця̀лото врѐме Милѐна гово̀реше (past imperfect) по телефо̀на.	*All that time Milena was talking on the phone.*
В това̀ врѐме мо̀ят позна̀т си купу̀ваше (past imperfect) вѐстник.	*Just then my acquaintance was buying himself a newspaper.*

На́дя оти́ваше (past imperfect) на ра́бота, кога́то я видя́х. ('ordinary' past')	*Nadya was going to work when I saw her.*

Аз продължа́вах да ка́рам кола́та *I went on driving the car*

The verb **продължа́вам** *to continue*, *to go on* is naturally used in the past imperfect because it describes the action as still going on. However, even without such a verb you can use the past imperfect forms to render English expressions such as *I went on* and *I kept (on)* (doing something):

На́дя опи́тваше да се оба́ди.	*Nadya kept (on) trying to get through (on the phone).*

Whenever you use time words like **все** *all the time* you also need the past imperfect:

Полица́ят **все** ми пока́зваше зна́ка.	*The policeman kept showing me the sign.*

Note too that a similar meaning of continuing for a period of time is present in the following examples:

От ня́колко дни мото́рът не рабо́теше добре́.	*(For) the past few days the engine has not been working properly*
Преди́ де́сет годи́ни г-н Анто́нов рабо́теше като́ журнали́ст.	*Ten years ago Mr Antonov was working as a journalist.*

Тя ви́наги и́дваше на вре́ме *She always used to come on time*

You also need to use past imperfect forms for actions that were habitual or were repeated in the past. Frequently, words like **мно́го пъ́ти** *many times,* **ко́лко пъ́ти** *how many times* and **че́сто** are used to reinforce this meaning:

Ко́лко пъти ѝ ка́звах!	*The times I've told her!*
Ка́звах ѝ мно́го пъти.	*I've told her many times.*

Very often you can conveniently use the past imperfect forms to convey the meaning of the phrase '*used to*' (do something):

Преди́ На́дя ви́наги **и́дваше** навре́ме.	*Before, Nadya always **used to come** on time.*
Тя че́сто **пъту́ваше** с трамва́й.	*She often **used to go** by tram.*
Че́сто я **ви́ждах** от трамва́я.	*I often **used to see** her from the tram.*

2 How to form the past imperfect

As you can see from the list below, the endings for the past imperfect are almost identical with those for the simple past tense, except for the *you* singular and *he*, *she*, *it* forms. The main difference lies in the vowel preceding the endings.

(**a**) Verbs adding past imperfect endings to **-а-**: all **а**-pattern verbs:

(аз)	оти̇в**ах**	*I used to go/ was going*	(ни̇е)	оти̇в**ахме**	*we used to go/ were going*
(ти)	оти̇в**аше**	*you used to go/ were going*	(ви̇е)	оти̇в**ахте**	*you used to go/ were going*
(той) (тя) (то)	оти̇в**аше**	*he/she/it used to go/was going*	(те)	оти̇в**аха**	*they used to go/ were going*

(**b**) Verbs adding past imperfect endings to **-е-**: most verbs of **е-** and **и**-pattern except those in (**c**) below:

(аз)	гово̀р**ех**	*I was speaking*	мо̀ж**ех**	(ни̇е)	гово̀р**ехме**	мо̀ж**ехме**
(ти)	гово̀р**еше**	*you were speaking*	мо̀ж**еше**	(ви̇е)	гово̀р**ехте**	мо̀ж**ехте**
(той) (тя) (то)	гово̀р**еше**	*he/she/it was speaking*	мо̀ж**еше**	(те)	гово̀р**еха**	мо̀ж**еха**

(**c**) Verbs adding past imperfect endings to a stressed **-я̀-** (**-а̀-** after **ж, ч, ш**): these can be either verbs of **е-** or of **и**-pattern with the stress on the final syllable. But do note the change of **-я̀-/-а̀-** to **-ѐ-** in the *you* (singular) and *he*, *she*, *it* forms, as shown below in *to stand* **стоя̀** and *to hold* **държа̀**:

(аз)	сто**я̀х**/ държ**а̀х**	*I was standing/ holding*	(ни̇е)	сто**я̀хме**/ държ**а̀хме**	*we were standing/ holding*
(ти)	сто**ѐше**/ държ**ѐше**	*you were standing/ holding*	(ви̇е)	сто**я̀хте**/ държ**а̀хте**	*you were standing holding*
(той) (тя) (то)	сто**ѐше**/ държ**ѐше**	*he/she/it was standing/holding*	(те)	сто**я̀ха**/ държ**а̀ха**	*they were standing/holding*

3 Compare 'ordinary' past with past imperfect

When you compare the two tenses you will see that the past imperfect goes most naturally with imperfective verbs since they, too, describe imcomplete actions (Unit 12). That is why some verbs which make no distinction in the past form between perfective/imperfective like **съм, ѝмам** (Unit 13) and **тря̀бва** (Unit 15) normally appear in the past imperfect only.

Compare the following examples based on the dialogue (left-hand column), with similar sentences in the right-hand column using the corresponding perfective 'twin':

Past imperfect tense (used with imperfective verb)	**Past tense** (used with perfective verb)
ѝдвам Тя ѝдваше наврѐме. *She used to come on time.*	**(да) до̀йда** Вчѐра тя дойдѐ наврѐме. *Yesterday she came on time.*
отѝвам На̀дя отѝваше на ра̀бота. *Nadya was going to work.*	**(да) отѝда** На̀дя отѝде на ра̀бота в сѐдем часа̀. *Nadya went to work at seven o'clock.*
пока̀звам Полица̀ят ми пока̀зваше зна̀ка. *The policeman was showing me the sign.*	**(да) пока̀жа** Полица̀ят ми пока̀за зна̀ка. *The policeman showed me the sign.*
купу̀вам Мо̀ят позна̀т си купу̀ваше вѐстник. *My acquaintance was buying (himself) a newspaper.*	**(да) ку̀пя** Мо̀ят позна̀т си ку̀пи вѐстник. *My acquaintance bought (himself) a newspaper.*
ка̀звам Ка̀звах ѝ мно̀го пъ̀ти. *I've told her many times.*	**(да) ка̀жа** Ка̀зах ѝ вчѐра. *I told her yesterday.*
опѝтвам На̀дя опѝтваше да се оба̀ди. *Nadya kept trying to get through.*	**(да) опѝтам** На̀дя опѝта да се оба̀ди. *Nadya tried to get through.*

4 Можа́х and мо́жех *I managed/I was able (to do it)*

Unlike the verbs used in the examples above, **мо́га** *can, be able,* has no proper perfective counterpart. It does, however, still have both a past tense form **можа́х** – as you saw in Unit 15 – and a past imperfect form **мо́жех**. It is not easy to make a clear distinction between the usage of the two forms in English, but the following examples will show in practice the difference in meaning in Bulgarian:

Past tense

можа́х

Можа́х да обясня́.	*I managed to explain.*
Не можа́х да чу́я какво́ ка́за.	*I did not manage to hear what you/he/she said.*

Here there is a sense of having a go and then bringing the action to an end, either, as in the first example, because you managed to achieve what you wanted, or, as in the second, because you did not.

Past imperfect

мо́жех

Ми́налата годи́на **не мо́жех** да говóря бъ́лгарски.	*Last year I couldn't/wasn't able to speak Bulgarian.*
Мо́жех да обясня́, но не обясни́х.	*I could have explained, but didn't.*

Here it is more a case of having – or not having! – the ability or potential to do something over a period of time. It is a state rather than an action.

5 Мо́га *Being allowed*

Finally, you should note that when *can* really means *being allowed* – or *not allowed*! – to do something, in the past you should always use the past imperfect form of **мо́га**. Compare these present and past usages:

Present	**Past**
Там (не) мо́же да се парки́ра. *One can/cannot park there.* (i.e. is/isn't allowed)	Там (не) мо́жеше да се парки́ра. *One could/n't park there.* (i.e. was/wasn't allowed)
Мо́га да парки́рам там. *I can park there.* (i.e. am allowed)	Мо́жех да парки́рам там. *I could park there.* (i.e. was allowed)

Exercises

1 In this story you will learn about Nadya's misfortunes with the car in a slightly different way. Can you choose the missing words from the list?

От ня́колко дни кола́та на На́дя не ______ добре́. И́маше ня́какъв шум (*noise*) ______. На́дя не оти́де на ______. Тя продължа́ваше да ______ кола́та, защо́то не оби́ча да хо́ди на ра́бота ______ трамва́й.

Вче́ра На́дя ______ неприя́тности. Кога́то оти́ваше на ра́бота, кола́та спря́ ______ бо́лницата. Тя ми́слеше, че кола́та и́ма повре́да, но не зна́еше каква́ е ______. Тя ______ да оста́ви кола́та там. Пред бо́лницата ______ е забране́но. Еди́н полица́й и́скаше На́дя да плати́ ______. На́дя и́скаше да му обясни́, че кола́та ______ повре́да, но той все ѝ пока́зваше зна́ка СПИ́РАНЕТО ______. Еди́н ______ на На́дя ѝ помо́гна. Той разбра́ веднáга, че ______ не е́ повре́дена. Про́сто (*simply*) ня́маше ______!

бензи́н	и́маше	серви́з	рабо́теше
гло́ба	ка́ра	повре́дата	с
ЗАБРАНЕ́НО	кола́та	позна́т	спи́рането
и́ма	в мото́ра	пред	тря́бваше

2 Complete the short dialogues below, inserting **Какво́ пра́веше?** or **Какво́ пра́веха?** and the right personal pronoun. Read the sentences out loud and then try to repeat them without looking.

a Вче́ра видя́х Никола́й и Миле́на. ______? Ни́що осо́бено. Оти́ваха на о́пера.

b Вче́ра видя́х твоя́ приятел. ______? Ни́що осо́бено. Ча́каше трамва́я.

c Вче́ра видя́х Неве́на. ______? Ни́що осо́бено. Гово́реше с еди́н англича́нин.

d Вче́ра видя́хме Са́шко. ______? Ни́що осо́бено. Игра́еше фу́тбол.

e Вче́ра видя́х Викто́рия и Джордж Ко́линс. ______? Ни́що осо́бено. Купу́ваха плодове́.

f Видя́хме гру́па америка́нци. ______? Ни́що осо́бено. Стоя́ха на пла́жа.

3 Somebody has stolen your suitcase and a policeman is taking evidence from you. Answer his questions.

Полица̀й Кога̀ ста̀на това̀?
Ві̀е (Say that it happened 15 minutes ago.)
Полица̀й Къдѐ бя̀хте Вѝе, кога̀то това̀ се слу̀чи?
Вѝе (Say you were in the hotel.)
Полица̀й Какво̀ пра̀вехте?
Вѝе (Say you were waiting for a taxi.)
Полица̀й Ѝмаше ли мно̀го хо̀ра във фоайѐто на хотѐла?
Вѝе (Say there was only one man.)
Полица̀й Какво̀ пра̀веше той?
Вѝе (Say that he was speaking on the phone.)
Полица̀й Къдѐ бѐше портиѐрът (*the doorman*)?
Вѝе (Say that he was standing in front of the hotel.)
Полица̀й Благодаря̀. Ще отѝда да гово̀ря с портиѐра.

4 Practise saying what you used to do for a job by changing the sentences to the *I* form:

a Предѝ те рабо̀теха в едѝн магазѝн.
b Предѝ две годѝни На̀дя рабо̀теше в музѐя.
c Предѝ той рабо̀теше като̀ сервитьо̀р. (Сервитьо̀рка is *waitress*, remember!)
d Викто̀рия и Джордж Ко̀линс рабо̀теха като̀ учѝтели предѝ мно̀го годѝни.
e Предѝ нѝе рабо̀техме в ба̀нката.

5 In this exercise you can check how good you are at distinguishing between repeated and single actions in the past. Do not forget that repeated actions usually go with an imperfective verb and single actions with a perfective one. Choose from the pair given with each set of sentences.

a **ѝдваше/дойдѐ**?
i На̀дя вѝнаги ______ ра̀но на ра̀бота.
ii Вчѐра На̀дя ______ къ̀сно на ра̀бота.

b **ка̀зваше/ка̀за**?
i Г-н Анто̀нов чѐсто ______ на На̀дя да не паркѝра пред бо̀лницата.
ii Милѐна ______, че не зна̀е къдѐ е На̀дя.

c **купу̀вах/ку̀пих**?
i Вчѐра ______ пода̀рък за бра̀т ми.
ii Предѝ аз чѐсто ______ вѐстници.

Do you understand?

Dialogue

In the Odessa Hotel outside the Collins' room, there is a bouquet of birthday surprises for Victoria.

г-жá Кóлинс	(*Rather flustered.*) Мóля Ви, кажéте на рецéпцията, че не мóга да спра дýша. Крáнът е повréден. Освéн товá, не знáя къдé е мъжът ми. Трябва да го намéря.
Камериéрка	Аз видях г-н Кóлинс предú мáлко. Отúваше към Мóрската градúна.
г-жá Кóлинс	Такá ли? Мнóго съм учýдена. Той нúкъде не хóди без мéне. Ще пúтам портиéра далú знáе къдé е мъжът ми.
Гост на хотéла	(*Overhearing and joining in.*) Аз същo видях г-н Кóлинс. Той говóреше с една женá пред вхóда на Мóрската градúна.
г-жá Кóлинс	Но той не познáва нúкого тук. Чýхте ли за каквó говóрят?
Гост на хотéла	Нúщо осóбено... Г-н Кóлинс пúташе за посóката, но не разбрáх къдé úскаше да отúде.
г-жá Кóлинс	Но той не знáе добрé бъ́лгарски. Кóлко пъ́ти му кáзвах да не излúза сам! Той е тóлкова разсéян. Ще пресечé ýлицата не кáкто трябва и ще úма неприятности. Ще трябва да платú глóба.
Портиéр	(*Seeing Mrs Collins in a state of agitation.*) Добрó ýтро, г-жá Кóлинс. Неприятности ли úмате?
г-жá Кóлинс	За съжалéние, да. Пъ́рво крáнът на дýша се развалú. Пóсле мъжът ми изчéзна. От някoлко дни дýшът не рабóтеше добрé, а сегá изóбщо не мóга да го спра.
Портиéр	Не сé безпокóйте, аз същo видях г-н Кóлинс. Изглéждаше съвсéм добрé. Купýваше нéщо, но не можáх да вúдя каквó.

(*Mr Collins appears at the end of the corridor.*)

г-жá Кóлинс	Джордж, каквó стáна? Защó излúзаш сам, без мéне? Страхýвах се, че ще загýбиш пъ́тя.
г-н Кóлинс	Е, мúсля, че мóга сам да кýпя букéт цветя́!

	(*Produces a bunch of flowers from behind his back.*) Чести́т рожде́н ден, ми́ла Ви́ки!
Всички	Чести́т рожде́н ден, госпо́жо Ко́линс! Ни́е вси́чки зна́ехме къде́ е г-н Ко́линс.
Камерие́рка	О́леле, забра́вихме за кра́на! Тря́бва бързо да се оба́дя на ма́йстора.

кран	*tap*
освéн	*apart from, besides*
гради́на	*garden*
дали́	*whether*
изли́зам, -заш	*to go out*
разсе́ян	*absent-minded*
кра́нът се развали́	*the tap is not working*
(да) изче́зна, -неш	*to disappear*
е!	*well, really!*
буке́т	*bunch*
мил	*dear*
камериéрка	*chambermaid*
о́леле!	*oh dear me!*
ма́йстор	*workman* (here: *plumber*)

Questions

1 Защо́ г-жа́ Ко́линс не мо́же да спре ду́ша?
2 Какво́ пра́веше г-н Ко́линс, кога́то го видя́ еди́н гост на хоте́ла?
3 Какви́ неприя́тности и́ма г-жа́ Ко́линс?
4 Какво́ пра́веше г-н Ко́линс, кога́то го видя́ портие́рът?
5 Какво́ зна́еха вси́чки?

ве́че съм реши́ла

I have already made up my mind

In this unit you will learn

- **how to talk about results: things that did or did not happen in the past and have affected the present**
- **how to say you have forgotten something**
- **how to talk about your leisure**

Dialogue

Nikolai has come to collect Milena for the opera but finds she is not yet dressed for going out.

Николáй Милéна, óще не сѝ готóва. Не сѝ забрáвила, че тáзи вéчер сме на óпера, нали́?

Милéна Не, не съм, но óще не съм се облякла.

Николáй Каквó прáви досегá?

Милéна Еднá приятелка дойдé на гóсти. Бях я покáнила преди́ да кýпиш билéти за óпера.

Николáй Óще ли не сѝ е оти́шла?

Милéна Оти́де си преди́ петнáйсет минýти.

Николáй Хáйде, ще закъснéем, акó не сé облечéш пó-бързо. Представлéнието запóчва в сéдем часá.

Милéна Няма да закъснéем. Ще бъдем там в сéдем.

Николáй Мнóго се съмнявам.

Милéна Вéче съм реши́ла каквó да облекá. Вечéрял ли си?

Николáй Не, не съм. Ми́сля да вечéряме зáедно след представлéнието.

Outside the opera house. They've made it for 7 o'clock but the place looks suspiciously empty. They go to the ticket office.

Милéна Запóчнало ли е представлéнието?

Касиéрка Óще не, госпóжице. Представлéнието е от сéдем и полови́на.

Николáй Милéна, съжалявам! Вината е мóя. Нямам представа как съм напрáвил такáва грéшка.

Милéна Няма значéние, слýчва се. Врéмето е хýбаво. Хáйде да се разхóдим.

Николáй Съглáсен съм. Такá ще бъдем зáедно полови́н час пóвече. Мóже да си кýпим сладолéд.

Милéна Разби́ра се. Няма да ни бъде скýчно.

Николáй О, не..! (*After a pause, groaning and throwing up his arms.*) Ами́ сегá?!

Милéна Каквó се е слýчило?

Николáй Не съм взел пари́! Забрáвил съм ги в джóба на джи́нсите си.

Милéна Мнóго си смéшен! Стáнал си мнóго разсéян. Си́гурно си се умори́л от мнóго ýчене...

Николáй Да, ни́кога не съм бил тóлкова разсéян. Но дали́ е сáмо от ýчене е друг въпрóс...

не си́ забрáвила	*you haven't forgotten*
Óще не съм се облякла.	*I haven't dressed yet.*
досегá	*until now*
еднá приятелка дойдé	*a friend came*
Бях я покáнила.	*I had invited her.*
Óще ли не си́ е оти́шла?	*Hasn't she gone yet?*
акó не сé облечéш	*if you don't get dressed*
представлéние	*performance*
Мнóго се съмнявам.	*I very much doubt it.*
Вéче съм реши́ла.	*I have already made up my mind.*
Вечéрял ли си?	*Have you had supper?*
Не, не съм.	*No, I haven't.*
Запóчнало ли е представлéнието?	*Has the performance started?*
Винáта е мóя.	*It's my fault.*
как съм напрáвил такáва грéшка	*how I made such a mistake*
Хáйде да се разхóдим.	*Let's go for a walk.*
Няма да ни бъде скýчно.	*We won't be bored.*
Ами́ сегá?!	*And now what?!*
Каквó се е слýчило?	*What's happened?/ What's the matter?*
Не съм взел пари́!	*I haven't taken any money!*
Забрáвил съм ги в джóба на джи́нсите си.	*I must have left it in the pocket of my jeans.*
смéшен	*funny*
Стáнал си мнóго разсéян.	*You have become very absent-minded.*
Си́гурно си се умори́л от мнóго ýчене...	*You must have got tired with all that studying...*
ни́кога не съм бил тóлкова разсéян.	*I have never been so absent-minded.*
друг въпрóс	*a different matter*

Questions

1 Try to answer the questions.

- **a** Каквó не é напрáвила Милéна?
- **b** Оти́шла ли си е приятелката на Милéна?
- **c** Когá предлáга Николáй да вечéрят?
- **d** Защó не é запóчнало представлéнието?
- **e** Какъ̀в е стáнал Николáй?
- **f** От каквó се е умори́л Николáй спорéд Милéна?

2 True or false?

- **a** Милéна бéше покáнила еднá приятелка предú Николáй да кýпи билéти.
- **b** Ще закъснéят, защóто Милéна óще не é решúла каквó да облечé.
- **c** Николáй вéче е вечéрял.
- **d** Представлéнието óще не é запóчнало.
- **e** Николáй няма предстáва как е напрáвил такáва грéшка.
- **f** На Николáй ще му е скýчно с Милéна.

How do you say it?

- Acknowledging guilt

Винáта е мóя.	*It's my fault.*
Мóя е винáта.	*The fault is mine.*

- Asking someone if they have eaten

Вечéрял(а) ли си?	*Have you had supper?*
Вечéряли ли сте?	*Have you had supper?*

- Expressing disbelief

Съмнявам се.	*I doubt it.*
Мнóго се съмнявам.	*I very much doubt it.*
Не é вярно.	*It's not true.*
Товá е друг въпрóс.	*That's a different matter.*

- Making little of something

Няма значéние.	*It doesn't matter./Never mind.*

- Expressing panic and confusion

Амú сегá?!	*Now what?!*
Óлеле!	*Oh dear me!*

- Saying *I've made up my mind*

Вéче съм решúл(а).	*I've already made up my mind.*

Grammar

1 Вéче съм решúл(а) *I have already made up my mind*

In Bulgarian, as in English, you need a special tense to talk about actions that happened in the past, but the results of which are still evident in the present. We can call this the **present perfect tense**. You usually use it when you are focusing on the effect a past action has on the here and now. You are not interested or not sure when it happened. Very often the meaning of result is reinforced by words like **вéче** *already* or **óще не** *not yet.*

Here are some examples based on the dialogue – all, notice, corresponding to an English form using *have* or *has*:

Не съм забрáвила.	*I haven't forgotten.*
Óще ли не сú е отúшла?	*Hasn't she gone yet?*
Запóчнало ли е представлéнието?	*Has the performance started?*
Óще не é запóчнало.	*It hasn't started yet.*

2 How to form the present perfect tense

As in English, the **present perfect** is made up of two parts. However, instead of *have* or *has*, Bulgarian uses the present forms of **съм** together with a distinct form of the main verb, called the **past participle**. (In English this is the form used with *have* or *has* in *have forgotten*, *have made* and *has started* in the translations of the sentences you have just read. The form often ends in *-ed* or *-en*.) The past participle in Bulgarian ends in **-л** in the masculine, but you can think of it as an adjective, for it changes its ending to **-ла** in the feminine, **-ло** in the neuter and **-ли** in the plural. You will find a list of past participles in the Appendix.

Here is a list of forms in all persons for **вечéрям**. Notice the word order!

вечéрял(а) съм/ не съм вечéрял(а)	*I have/have not had supper (i.e. dined!)*
вечéрял(а) си/ не сú вечéрял(а)	*you have/ have not had supper*
вечéрял(а) е/ не é вечéрял(а)	*he/she has/ has not had supper*
вечéряли сме/ не смé вечéряли	*we have/ have not had supper*

вечéряли сте/ не стé вечéряли	*you have/ have not had supper*
вечéряли са/ не cá вечéряли	*they have/ have not had supper*

Word order with this tense is awkward. Normally **съм** (or **си**, **е**, etc.) comes immediately before the past participle, as in the **не** (negative) forms above, and in the following examples:

Николáй е напрáвил грéшка.	*Nikolai has made a mistake.*
Милéна не é забрáвила.	*Milena hasn't forgotten.*

You will remember, however, that **съм** (or **си**, **е**, etc.) can never come first in a sentence. When the past participle comes first, **съм** (or **си**, **е**, etc.) comes immediately after it, as in the positive forms on the previous page.

Word order is particularly awkward when you have to use a verb with **се** like Óще не съ́м **се** облякла *I haven't got dressed yet.* In the Appendix you will find a table setting out the relative positions of **съм** and **се**.

3 How to form past participles

Regular past participles

To form regular past participles you start from the past *I* form of the verb and replace the ending **-х** by **-л**, **-ла**, **-ло-**, **-ли**. Again a look at the Appendix will help!

Past tense	Past participle
забрáвих	забрáвил, забрáвила, забрáвило, забрáвили (*forgotten*)
решúх	решúл, решúла, решúло, решúли (*decided*)
хóдих	хóдил, хóдила, хóдило, хóдили (*gone, walked*)
вечéрях	вечéрял, вечéряла, вечéряло, вечéряли (*dined*)
видя́х	видя́л, видя́ла, видя́ло, видéли (*seen*)
запóчнах	запóчнал, запóчнала, запóчнало, запóчнали (*begun*)

Irregular past participles

Now for some *irregular* past participles:

(**a**) With verbs ending in **-сох**, **-зох**, **-кох** (Unit 14), replace **-ох** by **-ъл** and drop the **-ъ-** in the feminine, neuter and plural:

обля́к**ох**	обля́к**ъл**, обля́к**ла**, обля́к**ло**, облéк**ли*** (*dressed*)
донéс**ох**	донéс**ъл**, донéс**ла**, донéс**ло**, донéс**ли** (*brought*)

(*See Unit 8 for the change from **я** to **е**.)

(**b**) **(да) оти́да** has **оти́шъл (-шла, -шло, -шли)** *gone* for its past participle, and **(да) дóйда** has **дошъ́л (-шлá, -шлó, -шли́)** *come, arrived.* You will recognize **дошъ́л** from the expression **Добрé дошъ́л!** (Unit 6). Here too, notice, you drop the **-ъ-** in the feminine, neuter and plural:

Прия́телката ми óще не си́ е оти́шла.	*My friend has not yet gone.*
Николáй óще не é дошъ́л.	*Nikolai has not yet come.*

(**c**) The past participle of **съм** is бил, билá, билó, били́

Ни́кога не съм бил тóлкова щастли́в.	*I've never been so happy.*
Ни́кога не съм билá в Москвá.	*I've never been to Moscow.*

4 *Ever* and *never* with the present perfect

The present perfect is frequently used in statements and questions including or implying the adverbs *ever* and *never*:

Хóдили ли сте в Пари́ж?	*Have you (ever) been to Paris?*
Не, ни́кога не съм хóдил в Пари́ж./ Не, не съм.	*No, I've never been to Paris./ No, I haven't.*
Да, хóдил съм.	*Yes, I have.*

Note that in Bulgarian the negative answer is, like the English, without the participle **хóдил**. (See Unit 11.5 for a special use of the Bulgarian present where English has present perfect *has/have been* – after **от**.)

5 The past perfect

Бях я **покáнила** (преди́ да кýпиш билéти).	*I had invited her* (*before you bought tickets*).

You need this form – the past perfect tense – to refer to events that took place before other past events. It differs from the present perfect tense only in that you use the past forms of *to be* instead of the present. Here is a list of all forms of the verb *to go*:

аз **бях оти́шъл/-шла**	*I had gone*	ние **бя́хме оти́шли**	*we had gone*
ти **бéше оти́шъл/-шла**	*you had gone*	вие **бя́хте оти́шли**	*you had gone*
той **бéше оти́шъл**	*he had gone*	те **бя́ха оти́шли**	*they had gone*
тя **бéше оти́шла**	*she had gone*		
то **бéше оти́шло**	*it had gone*		

6 (Да) Взéма *To take*

This verb loses the **-м-** in its past forms, and also in its past participle:

Past tense

аз взех	*I took*	**нúе взéхме**	*we took*
ти взе	*you took*	**вúе взéхте**	*you took*
(той) (тя) (то) } **взе**	*he/she/it took*	**те взéха**	*they took*

Past participle

взел, взéла, взéло, взéли (*taken*)

The verbs **(да) наéма** *to rent* (Unit 11) and **(да) приéма** *to accept* and some other verbs related to **(да) взéма** (Unit 16) also lose the **-м-** in the same way:

Мáйкъл Джóнсън наé колá и отúде в Бóровец.	*Michael Johnson rented a car and went to Borovets.*
Те приéха покáната.	*They accepted the invitation.*

7 (Да) се облекá *To get dressed;* (да) се съблекá *to get undressed*

A number of sound changes occur in these verbs and also in **(да) пресекá** *to cross* (the street). First, you replace **-к-** by **-ч-** before all endings containing **-е-**. Second, in the past, the shift of stress means that you have to change the first **-е-** to **-я́-** (Unit 8):

Present

Тря́бва да	се облекá	*I must get dressed*
	се облечéш	*you must get dressed*
	се облечé	*you/she/it must get dressed*
	се облечéм	*we must get dressed*
	се облечéте	*you must get dressed*
	се облекáт	*they must get dressed*

Past

Аз се обля́кох/обля́кох се	*I got dressed*
Ти се облéче	*You got dressed*
Той/тя/то се облéче	*He/she/it got dressed*
Нúе се обля́кохме	*We got dressed*
Вúе се обля́кохте	*You got dressed*
Те се обля́коха	*They got dressed*

What with the rules for positioning **се**, these sound changes may seriously undermine your desire to talk about getting dressed, or undressed, in Bulgarian. But it is still worth trying!

Exercises

1 Practise using the present perfect by rearranging the words so as to reproduce sentences from the dialogue.

a е, представлéнието, ли, запóчнало ...?
b се, не, óще, съм, облякла
c грéшка, как, нямам, съм, представа, напрáвил, такáва ...!
d слýчило, каквó, е, се ...?
e решúла, вéче, каквó, съм, да облекá

2 Read the sentences below in which a friend is inviting you to see what Nikolai has done:

a Виж, Николáй е дошъл!
b Виж, Николáй е донéсъл цветя!
c Виж, Николáй е кýпил бонбóни!
d Виж, Николáй е напрáвил кафé!

Now you say it is not true (**Не é вярно**), it is Nadya who has done all these things. Don't forget to make the participle feminine!

3 The receptionist at the Odessa hotel asks Mr and Mrs Collins whether they have been to Borovets: Хóдили ли сте в Бóровец?

Ask the following people the same question:

a a young girl
b the couple sharing your table
c an elderly gentleman
d a small boy

4 A friend, who has taken you out, suddenly says: Забрáвил съм да взéма парú. Стáнал съм мнóго разсéян! Now imagine:

a You are a woman and you have forgotten to take an umbrella.
b You are a man and you have forgotten to take a camera.
c You and your partner have forgotten to take any money.

What would you say? Don't forget the second half of the answer!

5 Read the sentences on the next page and then, using the model: Нямаше мляко. Милéна бéше забрáвила да кýпи мляко, complete the other sentences in the same way:

a Ня́маше бúра. Г-н Антóнов ______.
b Ня́маше хляб. Г-жá Антóнова ______.
c Ня́маше домáти. Г-н и г-жá Кóлинс ______.
d Ня́маше газúрана водá. Аз ______.

6 Continuing with our absent-minded, forgetful heroes, what would you say if you thought you'd taken, but now can't find:

(*a*) ФÓТОАПАРÁТ

(*b*) ШÁПКА

(*c*) СНÚМКИ

(*d*) БЕЛÉЖНИК

(*e*) КНÚГА

(*f*) BÉСТНИК

Base your answers on the model:
Взех чадъ́ра, но сегá го ня́ма. Сúгурно съм го загу́бил/а.

Do you understand?

Dialogue

Victoria Collins comes back from the beach. George, who still has not got over the mild sunstroke he suffered in Unit 15, has stayed back at the hotel. They increasingly speak Bulgarian to one another.

Викто́рия	Как се чу́вствaш, Джордж?
Джордж	Го́ре-до́лу. Но глава́та о́ще ме боли́.
Викто́рия	О́ще не си́ се облякъл. Какво́ си пра́вил ця́ла су́трин?
Джордж	Че́тох уче́бника по бъ́лгарски – *Teach Yourself Bulgarian*.
Викто́рия	Какво́ но́во нау́чи?
Джордж	В Бълга́рия и́ма ху́баво море́. В Бълга́рия и́ма ху́баво ви́но. И ве́че да́же и́ма ху́бава би́ра.
Викто́рия	Мно́го добре́, мно́го си нау́чил.
Джордж	Но ня́ма игри́ще за голф! Викто́рия, ти не мо́жеш да разбере́ш! Ску́чно ми е! I AM BORED!
Викто́рия	Съжаля́вам, Джордж. Вина́та е твоя́! Ако́ не бе́ше стоя́л на слъ́нце то́лкова, сега́ ще́ше да мо́жеш да хо́диш на плаж. И не е́ вя́рно. Тук и́ма игри́ще за голф.
Джордж	Така́ ли? Защо́ не си́ ми ка́зала досега́?
Викто́рия	Не си́ ме пи́тал.
Джордж	Къде́ и́ма игри́ще?
Викто́рия	На Зла́тни пя́съци. Това́ е бли́зо до Ва́рна. Ни́кога не сме́ хо́дили там.
Джордж	Ха́йде да оти́дем!
Викто́рия	Добре́, ще оти́дем. Но о́ще не сме́ обя́двали.
Джордж	А с какво́ ще игра́я? Не съм взел сти́ковете си.
Викто́рия	Предпола́гам, че ще мо́жеш да взе́меш сти́кове под на́ем. Пи́тай францу́зина от съсе́дната ста́я. Той ве́че е бил там.

го́ре-до́лу	*so-so* (lit. *up and down*)
(да) нау́ча, -чиш	*to learn*
игри́ще за голф	*golf course*
стик	*golf club*
съсе́ден, -дна	*next (door), neighbouring*
чета́, -те́ш	*to read*

Questions

1 Какво́ го боли́ Джордж о́ще?
2 Какво́ му е на не́го?
3 Какво́ не е́ ка́зала досега́ Викто́рия на Джордж?
4 Какво́ не е́ взел Джордж?
5 С какви́ сти́кове ще игра́е Джордж?
6 Кой ве́че е игра́л голф на Зла́тни пя́съци?

9

и́мате ли опла́квания?

is there anything wrong?

In this unit you will learn

- **how to complain if things go wrong**
- **how to distinguish between reporting what you know first hand and what you know from other sources**

Dialogue

Nevena is listening to the complaints of a businessman who has not been lucky with his room.

Би́знесмен Добро́ у́тро, госпо́жице! И́скам да сменя́ ста́ята си. Не съм дово́лен от ста́ята, коя́то сте ми да́ли.

Неве́на Какви́ опла́квания и́мате?

Би́знесмен Конта́ктът за самобръсна́чка не рабо́ти. Прозо́рецът е счу́пен, вентила́торът в ба́нята е развале́н. Сно́щи и телефо́нът се развали́! Осве́н това́, и́ма мно́го шум. Ста́ята е то́чно над рестора́нта и му́зиката не спи́ра ця́ла нощ!

Неве́на О, съжаля́вам, господи́не. Ще опи́там да Ви наме́ря по́-добра́ стая́. Мо́ля, поча́кайте във фоайе́то.

Би́знесмен Сега́ не мо́га да ча́кам, защо́то и́мам ва́жна сре́ща. Ще се вЪрна в хоте́ла към шест часа́.

Неве́на Добре́, не се́ безпоко́йте. Аз ще гово́ря с упра́вителя.

(*Later, in the manager's office.*)

Неве́на Господи́нът от стая́ сто и двана́йсета и́ска да смени́ ста́ята си.

Упра́вител От какво́ се опла́ква?

Неве́на Ка́зва, че конта́ктът за самобръсна́чка не рабо́тел, прозо́рецът бил счу́пен. Вентила́торът и телефо́нът били́ развале́ни.

Упра́вител Е, не е́ то́лкова стра́шно. Кажи́ му, че вси́чко ще попра́вим.

Неве́на Не́го го ня́ма. Ка́за, че и́мал ва́жна сре́ща. Щял да се върне към шест часа́.

Упра́вител Мно́го добре́. Като́ се върне, ста́ята му ще бъде наре́д.

Неве́на Страху́вам се, че пак ня́ма да бъде дово́лен. И́ска дру́га стая́, защо́то и́мало мно́го шум от рестора́нта.

Секрета́рка И дру́ги го́сти се опла́кват от шум. Ка́зват, че не мо́жели да спят от шума́ на трамва́ите.

Упра́вител Да, зна́я. Тога́ва ще го сло́жим в стая́ на двана́йсетия ета́ж. Там е по́-ти́хо.

Неве́на Добра́ иде́я. Да се надя́ваме, че асансьо́рите рабо́тят!

И́скам да сменя́ ста́ята си.	*I want to change my room.*
ста́ята, коя́то сте ми да́ли	*the room you have given me*
Какви́ опла́квания и́мате?	*What is wrong?*
конта́ктът за самобръсна́чка	*shaver socket*
счу́пен	*broken*
вентила́тор	*extractor fan*
е развале́н	*is broken/has gone wrong*
Сно́щи и телефо́нът се развали́.	*Last night the phone, too, went wrong.*
осве́н това́	*apart from that*
шум	*noise*
Му́зиката не спи́ра ця́ла нощ.	*The music doesn't stop all night.*
ще опи́там	*I'll try*
упра́вител	*manager, director*
От какво́ се опла́ква?	*What is he complaining about?*
конта́ктът за самобръсна́чка не рабо́тел	(he says) *the shaver socket doesn't work*
прозо́рецът бил счу́пен	(he says) *the window is broken*
вентила́торът и телефо́нът били́ развале́ни	(he says) *the extractor fan and the telephone aren't working*
Не е́ то́лкова стра́шно.	*That's not so terrible.*
Вси́чко ще попра́вим.	*We'll put everything right.*
и́мал ва́жна сре́ща	(he said) *he had an important meeting*
щял да се въ́рне	(he said) *he'd be back*
и́мало мно́го шум	(he said) *there was a lot of noise*
И дру́ги го́сти се опла́кват от шум.	*Other hotel residents too complain of the noise.*
не мо́жели да спят от шума́ на трамва́ите	(they say) *they couldn't sleep because of the noise from the trams*
Тога́ва ще го сло́жим в стá́я на двана́йсетия ета́ж.	*Then we'll put him in a room on the twelfth floor.*

Questions

1 Try to answer the questions.

- **a** Какво́ и́ска би́знесменът?
- **b** Какви́ опла́квания и́ма той?
- **c** Защо́ е шу́мна ста́ята му?
- **d** Защо́ би́знесменът не мо́же да ча́ка?

e От какъ̀в шум се опла́кват и дру́ги го́сти на хоте́ла?
f Къде́ предла́га упра́вителят да сло́жат би́знесмена?

2 True or false?

a Би́знесменът ка́за, че бил householdдово́лен от ста́ята, коя́то са му да́ли.
b Огледа́лото (*the mirror*) било́ счу́пено.
c Би́знесменът ка́за, че в ста́ята му и́мало мно́го шум от рестора́нта.
d Той щял да се въ̀рне след ма́лко.
e Дру́ги го́сти също се опла́квали от шума́ на трамва́ите.

How do you say it?

- Asking to have something changed

Ѝскам да сменя́ ста́ята си. — *I'd like to change my room.*

- Saying something *isn't working*

Асансьо́рът не рабо́ти. — *The lift isn't working.*
Ду́шът е развале́н. — *The shower has gone wrong.*
Прозо́рецът е счу́пен. — *The window is broken.*

- Recognizing requests for possible complaints

Ѝмате ли опла́квания? — *Is there anything wrong?*
Какви́ опла́квания и́мате? — *What complaints do you have?*
От какво́ се опла́квате? — *What is your complaint?* (The doctor may ask you this too!)

- Expressing dissatisfaction

Не съ̀м дово́лен/дово́лна от хоте́ла. — *I'm not happy with the hotel.*
Ѝскам да се опла́ча. — *I want to make a complaint.*

- Apologizing

Ѝскам да се извиня́. — *I want to apologize.*

- Reassuring someone

Не се́ безпоко́йте! — *Don't worry.*

Grammar

1 Renarrated forms

(Кáза, че) и́мало мнóго шум	*(He said) there was a lot of noise.*

You will have noticed in the dialogue that when Nevena repeats the businessman's complaints she puts them in a slightly different form:

Би́знесмен Контáктът... **не рабóти.**
Невéна Контáктът... **не рабóтел.**

Би́знесмен Прозóрецът **е счу́пен.**
Невéна Прозóрецът **бил счу́пен.**

Би́знесмен Сегá... **и́мам** вáжна срéща.
Невéна Кáза, че **и́мал** вáжна срéща.

In Bulgarian, you have to observe a clear distinction between what you know from first-hand experience and what you know from other sources. The form which Nevena uses shows that she is conveying second-hand information and that she has not herself been a witness to any of the events or facts she is presenting. She is only passing the information on, retelling the events. That is why the verb forms she is using are called renarrated forms.

Every so often in the book so far we have actually found it quite difficult to avoid these renarrated forms, especially in the exercises. Go back briefly to the questions after the dialogue in Unit 13, for example. You were asked there to imagine you were Mrs Collins and, as it were, to answer from 'first-hand experience':

Към кóлко часá присти́гнахте?	*What time did you arrive?*
Как бéше пъту́ването ви?	*How was your journey?*

It was not possible for us to ask you to talk about the journey yourself, because you were not a participant. You only read about it in the dialogue! Let's now compare Mrs Collins' answers with what you would need to say if you were 'renarrating' what she answered:

Г-жá Кóлинс **Присти́гнахме** към сéдем часá.
Ви́е Те (г-н и г-жá Кóлинс) **присти́гнали** към сéдем часá.
Г-жá Кóлинс Пъту́ването **бéше** приятно.
Ви́е Пъту́ването **билó** приятно.

Fairy tales are written using the renarrated forms. So are history books, unless, of course, the writer was an eye-witness to the events described.

2 How to construct the renarrated forms

Getting to grips with all the Bulgarian renarrated forms would be a pretty formidable task, as each tense has its equivalent renarrated version. For practical purposes, however, you will only need to use one or two of them, usually in the *he*, *she*, *it* and *they* forms, so it is on these that we will concentrate, both here and in the Appendix. In the Appendix, incidentally, you will find a slightly fuller set of tables enabling you to recognize some additional forms.

To start with, the renarrated forms are all based on the past participles ending in **-л**, **-ла**, **-ло**, **-ли**. This makes them look like the present perfect tense which you came across in Unit 18. The difference is that the renarrated form drops the **е** and **са**. Compare:

Present perfect tense

Той е пристѝгнал.	*He has arrived.*
Те са пристѝгнали.	*They have arrived.*

Renarrated

Той пристѝгнал.	(I hear/they said) *he has arrived.*
Те пристѝгнали.	(I hear) *they have arrived.*

3 Renarrating present and past events

Go back to the dialogue earlier in the unit. You will see that the secretary repeats a complaint made by other hotel residents: Не **мóжели** да спят от шумá на трамвáите. The form **мóжели** tells us that the original complaint was made in the present tense: Не **мóжем** да спим от шумá на трамвáите.

If the hotel residents had complained in the past tense (Не **можáхме** да спим от шумá), the secretary would have said: Не **можáли** да спя́т от шумá на трамвáите. To be technical for a moment, and if you've got this far, you'll surely manage to cope, the difference between **мóжели** and **можáли** is in the *type* of past participle being used. **Мóжел** (**-а**, **-о**, **-и**) comes from the past imperfect form **мóжех** (Unit 17). As an imperfective form it is suitable for reproducing the present or past imperfect tense. **Можáл** (**-а**, **-о**, **-и**) comes from the past form for ***completed*** actions **можáх** (Unit 15). It is therefore suitable for reproducing things said in the past tense. Luckily, for many verbs the two participles are identical.

4 Щял да се върне към шест *I will be back about six (he said)*

When you want to renarrate things said in the future tense, you merely replace **ще** with **щял (щя́ла, щя́ло** or **щя́ли/щéли) да...** You may remember Nevena saying the businessman would be back about six:

Бúзнесмен **Ще** се вър̀на към шест часá.
Невéна **Щял** да се вър̀не към шест часá.

5 The present perfect of (да) дам

Дал, дáла, дáло, дáли are the past participle forms of the verb **(да) дам** *to give*. It is an irregular form, because it is not directly derived from the past tense form **дáдох** (Unit 16). Instead of just replacing **-х** by **-л**, the past participle loses the last **three** letters: **-дох** and then adds **-л, -ла, -ло, -ли**:

стáята, коя́то сте ми дáли — *the room you've given me*

This happens with all verbs which end in **-дох** or **-тох** in the past, as with **четá** *to read* (past: **чéтох**) and **(да) преведá** *to translate* (past: **превéдох**):

Аз съм чел тáзи кнúга. — *I have read this book.*
Г-жá Кóлинс е превéла ня́колко кнúги. — *Mrs Collins has translated a number of books.*

6 Стáята, коя́то сте ми дáли: where to put the short indirect object pronoun

In present perfect sentences such as **стáята, коя́то сте ми дáли**, you put the short pronoun for the person who is given something between the appropriate form of **съм** and the past participle:

Аз **съм ти дал** еднá кнúга. — *I've given you a book.*
Ти **си ми дал** еднá кнúга. — *You've given me a book.*
Нúе **сме му дáли** еднá кнúга. — *We've given him a book.*
Вúе **сте им дáли** еднá кнúга. — *You've given them a book.*
Те **са ѝ дáли** еднá кнúга. — *They've given her a book.*

With **той, тя** and **то**, however, the short pronoun comes *before* the verb *to be*:

Той ми е дал еднó писмó. — *He's given me a letter.*
Тя му е дáла еднó писмó. — *She's given him a letter.*

When the past participle is the first word in the sentence, these sequences are preserved. The verb *to be* is followed by the pronoun in the *I*, *you*, *we* and *they* forms, but in the *he*, *she*, *it* form the pronoun comes *before* the verb *to be*. Compare:

Да́ла съм му ло́ша ста́я. — *I've given him a bad room.*

and

Да́ла му е ло́ша ста́я. — *She's given him a bad room.*

7 Introducing a reason or cause: от *because of*

The preposition **от** corresponds to a number of expressions in English. You have already come across **от** meaning *from* referring to time and space as in:

Магази́нът е отво́рен от 9 до 12.	*The shop is open from 9 to 12.*
Самоле́тът от Ло́ндон присти́га в о́сем часа́.	*The plane from London gets in at eight o'clock.*
И́ма шум от рестора́нта.	*There is noise from the restaurant.*

От is also frequently used to express reason or cause. Note the possible English equivalents in these expressions taken from the dialogue:

Не съм **дово́лен от ста́ята** си.	*I'm not happy with my room.*
И дру́ги го́сти се опла́кват **от шум**.	*Other hotel residents too complain of the noise.*
Не мо́гат да спя́т **от шума́** на трамва́ите.	*They can't sleep because of the noise from the trams.*

Exercises

1 If you were asked: **И́мате ли опла́квания?**, how would you answer if you were not happy with:

a the price
b the shop assistant
c the waiter
d the service station
e the food (use **храна́**)
f the quality of the photos (use **ка́чество**)
g the service (use **обслу́жване**)?

Model: Не съм дово́лен/дово́лна от камерие́рката.

2 Nothing is right in the restaurant. Complete the sentences using the model provided by the dissatisfied businessman in the dialogue:

Стáята, коя́то сте ми дáли, не ми харéсва.

Don't forget to change to **кóйто, коя́то, коéто, кои́то** where necessary (cf. Unit 5).

a Кюфтéто, ______, не ми́ харéсва.
b Сýпата, ______, не ми́ харéсва.
c Ви́ното, ______, не ми́ харéсва.
d Салáтите, ______, не ми́ харéсват.
a Сладолéдът, ______, не ми́ харéсва.

3 In this exercise you can practise using two different tenses of **(да) дам** and also putting the pronouns in the right order. First read out loud the short dialogue:

г-н и г-жá Кóлинс Не сте́ ни дáли клю́човете.
Портиéр Дáдох ви ги. Éто ги.

Now, still reading out loud, complete the dialogues below, making sure you have chosen the correct short pronouns. If necessary, look them up in the Appendix.

a – Не сте́ ни дáли паспóртите.
• ______.

b – Не сте́ ни дáли смéтката.
• ______.

c – Не сте́ ми дáли ключ.
• ______.

d – Не сте́ ми дáли Вáшата визи́тна кáртичка (*visiting card*).
• ______.

e – Не сте́ ни дáли билéтите.
• ______.

4 Read the following sentences in which you give several reasons why you cannot get off to sleep:

a Не мóга да спя от кафéто.
b Не мóга да спя от главобóлие.
c Не мóга да спя от горещинá (*heat*).
d Не мóга да спя от комáрите (*mosquitoes*).
e Не мóга да спя от мýзиката в ресторáнта.

Now, giving the same reasons, say why you couldn't get off to sleep last night:

Сно́щи не можа́х да спя от шума́ на трамва́ите.

5 The story below tells of Michael Johnson's trip to Plovdiv which you first learnt about at the end of Unit 13. It consists of two parts – one told by Nikolai, who was there with Mr Johnson, and one told by Nadya, who was not. Read the story and try to work out who is talking first and where the first part finishes.

В Пло́вдив било́ мно́го интере́сно. Ма́йкъл хо́дил в на́й-интере́сните къ́щи, разгле́дал Ри́мската стена́ и цъ́рквата «Свети́ Константи́н и Еле́на». Вре́мето било́ мно́го прия́тно. И́мало мно́го хо́ра на панаи́ра. Ма́йкъл и́маше възмо́жност да бъ́де превода́ч на една́ гру́па англича́ни. Той им помо́гна да наме́рят сво́я преводáч. Той ку́пи мно́го ка́ртички от Пло́вдив, защо́то ми́слеше, че е загу́бил фо́тоапара́та си.

6 This exercise is based on the conversation between John, Eli and Nevena at the end of Unit 14. We will ask questions in the special renarrated forms because we didn't take part in that conversation. Answer using the same forms – you weren't there either!

- **a** Кога́ била́ сва́тбата?
- **b** В кой рестора́нт празну́вали?
- **c** Къде́ се запозна́ли Джон и Е́ли?
- **d** Защо́ дошъ́л Джон в Со́фия?
- **e** Къде́ ще́ли да оти́дат сега́ Джон и Е́ли?

Do you understand?

Dialogue

Nadya receives a misdirected complaint from an agitated customer.

Клие́нт (*On the phone.*) До́бър ден. И́скам да гово́ря с дире́ктора на фи́рма «Търго́вска рекла́ма», мо́ля.

На́дя Г-н Анто́нов разгова́ря с клие́нти в моме́нта. Да му преда́м ли не́що?

Клие́нт Да, ако́ оби́чате. Оба́ждам се от фи́рма «Прогре́с». И́скам да се опла́ча. Преда́йте му, че не сме́ дово́лни от ва́шата ра́бота.

На́дя От какво́ по́-то́чно се опла́квате?

Клие́нт Поръ́чахме 1 200 (хиля́да и две́ста) рекла́мни брошу́ри, а полу́чихме са́мо 600 (ше́стстотин). Па́пките, който поръ́чахме, и́мат дефе́кти, а

	визи́тните ка́ртички са на лошока́чествена хартия.
На́дя	Ще преда́м на дире́ктора опла́кванията Ви. Ще Ви се оба́дя у́тре. Дочу́ване!
	(*Later, to the director.*)
На́дя	Г-н Анто́нов, оба́ди се еди́н не́рвен клие́нт от фи́рма «Прогре́с». И́маше цял куп опла́квания.
г-н Анто́нов	Какво́ е ста́нало?
На́дя	Пору̀чали 1 200 брошу́ри, а полу́чили са́мо 600. Па́пките и́мали дефе́кти, а визи́тните ка́ртички били́ на лошока́чествена харти́я.
г-н Анто́нов	Ча́кай, ча́кай! Тук и́ма ня́какава гре́шка. Фи́рма «Прогре́с» е пору̀чала 1 200 брошу́ри и ни́е сме изпра́тили 1 200 – в два кашо́на по 600. Си́гурно о́ще не са́ полу́чили вто́рия кашо́н. Пору̀чка за па́пки и визи́тни ка́ртички от тях не сме́ и́мали.
	(*Telephone rings.*)
Клие́нт	Оба́ждам се пак от фи́рма «Прогре́с». И́скам да се извиня́. Ока́за се, че вси́чко е наре́д.
На́дя	Г-н Анто́нов е тук. И́скате ли да гово́рите с не́го?
Клие́нт	Ня́ма ну́жда да го безпокои́те. Полу́чихме вси́чки брошу́ри. Ка́кто разбра́х от секрета́рката, па́пките и визи́тните ка́ртички били́ пору̀чани на дру́го мя́сто, в дру́га фи́рма. Гре́шката е мо́я. Извиня́вайте о́ще веднъ̀ж. Дочу́ване!
г-н Анто́нов	Не́рвният клие́нт ли бе́ше?
На́дя	Да, извини́ се. Бил напра́вил гре́шка.
г-н Анто́нов	Ни́що чу́дно. Ка́зват, че в та́зи фи́рма ста́вали мно́го гре́шки...

Търго́вска рекла́ма	*Trade Publicity*
(да) преда́м, -даде́ш	*to pass on/leave a message*
(да) се опла́ча, -чеш	*to make a complaint*
рекла́мен, -мна	*publicity* (adj.)
и́ма дефе́кт	*has something wrong with it*
не́рвен, -вна	*agitated, stressed out*
прогре́с	*progress*
цял куп	*a whole lot* (of)
лошока́чествен	*of inferior quality*
харти́я	*paper*

гре́шка	*mistake*
кашо́н	*cardboard box*
обáждам, -даш се	*to ring, phone*
(да) се извиня́, -ни́ш	*to apologize*
окáза се (*it* form)	*it turned out*
на дру́го мя́сто	*elsewhere*
о́ще веднъ́ж	*once again*

Questions

Try to use the renarrated forms in your answers!

1 Какво́ тря́бва да предаде́ На́дя на дире́ктора?
2 От какво́ се оплáква клие́нтът?
3 Защо́ се обáжда клие́нтът вто́ри път?
4 Какво́ е разбрáл клие́нтът от секретáрката?
5 Какво́ кáзват за фи́рма «Прогре́с»?

20

би́хме и́скали да до́йдем пак!

We would like to come again!

In this unit you will learn

- **how to take your leave of someone**
- **how to use some sentences with *if***
- **how to express wishes and requests being especially polite**
- **how to agree to stay in touch**

Dialogue

At Sofia airport Mrs Collins sees a young couple with a trolley.

г-жа́ Ко́линс Извине́те, би́хте ли ми ка́зали откъде́ взе́хте коли́чка за бага́ж?

Миле́на О, но ни́е се позна́ваме. Здраве́йте! Видя́хме се в една́ сладка́рница. По́мните ли?

г-жа́ Ко́линс Да, вя́рно – Ви́е сте моми́чето, кое́то ни пока́за Центра́лна по́ща. Миле́на, нали́?

Миле́на То́чно така́! Запозна́йте се – това́ е мо́ят коле́га Никола́й. Той замина́ва за А́нглия.

г-жа́ Ко́линс Зна́чи ще пъту́ваме за́едно. (*Shaking hands.*) Прия́тно ми е.

Миле́на Никола́й, би ли взел коли́чка за г-н и г-жа́ Ко́линс?

Никола́й Да, разби́ра се. Еди́н моме́нт.

Миле́на Дово́лни ли сте от престо́я във Ва́рна?

г-жа́ Ко́линс Да, прека́рахме чуде́сно. Ми́сля, че видя́хме по́вечето забележи́телности о́коло града́.

Миле́на Ще до́йдете ли пак в Бълга́рия сле́дващата годи́на?

г-жа́ Ко́линс Мно́го би́хме и́скали да до́йдем пак. Ако́ и́маме възмо́жност да до́йдем през зи́мата, би́хме оти́шли в Бо́ровец то́зи път.

Миле́на Ако́ и́двате пак, обаде́те ми се непреме́нно! Е́то, Никола́й и́два с коли́чката.

г-н Ко́линс Благодаря́, Никола́й. Викто́рия, тря́бва да бъ́рзаме. Дови́ждане, Миле́на! Ще Ви пи́шем от А́нглия.

Миле́на Вси́чко ху́баво, г-н Ко́линс! Г-жа́ Ко́линс, и́мам една́ молба́ към Вас. Би́хте ли помо́гнали на Никола́й на Хи́йтроу? Той се безпокои́, че не разби́ра англи́йски мно́го добре́.

г-жа́ Ко́линс Ще му помо́гна с удово́лствие. Дови́ждане, Миле́на!

Миле́на Прия́тен път! (*To Nikolai.*) Никола́й, ще ми пра́тиш ли ка́ртичка от Че́лмсфорд?

Никола́й Зна́еш, че ще ти пра́тя... (*With a sigh.*) Ко́лко бих и́скал ти да пъту́ваш с ме́не!

Миле́на Ха́йде, тръ́гвай! Ще закъсне́еш за самоле́та. Прия́тно прека́рване!

Никола́й Благодаря́! До ско́ро ви́ждане, Миле́на!

Бихте ли ми ка́зали?	*Could you please tell me?*
По́мните ли?	*Do you remember?*
зна́чи	*so* (lit. *that means*)
Би ли взел коли́чка?	*Could you please take a trolley?*
Еди́н моме́нт.	*Just a moment.*
Прека́рахме чуде́сно.	*We had a marvellous time.*
Видя́хме по́вечето забележи́телности о́коло града́.	*We saw most of the sights outside the town.*
Би́хме и́скали да до́йдем пак.	*We'd like to come again.*
би́хме оти́шли	*we would go*
обаде́те ми се непреме́нно	*don't fail to/do let me know*
Ще Ви пи́шем.	*We'll write to you.*
Вси́чко ху́баво.	*All the best.*
Би́хте ли помо́гнали?	*Could you please help?*
Ще ми пра́тиш ли ка́ртичка?	*Will you send me a card?*
Ко́лко бих и́скал ти да пъту́ваш с ме́не!	*How I wish you were going with me!*
Хайде, тръгвай.	*Come on, off you go.*

Questions

1 Try to answer the questions.

a Какво́ пока́за Миле́на на г-н и г-жа́ Ко́линс?
b Кога́ би́ха и́скали да до́йдат г-н и г-жа́ Ко́линс пак в Бълга́рия?
c Къде́ би́ха оти́шли те, ако́ и́маха възмо́жност?
d Каква́ молба́ и́ма Миле́на към г-жа́ Ко́линс?
e Какво́ би и́скал Никола́й?

2 True or false?

a Никола́й ня́ма да пъту́ва за́едно с г-н и г-жа́ Ко́линс.
b Г-н и г-жа́ Ко́линс са виде́ли вси́чки забележи́телности о́коло Ва́рна.
c Г-н и г-жа́ Ко́линс би́ха и́скали да до́йдат пак в Бълга́рия.
d Г-н и г-жа́ Ко́линс ня́ма да пи́шат на Миле́на от А́нглия.
e Никола́й ще пра́ти и́мейл на Миле́на от Че́лмсфорд.

How do you say it?

- Taking your leave

До скоро виждане!	*See you soon.*
Приятен път!	*Have a good journey.*

- Expressing a wish politely

Бих искал/а...	*I would like...*
(Много) бихме искали...	*We would (very much) like...*

- Intensifying a statement or a wish

Елате непременно!	*Do come!*
Непременно ще дойда.	*I certainly will come.*

- Making a polite request for assistance

Бихте ли ми казали...?	*Would you be so kind as to tell me...?*
Би ли взел количка?	*Would you be so kind as to take a trolley?*
Бихте ли ми помогнали?	*Could you please help me?*

- Asking someone to wait a moment

Един момент!	*Just a moment/hold on!*

- Saying you have enjoyed yourself very much

Прекарахме чудесно.	*We had a marvellous time.*

- Expressing eager expectation

Очаквам Николай с нетърпение.	*I'm looking forward to seeing Nikolai.*
С нетърпение очаквам да се обадите	*I'm looking forward to hearing from you.*

Grammar

1 Expressing wishes and requests more formally

Бих искал да... *I would like to...*

In Unit 6 you learned that the Bulgarian equivalent of *I want to* is **Искам да**, and you may have felt this way of expressing a wish rather rude. Although **искам** in Bulgarian is socially more acceptable than *I want* in English – ('I want never gets', remember!) – Bulgarian does also have more formal polite alternatives. These are based on a special form of **съм** and come close to English polite expressions with *would* and *could*. Compare:

Йскам да сменя́ ста́ята си.	*I want to change my room.*
and Бих и́скал(а) да сменя́ ста́ята си.	*I would like to change my room.*
Йскам да гово́ря с дире́ктора.	*I want to speak to the director.*
and Бих и́скал(а) да гово́ря с дире́ктора.	*I would like to speak to the director.*

The ultra-polite forms and also the conditionals about which you will discover more below consist of the special form of **съм** plus a past participle, usually from a verb of *wanting* or *wishing*.

would like

(аз) бих и́скал(а) да...	(ни́е) би́хме и́скали да...
(ти) би и́скал(а) да...	(ви́е) би́хте и́скали да...
(той) би и́скал да...	(те) би́ха и́скали да...
(тя) би и́скала да...	
(то) би и́скало да...	

Би́хте ли...? *Would you be so kind as to...? (Could you...?)*

You can use the same form of **съм** to make polite requests:

Би ли ми ка́зал(а) ко́лко е часъ́т?	*Could you tell me what the time is?*
Би́хте ли ми пока́зали пъ́тя за Ва́рна?	*Would you be so kind as to show me the way to Varna?*

These requests are a degree more formal than questions using **Мо́же ли...?** (see Unit 6).

2 Бих оти́шъл (ако́...) *I would go (if...)*

The same forms are used to express willingness to do something if the circumstances permit or if certain conditions are fulfilled. (Unlike constructions with **щях** in Unit 16, these are things that still can happen, they are 'open' conditions):

Би́хме оти́шли в Бо́ровец, ако́ до́йдем през зи́мата.	*We'd go to Borovets if we were to come in winter.*
Бих оти́шла в А́нглия (ако́ и́мам пари́)	*I'd go to England (if I were to have the money).*
Би́хме дошли́ с вас, ако́ не сме́ зае́ти.	*We will come with you if we aren't busy.*

In the last example the statement is more tentative and the Bulgarian expresses willingness and politeness as much as condition. In all three examples the Bulgarian polite form could be replaced by the normal future: **ще оти́дем, ще оти́да** and **ще до́йдем**, all of which are more assertive and definite – *I will* rather than *I would*.

3 Catching up with new verbs with 'се'

In Unit 6 you learned that some Bulgarian verbs, called reflexive verbs, are accompanied by the 'satellite' word **се**. Since then you have come across more reflexive verbs and they can be now summed up in three groups:

(**a**) when the object of the verb in English is *myself*, *yourself*, etc. (or such an object is implied) as in:

Момче́то се обле́че.	*The boy got (himself) dressed.*
Той се чу́вства по́-добре́ сега́.	*He feels better now.*
Той се безпокои́.	*He is worried.*

These verbs can usually also appear without **се** and with an object. Compare:

Неве́на обле́че момче́то.	*Nevena got the boy dressed.*
Чу́вствам бо́лка в кръ̀ста.	*I feel a pain in the back.*
Извиня́вай, че те безпокоя́.	*Forgive me for troubling you.*

Other similar verbs include:

(да) въ̀рна	*to return, give back*
(да) оже́ня	*to marry someone off*
(да) разваля́	*to break something*
(да) се въ̀рна	*to return, go back*
(да) се оже́ня	*to get married*
(да) се разваля́	*to break down, go wrong*

(**b**) when the object of the verb in English is *each other* or *one another*. These verbs can also be used without **се**:

Аз позна́вам Никола́й.	*I know Nikolai.*
but	
Ни́е се позна́ваме.	*We know each other.*
Миле́на видя́ г-жа́ Ко́линс.	*Milena saw Mrs Collins.*
but	
Те се видя́ха в една́ сладка́рница.	*They saw one another in a café.*

Ще запозна́я Никола́й с те́зи англича́ни.	*I'll introduce Nikolai to these Englishmen.*
but	
Те ще се запозна́ят на лети́щето.	*They'll get to know one another at the airport.*

(**c**) when the verb denotes feelings or emotions. These verbs never appear without **се**:

гри́жа се	*to look after*	страху́вам се	*to be afraid*
надя́вам се	*to hope*	съмня́вам се	*to be in doubt*
ра́двам се	*to be pleased*	шегу́вам се	*to joke*
сме́я се	*to laugh*		

4 To be doing something and to begin doing something

The difference in meaning of 'twin' verbs like **ра́двам се** *to be glad* and **(да) се зара́двам** *to rejoice* or **сме́я се** *to be laughing* and **да се засме́я** *to begin to laugh* is often difficult to render succinctly in English. One is imperfective, the other perfective (see Unit 12). When the prefix **за-** is added to a verb it often denotes the beginning of an action. Compare the beginning perceived as a moment in time A, with B, an action that is going on:

A	Тя го видя́ и се засмя́.	*She saw him and began to laugh.*
	Той я видя́ и веднáга го заболя́ главáта.	*He saw her and immediately got a headache.*
B	Тя пак се сме́е.	*She's laughing again.*
	Пак го боли́ главáта.	*He's having a headache again.*

Also compare the verb **по́мня** *to remember* with the verb **(да) запо́мня**. The first verb can be paraphrased as '*to be keeping something in one's memory*' (that is why it is imperfective) and the second one as '*to get something fixed in one's memory*' (that is why it is perfective).

5 Keeping in touch

(Да) се оба́дя *to get in touch*, *to phone* does not fit into any of the three groups and literally means '*to let oneself be heard*' (see Unit 11). When you use it in the phrase **обади́ ми се!** you have to remember where to put the two little unstressed words. The indirect object pronoun **(ми)** always comes before **се**, no matter whether they both follow or precede the verb (see Appendix):

Тря́бва да **ми се** оба́диш.	*You must get in touch/give me a ring/ call.*
Обаде́те **ми се**!	*Give me a ring/call.*

Exercises

1 Following the model, respond to the requests below. Watch the word order!

Request: Обади́ се на г-н Анто́нов, мо́ля те.
Responses: **a** Ще му се оба́дя
b Оба́дих му се ве́че
c Ве́че му се оба́дих

i Обаде́те се на секретáрката, мо́ля Ви.
ii Обади́ се на Николáй, мо́ля те.
iii Обади́ се на Джон и Е́ли, мо́ля те.
iv Обаде́те се на Неве́на Петко́ва, мо́ля Ви.

2 Make these requests, already quite decently civil, even more polite. The model may help:

Model: Покаже́те ми, мо́ля Ви, та́зи ва́за.
Би́хте ли ми пока́зали та́зи ва́за?

a Мо́ля Ви, каже́те ми Ва́шия адре́с.
b Обаде́те ми се по́-късно, мо́ля Ви.
c Мо́ля Ви, помогне́те ни да наме́рим пъ́тя за Ва́рна.
d Да́йте ми дру́га ста́я, ако́ оби́чате.
e Мо́ля Ви, поръ́чайте ми такси́ за де́сет часа́.

Here are the past participles to choose from. You won't need them all!

ка́зал дал доне́съл поръ́чал помо́гнал се оба́дил спрял

3 Answer these questions using the future form and, demonstrating your willingness to do what you are asked (provided certain conditions are met!), by using бих and the past participle.

Model: Ще оти́деш ли на мач (*match*)? Ще оти́да/бих оти́шъл, ако́ не вали́ дъжд.

a Ще ку́пите ли пода́ръци за жена́ Ви? (ако́ наме́ря не́що ху́баво)
b Ще се оба́диш ли от лети́щето? (ако́ и́мам вре́ме)
c Ще до́йдеш ли на те́нис? (ако́ се чу́вствам по́-добре́)
d Ще уча́ствате ли в конфере́нцията? (ако́ и́мам пари́)

Past participles to choose from (again, you won't need them all):

дошъ́л	ку́пил	уча́ствал	се оба́дил	разбра́л

4 If you have ever attended a conference in Bulgaria, you might find parts of the following brief address familiar. It contains several polite expressions which you yourself might have occasion to try out. Read the address out loud, then answer the questions in English.

Да́ми и господа́, скъ́пи прия́тели!
Бих и́скал(а) да ви поздравя́ с „Добре́ дошли́" в на́шата краси́ва сто́лица и да ви пожела́я успе́х в ра́ботата ви на та́зи конфере́нция. Мно́го се ра́дваме, че ви́ждаме тук то́лкова мно́го прия́тели на Бълга́рия от цял свят. Би́хме се ра́двали, ако́ та́зи конфере́нция е поле́зна за все́ки от вас.

О́ще веднъ́ж добре́ дошли́ в Бълга́рия! От все сърце́ (*all my heart*) ви пожела́вам прия́тна и плодотво́рна (*fruitful*) ра́бота и до но́ви тво́рчески (*creative*) и прия́телски (*friendly*) сре́щи.

a On what occasion is this address given?
b At what point in the proceedings is the speech made?
c How does the speaker address his audience?
d Where do the conference participants come from?
e What else do they have in common?
f In what city is this particular conference taking place?
g What benefit does the speaker hope the participants will derive from the conference?

5 Back in Britain, Michael Johnson is attending another conference. In the coffee break he dashes off a postcard to his friends in Bulgaria. Read aloud what he says:

Скъ́пи прия́тели!

Пи́ша ви от Ло́ндон, къде́то съм на конфере́нция. На конфере́нцията и́ма два́ма бизнесме́ни от Пло́вдив, който добре́ позна́ват г-жа́ Ко́линс. Ка́зват, че гово́ря ве́че не по́-ло́шо от не́я... Бих и́скал да ви благодаря́ о́ще веднъ́ж за помощта́ ви и за прия́тните дни в Бълга́рия. Оча́квам Никола́й с нетърпе́ние. Надя́вам се да се ви́дим ско́ро пак. Вси́чко ху́баво и до ско́ро ви́ждане!

С по́здрав (*kind regards*),
Ма́йкъл Джо́нсън

Ло́ндон, 6.VI. 2004

Now you write a postcard, also in Bulgarian, to Nikolai and Nadya.

Do you understand?

Dialogue

Sofia airport is not large, and shortly before taking off for Heathrow Mr and Mrs Collins bump into some more acquaintances.

г-н Ко́линс Викто́рия, виж! О́ще една́ позна́та.

г-жа́ Ко́линс А, да – моми́чето от реце́пцията в хоте́ла в Со́фия.

Неве́на Здраве́йте, г-н Ко́линс! Здраве́йте, г-жа́ Ко́линс! Каква́ изнена́да!

г-жа́ Ко́линс Здраве́йте, Неве́на. И Ви́е ли ще пъту́вате за А́нглия?

Неве́на Не, аз изпра́щам едни́ прия́тели – Марк Де́йвис и жена́ му. По́мните ли, аз Ви ка́зах за не́го.

г-жа́ Ко́линс Да, по́мня. Америка́нският журнали́ст, нали́?

Неве́на То́чно така́. Ела́те да Ви запозна́я с тях, те мно́го ще се ра́дват.

Марк Прия́тно ми е. Неве́на мно́го ми е разка́звала за Вас. Щях да Ви изпра́тя съобще́ние от Аме́рика, за да Ви пока́ня на една́ конфере́нция за Бълга́рия. Би́хте ли и́скали да уча́ствате?

г-жа́ Ко́линс Бих уча́ствала с удово́лствие, ако́ не съм зае́та по съ́щото вре́ме.

Марк Чуде́сно, ще Ви пра́тя пока́на и програ́мата. Би́хте ли ми да́ли и́мейла си, мо́ля.

г-жа́ Ко́линс Заповя́дайте, това́ е визи́тната ми ка́ртичка. Ви́е в Аме́рика ли живе́ете?

г-жа́ Де́йвис Да, по́вечето вре́ме прека́рваме в Аме́рика, но мно́го че́сто и́дваме в Бълга́рия.

г-жа́ Ко́линс Надя́вам се да се ви́дим пак! Обаде́те се!

(*The public address system crackles into life.*) Мо́ля за внима́ние! Вси́чки пъ́тници, замина́ващи за Ло́ндон, да се явя́т пред и́зход но́мер че́тири!

г-жа́ Ко́линс Сега́ тря́бва да бъ́рзаме. Дови́ждане на вси́чки!
Неве́на Дови́ждане! Прия́тен път и вси́чко ху́баво! Ела́те пак непреме́нно!
Вси́чки НЕПРЕМЕ́ННО!

(да) се зара́двам, -ваш	*to be pleased*
разка́звам, -ваш	*to tell, relate*
(да) уча́ствам, -ваш	*to take part*
пъ́тник, (pl) **-ици**	*passenger, traveller*
замина́ващ за	*travelling to*
(да) се явя́, яви́ш	*to present oneself*
и́зход	*gate; exit*
плодотво́рен, -рна	*fruitful*
съобще́ние	*message*

Questions

1 Коя́ позна́та ви́ждат г-н и г-жа́ Ко́линс на лети́щето?
2 Защо́ е на лети́щето Неве́на?
3 За кого́ е разка́звала мно́го Неве́на на Марк?
4 За какво́ щял Марк да изпра́ти съобще́ние на г-жа́ Ко́линс?
5 В какъ́в слу́чай би уча́ствала г-жа́ Ко́линс в конфере́нцията?
6 Какво́ да́ва г-жа́ Ко́линс на Марк?

taking it further

We hope you have found it fun working your way through *Teach Yourself Bulgarian*. We also hope you will wish to develop your knowledge of the language, the country and its people. Unfortunately, at present we cannot confidently direct you to any single book or course that takes you on from where you left off at the end of Unit 20. There are no modern, dedicated printed English-language materials for intermediate learners of Bulgarian. There is, for example, no advanced learner's dictionary of Bulgarian targeted at English-language learners. What you will have to do, therefore, is pick and mix from a variety of sources, combining limited printed materials with the expanding and ever-changing offerings of the internet. To help you on your way, we list here a few books and other sources you might find useful.

Dictionaries

Dictionaries that have been long in service are currently being updated and reissued. There are also a number of handy new dictionaries, mostly intended for Bulgarian learners of English, but nevertheless of value to English-language learners of Bulgarian. Try the two-way pocket dictionary by Levkova and Pishtalova: *English–Bulgarian, Bulgarian–English Dictionary*, Colibri, Sofia, 2001. For a good English–Bulgarian dictionary, look for *21st Century Reference English–Bulgarian Dictionary* by Shurbanova and Rangelova, published by Prozorets i Trud, Sofia. A Bulgarian–English dictionary by Shurbanova and Rangelova is promised soon. The German publisher Ernst Klett Verlag, operating in Bulgaria as 'PONS Bulgaria', has produced a number of English–Bulgarian dictionaries. These include a useful English–Bulgarian phrasebook, *Tematichen rechnik. Angliyski*. Try the PONS website: **http://www.pons.bg**.

Grammars, primers

For the intermediate learner the most appropriate primer is *Intensive Bulgarian: a textbook and reference grammar* by Ronelle Alexander, assisted by Olga Mladenova. Published by the University of Wisconsin Press in 2000, it comes in two hefty volumes, combines grammar and exercises and will both help you revise and take you further. Grammars of Bulgarian produced in Bulgaria are traditionally on the turgid side and are intended for a largely academic readership. They are also, of course, written in Bulgarian in an appropriate style!

Courses

A number of Bulgarian universities organize short courses in Bulgarian language and culture, usually in the summer, for keen and interested foreigners. Try the Sofia University website: **http://www.uni-sofia.bg** or, better, Bulgarian Links on the Oslo University site listed below. There are other established courses in Veliko Turnovo and Blagoevgrad.

Book buying

Most large internet booksellers can supply Bulgarian books. In the UK the specialist booksellers Grant & Cutler Ltd, 55–57 Great Marlborough Street, London W1F 7AY, supply a variety of learning materials produced by Western and Bulgarian publishers. They have dictionaries, including technical dictionaries, phrasebooks, literature in Bulgarian and even Bulgarian Scrabble. Try **http://www.grantandcutler.com**, or email to **G&C@grantandcutler.com** or phone 0044 (0)207 734 2012.

Ура (hurrah!) for the <.bg> internet address!

By far the most exciting source of authentic Bulgarian language material today is the internet. The '.bg' sites, and the information they provide, multiply by the minute. Here are just a few promising addresses for you to get started on.

An excellent site, primarily in Bulgarian but with English pages too, and a multitude of links, is **http://www.online.bg**. Here you will find newspapers, literary journals, theatre and cinema programmes and much else besides. Also try the lively **http://www.dir.bg**. It, too, has Bulgarian newspapers and even a Bulgarian **книжа́рница** (*bookshop*). Most Bulgarian newspapers also have their own websites. And if you are looking for authentic literature, try **http://liternet.bg**. A good general site with useful links and lots of information on Bulgaria is **http://www.kirildouhalov.net/**. For a thoroughly absorbing time and more substantial sustenance for

Bulgarian learners than on any other site, click into the Bulgarian language and literature offering at the University of Oslo on **http://www.hf.uio.no/east/bulg/mat/index.html**. Or explore its hugely rewarding Bulgarian Links. A long address, but it's well worth the journey!

Congratulations on completing *Teach Yourself Bulgarian*!

We hope you have enjoyed working your way through the course. We are always keen to receive feedback from people who have used our course, so why not contact us and let us know your reactions? We'll be particularly pleased to receive your praise, but we should also like to know if you think things could be improved. We always welcome comments and suggestions and we do our best to incorporate constructive suggestions into later editions.

You can contact us through the publishers at:

Teach Yourself Books, Hodder Headline Ltd, 338 Euston Road, London NW1 3BH.

So **прия́тен път! прия́тно река́рване!** and **на добър час!** (*farewell!*). And happy hunting!

Michael Holman and Mira Kovatcheva,
Tunbridge Wells and Sofia, 2003

Introduction

1 Alaska, address, Estonia, espresso, Canada, credit, Milan, minute, Ottawa, omelette, Texas, telephone. **2** Berlin, bar, Glasgow, garage, Dakota, vodka, Geneva, jury, Zambezi, Arizona, Istanbul, India, York, Mallorca, London, Balkan, Panama, police, Frankfurt, Sofia, Zurich, Donetsk, Chad, Churchill, Sheffield, show business, Stuttgart, Budapest, Updike, Bulgaria, chauffeur, signora, Yukon, Leeds United, Yalta, Yankee. **3** Vienna, Vivian, Namibia, Varna, Richard, Yorkshire, Sinatra, Amsterdam, Hungary, Liverpool, Hyde Park, Sahara. **4** Address, espresso, telephone, credit, Ottawa, garage, minute, Donetsk, show business, Budapest, Beatles, Vivian, Amsterdam.

Exercises

1 (*a*) iv, (*b*) xii, (*c*) v, (*d*) x, (*e*) xi, (*f*) iii, (*g*) i, (*h*) vi, (*i*) vii, (*j*) ii, (*k*) ix, (*l*) viii. **2** (*a*) v, (*b*) iii, (*c*) vii, (*d*) viii, (*e*) vi, (*f*) ix, (*g*) i, (*h*) x, (*i*) iv, (*j*) ii. **3** (*a*) viii, (*b*) xiv, (*c*) iii, (*d*) v, (*e*) vi, (*f*) xvi, (*g*) ix, (*h*) iv, (*i*) ii, (*j*) i, (*k*) xiii, (*l*) xv, (*m*) xi, (*n*) vii, (*o*) xii, (*p*) x. **4** 201 Fax, 202 Restaurant, 203 Reception, 204 Fitness centre, 205 Bar, 206 Taxi, 207 Information, 166 Police. **5** (*a*) Sirena Snack bar (*b*) Berlin Restaurant (*c*) Sheraton Hotel (*d*) Orient Café. **6** (*a*) 17.25, (*b*) 17.05, (*c*) 16.35, (*d*) 18.05, (*e*) 18.30, (*f*) 15.40, (*g*) 16.10.

Unit 1

Questions 1 (*a*) Да, и́ма (*b*) Не, ня́ма (*c*) Ка́звам се… **2** (*a*) T (*b*) F: Би́знесмен съм (*c*) T.

Exercises 1 (*a*) *agency* (f), (*b*) *address* (m), (*c*) *aspirin* (m) (*d*) *bank* (f), (*e*) *business* (m), (*f*) beer (f) (*g*) vodka (f) (*h*) *computer* (m), (*i*) *lemonade* (f), (*j*) *music* (f), (*k*) *pony* (n), (*l*) *problem* (m), (*m*) *soda water* (f), (*n*) *sport* (m), (*o*) *tonic* (m), (*p*) *tourist* (m), (*q*) *firm* (f), (*r*) *football* (m), (*s*) *chauffeur* (m), (*t*) *printer* (m), (*u*) *office* (m), (*v*) *fax* (m), (*w*) *video* (n), (*x*) *xerox* (m). **2** (*a*) здраве́й, (*b*) здраве́йте, (*c*) здраве́йте, (*d*) здраве́йте, (*e*) здраве́й, (*f*) здраве́й, (*g*) здраве́йте. **3** (*a*) Добро́ у́тро, (*b*) До́бър ден, (*c*) До́бър ден, (*d*) До́бър ве́чер. **4** i (*f*), ii (*e*), iii (*a*), iv (*c*), v (*d*), vi (*b*). **5** (*a*) Да, и́ма. (*b*) Да, и́ма. (*c*) Не, ня́ма. (*d*) Не, ня́ма. (*e*) Да, и́ма. (*f*) Не, ня́ма. **6** (*a*) И́ма ли уи́ски? (*b*) И́ма ли би́ра? (*c*) И́ма ли лимона́да? (*d*) И́ма ли чай? **7** (*a*) Уи́ски, мо́ля. Джин, мо́ля. (*b*) Би́ра, мо́ля. Ко́ка-ко́ла, мо́ля. (*c*) Капучи́но, мо́ля. Еспре́со, мо́ля. (*d*) Кафе́, мо́ля. Чай, мо́ля. **8** (*a*) a lovely hotel. (*b*) a good-looking man. (*c*) a beautiful sea. (*d*) lovely beer. (*e*) a beautiful name. (*f*) a beautiful Bulgarian (female!). (*g*) Ху́бава стáя! (*h*) Ху́бав апартаме́нт! (*i*) Ху́баво българско ви́но!

9

(*a*)	(*b*)
Майкъл Джонсън	България
4, Маунт Драйв	1000 София
Челмсфорд	хотел „Родина"
Есекс	апартамент 8
Англия	Майкъл Джонсън

Do you understand? (*a*) Evening. (*b*) Yes. (*c*) Scotch. (*d*) No. (*e*) No.

Unit 2

Questions 1 (*a*) Благодаря́, добре́ съм, (*b*) Това́ е те́лекс, (*c*) Да, това́ е те́лекс от Ло́ндон, (*d*) И́ма самоле́т от Ло́ндон в се́дем часа́, (*e*) Да, той присти́га днес. **2** (*a*) F: На́дя е добре́. (*b*) T, (*c*) T, (*d*) F: Господи́н Анто́нов ня́ма вре́ме за кафе́, (*e*) F: Господи́н Анто́нов и́ма мно́го ра́бота.
Exercises 1 (*a*) Къде́ е тя? (*b*) Той е добре́. (*c*) Как е той? (*d*) Къде́ са те? (*e*) Тя е в хоте́л «Роди́на». (*f*) Той и́ма ра́бота. (*g*) Тук ли са те? **2** (*a*) Ка́звам се Джу́ли Дже́ймсън; (*b*) Ка́звам се То́ни; (*c*) Ка́звам се Боя́н Анто́нов; (*d*) Ка́зваме се Ко́линс. **3** (*a*) Как се ка́зваш? (*b*) Как се ка́звате? (*c*) Как се ка́звате? **4** Трамва́й но́мер две, пет, шест, о́сем. Троле́й но́мер едно́, че́тири, се́дем, де́вет. **5** Не, аз съм г-жа́/г-н _____ (Try writing out your name!) Не, аз съм в стая но́мер

се́дем. **6** (*a*) Какво́ е това́? (*b*) Как е тя? (*c*) Как са те? (*d*) Какво́ е това́? (*e*) Как си? (*f*) Какво́ е това́ (*g*) Как сте? (*h*) Какво́ е това́? **7** i (*b*), ii (*d*), iii (*a*), iv (*e*), v (*c*). **8** (*a*) Това́ ли е ресторáнт «Кристáл»? Не, ресторáнт «Кристáл» е там. (*b*) Това́ ли е булевáрд «Ле́вски»? Не, булевáрд «Ле́вски» е там. (*c*) Това́ ли е Централна по́ща? Не, Централна по́ща е там. (*d*) Това́ ли е хоте́л «Хе́мус»? Не, хоте́л «Хе́мус» е там. (*e*) Това́ ли е у́лица «Рако́вски»? Не, у́лица «Рако́вски» е там. **9** (*a*) Не, ня́мам; (*b*) Да, и́мам; (*c*) Не, ня́мам; (*d*) Да, и́мам; (*e*) Да, и́мам. **10** (*a*) Мо́ля, къде́ и́ма ресторáнт? (*b*) Мо́ля, къде́ и́ма бáнка? (*c*) Мо́ля, къде́ и́ма телефо́н? (*d*) Мо́ля, къде́ и́ма тоале́тна? (*e*) Мо́ля, къде́ и́ма по́ща? (*f*) Мо́ля, къде́ и́ма фи́тнес це́нтър? **11** (*a*) съм, е; (*b*) съм, е; (*c*) съм, е; (*d*) сме, са; (*e*) съм, е.

Do you understand? **1** F: Булевáрд «Ви́тоша» не е́ бли́зо. **2** F: Г-н Джо́нсън ня́ма кáрта на Со́фия. **3** T. **4** F: И́ма трамвáй до булевáрд «Ви́тоша». **5** T. **6** T. **7** F: Той присти́га в Бо́ровец в де́сет часá.

Unit 3

Questions **1** (*a*) Тя е от Мáнчестър. (*b*) Тя е преводáчка. (*c*) Да, омъжена е. (*d*) Да, и́ма едно́ дете́. (*e*) Той е учи́тел. (*f*) Да, тя познáва България добре́. **2** (*a*) F: Г-жá Ко́линс е от Мáнчестър. (*b*) F: Г-жá Ко́линс и́ма едно́ дете́. (*c*) T (*d*) T (*e*) F: Г-жá Ко́линс не е́ за първи път в Бълга́рия. (*f*) T.

Exercises **1** (*a*) И́мам едно́ дете́. (*b*) Омъжена ли сте? (*c*) Г-жá Ко́линс е преводáчка. (*d*) Каквá е г-жá Ко́линс по наро́дност? (*e*) За първи път ли е г-жá Ко́линс в Бълга́рия? (*f*) Откъде́ са г-жá Ко́линс и г-н Ко́линс? (*g*) Познáвам странáта ви добре́. **2** i (*d*), ii (*f*), iii (*a*), iv (*b*), v (*c*), vi (*g*), vii (*h*), viii (*e*). **3** (*a*) Не, не съм ле́карка. Каквá сте по профе́сия? Секретáрка/учи́телка съм. (*b*) Не, не съм българка. Каквá сте по наро́дност? Ирлáндка/англичáнка/шотлáндка съм. (*c*) Не, не съм сервитьо́р. Какъв сте по профе́сия? Преводáч/ле́кар/студе́нт съм. (*d*) Не, не съм англичáнин. Какъв сте по наро́дност? Ирлáндец / шотлáндец /америкáнец съм. **4** (*a*) Марк Де́йвис е журнали́ст. Той е от Сáнта Бáрбара. Той е же́нен. (*b*) Миле́на е худо́жничка. Тя е от Со́фия. Тя не е́ омъжена. (*c*) А́ндрю е студе́нт. Той е от Глáзгоу. Той не е́ же́нен. (*d*) Г-жá Ко́линс е преводáчка. Тя е от Мáнчестър. Тя е омъжена. (*e*) Нáдя е секретáрка. Тя е от Пло́вдив. Тя не е́ омъжена. (*f*) Мáйкъл Джо́нсън е би́знесмен. Той е от Че́лмсфорд. Той е же́нен. (*g*) Г-н Анто́нов е дире́ктор. Той е от Бургáс. Той е жéнен. (*h*) Николáй е фотогрáф. Той е от Вáрна. Той не é жéнен. **5** (*a*) ът, (*b*) та, (*c*) ът, (*d*) та, (*e*) та, (*f*) ът, (*g*) ът, (*h*) ът. **6** (*a*) Лéкарят е шотлáндец. (*b*) Учи́телят е америкáнец. (*c*) Чáят е хýбав. Той е от Áнглия. **7** (*a*) Запознáйте се - мъжъ́т ми! (*b*) Запознáйте се - синъ́т ми! (*c*) Запознáйте се - дъщеря́ ми! (*d*) Запознáйте се - брат ми! (*e*) Запознáйте се - сестрá ми! **8** (*a*) Синъ́т ми се кáзва Áндрю. (*b*) Детéто ми се кáзва Ви́ктор. (*c*) Мáйка ми се кáзва Ири́на. (*d*) Женá ми се кáзва Мари́я. (*e*) Дъщеря́ ми се кáзва Си́лвия. (*f*) Бащá ми се кáзва Пол. **9** (*a*) Но тя е студéна! (*b*) Но той е студéн! (*c*) Но тя е тóпла! (*d*) Но то е тóпло! (*e*) Но тя е тóпла! (*f*) Но той е тóпъл. **10** Заповя́дайте, товá е ви́зата ми. Заповя́дайте, товá е резервáцията ми. Заповя́дайте, товá е билéтът ми. **11** (*a*) кáрта(та), (*b*) Чéрно морé, (*c*) Дýнав, (*d*) Гъ́рция и Тýрция. (*e*) Сóфия.

Do you understand? 1 T. **2** F: Милéна е худóжничката на фи́рмата. **3** T. **4** T. **5** F: Николáй и Милéна и́мат врéме за кафé.

Unit 4

Questions 1 (*a*) Той и́ма три писмá. (*b*) Не, господи́н Джóнсън не и́ска бъ́лгарски вéстници. (*c*) Не, той не разби́ра бъ́лгарски добрé. (*d*) Той и́ма пет минýти свобóдно врéме. (*e*) Той е в България за две сéдмици. (*f*) Той и́ма срéща тóчно в дванáйсет часá. **2** (*a*) T. (*b*) F: В хотéла и́ма англи́йски вéстници и списáния. (*c*) T. (*d*) F: Невéна и́ма сáмо еди́н въпрóс. (*e*) F: Часъ́т е единáйсет и полови́на. (*f*) F: Той е в Бългáрия за две сéдмици.

Exercises 1 Автобýсът за Мальóвица заминáва в шест (часá) и три́йсет и пет (минýти) и присти́га в дéвет (часá) и петнáйсет (минýти)./Автобýсът за Бáнкя заминáва в дéсет (часá) и дéсет (минýти) и присти́га в дéсет (часá) и чети́рисет и пет (минýти)./Автобýсът за Сáмоков заминáва в единáйсет (часá) и двáйсет (минýти) и присти́га в тринáйсет (часá) и три́йсет (минýти)./Автобýсът за Бóровец заминáва в тринáйсет (часá) и петдесéт (минýти) и присти́га в седемнáйсет (часá) и двáйсет и пет (минýти). **2** (*a*) Автобýсът за Сáмоков заминáва след пет минýти. (*b*) Автобýсът за Бóровец заминáва след двáйсет минýти. (*c*) Автобýсът за Мальóвица заминáва след дéсет минýти. **3** (*a*) Автобýсът за Плóвдив заминáва в единáйсет часá и двáйсет минýти.

(*b*) Самолéтът от Лóндон пристúга в деветнáйсет часá и четúрисет минýти. (*c*) Ѝма самолéт за Вáрна в дéсет часá и петнáйсет минýти. (*d*) Заминáвам за Сóфия в петнáйсет часá и трúйсет минýти (три и половúна). (*e*) Срéщата на г-н Джóнсън е тóчно в дванáйсет часá. **4** (*a*) Аз съм в България за дванáйсет/петнáйсет/двáйсет дни. (*b*) Аз съм в хотéла за три/тринáйсет нóщи. (*c*) Аз съм във Вáрна за еднá сéдмица/две сéдмици. **5** от сéдем часá до двáйсет часá и трúйсет минýти; от дéвет до двáйсет и едúн часá; от осемнáйсет до двáйсет и три часá; от óсем до дванáйсет и от шестнáйсет до двáйсет часá; от дéсет до тринáйсет и от четиринáйсет до деветнáйсет часá. (*a*) Пóщата рабóти от сéдем часá сутринтá до óсем и половúна вечертá. (*b*) Аптéката рабóти от дéвет часá сутринтá до дéвет часá вечертá. (*c*) Ресторáнтът рабóти от шест до единáйсет часá вечертá. (*d*) Сладкáрницата рабóти от дéсет часá сутринтá до едúн часá на óбед и от два часá следóбед до сéдем часá вечертá. **6** (*a*) Кóлко американки úма в хотéла? (*b*) За кóлко сéдмици е г-н Джóнсън в България? (*c*) След кóлко дни пристúга брат ти? (*d*) От кóлко дни са г-н и г-жá Кóлинс в Сóфия? (*e*) В кóлко часá заминáва автобýсът? (*f*) Кóлко писмá и кáртички úмам днес? (*g*) Кóлко децá úма г-н Джóнсън? **7** (*a*) Нáдя пúе кафé с Николáй и Милéна. (*b*) Нáдя пúе кафéто с мáлко зáхар. (*c*) Николáй пúе кафéто с мнóго зáхар. (*d*) Милéна úска кафé без зáхар. (*e*) Те обúчат кафéто с мáлко мля́ко. (*f*) Аз обúчам кафéто ______ **8** (*a*) В кафéто úма зáхар, налú? Да, úма мáлко зáхар. (*b*) В кафéто úма мля́ко, налú? Да, úма мáлко мля́ко. (*c*) В чáя úма мля́ко, налú? Да, úма мáлко мля́ко. **9** (*a*) В кафéто ня́ма мля́ко, налú? Не, ня́ма/Да, ня́ма. (*b*) В кафéто ня́ма зáхар, налú? Не, ня́ма/Да, ня́ма. (*c*) В чáя ня́ма зáхар, налú? Не, ня́ма/Да, ня́ма. **10** (*a*) две леглá; (*b*) чужденцú; (*c*) американци; (*d*) бъ́лгарски вéстници; (*e*) мнóго въпрóси; (*f*) мнóго езúци; (*g*) мнóго продавáчки; (*h*) трамвáи; (*i*) мнóго чужденкú. **11** (*a*) Хотéлът е до ресторáнта. (*b*) Ресторáнтът е до хотéла. (*c*) Теáтърът е до магазúна. (*d*) Магазúнът е до теáтъра. (*e*) Музéят е до пáрка. (*f*) Пáркът е до музéя.

Do you understand? 1 F: Николáй заминáва за Áнглия. **2** F: Той не разбúра англúйски. **3** T. **4** F: Фúрмата е в Чéлмсфорд. **5** T. **6** T. **7** F: Във фúрмата ня́ма мнóго фотогрáфи. **8** F: Той заминáва след три сéдмици.

Unit 5

Questions 1 (*a*) Англича́ни и́ма в мно́го стра́ни по света́. (*b*) Тя гово́ри мно́го добре́ бъ́лгарски ези́к (*c*) Г-жа́ Ко́линс е англича́нката в ста́я но́мер де́сет. (*d*) Неве́на зна́е три ези́ка. (*e*) Тя гово́ри фре́нски, ру́ски и испа́нски. (*f*) Той живе́е в Че́лмсфорд. **2** (*a*) F: Не мно́го англича́ни гово́рят бъ́лгарски. (*b*) F: Г-жа́ Ко́линс е анлича́нката, коя́то живе́е в ста́я но́мер де́сет. (*c*) T. (*d*) T. (*e*) F: Тя гово́ри фре́нски на́й-добре́. (*f*) F: Мно́го бъ́лгари гово́рят чу́жди ези́ци. **Exercises 1** (*a*) Мно́го англича́ни ли и́ма в хоте́ла? (*b*) Мно́го бъ́лгари ли гово́рят англи́йски? (*c*) Бъ́лгари ли са г-н Анто́нов и Никола́й? (*d*) Бъ́лгари и англича́ни ли рабо́тят във фи́рмата? (*e*) Англича́ни ли са г-н и г-жа́ Ко́линс? **2** (*a*) дру́ги; (*b*) дру́го; (*c*) дру́га; (*d*) дру́ги; (*e*) друг; (*f*) дру́ги; (*g*) друг; (*h*) дру́го; (*i*) дру́га; (*j*) дру́ги. **3** (i) (*a*) Тук на ка́ртата и́ма два рестора́нта. Кой (рестора́нт) е по́-бли́зо? (*b*) Тук на ка́ртата и́ма два гра́да. Кой (град) е по́-бли́зо? (*c*) Тук на ка́ртата и́ма два куро́рта. Кой (куро́рт) е по́-бли́зо? (*d*) Тук на ка́ртата и́ма два къ́мпинга. Кой (къ́мпинг) е по́-бли́зо? (*e*) Тук на ка́ртата и́ма два моте́ла. Кой (моте́л) е по́-бли́зо? (ii) (*a*) На ка́ртата и́ма две апте́ки. Коя́ (апте́ка) е по́-бли́зо? (*b*) На ка́ртата и́ма две бензиноста́нции. Коя́ (бензиноста́нция) е по́-бли́зо? (*c*) На ка́ртата и́ма две спи́рки. Коя́ (спи́рка) е по́-бли́зо? **4** (*a*) Кой, (*b*) Кой, (*c*) Коя́, (*d*) Кой, (*e*) Коя́, (*f*) Кой. **5** (*a*) Ко́лко чу́жди ези́ка гово́ри Неве́на? (*b*) Ко́лко биле́та и́скат те? (*c*) Ко́лко джи́на серви́ра сервитьо́рът? (*d*) Ко́лко чу́жди ези́ка зна́е Ма́йкъл Джо́нсън? **6** (*a*) **Тури́ст:** Извине́те, и́ма ли хоте́ли до га́рата? **Гра́жданин:** Да, до га́рата и́ма ня́колко хоте́ла. (*b*) **Тури́ст:** Извине́те, и́ма ли рестора́нти до га́рата? **Гра́жданин:** Да, до га́рата и́ма ня́колко рестора́нта. (*c*) **Тури́ст:** Извине́те, и́ма ли музе́и до га́рата? **Гра́жданин:** Да, до га́рата и́ма ня́колко музе́я. (*d*) **Тури́ст** Извине́те, и́ма ли о́фиси до га́рата? **Гра́жданин** Да, до га́рата и́ма ня́колко о́фиса. **7** (*a*) мъжа́, ко́йто присти́га от Ло́ндон; жена́та, коя́то гово́ри ху́баво бъ́лгарски; англича́ни, ко́ито живе́ят в Бълга́рия; семе́йството, koе́то живе́е в ста́я но́мер де́сет. (*b*) бъ́лгарина, ко́йто замина́ва за А́нглия? англича́ни, ко́ито са же́нени за бъ́лгарки?/ ко́ито не пи́ят уи́ски? шотла́ндци, ко́ито не пи́ят уи́ски?/ко́ито са же́нени за бъ́лгарки? бъ́лгарката, коя́то е омъ́жена за англича́нин? **8** (*a*) Е́то трамва́я. Е́то два трамва́я. (*b*) Е́то троле́я. Е́то два троле́я. (*c*) Е́то автобу́са. Е́то два автобу́са. (*d*) Е́то къ́мпинга. Е́то два къ́мпинга. (*e*)

Éто компю́търа. Éто два компю́търа. (*f*) Éто банкома́та, éто два банкома́та. **9** (*a*) Éто биле́та ми. (*b*) Éто паспо́рта ми. (*c*) Éто мъжа́ ми. (*d*) Éто сина́ ми. (*e*) Éто бага́жа ми. **10** Извине́те, ну́ла, о́сем, о́сем, о́сем, три, две, едно́, о́сем, де́вет, едно́ ли е? Извине́те, ну́ла, о́сем, де́вет, о́сем, едно́, пет, шест, се́дем, три, две ли е? Извине́те, се́дем, о́сем, де́вет, ну́ла, две, шест, шест ли е?

Do you understand? 1 F: Никола́й у́чи англи́йски, **2** T. **3** F: Миле́на позна́ва ня́колко учи́теля по англи́йски, **4** F: Миле́на и́ма два мно́го ху́бави уче́бника по англи́йски. **5** F: Никола́й и́ма ну́жда от уче́бници. **6** T. **7** F: Никола́й е на два́йсет и шест годи́ни.

Unit 6

Questions 1 (*a*) Ма́йкъл Джо́нсън и́ма сре́ща с г-н Анто́нов. (*b*) Г-н Анто́нов ача́ква г-н Джо́нсън. (*c*) Не, той ня́ма пробле́ми в Со́фия. (*d*) Той и́ска да оти́де първо в ба́нката. (*e*) Ма́йкъл Джо́нсън тря́бва да обмени́ пари́. (*f*) Той тря́бва да гово́ри по́-ба́вно. **2** (*a*) F: Г-н Джо́нсън е дово́лен от хоте́ла. (*b*) T. (*c*) F: Ба́нката и рестора́нтът не са́ дале́че от о́фиса. (*d*) T. (*e*) F: Г-н Анто́нов и г-н Джо́нсън ня́мат ну́жда от превода́ч. (*f*) T.

Exercises 1 И́мате ли **ви́за/биле́т/ бо́рдна ка́рта**? Не. Тря́бва ли да и́мам **ви́за/биле́т/бо́рдна ка́рта**? Да, тря́бва. **2** И́скате ли да оти́дем: (*a*) на о́пера? (*b*) на конце́рт? (*c*) на сладка́рница? (*d*) на дискоте́ка? (*e*) на теа́тър? (*f*) на екску́рзия? (*g*) на ски? (*h*) на плаж? **3** Никола́й тря́бва да оти́де в Че́лмсфорд след три се́дмици. **4** i (*g*), ii (*d*), iii (*a*), iv (*f*), v (*c*), vi (*b*), vii (*e*), viii (*a*), ix (*a*). **5** (*a*) не́я; (*b*) не́го; (*c*) тях. **6** (*a*) не́го; (*b*) не́я; (*c*) не́я; (*d*) не́го; (*e*) не́я; (*f*) не́го. **7** Ка́звам се (*your name*) И́мате ли писма́/факс/ве́стници/ма́са за ме́не? **8 Никола́й:** И́скам да/мо́же ли да гово́ря с Вас? **Г-н А** Съжаля́вам, но сега́ ня́мам вре́ме за те́бе. И́мам сре́ща с г-н Джо́нсън. **На́дя:** Г-н Анто́нов, и́мате ли ну́жда от ме́не? **Г-н А:** Ми́сля, че ня́маме ну́жда от превода́ч. Мо́же ли да напра́виш кафе́ за нас? **На́дя:** Ня́мам ни́що проти́в. **9** (*a*) ютия́, (*b*) чадър, (*c*) коли́чка, (*d*) такси́, (*e*) носа́ч, (*f*) пари́. **10** (*a*) се надя́вам; (*b*) се ра́двам; (*c*) се чу́вствам добре́.

Do you understand? 1 Еди́н клие́нт и́ска да гово́ри с дире́ктора. **2** Не, не е́ свобо́ден. **3** Той тря́бва да се оба́ди по́-къ́сно следо́бед. **4** Той и́ска да оти́де на те́нис. **5** Бра́тът на Миле́на и́ска да оти́де с не́я на конце́рт. **6** Да, На́дя и́ска да оти́де с тях.

Unit 7

Questions **1** (*a*) На́й-добре́ е да оти́дат на паза́ра. (*b*) Плодове́те и зеленчу́ците на паза́ра не са́ е́втини, но са на́й-пре́сни. (*c*) Г-жа́ Ко́линс не оби́ча ти́score kвички. (*d*) Той и́ска еди́н килогра́м дома́ти. (*e*) Тя прода́ва я́бълки, пра́скови и гро́зде. (*f*) Вси́чко стру́ва три́йсет и о́сем ле́ва и шейсе́т стоти́нки. **2** (*a*) F: Г-н и г-жа́ Ко́линс и́скат Неве́на да им пока́же магази́н за плодове́ и зеленчу́ци. (*b*) F: Г-н Ко́линс не и́ска да ку́пи ти́квички. (*c*) T. (*d*) T. (*e*) F: Г-жа́ Ко́линс не и́ска пра́скови. (*f*) T.

Exercises 1 (*a*) пли́кове, (*b*) два пли́ка, (*c*) два бана́на, (*d*) бана́ни, (*e*) два пъ́пеша. (*f*) пъ́пеши, (*g*) ножо́ве. (*h*) ня́колко но́жа, (*i*) ня́колко бъ́лгарски гра́да (*j*) градове́ **2** (*a*) Плате́те на ка́сата! Не пи́пай! (*b*) Пазе́те чистота́! Не газе́те трева́та! (*c*) Бутни́! Дръпни́ (*d*) Не пи́пай! **3** Мо́же ли да ми ка́жете: (*a*) къде́ и́ма телефо́н? (*b*) къде́ и́ма ба́нка? (*c*) къде́ и́ма апте́ка? (*d*) къде́ и́ма павилио́н? **4** Мо́же ли да ми пока́жете: (*a*) то́зи чадъ́р/крем? (*b*) та́зи ка́рта/ча́ша? (*c*) това́ списа́ние/ лека́рство? (*d*) те́зи ножо́ве/списа́ния/ кре́мове/ча́ши? **5** (*a*) Ко́лко стру́ват кра́ставиците? Да́йте ми еди́н килогра́м кра́ставици. (*b*) Ко́лко стру́ват ти́квичките? Да́йте ми еди́н килогра́м ти́квички. (*c*) Ко́лко стру́ват я́бълките? Да́йте ми еди́н килогра́м я́бълки. (*d*) Ко́лко стру́ват пра́сковите? Да́йте ми еди́н килогра́м пра́скови. **6** (*a*) Да, да оти́дем! (*b*) Да, да оти́дем! (*c*) Да, да плати́м! (*d*) Да, да се оба́дим! **7** (*a*) Да, мно́го оби́чам да пъту́вам. (*b*) Не, не оби́чам да игра́я на компю́тър. (*c*) Не, не оби́чам да пазару́вам. (*d*) Да, мно́го оби́чам да ка́рам ски. (*e*) Да, мно́го оби́чам да чета́. **8** (*a*) Купи́ мля́ко, мо́ля! (*b*) Ела́, мо́ля! (*c*) Седни́, мо́ля! (*d*) Ви́ж, мо́ля! (*e*) Кажи́, мо́ля! (*f*) Да́й, мо́ля! **9** (*a*) Да Ви дам ли солта́? (*b*) Мо́же ли да ни пока́жете ста́ята? (*c*) Да́йте ни клю́ча, мо́ля! (*d*) Мо́ля, покаже́те ми това́ списа́ние! (*e*) Мо́же ли да ми даде́те то́зи пъ́пеш? **10** (*a*) Я́бълките са по́-е́втини от пра́сковите, (*b*) Дома́тите са по́-пре́сни от ти́квичките, (*c*) Пъ́пешът е по́-сла́дък от гро́здето, (*d*) На́дя е по́-зае́та от Неве́на, (*e*) Кра́ставиците са по́-голе́ми от ти́квичките.

Do you understand? **1** T. **2** T. **3** F: Г-жа́ Ко́линс и́ска де́сет биле́та за трамва́й. **4** F: Г-жа́ Ко́линс и́ска два пли́ка и две ма́рки. **5** F: Ка́ртичките стру́ват лев и два́йсет **6** T.

Unit 8

Questions **1** (*a*) Г-н Джо́нсън и́ска да ви́ди меню́то. (*b*) Той препоръ́чва шо́пската сала́та. (*c*) Тарато́р е студе́на

су́па от ки́село мля́ко и кра́ставици. (*d*) Той предпочи́та то́пла су́па. (*e*) За пи́ене г-н Джо́нсън и́ска пло́дов сок. (*f*) Г-н Анто́нов поръ́чва ча́ша ви́но. **2** (*a*) F: Шо́пската сала́та е с дома́ти, кра́ставици и си́рене. (*b*) T. (*c*) T. (*d*) F: Г-н Анто́нов и г-н Джо́нсън поръ́чват че́тири бе́ли хле́бчета. (*e*) T. (*f*) F: На о́бед г-н Анто́нов поръ́чва ча́ша бя́ло ви́но.
Exercises 1 (*a*) Сервитьо́рът препоръ́чва пи́лзенска би́ра, но аз предпочи́там бъ́лгарска. Да поръ́чаме бъ́лгарска би́ра! (*b*) Сервитьо́рът препоръ́чва гро́здова раки́я, но аз предпочи́там сли́вова. Да поръ́чаме сли́вова раки́я! (*c*) Сервитьо́рът препоръ́чва пи́лешка су́па, но аз предпочи́там зеленчу́кова. Да поръ́чаме зеленчу́кова су́па! **2** (*a*) препоръ́чвате; (*b*) поръ́ча; (*c*) предпочи́тате; (*d*) препоръ́чва/предпочи́та; (*e*) поръ́чаме; (*f*) предпочи́та; (*g*) поръ́чате. **3** В тарато́ра и́ма ки́село мля́ко, кра́ставица, че́сън, сол, о́лио и о́рехи. **4** (*a*) И́ма не́скафе и еспре́со; (*b*) И́ма че́рен чай, ме́нтов чай и би́лков чай; (*c*) И́ма пло́дова то́рта, шокола́дова то́рта и о́рехова то́рта; (*d*) И́ма портока́лов сок, гро́здов сок, я́бълков сок и сок от я́годи. **5** (*a*) две, две; (*b*) два, две; (*c*) две; (*d*) две; (*e*) два, две; (*f*) два; (*g*) два́ма; (*h*) два; (*i*) две; (*j*) два́ма; (*k*) две; (*l*) два. **6** Try the following menus – other combinations will also do: (*a*) Една́ зеленчу́кова су́па и еди́н омле́т със си́рене; (*b*) Две вегетариа́нски су́пи и два пъ́ти омле́т с шу́нка/кюфте́та; (*c*) Че́тири зеленчу́кови су́пи и че́тири пъ́ти кюфте́та/пи́ца с кашкава́л. **7** Какви́ са́ндвичи и́мате?/Два са́ндвича с шу́нка и еди́н с кашкава́л, мо́ля./Еди́н портока́лов сок, две ко́ли и три кафе́та, мо́ля. **8** (i) (*a*) две кеба́пчета; (*b*) кеба́пчетата; (ii) (*a*) две хле́бчета; (*b*) хле́бчетата; (iii) (*a*) две кюфте́та; (*b*) кюфте́тата. **9** (*a*) вегетериа́нската су́па; (*b*) пълнените чу́шки; (*c*) бя́лото гро́зде; (*d*) пи́лешката су́па; (*e*) черве́ните я́бълки; (*f*) пло́довата то́рта; (*g*) бе́лите хле́бчета; (*h*) бъ́лгарското ки́село мля́ко. **10** (*a*) бя́лото ви́но; (*b*) сли́вовата раки́я; (*c*) вегетариа́нската су́па; (*d*) шокола́довата то́рта; (*e*) бъ́лгарските специалите́ти; (*f*) пи́лзенската би́ра.
Do you understand? 1 Часъ́т е о́сем и полови́на. **2** Да, о́ще е ра́но за ра́бота. **3** Не, сладка́рницата е отво́рена. **4** За заку́ска и́ма са́ндвичи, ки́фли и ба́нички. **5** За я́дене те поръ́чват два са́ндвича и две парче́та то́рта. **6** За пи́ене те поръ́чват две кафе́та еспре́со и два я́бълкови со́ка.

Unit 9

Questions 1 (*a*) Неве́на и́ска да гово́ри с г-жа́ Ко́линс.

(*b*) Момчéтата са на летúщето. (*c*) Те са от Амéрика. (*d*) Те úмат нýжда от преводáч. (*e*) Митничáрите не мóгат да намéрят багáжа на момчéтата. (*f*) Кен úма два кýфара. (*g*) Висóкият мъж нóси едúн чéрен кýфар и еднá сúня чáнта. **2** (*a*) F: Те са на летúщето. (*b*) F: Г-жá Кóлинс мóже да отúде на летúщето. (*c*) T. (*d*) T. (*e*) F: Кýфарите на Кен не сá голéми. (*f*) T.

Exercises 1 (*a*) С каквó мóга да Ви помóгна? (*b*) Момчéтата от Амéрика úмат нýжда от преводáч. (*c*) Митничáрите не мóгат да намéрят багáжа на момчéтата. (*d*) Товá не é мóят багáж. (*e*) Мáлката сúня чáнта е на Джон/Мáлката чáнта на Джон е сúня. **2** Да, мóга да/Не, не мóга да: (*a*) игрáя тéнис; (*b*) кáрам ски; (*c*) плýвам; (*d*) кáрам колá; (*e*) игрáя на кáрти. **3** Извинéте, мóжете ли да ми покáжете: (*a*) къдé е аптéката? (*b*) къдé е мúтницата? (*c*) къдé е хотéл «Шéратон»? (no definite article needed with names of hotels!) (*d*) къдé е спúрката на тролéй нóмер две? (*e*) къдé е Централна гáра? (no definite article here either.) **4** i (*e*); ii (*d*); iii (*a*); iv (*b*); v (*c*). **5** (**a**) Твóят кýфар ли е товá? Не, тóзи кýфар не é мой. Мóят кýфар е пó-голя́м. (**b**) Твóето портмонé ли е товá? Не, товá портмонé не é мóе. Мóето портмонé е пó-голя́мо. (**c**) Твóят чадъ́р ли е товá? Не, тóзи чадър не é мой. Мóят чадър е пó-голя́м. (**d**) Твóята пáпка ли е товá? Не, тáзи пáпка не é мóя. Мóята пáпка е пó-голя́ма. (**e**) Твóята писáлка ли е товá? Не, тáзи писáлка не é мóя. Мóята писáлка е пó-голя́ма. (**f**) Твóят молúв ли е товá? Не, тóзи молúв не é мой. Мóят молúв е пó-голя́м. (**g**) Твóят белéжник ли е товá? Не, тóзи белéжник не é мой. Мóят белéжник е пó-голя́м. (**h**) Твóята химикáлка ли е товá? Не, тáзи химикáлка не é мóя. Мóята химикáлка е пó-голя́ма. **6** Портмонéто ми го ня́ма! Багáжът ми го ня́ма! Чадъ́рът ми го ня́ма! Белéжникът ми го ня́ма! Пáпката ми я ня́ма! Парúте ми ги ня́ма! **7** (*a*) Турúстът не мóже да намéри свóя хотéл. (*b*) Не, турúстът не знáе úмето му/ úмето на хотéла. (*c*) Хотéлът е блúзо до спúрката на тролéй нóмер еднó и тролéй нóмер пет. (*d*) До Университéта úма два хотéла. (*e*) Нéговият хотéл се кáзва «Сéрдика». **Турúст** Извинéте, г-н полицáй, мóжете ли да ми помóгнете? Не мóга да намéря свóя хотéл. **Полицáй** Как се кáзва хотéлът Ви? **Турúст** За съжалéние, не знáя. Знáя сáмо, че е блúзо до спúрката на тролéй нóмер еднó и тролéй нóмер пет. **Полицáй** На коя́ ýлица е хотéлът? **Турúст** Не знáя на коя́ ýлица е, но е блúзо до Университéта. **Полицáй** Úма два хотéла блúзо до Университéта. Едúният се кáзва «Сóфия», дрýгият се кáзва

«Се́рдика». **Тури́ст** Ве́че зна́я и́мето на хоте́ла ми. Мо́ят хоте́л се ка́зва «Се́рдика». **8** (*a*) Ня́ма я; (*b*) Ня́ма го; (*c*) Ня́ма го; (*d*) Ня́ма ги; (*e*) Ня́ма я.
Do you understand? 1 F: До г-н и г-жа́ Ко́линс и́ма свобо́дни места́. **2** T. **3** T. **4** F: Г-н и г-жа́ Ко́линс и́мат ма́лко ра́бота в Со́фия. **5** T. **6** F: Еди́н не́ин коле́га замина́ва ско́ро за А́нглия. **7** F: Те не зна́ят къде́ е Центра́лна по́ща.

Unit 10

Questions 1 (*a*) Никола́й бъ́рза, защо́то тря́бва да поръ́ча такси́ и да запа́зи ма́са в рестора́нта за Ма́йкъл Джо́нсън и Боя́н Анто́нов. (*b*) Те мо́гат да чу́ят прогно́зата по ра́диото. (*c*) У́тре на Ви́тоша вре́мето ще бъ́де преди́мно слъ̀нчево, но ветрови́то. (*d*) На́дя предла́га да оти́дат в Ме́лник. (*e*) В кра́я на се́дмицата вре́мето ще бъ́де ху́баво. (*f*) На́дя ще гово́ри с ше́фа. **2** (*a*) T. (*b*) F: Никола́й тря́бва да поръ́ча такси́ и да запа́зи ма́са в рестора́нта. (*c*) T. (*d*) F: У́тре вре́мето на Ви́тоша ня́ма да бъ́де мно́го ху́баво. (*e*) F: Г-н Джо́нсън си́гурно не но́си туристи́чески обу́вки. (*f*) F: Ше́фът ще се съгласи́ да оти́де в Ме́лник.
Exercises 1 (*a*) У́тре ще бъ́де ли о́блачно и мра́чно? Не, у́тре ня́ма да бъ́де о́блачно и мра́чно. (*b*) У́тре ще бъ́де ли мъгли́во? Не, у́тре ня́ма да бъ́де мъгли́во. (*c*) У́тре ще бъ́де ли то́пло и слъ̀нчево? Не, у́тре ня́ма да бъ́де то́пло и слъ̀нчево. (*d*) У́тре ще бъ́де ли студе́но и вла́жно? Не, у́тре ня́ма да бъ́де студе́но и вла́жно. (*e*) У́тре ще бъ́де ли дъждо́вно? Не, у́тре ня́ма да бъ́де дъждо́вно. **2** (*a*) Наи́стина, мно́го е горе́що. Не съ́м съгла́сен/съгла́сна. Изо́бщо не е́ горе́що. (*b*) Наи́стина, мно́го е къ́сно. Не съ́м съгла́сен/съгла́сна. Изо́бщо не е́ къ́сно. (*c*) Наи́стина, мно́го е заба́вно. Не съ́м съгла́сен/съгла́сна. Изо́бщо не е́ заба́вно. (*d*) Наи́стина, мно́го е удо́бно. Не съ́м съгла́сен/съгла́сна. Изо́бщо не е́ удо́бно. (*e*) Наи́стина, мно́го е ле́сно. Не съ́м съгла́сен/съгла́сна. Изо́бщо не е́ ле́сно. **3** i (*d*); ii (*e*); iii (*a*); iv (*c*); v (*b*). **4** (*a*) Не, у́тре ще бъ́де я́сно и горе́що. (*b*) Не, вя́търът по Черномо́рието ще бъ́де слаб до уме́рен. (*c*) Ще бъ́де между́ два́йсет и о́сем и три́йсет и два гра́дуса. (*d*) Температу́рата на море́то ще бъ́де о́коло два́йсет и три гра́дуса. **5** Ня́ма да до́йда, защо́то ня́мам вре́ме./У́тре./Предла́гам да оти́дем на екску́рзия. Съгла́сна ли си?/Вре́мето ще бъ́де слъ̀нчево и то́пло. Добре́. И аз ще взе́ма мо́ето я́ке. **6** (*a*) Г-н Анто́нов ще се съгласи́ бъ́рзо/ле́сно/ тру́дно. (*b*) Ле́сно/тру́дно/

бъ́рзо ще наме́рим га́рата. (*c*) Тру́дно/ле́сно/бъ́рзо ще наме́рим бага́жа. (*d*) Ш-ш-ш! Гово́ри́ по́-ти́хо!
Do you understand? 1 T. **2** F: На Ви́тоша ви́наги е по́-студе́но. **3** F: Ме́лник е на юг. **4** T. **5** F: Миле́на не оби́ча да ста́ва ра́но. **6** T.

Unit 11

Questions 1 (*a*) Г-н Анто́нов и г-н Джо́нсън трябва да напра́вят план за сле́дващата се́дмица. (*b*) Г-н Джо́нсън и́ска да оти́де в Бо́ровец, за да разгле́да хоте́лите. (*c*) Г-н Джо́нсън и г-н Анто́нов са пока́нени на изло́жба във вто́рник преди́ о́бед. (*d*) Те ще оти́дат на панаи́ра на пъ́рвия ден, за да и́мат вре́ме да разгле́дат всичко. (*e*) Г-н Анто́нов тря́бва да се въ́рне в Со́фия на два́йсет и вто́ри май. **2** (*a*) F: Г-н Джо́нсън и́ска да оти́де сам. (*b*) T. (*c*) F: Пре́говорите ще бъ́дат на вто́рия и тре́тия ден. (*d*) F: Г-н Анто́нов ще посре́щне делега́ция, коя́то присти́га от Япо́ния. (*e*) T.
Exercises 1 (*a*) На па́ртера и́ма пода́ръци и козме́тика. (*b*) На пъ́рвия ета́ж и́ма вси́чко за дете́то. (*c*) На вто́рия ета́ж и́ма обу́вки. (*d*) На тре́тия ета́ж и́ма мъ́жка и да́мска конфе́кция. (*e*) На четвъ́ртия ета́ж и́ма кили́ми. (*f*) На пе́тия ета́ж и́ма рестора́нт и тоале́тна. **2** (*a*) Прода́ват марато́нки на вто́рия ета́ж. (*b*) Прода́ват парфю́ми на па́ртера. (*c*) Прода́ват я́кета на тре́тия ета́ж. (*d*) Прода́ват шампоа́ни на па́ртера. **3** (*a*) на не́го, го; (*b*) на не́я, я; (*c*) на не́го, го; (*d*) на тях, ги. **4** (*a*) съ́бота, за съ́бота; (*b*) пе́тък, в пе́тък; (*c*) сря́да, за у́тре. **5** (*a*) Еди́н прия́тен уи́кенд. (*b*) Луксо́зен автобу́с. (*c*) В хоте́л в це́нтъра на Бе́лград. (*d*) Два́йсет и о́сми апри́л; вто́ри ю́ни; четвъ́рти а́вгуст; о́сми септе́мври; трина́йсети окто́мври. (*e*) Екску́рзия до Но́ви Сад. (*f*) Бъ́лгарски ези́к. (*g*) Не. Цена́та не вклю́чва биле́ти за музе́и. **6** (*a*) В понеде́лник На́дя ще помо́гне на Никола́й с докуме́нтите. (*b*) Във вто́рник На́дя ще ка́же на ше́фа за да́тата на изло́жбата. (*c*) В сря́да На́дя ще отгово́ри на писмо́то на худо́жника. (*d*) В четвъ́ртък На́дя ще изпра́ти пока́ни на вси́чки, кои́то рабо́тят във фи́рмата. (*e*) В пе́тък На́дя ще се оба́ди на коле́гата в Пло́вдив. (*f*) В съ́бота На́дя ще ку́пи пода́рък на сина́ на Анто́нови. (*g*) В неде́ля На́дя ще пока́же на Миле́на но́вите плака́ти./**Dates**: Какво́ ще пра́виш на осемна́йсети, деветна́йсети, два́йсети, два́йсет и пъ́рви, два́йсет и вто́ри, два́йсет и тре́ти и два́йсет и четвъ́рти май?

Do you understand? **1** T. **2** F: Г-н и г-жá Кóлинс ще бъ̀дат във Вáрна до четвъ̀рти ю́ни. **3** T. **4** F: Кен не мóже да пътýва на двáйсет и втóри ю́ли. **5** T. **6** F: Кен тря́бва да отѝде в бюрó «Балкáн» в понедéлник.

Unit 12

Questions **1** (*a*) Нáдя не обѝча да чáка. (*b*) Милéна кáзва на Нáдя да не поръ̀чва óще, защóто Николáй ще дóйде след мáлко. (*c*) Спорéд Нáдя Николáй ще дóйде, защóто харéсва Милéна. (*d*) Милéна ѝска да се обáди на Николáй, за да го попѝта защó не ѝдва. (*e*) Не, тя ня́ма мобѝлен телефóн (GSM). (*f*) Николáй обѝча да ся́да до хýбави момѝчета. **2** (*a*) F: Николáй тря́бва да дóйде след мáлко. (*b*) F: Нáдя кáзва, че Николáй вѝнаги закъсня́ва. (*c*) T. (*d*) F: Милéна не обѝча да чáка. (*e*) T.
Exercises **1** (*a*) Оставѝ; (*b*) остáвя; (*c*) остáвяш. **2** (*a*) ii; (*b*) i; (*c*) v; (*d*) iv; (*e*) iii; (*f*) iv. **3** (*a*) помáга; (*b*) стáваме; (*c*) ѝдва; (*d*) поръ̀чва. **4** Ѝскам да вѝдя; хáйде да влéзем; Хáйде и нѝе да сéднем; и нѝе ще изберéм нéщо; ще отѝда пó-блѝзо; за да разглéдам блýзата ѝ; Ѝскам да поръ̀чаш. **5** Éто, тя ѝдва, вѝжда, влѝза. Éто вѝжда, ся́да. Éто избѝра, поръ̀чва. Éто нóси. Éто, не чáка. Éто, плáща, стáва и отѝва. **6** (*a*) обѝча; (*b*) харéсва/обѝча; (*c*) обѝча; (*d*) харéсва; (*e*) обѝча; (*f*) харéсате; (*g*) харéсват/обѝчат; (*h*) обѝчам; (*i*) обѝча; (*j*) харéса; (*k*) харéсва.
Do you understand? **1** Г-н Джóнсън не тря́бва да паркѝра до табéлката, защóто хотéлът е в ремóнт и поня́кога пáдат тéжки предмéти. **2** Пáркингът е зад хотéла. **3** Полицáят препоръ̀чва мáлкия ресторáнт, защóто г-н Джóнсън ня́ма да чáка дъ̀лго там. **4** Г-н Джóнсън не мóже да сéдне на мáсата в ъ̀гъла, защóто тя е запáзена. **5** Г-н Джóнсън кáзва „Мóля, недéйте да бъ̀рзате“. **6** Сервитьóрът ще помóгне на г-н Джóнсън, защóто той не разбѝра всѝчко в меню́то.

Unit 13

Questions **1** (*a*) Пристѝгнахме към сéдем часá. (*b*) Пътýването ни бéше прия́тно. (*c*) Ѝмахме проблéми, защóто ня́махме кáрта на градá. (*d*) Проблéмите ни запóчнаха, когáто пристѝгнахме в градá. (*e*) Не, когáто пристѝгнахме, бéше óще свéтло. (*f*) Не стѝгнахме до площáда с цъ̀рквата, защóто ýлицата бéше в ремóнт. **2** (*a*) F: Г-н и г-жá Кóлинс ще кáрат напрáво и ще стѝгнат едѝн площáд, на кóйто ѝма цъ̀рква. (*b*) F: Хотéл «Одéса» е вдя́сно, срещу́ Мо́рската гради́на. (*c*) F: Г-н и г-жа́ Ко́линс присти́гнаха във Ва́рна към се́дем часа́. (*d*) T. (*e*) F: Ресторáнтът е на па́ртера вля́во.

Exercises 1 i (*e*); ii (*f*); iii (*a*); iv (*c*); v (*d*); vi (*b*). **2** (*a*) Кога́ запо́чна да вали́? (*b*) Защо́ загу́бихте пъ́тя? (*c*) Къде́ е ба́нката? (*d*) Кого́ пи́тахте къде́ е магистра́лата? (*e*) Кой ви помо́гна да наме́рите пъ́тя? (*f*) Къде́ зави́хте надя́сно? **3** (*a*) обя́двах; (*b*) ку́пи; (*c*) зами́наха; (*d*) напра́ви; (*e*) запо́чна; (*f*) пи́тахме; (*g*) поръ́чах; (*h*) изпра́ти. **4** Въ́рнах се по съ́щата у́лица. Сти́гнах еди́н булева́рд. Зави́х надя́сно и ка́рах напра́во. Като́ сти́гнах площа́да, парки́рах на па́ркинга и пи́тах пак. Музе́ят не бе́ше дале́че от площа́да. **5** Върве́те напра́во по та́зи у́лица. На вто́рата у́лица зави́йте наля́во и по́сле ведна́га зави́йте надя́сно. Върве́те напра́во и ще сти́гнете до еди́н площа́д. На тре́тата у́лица вля́во зави́йте наля́во. Апте́ката е на о́коло два́йсет ме́тра вля́во. **6** Ка́рахме напра́во по та́зи у́лица. На вто́рата у́лица зави́хме наля́во и по́сле ведна́га зави́хме надя́сно. Ка́рахме напра́во и сти́гнахме еди́н площа́д. На тре́тата у́лица вля́во зави́хме наля́во. Апте́ката бе́ше на о́коло два́йсет ме́тра вля́во.

Do you understand? (*a*) Ня́мах предста́ва от бъ́лгарската исто́рия. (*b*) В ста́рия град разгле́дах Ри́мската стена́, ста́рия теа́тър и цъ́рквата «Свети́ Константи́н и Еле́на». (*c*) Вре́мето бе́ше прия́тно, защо́то не бе́ше мно́го горе́що. (*d*) Кога́то присти́гна гру́па англича́ни, и́мах възмо́жност да бъ́да преводá́ч. (*e*) Англича́ните тъ́рсиха превода́ча във фоайе́то вля́во от реце́пцията. (*f*) Ще пока́жа на На́дя ка́ртички, а не сни́мки, защо́то загу́бих фо́тоапара́та си.

Unit 14

Questions 1 (*a*) Кога́то се хо́ди на го́сти в Бълга́рия на домаки́нята се но́сят цветя́ и бонбо́ни. (*b*) Днес се празну́ва Ки́рил и Мето́дий, деня́т на бъ́лгарската култу́ра. (*c*) Ма́йкъл Джо́нсън не мо́же да ка́же на Са́шко „Чести́т рожде́н ден", защо́то днес не е́ рожде́ният ден да Са́шко. (*d*) Са́шко благодари́ на Ма́йкъл Джо́нсън за шокола́да и моли́вите. (*e*) Пода́ръци се получа́ват на рожде́н ден. (*f*) Боя́н Анто́нов ще донесе́ ви́ното от ку́хнята. **2** (*a*) F: Мно́го хо́ра купу́ват цветя́ днес. (*b*) T. (*c*) T. (*d*) F: Зла́тка Анто́нова ще пока́ни го́стите в хо́ла. (*e*) F: Са́шко оби́ча да пома́га. (*f*) T.

Exercises 1 Поздравя́вам Ви с но́вата ра́бота. Чести́то! Поздравя́вам Ви с но́вия апартаме́нт. Чести́то! Поздравя́-

вам Ви със сва́тбата. Чести́то! Поздравя́вам Ви с успе́ха. Чести́то! Поздравя́вам Ви с пра́зника. Чести́то! **2** (*a*) Миле́на е пока́нена на о́пера. (*b*) Пока́нен(а) съм на сва́тба. (*c*) Ма́йкъл Джо́нсън е пока́нен на изло́жба. (*d*) Те са пока́нени на па́рти. (*e*) Пока́нени ли сте на кокте́йла? **3** (*a*) Къде́ се обме́ня валу́та? (*b*) Какво́ не се прода́ва на малоле́тни? (*c*) Кога́ се пра́вят резерва́ции? (*d*) Къде́ се оти́ва с то́зи трамва́й? (*e*) Какво́ се ви́жда отту́к? (*f*) Какво́ се ви́жда отту́к? (Singular verb after **какво́**, remember?). **4** Видя́ ли катедра́лата «Свети́ Алекса́ндър Не́вски»? • Да, видя́х я. — Харе́са ли ти? • Мно́го ми харе́са. — Разгле́да ли кри́птата? • Да, разгле́дах и не́я. Пред кри́птата се прода́ваха ико́ни. Ку́пих една́ ма́лка ико́на. — Мо́же ли да я ви́дя? • Разби́ра се. Е́то я. Харе́сва ли ти? — Аз не разби́рам от ико́ни, но та́зи ми харе́сва. **5** (*a*) Да, компа́ктдискът с бъ́лгарска му́зика мно́го ми харе́сва. (*b*) Да, тарато́рът мно́го ми харе́сва. (*c*) Да, ба́ницата мно́го ми харе́сва. (*d*) Да, цветя́ мно́го ми харе́сват те́зи. (*e*) Да, бъ́лгарското ви́но мно́го ми харе́сва. (*f*) Да, пъ́лнените чу́шки мно́го ми харе́сват. (*g*) Да, бонбо́ните мно́го ми харе́сват. (*h*) Да, шо́пската сала́та мно́го ми харе́сва. **6** (*a*) Вче́ра Ма́йкъл Джо́нсън и Никола́й доне́соха ро́зи за Зла́тка Анто́нова. (*b*) Вче́ра Миле́на доне́се еди́н уче́бник за Никола́й. (*c*) Вче́ра доне́сохме брошу́ри от панаира в Пло́вдив. (*d*) Вче́ра доне́сохте ли пода́рък за сво́ите прия́тели? (*e*) Вче́ра Ма́йкъл Джо́нсън доне́се шокола́д за Са́шко. (*f*) Вче́ра г-н Анто́нов и синъ́т му доне́соха две бути́лки ви́но от ку́хнята.

Do you understand? 1 Те празну́ваха в рестора́нт «Берли́н». **2** Е́ли предла́га бонбо́ни на Неве́на по слу́чай сва́тбата. **3** Те се запозна́ха в Бо́ровец ми́налата годи́на. **4** Тя им пожела́ва мно́го ща́стие. **5** Кога́то запо́чват да пи́ят коня́к, Е́ли и Джон ка́зват „Наздра́ве!“.

Unit 15

Questions 1 (*a*) Миле́на не и́ска по́вече кекс, защо́то не ѝ се яде́. (*b*) Тя не се́ чу́вства добре́. От вче́ра я боли́ стома́хът. (*c*) Пи́е ѝ се вода́./На На́дя ѝ се пи́е вода́. (*d*) Ми́налата годи́на по това́ вре́ме тя и́маше грип с висо́ка температу́ра. (*e*) Чове́к тря́бва да се гри́жи за здра́вето си. **2** (*a*) F: Миле́на не и́ска кекс, защо́то я боли́ стома́хът/и́ма бо́лки в стома́ха. (*b*) F: Ке́ксът мно́го ѝ харе́са. (*c*) T. (*d*) F: Тя ня́ма хре́ма и ка́шлица. (*e*) T.

Exercises 1 i (*c*); ii (*g*); iii (*e*); iv (*f*); v (*a*); vi (*b*), (*d*), (*e*); vii (*b*), (*d*), (*e*). **2** (*a*) (i) Не, не гó болят очите. (ii) Не, не я́ боли́ зъб. (iii) Не, не ги́ болят крака́та. (iv) Не, не гó боли́ коля́ното. (v) Не, не я́ боли́ ръка́та. (*b*) (i) Не ми́ се хо́ди на плаж. (ii) Не ми́ се пи́е чай. (iii) Не ми́ се гово́ри български. (iv) Не ми́ се у́чи. (v) Не ми́ се рабо́ти на компю́тър. **3** Какво́ ти е?/Какво́ ти ка́за ле́карят?/Спи ли ти се?/Ску́чно ли ти е?/Не се́ безпоко́й! Ско́ро ще ти ми́не. **4** Ле́карят ми ка́за, че и́мам (*a*) грип; (*b*) апендиси́т; (*c*) висо́ка температу́ра; (*d*) хре́ма, (*e*) хепати́т. **5** (*a*) Не можа́ да оти́де, защо́то го боле́ше глава́та. (*b*) Не можа́х да я донеса́, защо́то ме боле́ше кръ́стът. (*c*) Не можа́ха да го разгле́дат, защо́то ги боля́ха крака́та. (*d*) Не можа́хме да го пра́тим, защо́то ня́махме ма́рки. (*e*) Не можа́х да ям от тях, защо́то и́мах бо́лки в стома́ха. **6** (*a*) Оти́дох да си ку́пя марато́нки. (*b*) Оти́дохме да си почи́нем. (*c*) Оти́дох да си ку́пя лека́рства. (*d*) Оти́дох да посре́щна дъщеря́ си. (*e*) Оти́дох на ле́кар. (*f*) Оти́дохме да пра́тим писмо́ на роди́телите си.

Do you understand? 1 Мъжъ́т на г-жа́ Ко́линс не се́ чу́вства добре́. **2** Той и́ма си́лно главобо́лие и все му е студе́но. **3** Ко́жата на г-н Ко́линс е черве́на, защо́то вче́ра цял ден бе́ше на пла́жа. **4** Г-н Ко́линс тря́бваше да сло́жи ша́пка. **5** Сега́ той тря́бва да сто́й на ся́нка ня́колко дни.

Unit 16

Questions 1 (*a*) После́дния ден в хоте́ла плати́хме сме́тката. (*b*) Той ѝ подари́ еди́н беле́жник. (*c*) За г-жа́ Джо́нсън избра́хме една́ сре́бърна гри́вна. (*d*) Да, да́дох го. (*e*) Той ще ми я пра́ти или́ по и́мейла или́ с факс. (*f*) Це́лия ден гово́рих на бъ́лгарски. **2** (*a*) T. (*b*) T. (*c*) F: Ма́йкъл Джо́нсън избра́ една́ сре́бърна гри́вна за жена́ си. (*d*) F: Той не му́ пока́за програ́мата. (*e*) F: Ако́ На́дя бе́ше на не́гово мя́сто, тя ня́маше да се безпокой. (*f*) F: Боя́н Анто́нов разбра́ това́, кое́то и́скаше да зна́е.

Exercises 1 (*a*) Ако́ ня́махме ва́жна сре́ща, щя́хме да оти́дем на плаж. (*b*) Ако́ ня́мах дру́га ра́бота, щях да оти́да на Ви́тоша. (*c*) Ако́ ня́махме дру́га ра́бота, щя́хме да оти́дем на те́нис. (*d*) Ако́ ня́мах ва́жна сре́ща, щях да оти́да на го́сти. (*e*) Ако́ ня́мах дру́га ра́бота, щях да оти́да на ски. **2** Ако́ и́сках да ку́пя пода́рък от Бълга́рия, щя́х да ку́пя кути́я бонбо́ни/календа́р/плака́т/бути́лка ви́но/кни́га/кути́я с луксо́зни пли́кове. **3** (*a*) Да, ако́ бях на тво́е мя́сто, щях да прие́ма пока́ната. Не, ако́ бях на тво́е мя́сто, ня́маше да прие́ма пока́ната. (*b*) Да, ако́ бях на твóе мя́сто, щях да кýпя цветя́. Не, акó бях на твóе мя́сто, ня́маше да кýпя цветя́. (*c*) Да, акó бях на твóе мя́сто, щях да изпрáтя момúчето. Не, акó бях на твóе мя́сто, ня́маше да изпрáтя момúчето. (*d*) Да, акó бях на твóе мя́сто, щях да донесá подáрък. Не, акó бях на твóе мя́сто, ня́маше да донесá подáрък. (*e*) Да, акó бях на твóе мя́сто, щях да посрéщна америкáнеца. Не, акó бях на твóе мя́сто, ня́маше да посрéщна америкáнеца. **4** (*a*) Невéна дáде две кáртички от Рúлския манастúр на Джон и Éли. Те úскаха óще, но тя ня́маше пóвече. (*b*) Нúе дáдохме две кáртички от Рúлския манастúр на турúстите. Те úскаха óще, но нúе ня́махме пóвече. (*c*) Г-н и г-жá Кóлинс дáдоха две кáртички от Рúлския манастúр на свóя прия́тел. Той úскаше óще, но те ня́маха пóвече. **5** (*a*) óще; (*b*) óще; (*c*) пóвече; (*d*) пóвече; (*e*) óще; (*f*) пóвече; (*g*) óще. **6** *You* Каквó úскаше да дадé г-жá Антóнова на Мáйкъл Джóнсън? *Your friend* Г-жá Антóнова úскаше да дадé на Мáйкъл Джóнсън мáлък подáрък. *You* Каквó разбрá тя от нéго? *Your friend* Тя разбрá от нéго, че женá му мнóго обúча кристáлни вáзи. *You* Къдé отúде тя вчéра сутринтá? *Your friend* Вчéра сутринтá тя отúде в магазúн за подáръци. *You* Каквó úскаше да изберé? *Your friend* Úскаше да изберé нáй-красúвата кристáлна вáза. *You* Защó тя не кýпи кристáлна вáза? *Your friend* Тя не кýпи кристáлна вáза, защóто кристáлните вáзи бя́ха ужáсно скъпи. *You* Каквó избрá г-жá Антóнова? *Your friend* Г-жá Антóнова избрá еднá красúва икóна. *You* На когó дáде тя пóсле подáръка за г-жá Джóнсън? *Your friend* Пóсле тя дáде подáръка за г-жá Джóнсън на Николáй. **7** (*a*) Г-н и г-жá Кóлинс пúтаха къдé úма магазúн за плодовé и зеленчýци. (*b*) Невéна попúта г-н Джóнсън далú úма/úма ли/свобóдно врéме. (*c*) Боя́н Антóнов попúта когá Мáйкъл Джóнсън ще изпрáти прогрáмата. (*d*) Милéна кáза, че úма срéща в два часá. (*e*) Марк и Éли кáзаха, че ще замúнат за Вáрна на двáйсет и óсми май. (*f*) Шéфът кáза, че не úска пóвече кафé.

Do you understand? **1** Мáйкъл Джóнсън ще изпрáти óще реклáми. **2** Той мóже да дадé реклáмите на Николáй. **3** Милéна разбрá за чудéсната възмóжност от Нáдя. **4** Акó бéше на мя́стото на Николáй, Милéна веднáга щéше да приéме. **5** Тя щéше да му ги донесé. **6** Николáй предпочúта да изпрáти Милéна.

Unit 17

Questions **1** (*a*) Не, не é бóлна. (*b*) Учýден съм, защóто та́зи су́трин я видя́х от трамва́я. (*c*) Кога́то я видя́х, На́дя оти́ваше на ра́бота. (*d*) На́дя не тря́бваше да парки́ра пред бо́лницата. (*e*) Мото́рът спря́ пред бо́лницата. (*f*) Ка́зах му, че кола́та и́ма повре́да. **2** (*a*) F: Полица́ят пока́зваше на На́дя зна́ка «Спи́рането забране́но». (*b*) F: На́дя ня́маше предста́ва какво́ му е на мото́ра. (*c*) T. (*d*) T. (*e*) F: Не́йният позна́т наме́ри повре́дата веdна́га. (*f*) F: Кола́та ня́маше бензи́н.

Exercises 1 не **рабо́теше** добре́, в **мото́ра,** на **серви́з,** да **ка́ра** кола́та, **с** трамва́й, **и́маше** неприя́тности, **пред** бо́лницата, **повре́дата, тря́бваше, спи́рането** е забране́но, **гло́ба, и́ма** повре́да, «Спи́рането **забране́но**», **позна́т, кола́та**, ня́маше **бензи́н**. **2** (*a*) Какво́ пра́веха те? (*b*) Какво́ пра́веше той? (*c*) Какво́ пра́веше тя? (*d*) Какво́ пра́веше той? (*e*) Какво́ пра́веха те? (*f*) Какво́ пра́веха те? **3** Това́ ста́на преди́ петна́йсет мину́ти. Аз бях в хоте́ла. Ча́ках такси́. И́маше са́мо еди́н мъж. Той гово́реше по телефо́на. Той стое́ше пред хоте́ла. **4** (*a*) Преди́ аз рабо́тех в еди́н магази́н. (*b*) Преди́ две годи́ни аз рабо́тех в музе́я. (*c*) Преди́ аз рабо́тех като́ сервитьо́р. (сервитьо́рка if you are a woman!) (*d*) Аз рабо́тех като́ учи́тел(ка) преди́ мно́го годи́ни. (*e*) Преди́ рабо́тех в ба́нката. **5** (*a*) (i) и́дваше, (ii) дойде́; (*b*) (i) ка́зваше, (ii) ка́за; (*c*) (i) ку́пих. (ii) купу́вах.

Do you understand? 1 Г-жа́ Ко́линс не мо́же да спре ду́ша, защо́то кра́нът е повре́ден. **2** Той гово́реше с една́ жена́ пред вхо́да на Мо́рската гради́на. **3** Пъ́рво кра́нът на ду́ша се развали́. По́сле мъжъ́т ѝ изче́зна. **4** Кога́то го видя́ портие́рът, г-н Ко́линс купу́ваше не́що. **5** Вси́чки зна́еха къде́ е г-н Ко́линс.

Unit 18

Questions 1 (*a*) Миле́на о́ще не се́ е обля́кла. (*b*) Да, прия́телката на Миле́на си е оти́шла. (*c*) Никола́й предла́га да вечеря́т след представле́нието. (*d*) Представле́нието не е́ запо́чнало, защо́то е о́ще ра́но. (*e*) Никола́й е ста́нал мно́го разсе́ян. (*f*) Споре́д Миле́на Никола́й се е умори́л от мно́го у́чене. **2** (*a*) T. (*b*) F: Ня́ма да закъсне́ят, защо́то Миле́на ве́че е реши́ла какво́ да облече́. (*c*) F: Никола́й о́ще не е́ вече́рял. (*d*) T. (*e*) T. (*f*) F: На Никола́й ня́ма да му е ску́чно с Миле́на.

Exercises 1 (*a*) Запо́чнало ли е представле́нието? (*b*) О́ще не съм се обля́кла. (*c*) Ня́мам предста́ва как съм напра́вил така́ва гре́шка! (*d*) Какво́ се е слу́чило? (*e*) Ве́че съм реши́ла какво́ да облека́. **2** (*a*) Не е́ вя́рно, На́дя е дошла́!

(*b*) Не е́ вя́рно, На́дя е доне́сла цветя́! (*c*) Не е́ вя́рно, На́дя е ку́пила бонбо́ни! (*d*) Не е́ вя́рно, На́дя е напра́вила кафе́! **3** (*a*) Хо́дила ли си в Бо́ровец? (*b*) Хо́дили ли сте в Бо́ровец? (*c*) Хо́дили ли сте в Бо́ровец? (*d*) Хо́дил ли си в Бо́ровец? **4** (*a*) Забра́вила съм да взе́ма чадъ̀р. Ста́нала съм мно́го разсе́яна! (*b*) Забра́вил съм да взе́ма фо́тоапара́т. Ста́нал съм мно́го разсе́ян! (*c*) Забра́вили сме да взе́мем пари́. Ста́нали сме мно́го разсе́яни! **5** (*a*) Ня́маше би́ра. Г-н Анто́нов бе́ше забра́вил да ку́пи би́ра. (*b*) Ня́маше хляб. Г-жа́ Анто́нова бе́ше забра́вила да ку́пи хляб. (*c*) Ня́маше дома́ти. Г-н и г-жа́ Ко́линс бя́ха забра́вили да ку́пят дома́ти. (*d*) Ня́маше гази́рана вода́. Аз бях забра́вил/а да ку́пя гази́рана вода́. **6** (*a*) Взех фо́тоапара́та, но сега́ го ня́ма. Си́гурно съм го загу́бил/а. (*b*) Взех ша́пката, но сега́ я ня́ма. Си́гурно съм я загу́бил/а. (*c*) Взех сни́мките, но сега́ ги ня́ма. Си́гурно съм ги загу́бил/а. (*d*) Взех беле́жника, но сега́ го ня́ма. Си́гурно съм го загу́бил/а. (*e*) Взех кни́гата, но сега́ я ня́ма. Си́гурно съм я загу́бил/а. (*f*) Взех ве́стника, но сега́ го ня́ма. Си́гурно съм го загу́бил/а.

Do you understand? **1** Джордж о́ще го боли́ глава́та. **2** На не́го му е ску́чно. **3** Тя не му́ е ка́зала досега́, че на Зла́тни пя́съци и́ма игри́ще за голф. **4** Джордж не е́ взел сти́ковете си. **5** Джордж ще взе́ме сти́кове под на́ем. **6** Францу́зинът от съсе́дната ста́я ве́че е игра́л голф на Зла́тни пя́съци.

Unit 19

Questions **1** (*a*) Би́знесменът и́ска да смени́ ста́ята си. (*b*) Конта́ктът за самобръсна́чка не рабо́ти, прозо́рецът е счу́пен и вентила́торът в ба́нята е развале́н. (*c*) Ста́ята му е шу́мна, защо́то е то́чно над рестора́нта. (*d*) Би́знесменът не мо́же да ча́ка, защо́то и́ма ва́жна сре́ща. (*e*) Дру́гите го́сти на хоте́ла се опла́кват от шума́ на трамва́ите. (*f*) Той предла́га да го сло́жат в ста́я на двана́йсетия ета́ж. **2** (*a*) F: Би́знесменът ка́за, че не би́л дово́лен от ста́ята, коя́то са му да́ли. (*b*) F: Прозо́рецът бил счу́пен. (*c*) T. (*d*) F: Той щял да се въ́рне към шест часа́. (*e*) T.

Exercises **1** Не съм дово́лен/дово́лна от: (*a*) цена́та, (*b*) продава́чката, (*c*) сервитьо́ра, (*d*) серви́за, (*e*) храна́та, (*f*) ка́чеството на сни́мките, (*g*) обслу́жването. **2** (*a*) Кюфте́то, коéто сте ми да́ли, не ми́ харе́сва. (*b*) Су́пата, коя́то сте ми да́ли, не ми́ харе́сва. (*c*) Ви́ното, кое́то сте ми да́ли, не ми́ харе́сва. (*d*) Сала́тите, кои́то сте ми да́ли, не ми́ харе́сват.

(*e*) Сладоле́дът, ко́йто сте ми да́ли, не ми́ харе́сва. **3** (*a*) Да́дох ви ги. Е́то ги. (*b*) Да́дох ви я. Е́то я. (*c*) Да́дох Ви го. Е́то го. (*d*) Да́дох Ви я. Е́то я. (*e*) Да́дох ви ги. Е́то ги. **4** (*a*) Сно́щи не можа́х да спя от кафе́то. (*b*) Сно́щи не можа́х да спя от главобо́лие. (*c*) Сно́щи не можа́х да спя от горещина́. (*d*) Сно́щи не можа́х да спя от кома́рите. (*e*) Сно́щи не можа́х да спя от му́зиката в рестора́нта. **5** Nadya is talking as far as „И́мало мно́го хо́ра на панаи́ра". Then Nikolai takes over. **6** (*a*) Сва́тбата била́ вче́ра. (*b*) Те празну́вали в рестора́нт «Берли́н». (*c*) Те се запозна́ли в Бо́ровец. (*d*) Той дошъ́л в Со́фия на го́сти на роди́телите на Е́ли. (*e*) Сега́ ще́ли да оти́дат на море́.

Do you understand? 1 На́дя тря́бва да предаде́ на дире́ктора, че клие́нтите не били́ дово́лни от тя́хната ра́бота. **2** Поръ́чали 1 200 брошу́ри, а полу́чили са́мо 600. Па́пките и́мали дефе́кти, а визи́тните ка́ртички били́ на лошока́чествена харти́я. **3** Клие́нтът се оба́жда за вто́ри път, за да се извини́. **4** Па́пките и визи́тните ка́ртички били́ поръ́чани на дру́го мя́сто в дру́га фи́рма. **5** Ка́зват, че в та́зи фи́рма ста́вали мно́го гре́шки.

Unit 20

Questions 1 (*a*) Миле́на пока́за Центра́лна поща на г-н и г-жа́ Ко́линс. (*b*) Г-н и г-жа́ Ко́линс би́ха и́скали да до́йдат в Бълга́рия през зи́мата. (*c*) Ако́ и́маха възмо́жност, те би́ха оти́шли в Бо́ровец. (*d*) Миле́на би и́скала г-жа́ Ко́линс да помо́гне на Никола́й на Хи́йтроу. (*e*) Никола́й би и́скал Миле́на да пъту́ва с не́го. **2** (*a*) F: Никола́й ще пъту́ва за́едно с г-н и г-жа́ Ко́линс. (*b*) F: Г-н и г-жа́ Ко́линс са видя́ли по́вечето забележи́телности о́коло Ва́рна. (*c*) T. (*d*) F: Г-н и г-жа́ Ко́линс ще пи́шат на Миле́на от А́нглия. (*e*) F: Никола́й ще пра́ти ка́ртичка на Миле́на от Че́лмсфорд.

Exercises 1 (i) (*a*) Ще ѝ се оба́дя, (*b*) Оба́дих ѝ се ве́че, (*c*) Ве́че ѝ се оба́дих; (ii) (*a*) Ще му се оба́дя, (*b*) Оба́дих му се ве́че, (*c*) Ве́че му се оба́дих; (iii) (*a*) Ще им се оба́дя, (*b*) Оба́дих им се ве́че, (*c*) Ве́че им се оба́дих; (iv) (*a*) Ще ѝ се оба́дя, (*b*) Оба́дих ѝ се ве́че, (*c*) Ве́че ѝ се оба́дих. **2** (*a*) Би́хте ли ми ка́зали Ва́шия адре́с? (*b*) Би́хте ли ми се оба́дили по́-къ́сно? (*c*) Би́хте ли ни помо́гнали да наме́рим пъ́тя за Ва́рна? (*d*) Би́хте ли ми да́ли дру́га ста́я? (*e*) Би́хте ли ми поръ́чали такси́ за де́сет часа́? **3** (*a*) Ще ку́пя/Бих ку́пил, ако́ наме́ря не́що ху́баво. (*b*) Ще се оба́дя/Бих се оба́дил(а), ако́ и́мам вре́ме. (*c*) Ще до́йда/Бих дошъ́л (дошла́), ако́ се чу́вствам по́-добре́. (*d*) Ще уча́ствам/Бих уча́ствал(а), ако́ и́мам пари́. **4** (*a*) At a conference in Bulgaria. (*b*) At the beginning of the conference. (*c*) Ladies and Gentlemen, Dear Friends. (*d*) From all over the world. (*e*) They are all friends of Bulgaria. (*f*) Sofia. (*g*) He hopes their deliberations will be enjoyable and fruitful.

Do you understand? 1 На лети́щето г-н и г-жа́ Ко́линс ви́ждат Неве́на. **2** Неве́на е на лети́щето, защо́то тя изпра́ща Марк Де́йвис и жена́ му. **3** Неве́на мно́го е разка́звала на Марк за г-жа́ Ко́линс. **4** Марк щял да изпра́ти съобще́ние на г-жа́ Ко́линс за една́ конфере́нция за Бълга́рия. **5** Г-жа́ Ко́линс би уча́ствала в конфере́нцията, ако́ не е зае́та по съ́щото вре́ме. **6** Г-жа́ Ко́линс да́ва на Марк визи́тната си ка́ртичка.

Pronunciation and spelling

Bulgarian letters are constant and reliable. English letters are fickle. In English, one letter can have many sounds and the right sound depends on the letters that come before and after it. This makes English spelling and pronunciation very difficult. Compare, for example, *laughter* and *slaughter* or *bough*, *cough* and *enough*. Bulgarian letters are altogether more trustworthy and their pronunciation only rarely depends on the company they keep. One letter has basically one sound. So you can usually pronounce Bulgarian correctly by moving logically through the words and combining the sounds of the individual letters as you go. This also makes spelling relatively straightforward.

A few Bulgarian letters do, however, alter their pronunciation depending on the company they keep and also on their position in the word. This particularly affects certain consonants which we can conveniently group in pairs. In each pair one of the letters is 'voiced' (i.e. pronounced with your vocal chords vibrating) and the other is 'voiceless' (i.e. pronounced without using your vocal chords, almost as if whispering). Read these letters out loud, holding your Adam's apple between your thumb and forefinger and you'll see the difference!

Voiced	**Voiceless**
б	**п**
в	**ф**
г	**к**
д	**т**
ж	**ш**
з	**с**

(Additional pairs are **дж/ч** and **дз/ц**. The consonant **х**, which has no partner, is also voiceless.)

Remember particularly that:

(**a**) When a voiced consonant is the last letter in a word, you usually pronounce it as if it were its voiceless partner:

Written		**Pronounced**
хля**б**	*bread*	хля**п**
ху́ба**в**	*beautiful*	ху́ба**ф**
Бо**г**	*God*	Бо**к**
мла**д**	*young*	мла**т**
мъ**ж**	*man*	мъ**ш**
вле**з**!	*come in*	вле**с**!

(Did you notice ху́ба**в** (ху́ба**ф**) and мла**д** (мла**т**) when you listened to the alphabet on the recording? And you will remember how Victoria Collins has to spell her name in Bulgarian: **Ко́линс**.) (See p. xv.)

(**b**) When **б**, **в**, **г**, **д**, **ж** or **з** come before a voiceless consonant, they too become voiceless: а**в**тобу́с (а**ф**тобу́с) *bus*, **вк**ъщи (**фк**ъщи) *at home*, командиро́**вк**а (командиро́**фк**а) *business trip*, ирла́н**дк**а (ирла́н**тк**а) *Irishwoman*, дъ**жд** (дъ**шт**) *rain*, и́**з**хо**д** (и́**с**хо**т**) *exit*.

(**c**) Bulgarian vowels are all single syllables and pure sounds, unlike the English vowels which begin on one sound and end on another (diphthongs). In Bulgarian, such sounds are formed by placing the vowels **а**, **е**, **и**, **о** or **у** before or after the letter **й**, which is itself not a vowel and fulfils the function of the English '*y*' (as in *yes*, *soya* or *York*): ха́**й**де! *come on!*; здраве́**й**! *hello!*; **й**од *iodine*.

(**d**) Bulgarians do tend to speak fast and the faster they speak the further they depart from 'standard' pronunciation. Listen, for example, how the letter '**о**', when unstressed, particularly when coming after a stressed syllable, is pronounced more like the letter '**у**', as in Ви́т**о**ша and бли́з**о** (pronounced Ви́т**у**ша and бли́з**у**). Similarly, the letter '**а**', especially when coming after or before a stressed syllable, gets 'reduced' to '**ъ**', as in ма́с**а**, ч**а**со́вник and р**а**зби́р**а** се (pronounced ч**ъ**со́вник and р**ъ**зби́р**ъ** се).

(**e**) The letter **ь** is only found after consonants and in combination with the letter **о**: шоф**ьо́**р *driver*.

(**f**) The diphthong **йо/йе** is only found after a vowel: фоа**йе́** *foyer* or at the beginning of a word: **Й**орк *York*.

Numerals

Cardinals

0	ну́ла	*23*	два́йсет и три
1	едно́ (еди́н, една́)	*24*	два́йсет и че́тири
2	две (два)	*25*	два́йсет и пет
3	три	*26*	два́йсет и шест
4	че́тири	*27*	два́йсет и се́дем
5	пет	*28*	два́йсет и о́сем
6	шест	*29*	два́йсет и де́вет
7	се́дем	*30*	три́йсет (три́десет)
8	о́сем	*40*	чети́рисет (чети́ридесет)
9	де́вет	*50*	петдесе́т
10	де́сет	*60*	шейсе́т (шестдесе́т)
11	едина́йсет	*70*	седемдесе́т
12	двана́йсет	*80*	осемдесе́т
13	трина́йсет	*90*	деветдесе́т
14	четирина́йсет	*100*	сто
15	петна́йсет	*101*	сто и едно́ (еди́н, една́)
16	шестна́йсет	*110*	сто и де́сет
17	седемна́йсет	*123*	сто два́йсет и три
18	осемна́йсет	*200*	две́ста
19	деветна́йсет	*300*	три́ста
20	два́йсет (два́десет)	*400*	че́тиристотин
21	два́йсет и едно́	*500*	пе́тстотин
22	два́йсет и две		

Numbers of four digits and more are separated by a space where English uses a comma.

1 000	хиля́да	*1 000 000*	еди́н милио́н
2 000	две хи́ляди	*2 000 000*	два милио́на
3 000	три хи́ляди		

Ordinals

1st	първи	*11th*	едина́йсети
2nd	вто́ри	*21st*	два́йсет и първи
3rd	тре́ти	*22nd*	два́йсет и вто́ри
4th	четвъ́рти		
5th	пе́ти		
6th	ше́сти		
7th	се́дми		
8th	о́сми		
9th	деве́ти		
10th	десе́ти		

Grammatical terms

1 Prepositions

Spatial prepositions

Location (*Where?*)		**Movement** (*Where to/from?*, etc.)	
в	*in*	към	*to(wards)*
върху́	*on top of*	о́коло	*(a)round*
до	*next to*	от	*from; out of*
зад	*behind*	по	*on; along*
между́	*between*	през	*through*
на	*on, at*	след	*after*
над	*above*		
под	*under*		
пред	*in front of*		
срещу́	*opposite*		

Bulgarian prepositions and their English equivalents

без	*without*	без превода́ч
	to	часъ́т е двана́йсет без пет
в (във)	*in*	в Пло́вдив
	to	(оти́вам) в ба́нката, в Ме́лник
	at	(рабо́тя) въ́в фи́рма „Прогре́с“, в двана́йсет часа́, в моме́нта
	on	в сря́да
до	*next to*	хоте́лът е до ба́нката
	to	(сти́гам) до площа́да, екску́рзия до Ви́тоша
	until	до четвъ́рти ю́ни
	till	до къ́сно
за	*for*	писмо́ за Вас, магази́н за плодове́, за две се́дмици, (замина́вам) за А́нглия
	about	(гово́ря) за англича́нката
	to	пъ́тят за Ва́рна
	—	(пи́там) за пъ́тя
към	*towards*	(оти́вам) към Мо́рската гради́на
	around	към шест часа́
	—	молба́ към Вас

на	*on*	на ка́ртата, на па́ртера, на почи́вка, на у́лица «Рако́вски», на Ви́тоша, на петна́йсети май
	at	на ма́сата, на лети́щето, на светофа́ра
	of	ка́рта на Со́фия, ча́нтата на Джон
	in	на юг; на англи́йски ези́к
	to	(оти́вам) на море́, на о́пера
	for	(да ку́пя) пода́рък на сина́ на Анто́нови
о́коло	*around*	о́коло града́
	about	о́коло пет часа́
от	*from*	писмо́ от Ло́ндон
	(made) of	су́па от зеленчу́ци
	with	дово́лен съм от хоте́ла
	since	в Со́фия съм от четвъ́рти май
	—	и́мам ну́жда от превода́ч
по	*on*	по ра́диото, по телефо́на
	over	по висо́ките планини́
	along	по пъ́тя, по Черномо́рието
под	*under*	под ма́сата
	—	(да взе́ма) кола́ под на́ем
преди́	*before*	преди́ о́бед
	ago	преди́ две се́дмици
през	*through*	през града́
	in/during	през зи́мата, през ме́сец май
	at	през нощта́
проти́в	*against*	проти́в не́го
с (със)	*with*	сре́ща с не́го, с удово́лствие
	on	(поздравя́вам) с пра́зника
	—	(да запозна́я) с г-н Анто́нов

след	{ *after*	след тéбе, след рáбота
	in	след две сéдмици
у	{ *at*	у нас
	with	кни́гата е у нéя

2 Nouns

Gender	Indefinite singular	Indefinite plural	Definite singular	Definite plural
Masculine				
consonant	хотéл	хотéли	хотéлът	хотéлите
	вéстник	вéстници	вéстникът	вéстниците
	лéкар	лéкари	лéкарят	лéкарите
	учи́тел	учи́тели	учи́телят	учи́телите
-й	музéй	музéи	музéят	музéите
one syllable	ключ	клю́чове	клю́чът	клю́човете
	NB Plural after numbers: хотéла вéстника лéкаря учи́теля музéя клю́ча		NB Non-subject definite: хотéла вéстника лéкаря учи́теля музéя клю́ча	
Feminine				
-а	женá	жени́	женáта	жени́те
-я	стáя	стáи	стáята	стáите
consonant	вéчер	вéчери	вечертá	вéчерите
	нарóдност	нарóдности	народносттá	нарóдностите
	нощ	нóщи	нощтá	нóщите
	прóлет	прóлети	пролеттá	прóлетите
	сýтрин	сýтрини	сутринтá	сýтрините
Neuter				
-о	писмó	писмá	писмóто	писмáта
-е	кафé	кафéта	кафéто	кафéтата
-ие	списáние	списáния	списáнието	списáнията
-и	такси́	такси́та	такси́то	такси́тата
-ю	меню́	меню́та	меню́то	меню́тата

Some irregular plurals

Masculine	**Feminine**	**Neuter**
брат-брáтя		
бъ́лгарин-бъ́лгари	ръкá-ръцé	детé-децá
господи́н-господá		и́ме-именá
гост-гóсти		окó-очи́
ден-дни		ухó-уши́
крак-кракá		
мъж-мъжé		

3 Adjectives and adverbs

	Masculine	Feminine	Neuter	Plural
without loss of vowel				
Indefinite	висóк син	висóка си́ня	висóко си́ньо	висóки си́ни
Definite	висóкият си́ният	висóката си́нята	висóкото си́ньото	висóките си́ните
with loss of vowel				
Indefinite	добър прия́тен	добрá прия́тна	добрó прия́тно	добри́ прия́тни
Definite	добри́ят прия́тният	добрáта прия́тната	добрóто прия́тното	добри́те прия́тните
ending in -ски				
Indefinite	български	българска	българско	български
Definite	българският	българската	българското	българските

Comparison of adjectives

добър	*good*	пó-добър	*better*	нáй-добър	*best*

Comparison of adverbs

бързо	*quickly*	пó-бързо	*quicker*	нáй-бързо	*quickest*
добрé	*well*	пó-добрé	*better*	нáй-добрé	*best*
мáлко	*little*	пó-мáлко	*less*	нáй-мáлко	*least*
мнóго	*much*	пóвече	*more*	нáй-мнóго	*most*

4 Pronouns

Subject form	Object form Full	Short	Indirect object form Full	Short
аз	мéне	ме	на мéне	ми
ти	тéбе	те	на тéбе	ти
той	нéго	го	на нéго	му
тя	нéя	я	на нéя	й
то	нéго	го	на нéго	му
ни́е	нас	ни	на нас	ни
*ви́е	*вас	*ви	на *вас	*ви
те	тях	ги	на тях	им

(*When the polite form for *you* is used referring to a single person, then you must use a capital letter in writing. This also applies to the possessives.)

Subject form		Possessive adjectival forms Masculine	Feminine	Neuter	Plural
аз	indefinite	мой	мóя	мóе	мóи
	definite	мóят	мóята	мóето	мóите
ти	indefinite	твой	твóя	твóе	твóи
	definite	твóят	твóята	твóето	твóите
той	indefinite	нéгов	нéгова	нéгово	нéгови
	definite	нéговият	нéговата	нéговото	нéговите
тя	indefinite	нéин	нéйна	нéйно	нéйни
	definite	нéйният	нéйната	нéйното	нéйните
то	indefinite	нéгов	нéгова	нéгово	нéгови
	definite	нéговият	нéговата	нéговото	нéговите
нѝе	indefinite	наш	нáша	нáше	нáши
	definite	нáшият	нáшата	нáшето	нáшите
вѝе	indefinite	ваш	вáша	вáше	вáши
	definite	вáшият	вáшата	вáшето	вáшите
те	indefinite	тéхен	тя́хна	тя́хно	тéхни
	definite	тéхният	тя́хната	тя́хното	тéхните
		own			
той тя то те	indefinite	свой	свóя	свóе	свóи
	definite	свóят	свóята	свóето	свóите

Definiteness and possession

(*a*) Short forms (noun + definite article + short indirect object pronoun)
(*b*) Full forms (possessive adjective + definite article + noun)

Singular Short		Full	Plural Short		full
лéкарят ми	=	мóят лéкар	кýфарите ми	=	мóите кýфари
стáята ми	=	мóята стáя	чáнтите ми	=	мóите чáнти
детéто ми	=	мóето детé	децáта ми	=	мóите децá

Other pronouns

	Persons					Things
	Subject form				Object form	
	Masc.	Fem.	Neuter	Plural		
Demonstrative pronouns	то́зи	та́зи	това́	те́зи		това́
Questions (interrogative pronouns)	кой какъ́в	коя́ каква́	кое́ какво́	кой какви́	кого́	какво́
Relative pronouns	ко́йто какъ́вто	коя́то каква́то	кое́то какво́то	ко́йто какви́то	кого́то	какво́то
Indefinite pronouns	ня́кой	ня́коя	ня́кое	ня́кои	ня́кого	не́що
Negative pronouns	ни́кой	ни́коя	ни́кое	ни́кои	ни́кого	ни́що
Generalizing pronouns	все́ки	вся́ка	вся́ко	всички	все́киго	вси́чко

Other question words and their relative equivalents

защо́?	*why?*	защо́то	*because*
как?	*how?*	ка́кто	*as*
кога́?	*when?*	кога́то	(the time) *when*
къде́?	*where?*	къде́то	(the place) *where*

5 Verbs

съм *to be*

Present		**Future** **Positive**	**Negative**
аз	съм	ще съм/бъ́да	ня́ма да съм/бъ́да
ти	си	ще си/бъ́деш	ня́ма да си/бъ́деш
той тя то	е	ще е/бъ́де	ня́ма да е/бъ́де
ни́е	сме	ще сме/бъ́дем	ня́ма да сме/бъ́дем
ви́е	сте	ще сте/бъ́дете	ня́ма да сте/бъ́дете
те	са	ще са/бъ́дат	ня́ма да са/бъ́дат

Past		**Present perfect**
аз	бях	бил съм/била́ съм/било́ съм
ти	бе́ше	бил си/била́ си/било́ си

той / тя / то	бе́ше	бил е / била́ е / било́ е
ни́е	бя́хме	били́ сме
ви́е	бя́хте	били́ сте
те	бя́ха	били́ са

Future in the past

	Positive	Negative
аз	щях да съм/бъ́да	ня́маше да съм/бъ́да
ти	ще́ше да си/бъ́деш	ня́маше да си/бъ́деш
той / тя / то	ще́ше да е/бъ́де	ня́маше да е/бъ́де
ни́е	щя́хме да сме/бъ́дем	ня́маше да сме/бъ́дем
ви́е	шя́хте да сте/бъ́дете	ня́маше да сте/бъ́дете
те	щя́ха да са/бъ́дат	ня́маше да са/бъ́дат

Present tense

	e-pattern (1st Conjugation)	и-pattern (2nd Conjugation)	a-pattern (3rd Conjugation)
аз	пи́ша	рабо́тя	и́мам
ти	пи́шеш	рабо́т**иш**	и́м**аш**
той / тя / то	пи́ше	рабо́т**и**	и́м**а**
ни́е	пи́шем	рабо́т**им**	и́м**аме**
ви́е	пи́шете	рабо́т**ите**	и́м**ате**
те	пи́шат	рабо́тят	и́м**ат**

Imperative (commands)

	Positive (Perfective and imperfective) Singular	Plural	Negative (Imperfective) Singular	Plural
e-pattern			**a-pattern**	
(да) се́дна	седни́! *sit down*	седне́те!	не ся́дай! неде́й да ся́даш	не ся́дайте! неде́йте да ся́дате
и-pattern				
платя́	плати́! *pay*	плате́те!	не пла́щай! неде́й да пла́щаш	не пла́щайте! неде́йте да пла́щате

a-pattern				
ча́кам	ча́кай! *wait*	ча́кайте!	не ча́кай! неде́й да ча́каш	не ча́кайте! неде́йте да ча́кате
Verbs with two vowels				
пи́я	пий! *drink*	пи́йте!	не пий! неде́й да пи́еш	не пи́йте! неде́йте да пи́ете
Irregular				
(да) ви́дя	виж! *look*	ви́жте!	не гле́дай! неде́й да гле́даш	не гле́дайте! неде́йте да гле́дате
(да) вля́за	влез! *go/come in*	вле́зте!	не вли́зай! неде́й да вли́заш	не вли́зайте! неде́йте да вли́зате
(да) до́йда	ела́! *come*	ела́те!	не и́двай! неде́й да и́дваш	не и́двайте! неде́йте да и́двате
(да) държа́	дръж! *hold*	дръ́жте!	не дръж! неде́й да държи́ш	не дръ́жте! неде́йте да държи́те
(да) изля́за	изле́з! *go out*	изле́зте!	не изли́зай! неде́й да изли́заш	не изли́зайте! неде́йте да изли́зате
(да) оти́да	иди́! *go*	иде́те!	не оти́вай! неде́й да оти́ваш	не оти́вайте! неде́йте да оти́вате
(да) ям	яж! *eat*	я́жте!	не яж! неде́й да яде́ш	не я́жте! неде́йте да яде́те

Past tense (personal endings*)

	Past				**Past imperfect**			
аз	-ах	-ях**	-их	-ох	-ех	-ах	-ях	-я́х
ти	-а	-я	-и	-е	-еше	-аше	-яше	-е́ше
той тя то	-а	-я	-и	-е	-еше	-аше	-яше	-е́ше
ни́е	-ахме	-яхме	-ихме	-охме	-ехме	-ахме	-яхме	-я́хме
ви́е	-ахте	-яхте	-ихте	-охте	-ехте	-ахте	-яхте	-я́хте
те	-аха	-яха	-иха	-оха	-еха	-аха	-яха	-я́ха

(*For the main conjugation patterns in the past see Verb Tables 1 and 2.)
(**With and without stress.)

Table 1 Ordinary past tense

Here are the main verb patterns of the ordinary past tense (+ past participles derived from them), arranged according to feaures 1–8 below. The verbs are mostly perfective. Imperfective verbs in the table are indicated with *.

1 Verbs ending in two vowels.
2 Verbs with **д/т**, **з/с** and **к** before the ending.
3 Verbs with **-на** before the ending.
4 Verbs with **ш** or **ж** before the ending change from them to **с** and **з** in the past.
5 Verbs with **-бер-/-пер-** lose the **е** in the past.
6 Irregular verbs.
7 Verbs *without* stress on the final syllable in the past.
8 Verbs *with* stress on the final syllable in the past.

Present	Past	Past participle			
		Masculine	Feminine	Neuter	Plural
e-pattern					
1 *живéя *live*	живя́х	живя́л	живя́ла	живя́ло	живéли
*пи́я *drink*	пих	пил	пи́ла	пи́ло	пи́ли
2 вля́за *go in*	вля́зох	вля́зъл	вля́зла	вля́зло	влéзли
дам *give*	да́дох	дал	да́ла	да́ло	да́ли
донеса́ *bring*	донéсох	донéсъл	донéсла	донéсло	донéсли
оти́да *go*	оти́дох	оти́шъл	оти́шла	оти́шло	оти́шли
облека́ *get dressed*	обля́кох	обля́къл	обля́кла	обля́кло	облéкли
3 запо́чна *begin*	запо́чнах	запо́чнал	запо́чнала	запо́чнало	запо́чнали
4 *пи́ша *write*	пи́сах	пи́сал	пи́сала	пи́сало	пи́сали
ка́жа *say*	ка́зах	ка́зал	ка́зала	ка́зало	ка́зали
5 разбера́ *understand*	разбра́х	разбра́л	разбра́ла	разбра́ло	разбра́ли
6 взéма *take*	взех	взел	взéла	взéло	взéли
*мо́га *can*	можа́х	могъ́л	могла́	могло́	могли́
спра *stop*	спрях	спрял	спря́ла	спря́ло	спрéли
и-pattern					
7 *рабо́тя *work*	рабо́тих	рабо́тил	рабо́тила	рабо́тило	рабо́тили
*у́ча *study*	у́чих	у́чил	у́чила	у́чило	у́чили
8 ви́дя *see*	видя́х	видя́л	видя́ла	видя́ло	видéли
*стоя́ *stand*	стоя́х	стоя́л	стоя́ла	стоя́ло	стоéли
a-pattern					
*вечéрям *have supper*	вечéрях	вечéрял	вечéряла	вечéряло	вечéряли
*ка́звам *say*	ка́звах	ка́звал	ка́звала	ка́звало	ка́звали

Table 2 Past imperfect

Main patterns of past imperfect + past participles derived from them.

The past imperfect endings depend on stress and not on the conjugation pattern (see Past endings above). Table 2 contains all the imperfective (starred) verbs from Table 1 together with the imperfective twins of the perfective verbs found there. Here the verbs are organized differently, for the conjugation patterns of the perfective and imperfective twins are often not the same. Most imperfectives, you will see, are 3rd Conjugation.

Present	Past imperfect	Past participle			
		Masculine	Feminine	Neuter	Plural
e-pattern					
живéя *live*	живéех	живéел	живéела	живéело	живéели
пúша *write*	пúшех	пúшел	пúшела	пúшело	пúшели
пúя *drink*	пúех	пúел	пúела	пúело	пúели
мóга *can*	мóжех	мóжел	мóжела	мóжело	мóжели
и-pattern					
нóся *carry*	нóсех	нóсел	нóсела	нóсело	нóсели
рабóтя *work*	рабóтех	рабóтел	рабóтела	рабóтело	рабóтели
ýча *study*	ýчех	ýчел	ýчела	ýчело	ýчели
стоя́ *stand*	стоя́х	стоя́л	стоя́ла	стоя́ло	стоéли
a-pattern					
взúмам *take*	взúмах	взúмал	взúмала	взúмало	взúмали
вúждам *see*	вúждах	вúждал	вúждала	вúждало	вúждали
влúзам *go in*	влúзах	влúзал	влúзала	влúзало	влúзали
дáвам *give*	дáвах	дáвал	дáвала	дáвало	дáвали
запóчвам *begin*	запóчвах	запóчвал	запóчвала	запóчвало	запóчвали
úмам *have*	úмах	úмал	úмала	úмало	úмали
кáзвам *say*	кáзвах	кáзвал	кáзвала	кáзвало	кáзвали
облúчам *get dressed*	облúчах	облúчал	облúчала	облúчало	облúчали
отúвам *go*	отúвах	отúвал	отúвала	отúвало	отúвали
разбúрам *understand*	разбúрах	разбúрал	разбúрала	разбúрало	разбúрали
спúрам *stop*	спúрах	спúрал	спúрала	спúрало	спúрали
вечéрям *have supper*	вечéрях	вечéрял	вечéряла	вечéряло	вечéряли

Table 3 Tense forms with the past participle

Present perfect *(I have had supper)*	**Past perfect** *(I had had supper)*	**Conditional** *(I would have had supper, if...)*
аз съм вечéрял(а)	бях вечéрял(а)	бих вечéрял(а), акó...
ти си вечéрял(а)	бéше вечéрял(а)	би вечéрял(а), акó...
той е вечéрял	бéше вечéрял	би вечéрял, акó...
тя е вечéряла	бéше вечéряла	би вечéряла, акó...
то е вечéряло	бéше вечéряло	би вечéряло, акó...
нúе сме вечéряли	бя́хме вечéряли	бúхме вечéряли, акó...
вúе сте вечéряли	бя́хте вечéряли	бúхте вечéряли, акó...
те са вечéряли	бя́ха вечéряли	бúха вечéряли, акó...

Table 4 Renarrated forms (3rd person only)

Tenses	**Statements**	**Renarrated forms** Кáзват, че... *(They say that...)*
Present	той пúше тя пúше то пúше те пúшат	той пúшел* тя пúшела то пúшело те пúшели
Past Imperfect	той пúшеше тя пúшеше то пúшеше те пúшеха	
Past	той пúса тя пúса то пúса те пúсаха	той пúсал** тя пúсала то пúсало те пúсали
Future	той ще пúше тя ще пúше то ще пúше те ще пúшат	той щял да пúше (ня́мало да пúше) тя щя́ла да пúше (ня́мало да пúше) то щя́ло да пúше (ня́мало да пúше) те щéли да пúшат) (ня́мало да пúшат)

(* See Table 2 for past participles (mainly imperfective).)
(**See Table 1 for past participles (mainly perfective).)

Table 5 Passive participles

Endings and verb group (Present)	Past form	Passive participle			
		Masculine	Feminine	Neuter	Plural
-ен					
и-pattern	затво́рих	затво́рен (*closed*)	затво́рена	затво́рено	затво́рени
е-pattern verbs with:					
т/д	да́дох	да́ден (*given*)	да́дена	да́дено	да́дени
с/з	доне́сох	доне́сен (*brought*)	доне́сена	доне́сено	доне́сени
к	обля́кох*	обле́чен (*dressed*)	обле́чена	обле́чено	обле́чени
-ан					
а-pattern	заплану́вах	заплану́ван (*planned*)	заплану́вана	заплану́вано	заплану́вани
е-pattern verbs with:					
-ая	игра́х	игра́н (*played*)	игра́на	игра́но	игра́ни
ш/ж	пи́сах	пи́сан (*written*)	пи́сана	пи́сано	пи́сани
	ка́зах	ка́зан (*said*)	ка́зана	ка́зано	ка́зани
-бер/пер	разбра́х	разбра́н (*understood*)	разбра́на	разбра́но	разбра́ни
-ян					
е-pattern verbs with:					
-ея	живя́х	живя́н (*lived*)	живя́на	живя́но	живе́ни
и-pattern verbs with: stressed ending	видя́х	видя́н (*seen*)	видя́на	видя́но	виде́ни
-т					
е-pattern verbs in:					
-ия, **-ея**	изпи́х	изпи́т (*drunk*)	изпи́та	изпи́то	изпи́ти
	изпя́х	изпя́т (*sung*)	изпя́та	изпя́то	изпя́ти
-на-	запо́чнах	запо́чнат (*begun*)	запо́чната	запо́чнато	запо́чнати
-ема	взех	взет (*taken*)	взе́та	взе́то	взе́ти

(*2nd person **ти обле́че**).

Passive forms

Reflexive

Вентила́торът се развали́. *The fan broke down.*
Тарато́рът се серви́ра студе́н. *Tarator is served cold.*
Биле́тите се прода́доха бързо. *The tickets sold out quickly.*

Resultative

Вентила́торът е развале́н. *The fan is broken.*
Тарато́рът е серви́ран. *The tarator has been served.*
Биле́тите са прода́дени. *The tickets have been sold.*

6 Word order

With subject noun or pronoun

Subject	Negative	Unstressed† (pronoun, *to be*, reflexive)		Main part of verb phrase	Object(s)
Аз	(не)			позна́вам	Ива́н
Аз	(не)	го		позна́вам	
Ни́е	(не)	се		позна́ваме	
Ива́н	(не)	е		добре́	
Ни́е	(не)	сме		англича́ни	
Кафе́то	(не)	ми		харе́сва	
На́дя	(не)			да́де	ча́нтата на Ива́н
Тя	(не)	я		да́де	на Ива́н
Тя	(не)	му		да́де	ча́нтата
Тя	(не)	му	я	да́де	
На́дя	(не)	се		оба́ди	на Никола́й
Тя	(не)	му	се	оба́ди	
Аз	(не)	съм		напра́вила	кафе́
Аз	(не)	съм	го	напра́вила	
Ти	(не)	си	го	напра́вил	
Той	(не)	*го	е	напра́вил	
Тя	(не)	*го	е	напра́вила	
Ни́е	(не)	сме	го	напра́вили	
Ви́е	(не)	сте	го	напра́вили	
Те	(не)	са	го	напра́вили	
Аз	(не)	съм	се	облякъл	
Ти	(не)	си	се	облякъл	
Той	(не)	*се	е	облякъл	
Тя	(не)	*се	е	облякла	
Ни́е	(не)	сме	се	облекли	
Ви́е	(не)	сте	се	облекли	
Те	(не)	са	се	облекли	

(†Stressed if after **не**.)
(*Note that *to be* changes places in the 3rd person singular.)

Without subject noun or pronoun

Other	Negative	Unstressed† (pronouns, *to be*, reflexive)	Main part of verb phrase	Unstressed (pronouns, *to be*, reflexive)	Object
	(Не)		Познáвам		Ивáн
			познáвам	го	
	Не	го	познáвам		
			Познáваме	се	
	Не	се	познáваме		
			Добрé	е	
	Не	е	добрé		
Мнóго		е	добрé		
			Англичáни	сме	
	Не	сме	англичáни		
			Харéсва	ми	
	Не	ми	харéсва		
Мнóго		ми	харéсва		
			Прия́тно	ми е	
	Не	ми е	прия́тно		
Мнóго		ми е	прия́тно		
На мéне	(не)	ми е	прия́тно		
			Дáде		чáнтата
					на Ивáн
			дáде	му	чáнтата
			дáде	му я	
	Не	му я	дáде		
			Обáдих	се	на Ивáн
	Не	се	обáдих		на Нáдя
	Не	й се	обáдих		
Вчéра		се	обáдих		на Ивáн
Вчéра	(не)	му се	обáдих		
			Напрáвила	съм	кафé
	Не	съм	напрáвила		кафé
Вéче		съм го	напрáвила		
			Облякъл	съм	се
	Не	съм се	облякъл		
Вéче		съм се	облякъл		

(†Stressed if after **не**.)

Bulgarian–English vocabulary

In this Vocabulary you should be able to find all the words used in this book with the meanings they have in the book. Occasionally, when a word has another very common meaning not used in the book, you will find the additional meaning.

The words are listed in a way that will be useful to you. The verbs, for example, show the *I* form followed by the final three letters of the *you* singular form. (Occasionally, with very short verbs, we have given the full *you* singular form.) All perfective verbs are preceded by (да). Where nouns have awkward plurals, the abbreviation (pl) is used and you will find either the last few letters — usually the last three — or the full plural form. The adjectives are listed in the masculine singular, but where the feminine, neuter and plural forms lose the letter **е**, we give you the last three letters of the feminine form too. Where a word has an odd gender, feminine nouns ending in consonants, for example, we give you the gender. The letter (f) means the word is feminine; the letter (n) that it is neuter.

Phrases are shown either under the most important word or according to the first word in the phrase.

Some words you will find in the Appendix rather than in the Vocabulary. You should look for most of the numerals, for example, and the different verb and pronoun forms, in the Appendix. The Appendix is really an addition to the Vocabulary, so use the two together.

а *but*
абонамéнт *subscription*
áвгуст *August*
авиокомпáния *airline*
автобýс *bus*
агéнция *agency*
администрáтор(ка) *receptionist*
адрéс *address*
аз *I*
акó *if*
алéргия *allergy*
алкохóл *alcohol*
áло *hello* (on the phone)
Амéрика *America*
америкáнец (pl) **-нци** *an American*
америкáнка *American woman*
америкáнски *American*
amú cerá *and now what*
амфитеáтър *amphitheatre*
англúйски *English*
англичáнин (pl) **-áни** *Englishman*
англичáнка *English woman*
Áнглия *England*

антибио́тик *an antibiotic*
апартаме́нт *flat*
апендиси́т *apendicitis*
апри́л *April*
апте́ка *chemist's, pharmacy*
асансьо́р *lift, elevator*
аспири́н *aspirin*
а-ха́ *a-ha*

ба́ба *grandmother*
ба́вно *slowly*
бага́ж *luggage*
бага́жник (pl) **-ици** *boot/trunk*
балка́нски *Balkan* (adj)
бана́н *banana*
ба́ница *cheese pasty*
ба́ничка *cheese roll*
ба́нка *bank*
банкома́т *cashpoint, ATM*
ба́ня *bathroom*
бар *bar*
баща́ *father*
без *without; less; to*
безпокоя́, -ои́ш *to worry, trouble*
безпокоя́, -ои́ш се *be anxious, to worry*
беле́жник (pl) **-ици** *diary, notebook*
бензи́н *petrol*
бензиноста́нция *petrol station*
би́знес *business*
би́знесмен (pl) **-ме́ни** *businessman*
биле́т *ticket*
би́лка *herb*
би́лков (made with) *herb(s)*
би́ра *beer*
би́ра-ска́ра *beer and grill*
благодаря́ *thank you*
благодаря́, -ри́ш *to thank*
бли́зо *near*
блок *block*
блу́за *blouse*
Бог *God*
(сла́ва) бо́гу *thank heavens*
бо́лен, -лна *ill*
боли́ (*it* form) *it hurts*
бо́лка *pain*
бо́лница *hospital*
бонбо́н (chocolate) *sweet*
брат (pl) **бра́тя** *brother*
братовче́д(ка) *cousin*
брой (pl) **бро́еве** *number; copy*
брошу́ра *brochure*
буке́т *bunch*
булева́рд *boulevard*
бути́лка *bottle*
бутни́ *push*
бъдеще *future*
българин (pl) **българи** *a Bulgarian*
Бълга́рия *Bulgaria*
българка *Bulgarian woman*
български *Bulgarian*
бързам, -заш *to be in a hurry*
бързо *quickly, fast*
бюро́ *agency, office*
бял (pl) **бе́ли** *white*

в/във *in; at; to; on*
в ремо́нт *under repair, reconstruction*
в такъв слу́чай *in that case*
ва́жен, -жна *important*
ва́жно (е) *(it's) important*
ва́за *vase*
вали́ *it's raining*
валу́та *hard currency*
ва́рненски *Varna* (adj)
ваш, Ваш *your(s)*
вдя́сно *on the right*
вегетариа́нски *vegetarian*
ведна́га *immediately*
веднъ́ж *once*
вентила́тор *extractor fan*
ве́сел *merry, happy*
ве́стник (pl) **-ици** *newspaper*
ветрови́то *windy*
ве́че *already*
ве́чер (f) *evening*
вечерта́ *in the evening*
вече́ря *dinner, supper*
вече́рям, -ряш *to have supper*
(да) взе́ма, -меш *to take*
взи́мам, -маш *to take*
ви́део *video*
(да) ви́дя, -диш *to see*
ви́е (or) **Ви́е** *you*
ви́ждам, -даш *to see*
ви́за *visa*
визи́тна ка́ртичка *visiting card*
ви́лица *fork*
вина́ *fault*
ви́наги *always*
ви́но *wine*
висо́к *high, tall*
вклю́чвам, -ваш *to include*
вку́сен, -сна *nice* (to eat), *delicious*
вкъ́щи *at home/*(go) *home*
вла́жен, -жна *damp*

вли́зам, -заш *to go in*
вля́во *on the left*
(да) вля́за, вле́зеш *to go in*
вме́сто *instead of*
внима́вам, -ваш *to watch out*
внима́ние! *danger!; attention!*
вода́ *water*
во́дка *vodka*
врата́ *door*
вре́ме (pl) **времена́** *time*
вре́ме *weather*
все *all the time*
все едно́ *all the same*
все́ки, вся́ка *each*
всі́чки *everybody*
всі́чко *all*
вто́рник *Tuesday*
вход *entrance*
вче́ра *yesterday*
въ́здух *air*
възмо́жно (е) *(it's) possible*
възмо́жност (f) *possibility*
въпро́с *question*
вървя́, -ви́ш *to walk*
(да) въ́рна, -неш *to return, give back*
(да) се въ́рна, -неш *to return, go back*
върху́ *on top of*
вя́рвам, -ваш *to believe*
вя́рно (е) *(it's) true*
вя́тър (pl) **ветрове́** *wind*

гази́рана вода́ *soda water*
гале́рия *gallery*
га́ра *railway station*
гара́ж *garage*
гардеро́б *cloakroom; wardrobe*
г-жа́ = госпожа́ *Mrs*
глава́ *head*
главобо́лие *headache*
гла́ден, -дна *hungry*
гле́дам, -даш *to look*
гло́ба *fine*
глу́пости! (pl) *nonsense!*
г-н = господи́н *Mr*
говоря́, -риш *to speak, talk*
годи́на *year*
големина́ *size*
голф *golf*
голя́м (pl) **голе́ми** *big*
го́ре-до́лу *so-so*
горещина́ *heat*
горе́що (е) *(it's) hot*
господи́н (pl) **-да́** *Mr*
госпожа́ *Mrs*
госпо́жица *Miss*
гост (pl) **го́сти** *guest, resident*
гото́в *ready*
гото́во (е) *(it's) ready*
град (pl) **градове́** *town, city*
гради́на *garden, park*
гра́дус *degree*
градче́ *little town*
гра́жданин (pl) **-ани** *citizen*
грам *gram*
гра́ница *border*
гре́шка *mistake*
гри́вна *bracelet*
гри́жа, -жиш се *to look after, worry about*
грип *flu*
гро́зде *grapes*
гро́здов (made with) *grapes*
гру́па *group*
гъ́рло *throat*
Гъ́рция *Greece*

да *yes; to*
да́вам, -ваш *to give*
да́же *even*
дале́че *far*
дали́ *whether, if*
(да) дам, даде́ш *to give*
да́ми и господа́ *ladies and gentlemen*
да́мски *women's*
да́та *date*
два́ма (ду́ши) *two (people)*
дво́ен, дво́йна *double*
дворе́ц (pl) **дворци́** *palace*
деке́мври *December*
делега́ция *delegation*
ден, деня́т (pl) **дни** *day*
дете́ (pl) **деца́** *child*
дефе́кт *defect, flaw*
джин *gin*
джи́нси (pl) *jeans*
джоб *pocket*
дие́та *diet*
дире́ктор *director*
дискоте́ка *disco*
днес *today*
до *next to; until, till; to*
до на́шата е́ра *BC*
добре́ *well; OK, fine*
добре́ дошъ́л, -шла́, -шли́! *welcome!*

добре́ зава́рил! lit. *well met!* (response to добре́ дошъ́л!)
добъ́р, -бра́ *good*
до́бър ден! *good morning/afternoon!*
добъ́р път! *have a good/safe journey!*
дови́ждане! *goodbye!*
дово́лен, -лна (от) *happy* (with)
(да) до́йда, -деш *to come*
докато́ *while*
до́ктор *doctor*
докуме́нт *document; paper*
до́лар *dollar*
домаки́н *host*
домаки́ня *hostess, lady of the house*
дома́т *tomato*
(да) донеса́, -се́ш *to bring*
дори́ *even*
досега́ *until now*
до́ста *quite, pretty (very)*
дочу́ване *goodbye* (on the phone)
дошъ́л: добре́ дошъ́л! *welcome!*
друг *another; other*
дру́го? *anything else?*
дръпни́ *pull*
ду́ма *word*
Ду́нав *Danube*
(два́ма) ду́ши *two people*
душ *shower*
дъжд (pl) **дъждове́** *rain*
дъждо́вно (е) *(it's) rainy*
дъ́лъг, дъ́лга *long*
държа́, -жи́ш *to hold*
дъщеря́ *daughter*
дя́до *grandfather*

е *well; really*
е́вро *euro*
Евро́па *Europe*
е́втин *cheap*
ези́к (pl) **ези́ци** *language, tongue*
екску́рзия *outing, excursion*
екскурзово́д *guide*
е́сен (f) *autumn*
еспре́со *espresso*
ета́ж *floor*
е́то *here is*

Ж *ladies (toilet)*
жа́лко *it's a pity*
жена́ *woman; wife*
же́нен *married*
живе́я, -е́еш *to live*
живо́т *life*
жу́ри *jury*
журнали́ст *journalist*

за *for; to; at; about*
за да *(in order) to*
заба́вен, -вна *amusing*
заба́вно (е) (it's) *fun, amusing*
забележи́телност (f) *sight, tourist attraction*
(да) заболи́ (*it* form) *begins to hurt*
(да) забра́вя, -виш *to forget*
забране́но *prohibited*
(да) зави́я, -и́еш *to turn*
загу́бен *lost*
(да) загу́бя, -биш *to lose*
зад *behind*
за́едно *together*
зае́т *busy, engaged*
закусва́лня *snack bar*
заку́ска *breakfast, snack*
закъсне́ние *delay*
(да) закъсне́я, -е́еш *to be late*
закъсня́вам, -ваш *to be late*
за́ла *hall*
(да) зами́на, -неш *to leave*
замина́вам, -ваш *to leave*
замина́ване *departure*
замина́ващ за *leaving for, travelling to*
(на) за́пад *(to the) west*
запа́зен *reserved; preserved*
(да) запа́зя, -зиш *to reserve, book*
(да) запа́ли (*it* form) *to start* (car)
(да) заплану́вам, -ваш *to plan*
заплану́ван *planned*
заповя́дай(те)! *here you are, there you go; welcome*
запозна́вам, -ваш се *to get to know one another*
запозна́йте се! *meet …*
(да) запозна́я, -а́еш *to introduce*
(да) се запозна́я, -а́еш *to get to know one another*
(да) запо́мня, -ниш *to remember*
запо́чвам, -ваш *to begin*
(да) запо́чна, -неш *to begin*
(да) се зара́двам, -ваш *to be pleased*
засега́ *for now*
(да) се засме́я, -е́еш *to begin to laugh*

затва́рям, -ряш *to close*
затво́рен *closed*
(да) затво́ря, -риш *to close*
затова́ *that's why*
за́хар (f) *sugar*
защо́ *why*
защо́то *because*
здра́ве *health*
здраве́й(те)! *hello!*
зеленчу́к (pl) **-у́ци** *vegetable*
зеленчу́ков (made with) *vegetable(s)*
зи́ма *winter*
Зла́тни пя́съци *Golden Sands*
зле *poorly*
знак (pl) **зна́ци** *sign*
значе́ние *significance, meaning*
зна́чи *so, that means, that is to say*
зна́я, -а́еш *to know*
зъб (pl) **зъ́би** *tooth*
зъболе́кар (ка) *dentist*

и *and, too, as well*
игра́я, -а́еш *to play*
игри́ще за голф *golf course*
и́двам, -ваш *to come*
иде́я *idea*
(да) избера́, -ре́ш *to choose*
изби́рам, -раш *to choose*
извине́те! *excuse me!*
(да) се извиня́, -ни́ш *to apologize*
извиня́вай(те)! *excuse/forgive me!*
и́зглед *view*
изгле́ждам, -даш *to look*
изго́ден, -дна *favourable*
изключи́телен, -лна *exceptional*
изли́зам, -заш *to go out, leave*
изло́жба *exhibition*
(да) изля́за, -ле́зеш *to go out, leave*
изнена́да *surprise*
изо́бщо *at all*
изо́бщо не é... *it's not at all...*
(да) изпе́я, -е́еш *to sing*
(да) изпи́я, -и́еш *to drink*
(да) изпра́тя, -тиш *to accompany, to see off; to send*
изпра́щам, -щаш *to accompany, to see off; to send*
(на) и́зток *(to the) east*
и́зточен, -чна *(from/to the) east*
и́зход *exit; gate*
(да) изче́зна, -неш *to disappear*
ико́на *icon*
или́ *or*
и́ма (*it* form) *there is, are*
и́мам, -маш *to have*
и́ме (pl) **имена́** *name*
и́мейл *email*
интервю́ *interview*
интере́сен, -сна *interesting*
информа́ция *information (desk)*
ирла́ндец (pl) **-дци** *Irishman*
Ирла́ндия *Ireland*
ирла́ндка *Irishwoman*
и́скам, -каш *to want*
испа́нец (pl) **-нци** *Spaniard*
испа́нка *Spanish woman*
испа́нски *Spanish*
исто́рия *history*
италиа́нец (pl) **-нци** *an Italian*
италиа́нка *Italian woman*
италиа́нски *Italian*

йод *iodine*

(да) ка́жа, -жеш *to say*
ка́звам, -ваш *to say*
ка́звам, -ваш се *my (your) name is*
каже́те? *can I help you?*
как *how*
какво́ *what*
ка́кто *as*
какъ́в, каква́ *what (kind of)*
календа́р *calendar, diary*
камерие́рка *chambermaid*
капучи́но *capuccino*
ка́рам, -раш *to drive*
ка́рам, -раш ски *to ski*
ка́рта *map; card*
(бо́рдна) ка́рта *boarding card/pass*
ка́ртичка *(post) card*
ка́са *checkout; ticket office; till*
касие́рка *cashier, checkout operator*
катедра́ла *cathedral*
като́ *as; when; like*
кафе́ *coffee; café*
ка́чество *quality*
кашкава́л *(yellow) cheese*
ка́шлица *cough*
кашо́н *cardboard box*
кеба́пче *'kebapche' sausage*
кекс *(sponge) cake*
кили́м *carpet, rug*
килогра́м *kilogram*
ки́село мля́ко *yoghurt*
кита́йски (adj) *Chinese*

ки́фла *bun*
класи́чески *classical*
клие́нт(ка) *customer*
клуб *club*
ключ *key*
кни́га *book*
кога́(то) *when*
ко́жа *skin*
козме́тика *cosmetics*
кой, коя́, кое́, кои́ *who*
ко́йто, коя́то, кое́то, кои́то (the one) *who*
ockте́йл *cocktail party*
ко́ла *coke*
кола́ *car*
коле́га *colleague*
Ко́леда *Christmas*
коли́чка *trolley, shopping cart*
ко́лко *how many, how much*
коля́но (pl) **колена́** *knee*
командиро́вка *business trip*
кома́р *mosquito*
комбина́ция *combination*
компа́ктдиск (pl) **-кове** *CD*
компю́тър (pl) **-три** *computer*
конта́кт *socket*
конфе́кция *ready-made clothes*
конфере́нция *conference*
конце́рт *concert*
коня́к *brandy*
ко́раб(че) *(small) boat*
коридо́р *corridor*
край (pl) **кра́ища** *end*
крак (pl) **крака́** *foot; leg*
кран *tap*
краси́в *beautiful*
кра́ставица *cucumber*
кре́дит *loan, credit*
крем *cream*
кре́постен, -тна *fortification* (adj)
кри́пта *crypt*
криста́лен, -лна *crystal*
кръст *(small of the) back; cross*
ксе́рокс *photocopier, xerox*
култу́ра *culture*
купу́вам, -ваш *to buy*
(да) ку́пя, -пиш *to buy*
куро́рт *resort, spa*
кути́я *box*
ку́фар *suitcase*
ку́хня *kitchen*
къде́(то) *where*
към *about; around; towards; to*
къ́мпинг *campsite*
къ́сно *late*
къ́ща *house*
кюфте́ *meatball*

лев *lev*
легло́ *bed*
лек *light* (adj)
ле́ка нощ! *good night!*
ле́кар(ка) *doctor*
лека́рство *medicine*
ле́сно *easily*
лети́ще *airport*
ли (question word)
лимо́н *lemon*
лимона́да *lemonade*
лимо́нов (made with) *lemon*
(англи́йска) ли́ра *pound sterling*
литерату́ра *literature*
ли́тър (pl) **ли́три** *litre*
лифт *(ski/chair) lift*
ло́ндонски *London* (adj)
лондонча́нин (pl) **-а́ни** *Londoner*
лош *bad*
лошока́чествен *of inferior quality*
луксо́зен, -зна *deluxe*
ля́то *summer*

М *gents (toilet)*
магази́н *shop*
магистра́ла *motorway*
май *May*
ма́йка *mother*
ма́йстор *workman*
Македо́ния *Macedonia*
ма́лко *a little*
малоле́тен, -тна *juvenile, young*
ма́лък, ма́лка *small*
ма́ма *mum, mother*
манасти́р *monastery*
марато́нки *trainers, athletic shoes*
ма́рка *(postage) stamp*
март *March*
маршру́тка *minibus (taxi)*
ма́са *table*
мач *match*
маши́на *machine*
между́ *between*
междунаро́ден, -дна *international*
ме́нта *mint*
ме́нтов (made with) *mint*
меню́ *menu*
мерси́ *thank you*
ме́сец *month*
ме́тър (pl) **ме́три** *metre*

механá *tavern*
мил *dear*
(да) мúна, -неш *to go, pass* (of time)
(ще ми) мúне *I'll be OK*
мúнал *past*
минерáлна водá *mineral water*
минýта *minute*
мúсля, -лиш *to think*
мúтница *customs*
митничáр *customs officer*
млад *young*
млякo *milk*
мнóго *a lot, much, many*
мóга, мóжеш *I can, am able*
модéрен, -рна *modern, latest, fashionable*
мóже *it is possible*
мóже би *maybe*
мóже ли? *may I?, could you?*
мой *my, mine*
молбá *request*
молúв *pencil*
мóля *please; I beg your pardon; don't mention it*
момéнт *moment*
момúче (n) *girl*
момчé (n) *boy*
морé *sea*
мóрски (of the) *sea*
мотéл *motel*
мотóр *engine*
мрáчен, -чна *dull*
музéй *museum*
мýзика *music*
музикáнт *musician*
мъглúво *foggy*
мъж (pl) **мъжé** *man; husband*
мъ́жки *man's*
мя́сто (pl) **местá** *place*

на *on; of; at; in; to; for*
наблúзо *nearby*
наврéме *in time*
нався́къде *everywhere*
навъ́н *outside*
над *above*
надя́вам, -ваш се *to hope*
надя́сно *to the right*
наздрáве! *cheers!*
(под) нáем *hired*
(да) наéма, -меш *to rent*
наúстина *really, indeed*
нáй-пóсле *at last*
(да) накáрам, -раш *to make* (someone do something)
налú? *isn't that so?*
наля́во *to the left*
(да) намéря, -риш *to find*
наóколо *nearby*
напрáво *straight ahead*
(да) напрáвя, -виш *to make; to do*
напрéдвам, -ваш *to make progress*
нарéд *in order*
нарéдéн *arranged*
(да) наредя́, -дúш *to arrange*
нарóден, -дня *national*
нарóдност (f) *nationality*
(да) наýча, -чиш *to learn*
национáлен, -лна *national*
нáция *nation*
начáло *beginning*
наш *our(s)*
не *no, not*
невя́рно *false*
нéгов *his*
недéй! *don't!*
недéля *Sunday*
нéин *her(s)*
нéмец (pl) **нéмци** *a German*
немкúня *German woman*
нéмски *German*
непрекъ́снато *all the time*
непремéнно *certainly; don't fail to*
неприя́тно *unpleasant*
неприя́тност (f) *unpleasantness, trouble*
нéрвен, нéрвна *agitated, stressed out*
нéс(кафе) *instant (coffee)*
с нетърпéние *eagerly*
нéщо *something*
нéщо дрýго *some/anything else*
нéщо за пúене *something to drink*
нéщо за я́дене *something to eat*
нúе *we*
нúсък, -ска *short* (stature)
нúто..., нúто... *neither, nor...*
нúщо *nothing; no matter; never mind*
нúщо чýдно *that's hardly surprising*
но *but*
нов *new*
Нóва годúна *New Year*
новинá *news* (item)
нож (pl) **ножóве** *knife*
ноéмври *November*

но́мер *number*
норма́лно *normally; OK*
носа́ч *porter*
но́ся, -сиш *to carry, have with one, bring*
нощ (f) *night*
(ле́ка) нощ! *good night!*
ну́жда *need*
ну́ла *zero, nought*
ня́как *somehow*
ня́какъв, ня́каква *some kind of*
ня́кога *sometime*
ня́кой *somebody, some*
ня́колко *some, a few*
ня́къде *somewhere*
ня́ма *there isn't*
ня́ма защо́ *you're welcome, don't mention it*
ня́мам, -маш *not to have*

(да) се оба́дя, -диш *to ring, phone, call*
оба́ждам, -даш се *to ring, phone, call*
о́бед and **обя́д** *lunch (time), noon*
обикнове́но *usually*
оби́чам, -чаш *to love, like*
о́блачно *cloudy*
(да) се облека́, -че́ш *to get dressed*
(да) обменя́, -ни́ш *to change*
обмя́на на валу́та *currency exchange*
обра́тен, -тна *opposite*
обслу́жване *service* (e.g. in a restaurant)
(туристи́чески) обу́вки *(walking) shoes, footwear*
обя́двам, -ваш *to have lunch*
(да) обясня́, -ни́ш *to explain*
огледа́ло *mirror*
(да) оже́ня, -ниш *to marry off*
(да) се оже́ня, -ниш *to get married*
ока́за се *it turned out*
око́ (pl) **очи́** *eye*
о́коло *about, around*
окто́мври *October*
о́леле! *oh dear me!*
о́лио *vegetable oil*
омле́т *omelette*
омъ̀жена *married* (for a woman)
о́нзи *that*
опа́сен, -сна *dangerous*
о́пера *opera*
о́перен, -рна *opera* (adj)
о́пит *practice, experience*
(да) опи́там, -таш *to try*
опи́твам, -ваш *to try*
о́питен, -тна *experienced*
опла́квам, -ваш се *to complain*
опла́кване (pl) **-ния** *complaint*
(да) се опла́ча, -чеш *to complain*
(да) се опра́вя, -виш *to get better*
организи́ра се (*it* form) *is organized*
организи́рам, -раш *to organize*
о́рех(ов) (made with) *walnut(s)*
ориента́лски *oriental*
осве́н *apart from, besides*
осо́бено *especially*
(ни́що) осо́бено *nothing special*
оста́ва(т) *is/are left*
(да) оста́вя, -виш *to leave*
оста́вям, -вяш *to leave*
от *from; (because) of; than; made of; with; since; out of*
от ня́колко дни *(for) the past few days*
отво́рен *open*
отгова́рям, -ряш *to answer*
(да) отгово́ря, -риш *to answer*
отда́вна *long since, long ago*
отдале́че *from afar*
оти́вам, -ваш *to go*
(да) оти́да, -деш *to go (there)*
отклоне́ние *diversion*
отко́лкото *than*
откъде́ *where from*
отли́чно! *excellent!*
отпа́дък (pl) **отпа́дъци** *litter, rubbish*
оттýк *from here*
о́фис *office*
оча́квам, -ваш *to expect*
о́ще *more; still; even; yet*
о́ще веднъ̀ж *once again*
о́ще не *not yet*

павилио́н *kiosk*
па́дам, -даш *to fall*
па́дащи предме́ти *falling objects*
(да) па́дна, -неш *to fall*
паза́р *market*
пазару́вам, -ваш *to do the shopping*
па́зя, -зиш *to keep, preserve*
пак *again*

панаи́р *fair*
па́пка *folder, file*
пари́ (pl) *money*
парк *park; garden*
па́ркинг *car park*
парки́рам, -раш *to park*
па́ртер *ground floor*
па́рти *party*
парфю́м *perfume*
парче́ *piece*
паспо́рт *passport*
(брита́нски) па́унд *pound sterling*
пе́тък *Friday*
(не́що за) пи́ене *something to drink*
пи́во *ale*
пи́лзенска би́ра *Pilsner (beer)*
пи́лешки (made with) *chicken*
пи́пам, -паш *to touch*
писа́лка *pen*
писмо́ *letter*
пи́там, -таш *to ask*
пи́ца *pizza*
пицари́я *pizzeria*
пи́ша, -шеш *to write*
пи́я, пи́еш *to drink*
плаж *beach*
плака́т *poster*
план *plan*
планина́ *mountain(s)*
(да) платя́, -ти́ш *to pay*
пла́щам, -щаш *to pay*
плик *envelope*
плод (pl) **плодове́** *fruit*
пло́дов (made of) *fruit*
плодотво́рен, -рна *fruitful*
площа́д *square*
плу́вам, -ваш *to swim*
плюс *plus*
по *along; over; on*
по́вече *more*
по́вечето *most of*
повре́да *fault*
повре́ден *out of order*
под *under*
пода́рък (pl) **-ъци** *present*
(да) подаря́, -ри́ш *to give*
подходя́щ *suitable*
пожела́вам, -ваш *to wish*
(да) пожела́я, -а́еш *to wish*
(с) по́здрав *kind regards*
поздравле́ния! *congratulations!*
(да) поздравя́, -ви́ш *to welcome, greet; congratulate*
поздравя́вам, -ваш *to welcome, greet; congratulate*
позна́вам, -ваш *to know* (someone, one another)
позна́т(а) *acquaintance*
(да) пока́жа, -жеш *to show, point*
пока́звам, -ваш *to show, point*
пока́на *invitation*
пока́нен *invited*
(да) пока́ня, -ниш *to invite*
поле́зен, -зна *useful*
полица́й *policeman*
поли́ция *police*
полови́н *half*
полови́на *a half*
(да) полу́ча, -чиш *to receive*
получа́вам, -ваш *to receive*
пома́гам, -гаш *to help*
(да) поми́сля, -лиш *to think over*
(да) помо́гна, -неш *to help*
по́мня, -ниш *to remember*
по́мощ (f) *help, assistance*
понеде́лник *Monday*
по́ни (n) *pony*
поня́кога *sometimes*
(да) попи́там, -таш *to ask*
(да) попра́вя, -виш *to mend*
портие́р *doorman*
портмоне́ *purse, bag*
портока́л(ов) (made with) *orange(s)*
(да) пора́чам, -чаш *to order*
пора́чвам, -ваш *to order*
пора́чка *order*
по́сле *after that, then*
после́ден, -дна *final, last*
посо́ка *direction*
(да) посре́щна, -неш *to meet*
(да) почáкам, -каш *to wait a little*
почи́вам, -ваш си *to be resting*
почи́вка *rest, break*
(да) си почи́на, -неш *to have a rest*
почти́ *almost*
по́ща *post office*
прав *right*
пра́вя, -виш *to do; to make*
пра́зник (pl) **-ици** *festival, holiday*
празну́вам, -ваш *to celebrate*
пра́скова *peach*
(да) пра́тя, -тиш *to send*
преваля́ване (pl) **-ния** *shower*
(да) преведа́, -де́ш *to translate*
превода́ч(ка) *translator;*

interpreter
пре́говори (pl) *negotiations; talks*
пред *in front of*
(да) преда́м, -даде́ш *to leave/pass on/a message*
преди́ *before; ago*
preди́мно *mainly*
предла́гам, -гаш *to suggest, make an offer*
(да) предло́жа, -жиш *to suggest; make an offer*
предпола́гам, -гаш *to suppose*
предпочи́там, -таш *to prefer*
предста́ва *idea*
представле́ние *performance*
през *during; through; in; at*
(да) река́рам, -раш *to spend* (time)
река́рвам, -ваш *to spend* (time)
(да) пренеса́, -се́ш *to take* (somewhere)
препоръ́чвам, -ваш *to recommend*
(да) пресека́, -ече́ш *to cross*
пре́сен, пря́сна, пре́сни *fresh*
престо́й (duration of) *stay*
(да) прете́гля, -лиш *to weigh*
(да) придружа́, -жи́ш *to accompany*
(да) прие́ма, -меш *to accept*
при́нтер *printer*
присти́гам, -гаш *to arrive*
присти́гащ *arriving*
(да) присти́гна, -неш *to arrive*
прия́тел(ка) *friend*
прия́телски *friendly*
прия́тен, -тна *pleasant*
прия́тен път! *have a good journey!*
прия́тно река́рване! *have a nice time!*
пробле́м *problem*
прогно́за *forecast*
програ́ма *program(me)*
прогре́с *progress*
прода́вам, -ваш *to sell*
продава́ч(ка) *shop assistant, sales person*
прода́ден *sold*
проду́кт *product*
продължа́вам, -ваш *to continue*
прозо́рец (pl) **-рци** *window*
про́лет (f) *spring*
про́сто *simply*
проти́в *against*
профе́сия *occupation*
пу́ша, -шиш *to smoke*
пу́шене *smoking*
пъ́лен, -лна с *full of*
пъ́лнени чу́шки *stuffed peppers*
пъ́пеш *melon*
пъ́рво *firstly*
път (pl) **пъ́ти** *time*
път (pl) **пъ́тища** *road, way*
пъ́тник (pl) **-ици** *passenger, traveller*
пъту́вам, -ваш *to travel*
пъту́ване *journey*

ра́бота *work*
рабо́тник (pl) **-ици** *worker*
рабо́тно вре́ме *opening hours*
рабо́тя, -тиш *to work*
ра́двам, -ваш се *to enjoy, be glad*
ра́дио *radio*
ра́достен, -тна *joyous, glad*
(да) разбера́, -ре́ш *to understand*
разби́ра се *of course*
разби́рам, -раш *to understand*
развале́н *broken, not working*
(да) разваля́, -ли́ш *to break* (something)
(да) се разваля́, -ли́ш *to go wrong; to break down*
разве́ден *divorced*
(да) разгле́дам, -даш *to look at/around*
разглѐждам, -даш *to look at/round*
ра́зговор *conversation*
разка́звам, -ваш *to tell*
разкъ́сана о́блачност *broken cloud*
разписа́ние *timetable*
разсе́ян *absent-minded*
разхо́дка *trip, walk*
(да) се разхо́дя, -диш *to have a walk*
разчи́там, -таш на *to rely on*
раки́я *rakiya, brandy*
ра́но *early*
резерва́ция *reservation*
река́ *river*
рекла́ма *publicity* (adj)
рекла́мен, -мна *publicity, advertisement*
рели́гия *religion*
(в) ремо́нт (*under*) *repair*
рестора́нт *restaurant*
реце́пция *reception*

ре́чник (pl) **-ици** *vocabulary, dictionary*
(да) реша́, -ши́ш *to decide*
Ри́ла планина́ *the Rila Mountains*
ри́мски *Roman* (adj)
роде́н(а) съм *I was born*
роди́на *fatherland, motherland*
роди́тел *parent*
рожде́н ден *birthday*
ро́за *rose*
ро́кля *dress*
романти́чно *romantic*
Румъ́ния *Romania*
ру́ски *Russian* (adj)
ръка́ (pl) **ръце́** *hand; arm*
ря́дко *rarely*

с/със *with; on*
сала́та *salad*
салфе́тка *serviette, napkin*
сам *alone*
са́мо *only, just*
самобръсна́чка *razor, shaver*
самоле́т *airplane*
са́ндвич *sandwich*
сва́тба *wedding*
(по) света́ *around the world*
свети́, света́ *Saint, holy*
све́тло *light*
све́тло пи́во *lager*
светофа́р *traffic light*
свобо́ден, -дна *free*
свой *one's own*
свят *world*
(на) се́вер *(to the) north*
се (reflexive particle) *-self*
сега́ *now*
се́дмица *week*
(да) се́дна, -неш *to sit*
секрета́р(ка) *secretary*
се́ло *village*
семе́йство *family*
септе́мври *September*
серви́з *garage, service station*
сервитьо́р(ка) *waiter, waitress*
серви́рам, -раш *to serve*
серио́зно *seriously*
сестра́ *sister*
сигна́л *beep, signal*
си́гурен, -рна съм *I am sure*
си́гурно *most probably; certainly*
си́лен, -лна *strong*
син, (pl) **синове́** *son*
син, си́ня, си́ньо, си́ни *blue*
си́рене *white cheese, feta*
ски (pl) *skis*
на ски *skiing*
ско́ро *soon*
ску́чно *boring*
скъп *dear; expensive*
сла́б *light; weak*
сла́ва бо́гу! *thank heavens!*
славя́нски *Slavonic*
сладка́рница *café, cakeshop, patisserie*
сладоле́д *ice-cream*
сла́дък, сла́дка *sweet*
след (като́) *after; in*
сле́дващ *(up)coming, following*
сле́дващия(т) път *next time*
следо́бед *(in the) afternoon*
сли́ва *plum*
сли́вов (made of*) plums*
(да) сло́жа, -жиш *to put*
служе́бен, -бна *official; for staff only*
служи́тел(ка) *counter assistant, clerk*
(по) слу́чай *(on the) occasion (of)*
слу́чва се *it happens*
(да) се слу́чи (*it* form) *happen*
слъ́нце *sun*
Слъ́нчев бряг *Sunny Beach*
слъ́нчево *sunny*
(да) сменя́, -ни́ш *to change*
смета́на *cream*
сме́тка *bill*
сме́я, -е́еш се *to laugh*
сме́шен, -шна *funny*
сни́мка *photo*
сно́щи *last night*
сняг *snow*
со́да *soda water*
сок *juice*
сол (f) *salt*
софи́йски *Sofia* (adj)
спа́лня *bedroom*
специалите́т *speciality*
специа́лно *specially*
спи́рам, -раш *to stop*
спи́ране *stopping*
спи́рка *(bus) stop*
списа́ние *magazine*
споко́йно *calmly*
спо́мен *memento*
спо́мням, -няш си *to remember*
споре́д *according to*
спорт *sport*

(да) спра, спреш *to stop*
спя, спиш *to sleep*
сре́бърен, -рна (made of) *silver*
сре́ща *appointment, meeting, get-together*
срещу́ *opposite*
сря́да *Wednesday*
ста́вам, -ваш *to stand/get up; to happen; become*
(да) ста́на, -неш *to stand/get up; to happen; become*
стар *old*
старт *start*
ста́я *room*
стена́ *wall*
сти́га! *stop it! enough!*
(да) сти́гна, -неш *to reach*
стик *golf club*
сто *hundred*
сто́лица *capital*
стома́х (pl) **стома́си** *stomach*
стоти́нка *stotinka*
стоя́, стои́ш *to stand; stay*
страна́ *country*
страху́вам, -ваш се *to be afraid*
стра́шен, -шна *incredible; terrible*
(ко́лко) стру́ва? *how much does it cost?*
студе́н *cold*
студе́нт(ка) *student*
стъкло́ *glass*
су́па *soup*
су́пермаркет *supermarket*
су́трин (f) *morning*
сутринта́ *in the morning*
счу́пен *broken, not working*
(да) счу́пя, -пиш *to break*
(да) съберá, -ре́ш *to gather*
съ́бота *Saturday*
съве́т *advice*
съвре́менен, -менна *contemporary*
съгла́сен, -сна съм *I agree*
(да) се съглася́, -си́ш *to agree*
(за) съжале́ние *unfortunately*
съжаля́вам, -ваш *to be sorry, regret*
(да) създа́м, -даде́ш *to create*
съм *I am* (to be)
съмня́вам, -ваш се *to doubt*
съобще́ние *message*
Съ́рбия *Serbia*
(от все) сърце́ *with all my heart*
съсе́ден, -дна *next door, neighbouring*
същ, съ́ща *same*
съ́що *also*
ся́дам, -даш *to sit down*
ся́нка *shade, shadow*

табе́лка *notice*
та́зи (f) *this*
така́ *right, just so, likewise*
така́ ли? *really?, is that so?*
та́кса *fee*
такси́ (n) *taxi*
таки́в, така́ва *such*
там *there*
танц *dance*
тарато́р *tarator* (Bulgarian cold summer soup)
твой *your(s)*
тво́рчески *creative*
те *they*
теа́тър (pl) **-три** *theatre*
те́жък, -жка *heavy*
те́зи (pl) *these*
телефо́н *telephone*
телефо́нен секрета́р *answerphone*
те́лекс *telex*
температу́ра *temperature*
те́нис *tennis*
те́хен, тя́хна *their(s)*
те́хника *equipment, technology*
ти *you*
ти́квичка *courgette, zucchini*
типи́чно *typically*
ти́хо *quietly*
то *it*
тоале́тна *toilet, bathroom*
това́ (n) *this*
тога́ва *then*
то́зи (m) *this*
той *he*
то́лкова *so*
то́ник *tonic water*
то́пъл, -пла *warm, hot*
то́рта *gateau, cake*
то́чен, -чна *punctual*
то́чно *exact(ly)*
трамва́й *tram*
транспо́рт *transport(ation)*
трева́ *grass*
три́ма (ду́ши) *three people*
триме́сечие *quarter, three-month period*
троле́й *trolleybus*
тру́ден, -дна *difficult*
тръ́гвам, -ваш *to set off*

тря́бва *have to; must*
ту́ба *canister, gas can*
тук *here*
тури́ст(ка) *tourist*
ту́рски *Turkish*
Ту́рция *Turkey*
тъ́мно *dark*
търго́вски *trade* (adj)
търго́вски це́нтър *shopping mall*
тъ́рся, -сиш *to look for*
тя *she*

у *at, with*
удо́бен, -бна *convenient, comfortable*
удово́лствие *pleasure*
ужа́сен, -сна *terrible, awful*
ужа́сно *terribly*
у́йкенд *weekend*
у́иски (n) *whisky*
у́лица *street*
уме́рен *moderate*
уми́рам, -раш за *to be dying for*
уморе́н *tired*
(да) се уморя́, -ри́ш *to get tired*
университе́т *university*
упра́вител *manager, director*
упражне́ние *exercise*
уро́к (pl) **уро́ци** *lesson*
успе́х *success*
у́тре *tomorrow*
у́тро *morning*
ухо́ (pl) **уши́** *ear*
у́ча, -чиш *to study, learn*
уча́ствам, -ваш *to take part*
уче́бник (pl) **-ници** *textbook*
у́чене *studying*
учени́к (pl) **и́ци** *pupil*
учи́тел(ка) *teacher*
учу́ден *surprised*

факс *fax*
(не е́) фата́лно *it's not fatal*
февруа́ри *February*
фина́л *finish*
фи́рма *firm*
фи́тнес це́нтър/клуб *fitness centre*
фоайе́ *foyer; lounge*
фолкло́р *folklore*
фолкло́рен фестива́л *folklore festival*
фо́нока́рта *phone-card*
фонта́н *fountain*
фо́рма *shape*
фо́тоапара́т *camera*
фотогра́ф *photographer*
францу́зин (pl) **-зи** *Frenchman*
французо́йка *Frenchwoman*
фре́нски *French*
фу́тбол *football*

ха́йде! *come on!*
(да) харе́сам, -саш *to like*
харе́свам, -ваш *to like*
харти́я *paper*
ха-ха! *ha-ha!*
хвъ́рлям, -ляш *to throw*
хепати́т *hepatitis*
хиля́да (pl) **хи́ляди** *thousand*
Хи́йтроу *Heathrow*
химика́лка *(ball-point) pen, biro*
хле́бче *bread roll*
хля́б *bread*
хо́дя, -диш *to go, walk*
хол *sitting/living room*
хо́ра (pl) *people*
хоте́л *hotel*
храна́ *food*
хре́ма (head) *cold*
христия́нски *Christian*
ху́бав *nice, beautiful, handsome*
худо́жник (pl) **-ици** *artist*
худо́жничка *artist* (woman)
ху́мор *humour*
хълм *hill*

цве́те (pl) **цветя́** *flower*
целодне́вен, -вна *whole day*
цена́ *price*
це́нност (f) (something) *valuable*
це́нтър (pl) **це́нтрове** *centre*
цига́ра *cigarette*
цъ́рква *church*
цял (pl) **це́ли** *all; whole*
цял куп *a whole lot of*

чадъ́р *umbrella*
чай *tea*
ча́кам, -каш *to wait*
ча́нта *bag*
час *hour*
часа́ *o'clock*
часо́вник (pl) **-ици** *watch; clock*
част (f) *part*
ча́ша *cup; glass*
че *that*
черве́н *red*
че́рен, -рна *black*

че́рква *church*
Черномо́рието *the Black Sea coast*
че́сън *garlic*
чести́т рожде́н ден! *happy birthday!*
чести́то! *congratulations!*
че́сто *often*
чета́, -те́ш *to read*
че́твърт (f) *quarter*
четвъ́ртък *Thursday*
чистота́ *cleanliness*
чове́к (pl) **хо́ра** *person, human being*
чу́вам, -ваш *to hear*
чу́вствам, -ваш (се) *to feel*
чу́вство *feeling, sense*
чуде́сен, -сна *wonderful, marvellous*
чужд *foreign*
чужденéц (pl) **-нци́** *foreigner*
чужденка́ *foreigner* (woman)
чу́шка *bell pepper, capsicum*
(да) чу́я, чу́еш *to hear*

шампа́нско *champagne*
шампоа́н *shampoo*
ша́пка *hat*
шегу́вам, -ваш се *to joke*
шеф *boss*
шокола́д *bar of chocolate*
шокола́дов (made of) *chocolate*
шо́пска сала́та *'shopska' salad*
шотла́ндец *Scot*
Шотла́ндия *Scotland*
шотла́ндка *Scotswoman*
шотла́ндски *Scottish*
шофьо́р *driver*
шум *noise*
шу́мен, -мна *noisy*
шу́нка *ham*
шшш! *sh-sh-sh!*

ща́стие *happiness*
(за) ща́стие *fortunately, luckily*
щастли́в *happy*
щом *since, seeing that*

ъ́гъл (pl) **ъ́гли** *corner*

(на) юг *(to the) south*
ю́ли *July*
ю́ни *June*
юти́я *iron*

я́бълка *apple*
я́бълков (made with*) apple*
(да) се явя́, -ви́ш *to present oneself*
я́года *strawberry*
я́годов (made with) *strawberry*
(не́що за) я́дене *something to eat*
я́ке *jacket*
ям, яде́ш *to eat*
януа́ри *January*
Япо́ния *Japan*
я́сен, я́сна *clear, obvious*
я́сно защо́ *it's obvious why; now I see why*

English–Bulgarian vocabulary

This is a 'survival' vocabulary and you should use it in conjunction with the Appendix and the Bulgarian–English Vocabulary. It includes most of the Bulgarian words you came across in the course – and a good few more besides. You'll be pleased to see that we have given most verbs in both imperfective and perfective forms. All other words we have listed in their basic form only, so for irregularities of form in nouns and adjectives, for example, or, indeed, for verb patterns, you'll have to turn to the Bulgarian–English vocabulary. If an English word has more than one equivalent in Bulgarian, we have attempted to list the more common word first. Where you might confuse forms, we have listed nouns before adjectives and verbs.

Although we trust that the Bulgarian equivalents of the 900 or so English words listed here will ensure your linguistic survival in a Bulgarian environment, do not expect it to replace a good English–Bulgarian dictionary.

Some words you will find in the Appendix rather than in the Vocabulary. You should look for most of the numerals, for example, and the different verb and pronoun forms, in the Appendix. The Appendix is really an addition to the Vocabulary, so use the two together.

able, be ~ *мóга*
about *óколо, към*
above *над*
accept *приéмам, (да) приéма*
accompany *изпрáщам, (да) изпрáтя; придружáвам, (да) придружá*
according to *сперéд*
acquaintance *познáт*
address *адрéс*
advertisement *реклáма*
advice *съвéт*
afraid, be ~ *страхýвам се*
after *след*
afternoon *следóбед;* **in the ~** *следóбед*
again *пак*
against *срещý*
agency *агéнция*
agitated *нéрвен*
ago *преди́*
agree, I ~ *съглáсен съм*
aim *цел*
air *вѝздух*
airline *авиокомпáния*
airplane *самолéт*
airport *лети́ще, аерогáра*
all *всѝчко;* **~ of us** *всѝчки*
almost *почти́*
alone *сам*
along *по, покрáй*
already *вéче*
also *сѝщо*
always *ви́наги*

America *Аме́рика*
American *америка́нец; америка́нски*
amusing *заба́вен*
and *и, а*
another *друг*
answer *о́тговор; отгова́рям, (да) отгово́ря*
anxious, be ~ *безпокоя́ се*
anybody *ня́кой*
anything *не́що*
apart from *осве́н*
apartment *апартаме́нт*
apologize *извиня́вам се, (да) се извиня́*
apple *я́бълка*
appointment *сре́ща*
arm *ръка́*
around *о́коло, към*
arrival *присти́гане*
arrive *присти́гам, (да) присти́гна*
artist *худо́жник*
as *ка́кто, като́*
ask *пи́там, (да) попи́там*
assistance *по́мощ*
at *на, у, в, през*
attention *внима́ние*
attraction (tourist) *забележи́телност*
Australia *Австра́лия*
Australian *австрали́ец; австрали́йски*
autumn *е́сен*
awful *ужа́сен*

back *гръб;* **small of the ~** *кръст*
bad *лош*
bag *ча́нта*
banana *бана́н*
bank *ба́нка*
bar *бар;* **~ of chocolate** *шокола́д*
bathroom *ба́ня, тоале́тна*
be *съм*
beach *плаж*
beard *брада́*
beautiful *краси́в, ху́бав*
because *защо́то*
become *ста́вам, (да) ста́на*
bed *легло́*
bedroom *спа́лня*
beer *би́ра, пи́во*
before *преди́*
begin *запо́чвам, (да) запо́чна*
beginning *нача́ло*
behind *зад*
beside *до*
besides *осве́н*
between *между́*
big *голя́м*
bill *сме́тка*
birth *ра́ждане*
birthday *рожде́н ден*; **happy ~!** *чести́т ~!*
black *че́рен*
block *блок*
blond *рус*
blue *син*
boarding card *бо́рдна ка́рта*
book *кни́га; запа́звам, (да) запа́зя*
boot, car-~ *бага́жник*
border *гра́ница*
boring *ску́чен*
born, I was ~ *роде́н съм*
boss *шеф*
bottle *бути́лка*
boulevard *булева́рд*
box *кутия́*
boy *момче́*
brandy *коня́к*; **Bulgarian ~** *раки́я*
bread *хляб*; **~ roll** *хле́бче*
break (something) *чу́пя (да) счу́пя; почи́вка, вака́нция*
break down *разва́лям се, (да) се разваля́*
breakfast *заку́ска*
bring *но́ся, (да) донеса́*
Britain *Великобрита́ния*
British *брита́нски*; **the ~** *брита́нците*
broken *счу́пен, развале́н*
brother *брат*
Bulgaria *Бълга́рия*
Bulgarian *бъ́лгарин; бъ́лгарски*
bun *ки́фла*
bus *автобу́с*
business *би́знес*; **~ card** *визи́тна ка́ртичка*; **~man** *би́знесмен*
busy *зае́т*
but *но, а, оба́че*
butter *ма́сло*
buy *купу́вам, (да) ку́пя*

café *кафе́, кафене́*
cake *то́рта, кекс*
calendar *календа́р*
call *оба́ждам се, (да) се оба́дя*

calmly *спокóйно*
camera *фóтоапарáт*
campsite *къ́мпинг*
can *мóга; мóже*
Canada *Канáда*
Canadian *канáдец; канáдски*
candy *бонбóн*
car *колá, автомобúл;* **~ park** *пáркинг*
card *кáрта;* **credit ~** *крéдитна ~,* **post~** *кáртичка*
carry *нóся, (да) донесá*
case *слу́чай; ку́фар*
celebrate *празну́вам, (да) отпразну́вам*
central *централен*
centre *цéнтър*
certainly *сúгурно; разбúра се; непремéнно*
chambermaid *камериéрка*
champagne *шампáнско*
change *обмéням, (да) обменя́; промéням, (да) променя́*
cheap *éвтин*
checkout *кáса*
cheers! *наздрáве!*
cheese (white, feta) *сúрене,* **(yellow)** *кашкавáл*
chemist's *аптéка*
chicken *пúле;* **grilled ~** *пúле на грил*
child *детé*
China *Китáй*
Chinese *китáец; китáйски*
chocolate *бонбóн;* **bar of ~** *шоколáд*
choose *избúрам, (да) изберá*
Christmas *Кóледа;* **merry ~ !** *честúта ~!*
cinema *кúно*
church *цъ́рква*
cigarette *цигáра*
citizen *грáжданин*
city *град*
clean *чист*
clear *я́сен*
cloakroom *гардерóб*
clock *часóвник*
close *затвáрям, (да) затвóря;* **~d** *затвóрен*
clothes *дрéхи*
cloud *óблак;* **it's ~y** *óблачно е*
coffee *кафé;* **instant ~** *нéскафе*
cold *студéн;* **head ~** *хрéма*
colleague *колéга*
come *úдвам, (да) дóйда;* **~ on!** *хáйде!*
come in *влúзам, (да) вля́за*
come out *излúзам, (да) изля́за*
comfortable *удóбен*
complain *оплáквам се, (да) се оплáча*
computer *компю́тър*
concert *концéрт*
conference *конферéнция*
congratulate *поздравя́вам, (да) поздравя́*
congratulations! *поздравлéния! честúто!*
continue *продължáвам, (да) продължá*
continuously *непрекъ́снато*
convenient *удóбен*
conversation *рáзговор*
corner *ъ́гъл*
cost, how much does it ~? *кóлко стру́ва?*
cough *кáшлица*
cousin *братовчéд*
country *странá*
cream *крем; сметáна*
create *създáвам, (да) създáм*
cross *кръст; пресúчам, (да) пресекá*
cucumber *крáставица*
culture *култу́ра*
cup *чáша*
currency *валу́та;* **~ exchange office** *обмéнно бюрó*
customer *клиéнт*
customs *мúтница;* **~ officer** *митничáр*

damp *влáжен*
dance *танцу́вам*
danger *опáсност; вниманúе!*
dangerous *опáсен*
dark *тъ́мен*
date *дáта*
daughter *дъщеря́*
day *ден*
dear *скъп*
decide *решáвам, (да) решá*
degree *грáдус*
delay *закъснéние*
delegation *делегáция*
delicious *вку́сен*
dentist *зъболéкар*
departure *заминáване*

dialogue *ра́зговор, диало́г*
diary *дне́вник, беле́жник*
dictionary *ре́чник*
die *уми́рам, (да) умра́*
diet *дие́та, режи́м*
different *разли́чен*
difficult *тру́ден*
dinner *вече́ря*
direction *посо́ка*
director *дире́ктор*
disappear *изче́звам, (да) изче́зна*
disco *дискоте́ка*
distance *разстоя́ние*
diversion *отклоне́ние*
do *пра́вя, (да) напра́вя*
doctor *ле́кар*
document *докуме́нт*
don't! *неде́й!*
door *врата́;* **~man** *портие́р*
doubt *съмня́вам се*
dress (oneself) *обли́чам се, (да) се облека́*
drink *напи́тка, не́що за пи́ене; пи́я, (да) изпи́я*
drive *ка́рам;* **~r** *шофьо́р*
dull *мра́чен*
during *през*

each *все́ки*
ear *ухо́*
early *ра́но*
east *и́зток;* **in/to the ~** *на и́зток*
easy *ле́сен*
eat *ям, (да) изя́м;* **something to ~** *не́що за я́дене*
elevator *асансьо́р*
email *и́мейл, електро́нна по́ща*
end *край*
engaged *зае́т*
engine *мото́р*
England *А́нглия*
English *англи́йски*
Englishman *англича́нин*
enough *доста́тъчно; сти́га!*
entrance *вход*
envelope *плик*
especially *специа́лно, осо́бено*
even *дори́, да́же; ра́вен*
evening *ве́чер;* **in the ~** *вечерта́*
every *все́ки;* **~body** *все́ки;* **~thing** *вси́чко;* **~where** *нався́къде*
exact *то́чен;* **~ly!** *то́чно така́!*
excellent *отли́чен*
except *осве́н*
exceptional *изключи́телен*
excursion *екску́рзия*
excuse *извине́ние;* **~ me!** *извине́те! извиня́вайте!*
exhibition *изло́жба*
exit *и́зход*
expect *оча́квам*
expensive *скъп*
explain *обясня́вам, (да) обясня́*
eye *око́*

fall *па́дам, (да) па́дна*
false *невя́рно*
far *дале́че*
family *семе́йство*
fast *бърз*
fat *слани́на;* (adj) *дебе́л*
father *баща́*
fault *дефе́кт, повре́да; вина́*
favour *услу́га*
fax *факс*
feel *чу́вствам;* **~ing** *чу́вство*
festival *пра́зник, фестива́л*
few *ма́лко* **a ~** *ня́колко*
file *па́пка, файл*
final *после́ден;* **~ly** *на́й-накра́я*
find *нами́рам, (да) наме́ря*
fine *гло́ба;* **~!** *добре́!*
finish *свъ́ршвам, (да) свъ́рша*
firm *фи́рма*
fish *ри́ба*
flat *апартаме́нт,* (adj) *ра́вен*
floor *ета́ж*
flower *цве́те*
flu *грип*
fly *муха́;* (vb) *летя́*
fog *мъгла́*
folklore *фолкло́р; фолкло́рен*
food *храна́*
foot *крак*
for *за*
forbidden *забране́н*
forecast *прогно́за*
foreign *чужд;* **~er** *чужденец*
forget *забра́вям, (да) забра́вя*
forgive *проща́вам, (да) простя́;* **~ me** *извине́те! извиня́вайте!*
fork *ви́лица*
fortunately *за ща́стие*
free *свобо́ден; безпла́тен*
France *Фра́нция*
French *фре́нски*
Frenchman *францу́зин*
frequent *чест*

fresh *свеж, пре́сен*
friend *прия́тел;* **~ly** *прия́телски*
from *от*
front *пре́дна част;* **in ~** *отпре́д*
fruit *плод;* **~ful** *плодотво́рен*
full of *пълен с*
fun, it's ~ *заба́вно е*
funny *сме́шен*
future *бъдеще*

game *игра́*
garage *гара́ж; серви́з*
garden *гради́на*
garlic *че́сън*
gas *бензи́н; газ*
German *герма́нец, не́мец; герма́нски, не́мски*
Germany *Герма́ния*
get *получа́вам, (да) полу́ча*
get to know one another *запозна́вам се, (да) се запозна́я*
get up *ста́вам, (да) ста́на*
girl *моми́че*
give *да́вам, (да) дам*
give back *връ́щам, (да) върна*
glad *дово́лен;* **be ~** *ра́двам се*
glass *ча́ша*
go *хо́дя;* (somewhere) *оти́вам, (да) оти́да*
go back *връ́щам се, (да) се върна*
go in *вли́зам, (да) вля́за*
go out *изли́зам, (да) изля́за*
God *Бог*
good *добър*
goodbye *дови́ждане;* (on the phone) *дочу́ване*
gram *грам*
grandmother *ба́ба*
grapes *гро́зде*
grass *трева́*
great *голя́м;* **~!** *чуде́сно!*
green *зеле́н*
Greece *Гъ́рция*
Greek *грък; гръ́цки*
greet *поздравя́вам, (да) поздравя́;* **~ing** *по́здрав*
grey *сив*
grill *ска́ра*
ground floor *па́ртер*
group *гру́па*
guest *гост*
guide *екскурзово́д*

hair *коса́; ко́съм*
half *полови́н;* **a ~** *полови́на*
hall *за́ла*
ham *шу́нка*
hand *ръка́*
handsome *ху́бав, краси́в*
happen, it ~s *ста́ва, (да) ста́не*
happiness *ща́стие*
happy *щастли́в, ве́сел;* **~ with** *дово́лен от; чести́т*
hard *твърд, тру́ден*
hat *ша́пка*
have *и́мам;* **not to ~** *ня́мам;* **~ to** *тря́бва*
he *той*
head *глава́*
headache *главобо́лие*
health *здра́ве*
hear *чу́вам, (да), чу́я*
heart *сърце́*
heat *топлина́; горещина́*
heavy *те́жък*
hello! *здраве́й(те)!;* (on the phone) *а́ло!*
help *по́мощ; пома́гам, (да) помо́гна*
her(s) *не́ин*
here *тук;* **~ is** *е́то;* **~ you are** *заповя́дай(те)*
high *висо́к;* **~way** *магистра́ла*
hill *хълм*
his *не́гов*
history *исто́рия*
hold *държа́ (се), (да) се хва́на*
holiday *пра́зник, почи́вка*
home *дом;* **go ~/at ~** *вкъ́щи*
hope *наде́жда; надя́вам се*
hospital *бо́лница*
host *домаки́н*
hot *горе́що*
hotel *хоте́л*
hour *час*
house *къ́ща*
how *как;* **~ many/much** *ко́лко*
however *оба́че*
hungry *гла́ден*
hurry, be in a ~ *бъ́рзам*
hurt, it ~s *боли́*
husband *съпру́г, мъж*

I *аз*
ice-cream *сладоле́д*
icon *ико́на*
idea *иде́я, предста́ва*

if *ако́*
ill *бо́лен*
immediately *веднáга*
important *ва́жен;* **it's ~** *ва́жно е*
impossible *невъзмо́жен;* **it's ~** *невъзмо́жно е*
in *в/във, на, през, след;* **~ front of** *пред*
indeed *наи́стина*
information *информа́ция*
instead of *вме́сто*
interesting *интере́сен*
international *междунаро́ден*
interpreter *превода́ч*
introduce *запозна́вам, (да) запозна́я*
invitation *пока́на*
invite *ка́ня, (да) пока́ня* **~d** *пока́нен*
Ireland *Ирла́ндия*
Irish *ирла́ндски* **~ man** *ирла́ндец*
iron *юти́я*
it *то*
Italian *италиа́нец; италиа́нски*
Italy *Ита́лия*
its *не́гов*

jacket *сако́, я́ке*
jeans *джи́нси*
job *ра́бота*
joke *шегу́вам се*
journalist *журнали́ст*
journey *пъту́ване*
juice *сок*
just *са́мо*

keep *па́зя, (да) запа́зя*
key *ключ*
kilogram *килогра́м*
kind *добъ́р, любе́зен; вид, род*
kitchen *ку́хня*
knee *коля́но*
knife *нож*
know *зна́я, позна́вам;* **get to ~ one another** *(да) се запозна́я*

lady *да́ма;* **~ of the house** *домаки́ня*
land *земя́*
language *ези́к*
last *после́ден;* **at ~** *на́й-по́сле*
late *къ́сно;* **to be ~** *закъсня́вам, (да) закъсне́я*
laugh *сме́я се*
learn *у́ча, (да) нау́ча*
leave (go out) *изли́зам, (да) изля́за; тръ́гвам, (да) тръ́гна; замина́вам, (да) зами́на*
leave (behind) *оста́вям, (да) оста́вя*
left *ляв;* **on/to the ~** *наля́во*
leg *крак*
lemon *лимо́н;* **~ade** *лимона́да*
lesson *уро́к*
let's! *(ха́йде) да!*
letter *писмо́, бу́ква*
lie *лъжа́; лъ́жа, (да) излъ́жа*
lie *лежа́*
lie down *ля́гам, (да) ле́гна*
life *живо́т*
lift *асансьо́р;* **ski/chair ~** *лифт*
light *светлина́;* (adj) *све́тъл, лек, слаб*
like *като́*
like *харе́свам, (да) харе́сам, оби́чам*
likewise *така́*
line *ли́ния*
lion *лъв*
listen *слу́шам*
litre *ли́тър*
little *ма́лък;* **a ~** *ма́лко*
live *живе́я*
long *дъ́лъг;* **~ ago** *отда́вна*
look *гле́дам; разгле́ждам, (да) разгле́дам*
look after *гри́жа се (за)*
look at/round *разгле́ждам, (да) разгле́дам*
look for *тъ́рся*
lose *гу́бя, (да) загу́бя*
lot, a ~ of *мно́го*
love *любо́в; оби́чам*
luckily *за ща́стие*
luggage *бага́ж*
lunch *обя́д;* **have ~** *обя́двам*

machine *маши́на*
make *пра́вя, (да) напра́вя; ка́рам, (да) нака́рам*
man *мъж; чове́к*
manager *дире́ктор, ме́ниджър*
many *мно́го*
map *ка́рта*
market *паза́р*
married *же́нен/омъ́жена*
marry *(да) се оже́ня/омъ́жа*
may I? *мо́же ли?*

maybe *мо́же би*
meaning *значе́ние*
mean, I ~ *и́скам да ка́жа*
meat *месо́*
medicine *лека́рство*
meet *сре́щам, (да) сре́щна; посре́щам, (да) посре́щна*
meeting *сре́ща*
melon *пъ́пеш*
memory *па́мет*
mend *попра́вям, (да) попра́вя*
mention *споменა́вам, (да) спомена́*
menu *меню́*
merry *ве́сел*
message *съобще́ние*
metre *ме́тър*
mile *ми́ля*
milk *мля́ко*
mine *мой*
minute *мину́та*
mirror *огледа́ло*
Miss *госпо́жица*
mistake *гре́шка*
mobile (phone) *моби́лен телефо́н,* **GSM** *(джиесе́м)*
monastery *манасти́р*
money *пари́*
month *ме́сец*
more *по́вече, о́ще*
morning *су́трин, у́тро;* **in the ~** *сутринта́*
most *на́й-мно́го;* **~ of** *по́вечето*
mother *ма́йка*
motorway *магистра́ла*
mountain(s) *планина́*
mouth *уста́*
Mr *господи́н*
Mrs *госпожа́*
much *мно́го*
museum *музе́й*
music *му́зика*
must *тря́бва*
my *мой*

name *и́ме*
napkin *салфе́тка*
nation *на́ция*
national *национа́лен, наро́ден;* **~ity** *наро́дност*
natural *натура́лен, есте́ствен;* **~ly** *есте́ствено*
near *бли́зо;* **~by** *набли́зо*
need *ну́жда*
neither... nor... *ни́то ... ни́то*
nervous *не́рвен, притесне́н*
never *ни́кога*
new *нов*
news (item) *новина́;* **~paper** *ве́стник*
next *сле́дващ;* **~ to** *до*
nice *ху́бав*
night *нощ;* **last ~** *сно́щи*
no *не*
noise *шум*
noisy *шу́мен*
none *ни́какъв*
nose *нос*
normally *норма́лно, обикнове́но*
north *се́вер;* **in/to the ~** *на се́вер*
not *не;* **~ yet** *о́ще не*
note *беле́жка;* **~book** *беле́жник*
nothing *ни́що*
nought *ну́ла*
now *сега́*
number *но́мер, брой*
nurse *сестра́*

object *предме́т*
obvious *я́вен, я́сен*
occasion *слу́чай*
occupation *профе́сия*
of *на;* **~ course** *разби́ра се*
offer *предложе́ние; предла́гам, (да) предло́жа*
office *о́фис, бюро́*
official *служе́бен*
often *че́сто*
OK *добре́, мо́же*
old *стар*
on *на, върху́, по, в*
once *ведня́ж;* **~ again** *о́ще ведня́ж*
only *са́мо*
open *отво́рен; отва́рям, (да) отво́ря;* **~ing hours** *рабо́тно вре́ме*
opposite *срещу́*
or *или́*
orange (nn) *портока́л*
order *ред;* **out of ~** *повре́ден; пора́чка; пора́чвам, (да) пора́чам*
ordinary *обикнове́н*
organize *организи́рам;* **~d** *организи́ран*
other (pl) *дру́ги*
our(s) *наш*

outside *навъ́н*
over *над*
own *свой*

pain *бо́лка*
paper *харти́я, докуме́нт*
pardon? *мо́ля?*
parent *роди́тел*
park *парк; парки́рам*
part *част*
pass *мина́вам, (да) ми́на*
passenger *пъ́тник*
passport *паспо́рт*
pay *пла́щам, (да) платя́*
peach *пра́скова*
pen *химика́лка*
pencil *моли́в*
people *хо́ра*
pepper *чу́шка; че́рен пипе́р*
performance *представле́ние*
petrol *бензи́н;* **~ station** *бензиноста́нция*
pharmacy *апте́ка*
phone *оба́ждам се, (да) се оба́дя*
photo *сни́мка;* **~grapher** *фотогра́ф*
piece *парче́*
pity, it's a ~ *жа́лко*
place *мя́сто*
plate *чини́я*
pleasant *прия́тен*
please *мо́ля*
pleased *дово́лен;* **be ~** *ра́двам се*
pleasure *удово́лствие*
plum *сли́ва*
pocket *джоб*
point *пока́звам, (да) пока́жа*
police *поли́ция;* **~man** *полица́й*
possible *възмо́жен;* **it's ~** *възмо́жно е, мо́же*
post (office) *по́ща;* **~card** *ка́ртичка*
prefer *предпочи́там, (да) предпочета́*
present *пода́рък*
price *цена́*
private *ча́стен*
probably *си́гурно*
problem *пробле́м*
programme *програ́ма*
punctual *то́чен*
pupil *учени́к*
purpose *цел*
purse *портмоне́, ча́нта*
put *сла́гам, (да) сло́жа*

quality *ка́чество*
quarter *че́твърт*
question *въпро́с*
quick *бърз*
quiet *тих*
quite *до́ста*
railway station *га́ра*
rain *дъжд;* **it's ~ing** *вали́*
rarely *ря́дко*
reach *сти́гам, (да) сти́гна*
read *чета́, (да) прочета́*
ready *гото́в*
really *наи́стина;* **~?** *така́ ли?*
receive *получа́вам, (да) полу́ча*
reception *реце́пция, при́ем*
receptionist *администра́тор*
recommend *препоръ́чвам, (да) препоръ́чам*
red *черве́н*
regret *съжаля́вам, (да) съжаля́*
religion *рели́гия*
rely on *разчи́там на*
remember *по́мня, (да) запо́мня; спо́мням си, (да) си спо́мня*
rent *на́ем; нае́мам, (да) нае́ма;* **~ed** *под на́ем*
repeat *повта́рям, (да) повто́ря*
repair *ремо́нт*
request *молба́*
reserve *запа́звам, (да) запа́зя;* **~d** *запа́зен, резерви́ран*
rest *почи́вам си, (да) си почи́на;* **~ room** *тоале́тна*
restaurant *рестора́нт*
return *връ́щам (се), (да) (се) въ́рна*
right *прав, де́сен;* **on/to the ~** *надя́сно*
river *река́*
road *път*
room *стя́а*
route *маршру́т, път*
Russia *Руси́я*
Russian *русна́к; ру́ски*

salad *сала́та*
sales person *продава́ч*
salt *сол*
same, the ~ *съ́щият*
sandwich *са́ндвич*
say *ка́звам, (да) ка́жа*
school *учи́лище*

Scot *шотла́ндец*
Scotland *Шотла́ндия*
Scottish *шотла́ндски*
sea *море́*
see *ви́ждам, (да) ви́дя*
sell *прода́вам, (да) прода́м*
send *пра́щам, (да) пра́тя; изпра́щам, (да) изпра́тя*
serious *серио́зен*
service (in a restaurant) *обслу́жване*
service station *серви́з*
serviette *салфе́тка*
several *ня́колко*
shape *фо́рма*
shaver *самобръсна́чка*
she *тя*
shoe *обу́вка*
shop *магази́н*
shop assistant *продава́ч*
shopping, do the ~ *пазару́вам*
short (stature) *ни́сък* (time) *кра́тък*
show *пока́звам, (да) пока́жа*
shower *душ*
sick *бо́лен*
side *страна́*
sight, tourist ~ *забележи́телност*
sign *знак, табе́лка*
simply *про́сто*
since *тъй като́,* (time) *от*
sing *пе́я, (да) изпе́я*
single *едини́чен; неже́нен/неомъ́жена*
sister *сестра́*
sit *седя́*
sit down *ся́дам, (да) се́дна*
size *големина́, разме́р*
ski *ка́рам ски;* **~ run** *пи́ста*
skin *ко́жа*
sleep *спя*
slow *ба́вен*
small *ма́лък*
smoke (vb) *пу́ша*
smoking *пу́шене*
snack *заку́ска;* **~ bar** *бъ́рза заку́ска, закусва́лня*
snow *сняг*
so *така́; то́лкова*
sock *чора́п*
soda water *гази́рана вода́, со́да*
soft *мек;* **~ drink** *безалкохо́лна напи́тка*
some *ня́кои, ня́колко; ня́какъв;* **~body** *ня́кой;* **~how** *ня́как;* **~thing** *не́що;* **~ time** *ня́кога,* **~times** *поня́кога* **~where** *ня́къде*
son *син*
soon *ско́ро*
sorry, to be ~ *съжаля́вам, (да) съжаля́*
soup *су́па*
south *юг;* **in/to the ~** *на юг*
Spain *Испа́ния*
Spaniard *испа́нец*
Spanish *испа́нски*
speak *гово́ря*
special *специа́лен, осо́бен*
spend (time) *прека́рвам, (да) прека́рам;* **(money)** *ха́рча, (да) поха́рча*
spoon *лъжи́ца*
spring *про́лет*
square *площа́д*
stamp, postage ~ *ма́рка*
stand *стоя́*
stand up *ста́вам, (да) ста́на*
stomach *стома́х, коре́м*
stop *спи́рам, (да) спра;* **bus ~** *спи́рка*
straight *прав*
strawberry *я́года*
street *у́лица*
strong *си́лен*
student *студе́нт, учени́к*
study (vb) *у́ча*
success *успе́х*
such *такъ́в*
sugar *за́хар*
suggest *предла́гам, (да) предло́жа*
suit *костю́м*
suitcase *ку́фар*
summer *ля́то*
sun *слъ́нце*
supper *вече́ря;* **have ~** *вече́рям*
suppose *предпола́гам, (да) предполо́жа*
sure *си́гурен*
surname *пре́зиме, фами́лно и́ме*
surprise *изнена́да*
sweet *бонбо́н;* (adj) *сла́дък*
swim *плу́вам*

table *ма́са*
take *взи́мам, (да) взе́ма;* **~ part** *уча́ствам*
take away (nn) *(храна́) за вкъ́щи*
talk *гово́ря*

tall *висóк*
taxi *такси́*
tea *чай*
teacher *учи́тел*
telephone *телефóн;* **mobile ~** *мобúлен телефóн, джúесéм*
tell *кáзвам, (да) кáжа*
temperature *температýра*
terrible *ужáсен, стрáшен*
than *от, откóлкото*
thank *благодаря́;* **~ you** *благодаря́, мерси́*
that *товá; оновá;* че
theatre *теáтър*
their(s) *тéхен*
then *тогáва*
there *там;* **~ is/are** *и́ма;* **~ isn't/aren't** *ня́ма*
these *тéзи*
they *те*
thin *тъ́нък, слаб*
think *ми́сля*
this *товá*
throat *гъ́рло*
through *през*
ticket *билéт;* **~-office** *кáса*
till *кáса*
time *врéме;* **in ~** *наврéме;* **two ~s** *два пъ́ти*
timetable *разписáние*
tired *уморéн*
to *до, към;* **in order ~** *за да*
today *днес*
together *зáедно*
toilet *тоалéтна*
tomato *домáт*
tomorrow *ýтре*
tongue *ези́к*
too *съ́що, и; прекалéно*
tooth *зъб*
touch *пи́пам, (да) пи́пна*
tourist *тури́ст*
toward(s) *към*
town *град*
tram *трамвáй*
translate *превéждам, (да) преведá*
travel *пътýвам*
tree *дървó*
trip *екскýрзия*
trolleybus *тролéй*
trouble *неприя́тност*
trousers *панталóн*
true, it's ~ *вя́рно (е)*
trunk (car) *багáжник*
try *опи́твам, (да) опи́там*
Turk *тýрчин*
Turkey *Тýрция*
Turkish *тýрски*
turn *зави́вам, (да) зави́я*

umbrella *чадъ́р*
under *под;* **~ground** *метрó*
understand *разби́рам, (да) разберá*
unfortunately *за съжалéние*
university *университéт*
unpleasant *неприя́тен*
until *до, доказó;* **~ now** *досегá*
useful *полéзен*
usually *обикновéно*

vegetable *зеленчýк*
vegetarian *вегетариáнец; вегетариáнски*
very *мнóго, твъ́рде, дóста*
village *сéло*
visit *престóй*

wait *чáкам*
waiter *сервитьóр*
Wales *Уéлс*
walk *разхóдка; вървя́, хóдя*
wall *стенá*
wallet *портфéйл, портмонé*
want *и́скам*
war *войнá*
warm *тóпъл*
wash *ми́я (се), (да) (се) изми́я*
watch *часóвник*
water *водá;* **mineral ~** *минерáлна ~*
way *път*
we *ни́е*
weak *слаб, лек*
wear *нóся*
weather *врéме*
week *сéдмица*
welcome! *добрé дошъ́л! заповя́дай(те)!*
well *добрé*
Welsh *уéлсец; уéлски*
west *зáпад;* **in/to the ~** *на зáпад*
what *каквó, каквóто;* **~ kind of** *какъ́в*
when *когá; когáто*
where *къдé; къдéто;* **~ from** *откъдé*

whether *дали́*
which *кой; ко́йто*
while *докато́*
white *бял*
who *кой; ко́йто*
whole *цял*
why *защо́*
wife *съпру́га, жена́*
wind *вя́тър*
window *прозо́рец*
wine *ви́но*
winter *зи́ма*
wish *жела́ние; жела́я; пожела́вам, (да) пожела́я*
with *с/със*
without *без*
woman *жена́*
wonderful *чуде́сен*
word *ду́ма*
work *ра́бота; рабо́тя*
world *свят*
worry *гри́жа; безпокоя́ се*
write *пи́ша, (да) напи́ша*

year *годи́на*
yellow *жълт*
yes *да*
yesterday *вче́ра*
yet *о́ще; все пак*
yoghurt *ки́село мля́ко*
you *ти; ви́е*
young *млад*
your(s) *твой; ваш*

zero *ну́ла*

index to grammar and usage

Although the grammatical explanations in this course are based on a pragmatic, need-to-know basis and we try to avoid grammatical jargon, grammatical categories are a very useful aid to learning. We hope, therefore, that this index, arranged according to grammatical features, will be a handy additional aid to finding your way around the book and the Bulgarian language.

The numbers refer you to the units. An asterisk indicates that you will find further material in the Appendix.